IMF GLOSSARY

ENGLISH-FRENCH-SPANISH

SEVENTH EDITION

International Monetary Fund
Washington, D.C.
2007

Production: IMF Multimedia Services Division
Cover and Design: Jorge Salazar
Typesetting: Maryse Schutt-Ainé Rickford

Cataloging-in-Publication Data

IMF glossary : English-French-Spanish. – 7th ed. -- Washington, D.C. :
International Monetary Fund, 2007.
        p. ;   cm.

    ISBN 978-158906-645-8
    Includes indexes.

1. International Monetary Fund-Dictionaries-Polyglot.
2. International finance-Dictionaries-Polyglot.
3. Dictionaries-Polyglot.
4. Associations, institutions, etc.-Abbreviations.
5. Money.

I. Title. II. International Monetary Fund. Reference, Terminology, and
Documentation Section.

HG3881.5.I58 I63 2007

Price: US$49.00

Please send orders to:
International Monetary Fund, Publications Services
700 19th Street, N.W., Washington D.C. 20431, U.S.A.
Telephone: (202) 623-7430   Telefax: (202) 623-7201
E-mail: publications@imf.org
Internet: http://www.imf.org

TABLE OF CONTENTS

PREFACE

This ***Glossary*** is based on the work done over the years by the IMF Terminology Working Group (TWG). In the preparation of this ***Glossary***, the **IMF terminology database** (database), which currently contains approximately 20,000 entries, was thoroughly reviewed. This seventh revised edition of the ***IMF Glossary: English-French-Spanish*** contains some 4,000 records, which are believed to be the most useful to translators dealing with IMF material.

The main body of the ***Glossary*** consists of terms, phraseological units, and institutional titles covering a broad variety of areas, such as macroeconomics, money and banking, public finance, taxation, balance of payments, statistics, accounting, and economic development. It contains terminology from the *IMF Articles of Agreement, By-Laws, Rules and Regulations*, as well as other major IMF publications.

Since this ***Glossary*** is concept-based, synonyms are consolidated into one single entry. Cross references ***"see"*** refer to the main entry under which the various synonyms are listed, and cross references ***"see also"*** draw the user's attention to terms that are related but not synonyms. Notations indicated in square brackets **[ ]** denote the source of the term **[OECD]**, the subject **[balance of payments]**, or a specific regional usage indicated by the ISO-3 country code **[ESP]**. Acronyms are cross-referenced in the main body of the ***Glossary*** and in the language indexes.

Terms relating to IMF organization and structure, as well as senior staff titles, are included in this ***Glossary.*** In **Appendices III** and **IV**, color-coded **French** and **Spanish indexes** are provided for the convenience of users who work from these languages. **Currency Units** of the various countries and areas are contained in **Appendix I**. An **IMF Organizational Chart**, in all three languages, is found in **Appendix II**.

As a complement to the **IMF's series of glossaries**, TWG produces several topical Terminology Bulletins and specialized glossaries (*Organizational Structure*, *Currency Units*, *Staff Titles*, *Statistical Glossary*, *Financial Glossary*, and others). An updated CD-ROM edition of the **IMF Glossary** including Arabic, Chinese, English, French, German, Portuguese, Russian, and Spanish is in preparation.

This edition benefited from an extensive review conducted in the English, French, and Spanish Divisions, under the coordination of Adriana Russo, Marc Servais, and William Ford. Hubertus Hesse provided research assistance and coordinated the glossary production in Language Services. Annette Berthail-Costa, Virginia Masoller, Van Kieu Tran, and Adriana Vilar de Vilariño were in charge of the proofreading. Maryse Schutt-Ainé Rickford, Krishna Kanth, and Randall Emmelhainz managed the database and the computer systems. James McEuen of the External Relations Department edited the content of the glossary and coordinated the production of this publication.

This glossary has also benefited greatly from comments and suggestions received from IMF departments, the Executive Directors' offices, and Language Services staff.

Please address any comments to: **RTD Section, Language Services, Technology and General Services Department, International Monetary Fund**, Washington, DC 20431, USA, or via e-mail at <u>terminology@imf.org</u>.

April 2007

A

A-1	AAA debtor	débiteur de premier ordre	deudor con calificación AAA deudor con clasificación AAA
A-2	AAA rating *see also:* rating	cotation AAA cotation triple A	calificación AAA clasificación AAA
A-3	AAD, *see* Arab accounting dinar		
A-4	ABEDA, *see* Arab Bank for Economic Development in Africa		
A-5	ability to pay, *see* taxable capacity		
A-6	above par [securities]	au-dessus du pair au-dessus de la valeur nominale	por encima del par por encima del valor nominal con prima
A-7	above par value [currency]	au-dessus de la parité	por encima de la paridad
A-8	above the line	«au-dessus de la ligne»	por encima de la línea
A-9	above-the-line entry, *see* above-the-line item		
A-10	above-the-line item above-the-line entry	poste au-dessus de la ligne poste ordinaire	partida ordinaria partida por encima de la línea
A-11	absolute advantage *see also:* comparative advantage	avantage absolu	ventaja absoluta
A-12	absolute return fund, *see* hedge fund		
A-13	absorptive capacity	capacité d'absorption	capacidad de absorción
A-14	accelerated depreciation accelerated rate of depreciation	amortissement accéléré taux d'amortissement accéléré	depreciación acelerada amortización acelerada tasa de depreciación acelerada tasa de amortización acelerada
A-15	accelerated purchase	achat accéléré	compra acelerada
A-16	accelerated rate of depreciation, *see* accelerated depreciation		
A-17	accelerated set-aside amounts repurchase, *see* repurchase of accelerated set-aside amounts		
A-18	acceleration clause *see also:* nonacceleration clause	clause de remboursement accéléré	cláusula de aceleración cláusula de opción de pago anticipado cláusula de anticipación de pagos cláusula de caducidad de plazos
A-19	acceptance credit	crédit d'acceptation crédit par acceptation	crédito de aceptación crédito por aceptación
A-20	acceptance error, *see* type II error		
A-21	acceptance limit [IMF]	limite d'acceptation	límite de aceptación

1

A-22	acceptance of membership [IMF]	acceptation de la qualité de membre	aceptación de la calidad de miembro
A-23	access limit [IMF]	limite d'accès limite d'accès aux ressources du FMI	límite de acceso a los recursos del FMI límite de acceso
A-24	access policy [IMF]	politique d'accès	política de acceso a los recursos del FMI política de acceso
A-25	access to a facility [IMF]	accès à une facilité accès à un mécanisme	acceso a un servicio financiero
A-26	accommodating policy, *see* accommodative monetary policy		
A-27	accommodating stance, *see* accommodative monetary policy		
A-28	accommodation, *see* accommodative monetary policy		
A-29	accommodative monetary policy *see also:* monetary tightening accommodating policy accommodating stance monetary accommodation accommodation easy monetary policy easing of monetary policy monetary easing easing	politique d'accompagnement monétaire politique monétaire accommodante	política monetaria acomodaticia distensión de la política monetaria adopción de una política monetaria menos restrictiva adopción de una política monetaria más expansiva política acomodaticia acomodación monetaria
A-30	account statement, *see* statement of account		
A-31	accountability	responsabilisation obligation de rendre compte éthique de responsabilité responsabilité responsabilité financière responsabilité de la gestion	rendición de cuentas responsabilización responsabilidad obligación de rendir cuentas
A-32	accounting concept	postulat comptable convention comptable convention comptable de base règle comptable	concepto contable
A-33	accounting entity, *see* accounting unit		
A-34	accounting exchange rate, *see* shadow exchange rate		
A-35	accounting identity	identité comptable	identidad contable
A-36	accounting methods, *see* accounting practices		
A-37	accounting practices accounting methods accounting procedures	pratiques comptables méthodes comptables procédés comptables usages comptables	prácticas contables métodos contables procedimientos contables
A-38	accounting principles, *see* accounting standards		
A-39	accounting procedures, *see* accounting practices		

A-40	accounting rate book rate	taux comptable	tipo de cambio contable tipo para fines contables
A-41	accounting standards accounting principles	normes comptables principes comptables règles comptables	normas contables principios de contabilidad
A-42	accounting unit accounting entity	unité comptable division comptable entité comptable	unidad contable entidad contable
A-43	accounting unit [IMF] *see also:* numeraire unit of account	unité de compte	unidad de cuenta
A-44	accounts of the IMF in member countries IMF accounts in member countries	comptes du FMI dans les pays membres	cuentas del FMI en los países miembros
A-45	accounts payable	comptes de tiers créditeurs effets à payer comptes à payer montants à payer	cuentas por pagar
A-46	accounts receivable	comptes de tiers débiteurs effets à recevoir comptes à recevoir montants à recevoir	cuentas por cobrar
A-47	accrual accounting accrual basis accounting	comptabilité sur la base des droits et obligations comptabilité sur la base des droits constatés comptabilité d'exercice comptabilité d'engagements comptabilité patrimoniale	contabilidad en base devengado registro en base devengado contabilidad en valores devengados
A-48	accrual basis *see also:* commitment basis, on a	sur la base des droits constatés sur la base des droits et obligations	base devengado valores devengados
A-49	accrual basis accounting, *see* accrual accounting		
A-50	accruals	comptes de régularisation	valores devengados devengado
A-51	accruals, *see* provision		
A-52	accrued charges [IMF]	commissions courues commissions échues	cargos devengados
A-53	accrued income	revenu gagné revenu cumulé produits à recevoir	ingreso devengado
A-54	accrued interest	intérêts courus intérêts cumulés intérêts acquis coupon couru CC	intereses devengados intereses acumulados cupón corrido

	English	French	Spanish

A-55	accumulated depreciation	provision pour dépréciation
		amortissement(s)
		amortissement cumulé
		montant cumulé des
		  amortissements
		provision pour amortissement
		dotation aux comptes
		  d'amortissement
			amortización acumulada
			depreciación acumulada
			partida de depreciación
			partida de amortización
			depreciación acumulada

A-56	acid-test ratio, *see* quick asset ratio		
A-57	ACP Group, *see* African, Caribbean and Pacific Group of States		
A-58	ACP States, *see* African, Caribbean and Pacific Group of States		

A-59	ACP-EEC Convention (between
	  the African, Caribbean and
	  Pacific States and the European
	  Economic Community)
	Lomé Convention
		Convention ACP–CEE (entre les
		  États de l'Afrique, des Caraïbes
		  et du Pacifique et la
		  Communauté économique
		  européenne)
		Convention de Lomé
			Convenio ACP–CEE (entre los
			  Estados de África, el Caribe y el
			  Pacífico y la Comunidad
			  Económica Europea)
			Convención de Lomé

A-60	acquaintance mission [IMF] *see also:* advance mission exploratory mission	mission exploratoire mission d'évaluation mission de prise de contact	misión inicial misión exploratoria
A-61	acquired rights clause grandfather clause	clause des droits acquis	cláusula de derechos adquiridos
A-62	acquisition of SDRs [IMF]	acquisition de DTS	adquisición de DEG
A-63	act of consent [IMF quotas] *see also:* consent	notification donnant acte du consentement notification de l'acceptation	notificación de la aceptación manifestación de consentimiento
A-64	act of God *see also:* force majeure natural disaster	catastrophe naturelle force majeure	caso fortuito catástrofe natural desastre natural fuerza mayor
A-65	Acting ... [IMF]	... par intérim	... Interino
A-66	Acting Managing Director, *see* Managing Director, Acting [IMF]		
A-67	activate *see also:* trigger	mettre en œuvre mettre en application faire intervenir activer	activar poner en marcha
A-68	active claim	créance vive créance productrice de revenu	activo productivo activo que devenga intereses
A-69	activist policy *see also:* automatic stabilizer discretionary policy	politique volontariste politique volontaire mesure discrétionnaire	política discrecional
A-70	activity report [IMF] *see also:* advisory report	rapport d'activité	informe de actividades

A-71	actual final consumption	consommation finale effective	consumo final efectivo
A-72	actual income	revenu effectif revenu effectivement gagné	ingreso efectivo
A-73	actual interest yield *see also:* nominal interest rate effective yield	rendement effectif taux de rendement effectif	rentabilidad efectiva rendimiento efectivo tasa de interés efectiva
A-74	actual quota share, *see* quota share		
A-75	actual rate of return	taux de rentabilité effectif taux de rentabilité observé rendement effectif taux de rendement effectif	tasa de rendimiento efectivo tasa de rentabilidad efectiva tasa de retorno efectiva
A-76	actuals	chiffres effectifs	cifras efectivas
A-77	actuarial reserve	réserve actuarielle réserve technique réserve mathématique	reserva actuarial reserva matemática reservas técnicas
A-78	actuarial valuation actuary's valuation	calcul actuariel évaluation actuarielle	valuación actuarial valoración actuarial
A-79	actuary's valuation, *see* actuarial valuation		
A-80	ad hoc request [IMF]	demande ponctuelle demande *ad hoc*	solicitud ad hoc solicitud especial
A-81	ad valorem [taxation]	*ad valorem* à la valeur sur la valeur	ad valórem
A-82	adaptive expectations	anticipations évolutives anticipations adaptatives	expectativas adaptables
A-83	ADB, *see* African Development Bank		
A-84	ADB, *see* Asian Development Bank		
A-85	additional charges, *see* special charges		
A-86	adequacy of financing	ressources suffisantes financement suffisant existence d'un financement suffisant	suficiencia del financiamiento nivel adecuado de financiamiento
A-87	adequacy of reserves reserves adequacy	réserves suffisantes existence de réserves suffisantes adéquation des réserves	suficiencia de las reservas nivel adecuado de reservas
A-88	adequate safeguards [IMF] *see also:* safeguards (on the use of Fund resources)	garanties adéquates	salvaguardias adecuadas
A-89	ADF, *see* African Development Fund		
A-90	adjustable peg fixed but adjustable exchange rate	taux de change ajustable taux de change fixe mais ajustable	paridad ajustable tipo de cambio fijo pero ajustable

A-91	adjustable rate, *see* floating interest rate		
A-92	adjustment equation	équation d'ajustement	ecuación de ajuste
A-93	adjustment fatigue	fatigue de l'ajustement	fatiga del ajuste fatiga causada por el ajuste
A-94	adjustment of charges [IMF]	ajustement des commissions	ajuste de los cargos
A-95	adjustment of quotas [IMF] *see also:* quota review	ajustement des quotes-parts révision des quotes-parts réalignement des quotes-parts	ajuste de las cuotas
A-96	adjustment path	trajectoire de l'ajustement profil de l'ajustement	trayectoria del ajuste perfil del ajuste
A-97	adjustment process	processus d'ajustement	proceso de ajuste
A-98	adjustment program [IMF]	programme d'ajustement	programa de ajuste

A-99	adjustment to cash
	adjustment to cash basis
		ajustement à la base caisse
		ajustement à la base
		  encaissements-décaissements
			ajuste a base caja
			ajuste a valores de caja
			ajuste de las cifras a valores de
			  caja

A-100	adjustment to cash basis, *see* adjustment to cash		
A-101	adjustment transaction	transaction d'ajustement opération d'ajustement	transacción de ajuste
A-102	adjustment with growth	ajustement dans la croissance	ajuste con crecimiento
A-103	Administered Account [IMF]	compte administré	Cuenta Administrada
A-104	Administered Account -*country* [IMF - contribution from a country]	compte administré (au nom de ...)	Cuenta Administrada (correspondiente a ...)
A-105	Administered Account -*country* [IMF - contribution for a country]	compte administré (en faveur de ...)	Cuenta Administrada [nombre del país]
A-106	administered price controlled price administrative price	prix administré prix réglementé prix imposé prix contrôlé prix fixé par le producteur	precio administrado precio controlado precio regulado
A-107	administration of control	organisation administrative du contrôle des changes	administración de los controles cambiarios
A-108	administration of restrictions [IMF]	application de restrictions	aplicación de restricciones
A-109	administrative action	mesure administrative décision administrative	medida administrativa decisión administrativa
A-110	administrative budget [IMF] *see also:* capital budget	budget administratif	presupuesto administrativo

A-111	Administrative Division [IMF]	Division administrative	División Administrativa
A-112	Administrative Expenditures and Control Division [IMF] AECD	Division des dépenses et du contrôle administratifs	División de Gastos y Controles Administrativos
A-113	administrative fees and charges	droits et frais administratifs	tasas y derechos administrativos
A-114	administrative price, *see* administered price		
A-115	administrative receivership [GBR]	mise sous séquestre	sindicatura
A-116	Administrative Services [IMF]	Services administratifs	Servicios Administrativos
A-117	Administrative Tribunal [IMF]	Tribunal administratif	Tribunal Administrativo
A-118	administrative value, *see* official value		
A-119	advance	avance	anticipo pago anticipado adelanto
A-120	advance deposit import deposit	dépôt préalable à l'importation dépôt préalable caution préalable	depósito previo a la importación
A-121	advance mission [IMF] *see also:* acquaintance mission	mission préparatoire	misión preparatoria
A-122	advance redemption advance repayment	remboursement par anticipation remboursement anticipé règlement anticipé	rescate anticipado reembolso anticipado amortización anticipada
A-123	advance repayment, *see* advance redemption		
A-124	advance repurchase, *see* early repurchase		
A-125	advanced economy	économie avancée pays avancé	economía avanzada
A-126	adverse selection	antisélection sélection adverse «sélection négative»	selección adversa
A-127	adversely classified asset, *see* classified loan		
A-128	Advisor on Diversity, Senior [IMF]	Conseiller principal pour la diversité	Asesor Principal sobre Diversidad
A-129	Advisor, Special, *see* Special Advisor [IMF]		
A-130	Advisor to the Executive Director [IMF]	Conseiller de l'administrateur	Asesor del Director Ejecutivo
A-131	advisory committee, *see* bank advisory committee		

A-132	advisory report [IMF] *see also:* activity report	rapport d'assistance technique	informe de asistencia técnica
A-133	AECD, *see* Administrative Expenditures and Control Division		
A-134	AfDB, *see* African Development Bank		
A-135	AfDF, *see* African Development Fund		
A-136	AFESD, *see* Arab Fund for Economic and Social Development		
A-137	affiliate *see also:* associate, subsidiary affiliated enterprise	entreprise apparentée entreprise affiliée	filial empresa filial afiliada empresa afiliada
A-138	affiliated enterprise, *see* affiliate		
A-139	affluent society	société d'abondance société de consommation société d'opulence	sociedad opulenta sociedad de consumo
A-140	AFR, *see* African Department		
A-141	Africa Facility, *see* Special Facility for Sub-Saharan Africa		
A-142	Africa Group I Constituency, *see* African Group I		
A-143	Africa Group II Constituency, *see* African Group II		
A-144	Africa Regional Division [IMF]	Division Afrique	División de la Región de África
A-145	African, Caribbean and Pacific Group of States ACP Group ACP States	États de l'Afrique, des Caraïbes et du Pacifique États ACP Groupe des États ACP	Grupo de Estados de África, el Caribe y el Pacífico Grupo ACP Estados ACP
A-146	African Caucus, *see* African Group		
A-147	African Caucus [IMF] *see also:* African Group [IMF-IBRD]	Groupe africain Groupe africain du FMI Caucus africain	Grupo Africano del FMI
A-148	African Department [IMF] AFR	Département Afrique	Departamento de África
A-149	African Development Bank AfDB ADB	Banque africaine de développement BAfD BAD	Banco Africano de Desarrollo BAfD BAD
A-150	African Development Fund AfDF ADF	Fonds africain de développement FAfD FAD	Fondo Africano de Desarrollo FAfD FAD
A-151	African Division [IMF]	Division Afrique	División de África

A-152	African Financial Community [BCEAO] CFA	Communauté financière africaine CFA	Comunidad Financiera Africana CFA
A-153	African Group [IMF-IBRD] *see also:* African Caucus [IMF] Group of African Governors African Caucus	Groupe africain Groupe des gouverneurs africains	Grupo Africano Grupo de Gobernadores Africanos
A-154	African Group I [IMF-IBRD] Africa Group I Constituency	Gouverneurs africains du Groupe I	Grupo I de Gobernadores Africanos
A-155	African Group II [IMF-IBRD] Africa Group II Constituency	Gouverneurs africains du Groupe II	Grupo II de Gobernadores Africanos
A-156	African Regional Technical Assistance Center *see also:* East AFRITAC; regional technical assistance center; West AFRITAC AFRITAC	Centre régional d'assistance technique en Afrique AFRITAC	Centro Regional de Asistencia Técnica en África AFRITAC
A-157	African Union AU	Union africaine UA	Unión Africana UA
A-158	AFRITAC, *see* African Regional Technical Assistance Center		
A-159	AFSSR, *see* Assessment of Financial Sector Supervision and Regulation		
A-160	after taxes	net d'impôt(s) après impôt(s)	neto de impuestos deducidos los impuestos después de impuestos
A-161	age pyramid, *see* population pyramid		
A-162	agency	administration services administratifs organisme public organe ministère commissariat commission office	entidad organismo órgano dependencia agencia
A-163	agency bond *see also:* treasury bond	titre émis par un organisme parrainé par l'État	título emitido por un organismo autorizado
A-164	agency fee	commission de gestion commission de mandataire commission d'agent	comisión de gestión comisión de agente
A-165	Agency for International Development [USA] AID USAID	Agence pour le développement international AID USAID	Agencia para el Desarrollo Internacional USAID
A-166	agency transaction	opération pour le compte de tiers	transacción por cuenta de terceros

A-167	Agenda and Procedures Committee [IMF] APC	Comité de l'ordre du jour et des procédures	Comisión sobre Temarios y Procedimientos
A-168	aggregate real GNP, *see* aggregate real gross national product		
A-169	aggregate real gross national product aggregate real GNP	produit national brut global en valeur réelle PNB global réel	producto nacional bruto agregado real PNB agregado real
A-170	aggregation bias	biais résultant de l'agrégation biais dû à l'agrégation	sesgo de agregación sesgo causado por la agregación
A-171	aggregation, degree of	niveau d'agrégation degré d'agrégation	nivel de agregación grado de agregación
A-172	agrarian reform, *see* land reform		
A-173	agreed minute [Paris Club]	procès-verbal agréé	acta aprobada
A-174	agreement, use by [SDR]	utilisation en vertu d'un accord	uso mediante acuerdo
A-175	agricultural exporter	pays exportateurs de produits agricoles	país exportador de productos agrícolas
A-176	agricultural extension agricultural extension services extension services	vulgarisation agricole services de vulgarisation agricole	extensión agrícola servicios de extensión agraria
A-177	agricultural extension services, *see* agricultural extension		
A-178	agriculture, forestry, fishing, and hunting	agriculture, sylviculture, pêche et chasse	agricultura, silvicultura, pesca y caza
A-179	.../AI, *see* Immediate Office		
A-180	AID, *see* Agency for International Development		
A-181	aid flows	apports d'aide flux d'aide	flujos de ayuda flujos de asistencia financiera
A-182	aide-mémoire [IMF]	aide-mémoire	ayuda memoria
A-183	all other things being equal, *see* *ceteris paribus*		
A-184	allocate	allouer assigner affecter attribuer répartir	asignar distribuir atribuir
A-185	allocation *see also:* appropriation	allocation de crédits budgétaires	partida presupuestaria asignación presupuestaria asignación
A-186	allocation of resources, *see* resource allocation		
A-187	allocation of SDRs, *see* SDR allocation		

A-188	allocative efficiency of resources	efficience de l'allocation des ressources	eficiencia en la asignación de recursos
A-189	allotted number of votes [IMF] *see also:* voting power	nombre de voix attribuées	número de votos asignados
A-190	allowance, *see* depreciation allowance		
A-191	allowance for bad debts, *see* loan loss provision		
A-192	allowance for depreciation, *see* depreciation allowance		
A-193	allowance for loan losses, *see* loan loss provision		
A-194	all-purpose bank, *see* multipurpose bank		
A-195	Alternate ..., *see* ..., Alternate [IMF]		
A-196	amended Articles of Agreement [IMF] Articles of Agreement as amended	Statuts amendés Statuts du FMI, tels qu'ils ont été modifiés	Convenio Constitutivo enmendado Convenio Constitutivo con sus enmiendas texto enmendado del Convenio Constitutivo
A-197	amendment	amendement	enmienda modificación reforma
A-198	amendment (to the Articles of Agreement) [IMF]	amendement (des Statuts)	enmienda (del Convenio Constitutivo)
A-199	AMF, *see* Arab Monetary Fund		
A-200	AML, *see* anti-money laundering		
A-201	AML Methodology Document joint Fund/World Bank AML Methodology Document	Document de méthodologie sur la lutte contre le blanchiment d'argent Document de méthodologie conjoint FMI/Banque mondiale sur la lutte contre le blanchiment d'argent	documento de metodología sobre la lucha contra el lavado de dinero documento conjunto del Banco Mundial y el FMI de metodología sobre la lucha contra el lavado de dinero
A-202	AML supervisory principles	principes de contrôle financier	principios de supervisión contra el lavado de dinero
A-203	amortization *see also:* depreciation	amortissement	amortización financiera amortización
A-204	amortization	amortissement financier remboursement recouvrement	amortización
A-205	amortization profile	structure de l'amortissement structure des remboursements	perfil de la amortización estructura de los pagos de amortización
A-206	amount of access [IMF]	montant de l'accès (aux ressources du FMI)	monto del acceso a los recursos del FMI monto del acceso

A-207	amount outstanding	encours solde	saldo deuda viva deuda pendiente
A-208	amount payable forthwith	montant immédiatement exigible	cantidad pagadera de inmediato
A-209	anchor	point d'ancrage	ancla anclaje
A-210	ancillary meetings [IMF/World Bank]	réunions annexes	reuniones conexas
A-211	ancillary services	services auxiliaires	servicios auxiliares
A-212	Andean Subregional Integration Agreement, *see* Cartagena Agreement		
A-213	annual arrangement [IMF]	accord annuel	acuerdo anual
A-214	annual basis, on an *see also:* year-to-year basis, on a annualized basis, on an full-year basis, on a	annuel en année pleine en année complète	elevado a cifras anuales en cifras anualizadas tomando como base el año completo con base anual
A-215	Annual Meetings, *see* Annual Meetings (of the Boards of Governors) of the International Monetary Fund and the World Bank		
A-216	Annual Meetings of the Board of Governors, *see* Annual Meetings (of the Boards of Governors) of the International Monetary Fund and the World Bank		
A-217	Annual Meetings (of the Boards of Governors) of the International Monetary Fund and the World Bank [IMF/World Bank] Annual Meetings of the Board of Governors Annual Meetings	Assemblée annuelle (des Conseils des gouverneurs) du Fonds monétaire international et de la Banque mondiale Assemblée annuelle	Reuniones Anuales (de las Juntas de Gobernadores) del Fondo Monetario Internacional y del Banco Mundial
A-218	Annual PRSP Progress Report, *see* PRSP Progress Report		
A-219	*Annual Report, see Annual Report of the Executive Board*		
A-220	*Annual Report of the Executive Board* [IMF] *Annual Report*	*Rapport annuel du Conseil d'administration* *Rapport annuel*	*Informe Anual del Directorio Ejecutivo* *Informe Anual*
A-221	*Annual Report on Exchange Arrangements and Exchange Restrictions* [IMF] *AREAER* *ARER*	Rapport annuel sur les régimes et les restrictions de change AREAER	Informe anual sobre regímenes de cambio y restricciones cambiarias
A-222	annualized basis, on an, *see* annual basis, on an		
A-223	annuity	annuité paiement périodique rente	anualidad renta vitalicia pensión vitalicia seguro de renta vitalicia seguro de rentas

A-224	annuity bond, *see* perpetual bond		
A-225	antibounty duty, *see* countervailing duty		
A-226	anticipated growth rate	taux de croissance prévu taux de croissance escompté	tasa de crecimiento prevista
A-227	anticyclical measure, *see* countercyclical action		
A-228	anticyclical reserve fund	fonds de stabilisation de la conjoncture	fondo de estabilización anticíclica
A-229	anticyclical tax	impôt conjoncturel prélèvement conjoncturel	impuesto anticíclico
A-230	antidumping duty	droit antidumping	derecho *antidumping*
A-231	anti-money laundering AML	lutte contre le blanchiment d'argent lutte contre le blanchiment des capitaux	prevención del lavado de dinero lucha contra el lavado de dinero
A-232	APC, *see* Agenda and Procedures Committee		
A-233	APD, *see* Asia and Pacific Department		
A-234	APEC, *see* Asia-Pacific Economic Cooperation		
A-235	APEC Council, *see* Asia-Pacific Economic Cooperation		
A-236	APEC Forum, *see* Asia-Pacific Economic Cooperation		
A-237	application for membership [IMF]	demande d'admission	solicitud de admisión
A-238	appointed Executive Director [IMF]	administrateur nommé	Director Ejecutivo Nombrado
A-239	apportionment of appropriations [USA]	répartition des crédits	distribución de las asignaciones presupuestarias distribución de los créditos presupuestarios
A-240	appreciate	s'apprécier se valoriser	apreciarse valorizarse
A-241	appropriation, *see* budget appropriation		
A-242	appropriation *see also:* allocation; budget appropriation	crédit crédit budgétaire dotation autorisation de crédits budgétaires	autorización presupuestaria partida presupuestaria crédito presupuestario afectación presupuestaria consignación presupuestaria
A-243	appropriation ceiling	enveloppe budgétaire	tope de la autorización presupuestaria
A-244	appropriation-in-aid	fonds affectés recettes affectées à des dépenses particulières recettes en atténuation de dépenses	autorizaciones presupuestarias de ayuda
A-245	approved budget, *see* budget law		

A-246	APR, *see* PRSP Progress Report		
A-247	Arab accounting dinar [AMF] AAD	dinar arabe dinar comptable arabe	dinar árabe dinar árabe contable

A-248	Arab Bank for Economic
	   Development in Africa
	ABEDA
	BADEA
		Banque arabe pour le
		   développement économique en
		   Afrique
		BADEA
			Banco Árabe para el Desarrollo
			   Económico de África
			BADEA

A-249	Arab Fund for Economic
	   and Social Development
	AFESD
		Fonds arabe pour le
		   développement économique et
		   social
		FADES
			Fondo Árabe de Desarrollo
			   Económico y Social
			FADES

A-250	Arab Monetary Fund AMF	Fonds monétaire arabe FMA	Fondo Monetario Árabe FMA
A-251	Arabic and Russian Division [IMF]	Division arabe et russe	División de Árabe y Ruso
A-252	arbitrager arbitrageur	arbitragiste	arbitrajista
A-253	arbitrageur, *see* arbitrager		
A-254	arbitration clause	clause compromissoire clause d'arbitrage	cláusula de arbitraje
A-255	area department [IMF]	département géographique	departamento regional
A-256	AREAER, *see* Annual Report on Exchange Arrangements and Exchange Restrictions		
A-257	ARER, *see* Annual Report on Exchange Arrangements and Exchange Restrictions		
A-258	arithmetic mean mean	moyenne arithmétique moyenne	media aritmética media
A-259	arm's length	de pleine concurrence sur un pied d'égalité à armes égales	en pie de igualdad sin favoritismo en condiciones de igualdad entre partes independientes
A-260	arranged transaction [IMF] *see also:* transaction by agreement transaction arranged by the IMF	transaction organisée par le FMI	transacción concertada por el FMI
A-261	arrangement [IMF] *see also:* Extended Arrangement; Stand-By Arrangement	accord	acuerdo
A-262	arrangements	dispositions dispositif	mecanismo disposiciones régimen arreglo

A-263	arrears	arriérés impayés	atrasos mora atrasos de pagos
A-264	arrears [IMF] payment arrears	arriérés arriérés de paiements	atrasos atrasos en los pagos pagos en mora
A-265	arrears country [IMF] *see also:* overdue country country with payment arrears	pays ayant des arriérés de paiements pays en situation d'arriérés	país en mora país miembro con atrasos en los pagos
A-266	arrears strategy, *see* intensified cooperative approach		
A-267	Article IV consultation [IMF]	consultations au titre de l'article IV	consulta del Artículo IV
A-268	Article IV consultation discussions [IMF] consultation discussions	entretiens dans le cadre des consultations au titre de l'article IV	conversaciones en el marco de la consulta del Artículo IV
A-269	Article IV surveillance, *see* bilateral surveillance		
A-270	Article VIII country [IMF]	pays remplissant les conditions de l'article VIII	país que cumple las condiciones del Artículo VIII
A-271	Article VIII obligations [IMF]	obligations (au titre) de l'article VIII obligations visées à l'article VIII	obligaciones del Artículo VIII
A-272	Articles of Agreement, *see* Articles of Agreement of the International Monetary Fund		
A-273	Articles of Agreement as amended, *see* amended Articles of Agreement		
A-274	*Articles of Agreement of the* *International Monetary Fund* [IMF] Articles of Agreement Articles of the Fund Fund Agreement	*Statuts du Fonds monétaire* *international* Statuts du FMI Statuts	*Convenio Constitutivo del Fondo* *Monetario Internacional* Convenio Constitutivo del FMI Convenio Constitutivo
A-275	Articles of the Fund, *see* Articles of Agreement of the International Monetary Fund		
A-276	artificial person *see also:* natural person legal entity corporation corporate body	personne morale	persona jurídica entidad jurídica
A-277	artisanal industry cottage industry	industrie artisanale industrie familiale	industria artesanal industria familiar industria casera industria doméstica
A-278	AsDB, *see* Asian Development Bank		
A-279	ASEAN, *see* Association of Southeast Asian Nations		
A-280	Asia and Pacific Department [IMF] APD	Département Asie et Pacifique	Departamento de Asia y el Pacífico

A-281	Asia and Pacific Regional Division [IMF]	Division Asie et Pacifique	División de la Región de Asia y el Pacífico
A-282	Asian Development Bank AsDB ADB	Banque asiatique de développement BAsD BAD	Banco Asiático de Desarrollo BAsD BAD
A-283	Asian Division [IMF]	Division Asie	División de Asia
A-284	Asia-Pacific Economic Cooperation *see also:* Pacific Economic Cooperation Council APEC Asia-Pacific Economic Cooperation Council APEC Council Asia-Pacific Economic Forum APEC Forum	Coopération économique Asie–Pacifique CEAP Coopération des économies de l'Asie–Pacifique APEC Forum économique Asie–Pacifique Conseil de l'Association de coopération économique Asie–Pacifique	Foro de Cooperación Económica Asia-Pacífico APEC
A-285	Asia-Pacific Economic Cooperation Council, *see* Asia-Pacific Economic Cooperation		
A-286	Asia-Pacific Economic Forum, *see* Asia-Pacific Economic Cooperation		
A-287	assessment, *see* SDR assessment		
A-288	assessment	prélèvement	contribución directa contribución derrama gravamen tributo
A-289	assessment, *see* tax assessment		
A-290	assessment letter [IMF] comfort letter assessment statement	lettre de confort lettre d'évaluation	carta de evaluación informe de evaluación
A-291	assessment list, *see* assessment roll		
A-292	assessment mission [IMF-IBRD]	mission d'évaluation	misión de evaluación
A-293	Assessment of Financial Sector Supervision and Regulation [IMF] AFSSR	Évaluation du contrôle et de la réglementation du secteur financier	Evaluación de la Supervisión y Regulación del Sector Financiero
A-294	assessment roll [taxation] assessment list	rôle	registro tributario
A-295	assessment statement, *see* assessment letter		
A-296	assessor [taxation]	agent de perception agent d'assiette contrôleur des contributions inspecteur des impôts	tasador inspector de impuestos aforador

A-297	asset	actif avoir élément d'actif	activo elemento del activo rubro del activo
A-298	asset operation	opération sur actifs	operación activa
A-299	asset position, *see* creditor position		
A-300	asset price bubble	bulle des prix des actifs	burbuja de precios de los activos
A-301	assets	actifs avoirs	activos
A-302	assignment *see also:* secondment	affectation mise à disposition mission	destino comisión de servicios misión
A-303	Assistant ..., *see* ..., Assistant [IMF]		
A-304	Assistant to the Director [IMF]	Assistant du Directeur	Asistente del Director
A-305	Assistant to the Secretary [IMF]	Assistant du Secrétaire	Asistente del Secretario
A-306	associate, *see* associated enterprise		
A-307	Associate ..., *see* ..., Associate [IMF]		
A-308	associated agreement, *see* associated borrowing arrangement		
A-309	associated borrowing arrangement [IMF] associated agreement	accord d'emprunt associé (aux AGE)	acuerdo de obtención de préstamo paralelo a los AGP acuerdo paralelo
A-310	associated enterprise *see also:* affiliate associate	entreprise affiliée entreprise apparentée	empresa asociada asociada
A-311	Association of Southeast Asian Nations ASEAN	Association des nations de l'Asie du Sud-Est ASEAN	Asociación de Naciones del Asia Sudoriental ASEAN
A-312	Atlantic Division [IMF]	Division Atlantique	División del Atlántico
A-313	attendance list	liste des participants	lista de participantes
A-314	attracting deposits, *see* deposit taking		
A-315	attrition rate	taux d'usure	tasa de desgaste
A-316	AU, *see* African Union		
A-317	auction rate [exchange rates]	taux d'adjudication	tipo de cambio de adjudicación

A-318	audit auditing	vérification des comptes examen des comptes contrôle des comptes inspection des comptes audit apurement des comptes	auditoría revisión de cuentas verificación de cuentas comprobación de cuentas
A-319	audit committee	commission de vérification des comptes	comité de auditoría
A-320	audit office auditing department	Cour des comptes organisme de vérification des comptes publics commission de vérification des comptes publics	Tribunal de Cuentas Oficina de Auditoría
A-321	audit opinion	avis des commissaires aux comptes	dictamen de auditoría
A-322	audited financial statements	états financiers vérifiés état comptable vérifié	estados financieros auditados estados financieros verificados por auditores
A-323	auditing, *see* audit		
A-324	auditing department, *see* audit office		
A-325	Auditor [IMF]	vérificateur	Auditor
A-326	Auditor, Senior [IMF]	Vérificateur principal	Auditor Principal
A-327	augmentation of resources [IMF]	augmentation des ressources	aumento de los recursos complemento de los recursos
A-328	augmented Fund resources, *see* augmented resources		
A-329	augmented resources [IMF] augmented Fund resources	ressources d'appoint complément de ressources	aumento de los recursos complemento de los recursos recursos aumentados recursos complementarios
A-330	authorized bank	banque agréée	banco autorizado banca delegada
A-331	authorized capital	capital social capital autorisé capital déclaré capital nominal	capital autorizado capital social capital nominal
A-332	automatic stabilizer, *see* built-in stabilizer		
A-333	average daily balance	moyenne des soldes quotidiens	promedio de los saldos diarios saldo medio diario
A-334	average-inflation country	pays à inflation moyenne	país de mediana inflación país de inflación media
A-335	avoidance of cross-conditionality [IMF] *see also:* collaboration with the World Bank	modalités visant à éviter la conditionnalité croisée	necesidad de evitar la condicionalidad cruzada necesidad de evitar la doble condicionalidad

B

B-1	back office	postmarché service-titres back-office	*back office* servicio auxiliar oficina de servicios auxiliares
B-2	backed loan, *see* guaranteed loan		
B-3	background paper	document de référence document d'information	documento de antecedentes documento de información básica documento de referencia
B-4	back-loading [IMF] *see also:* flat-loading; front-loading	concentration des décaissements en fin de période concentration en fin de programme	concentración de desembolsos al final del período del acuerdo concentración (de medidas, gastos, etc.) al final del período concentración al final del programa
B-5	back-to-back credit back-to-back loan	prêts croisés en devises contre-crédit crédit adossé financements couplés	préstamos cruzados en divisas crédito con garantía de otro crédito
B-6	back-to-back loan, *see* back-to-back credit		
B-7	back-to-back missions [IMF]	missions successives sans retour au siège	misiones consecutivas sin regresar a la sede
B-8	back-to-office report BTO forty-eight-hour report debrief [IMF]	compte rendu de retour de mission rapport sous quarante-huit heures	informe al regreso de una misión informe dentro de las cuarenta y ocho horas
B-9	backward shifting *see also:* forward shifting	répercussion en amont	traslación hacia atrás traslación del impuesto hacia atrás
B-10	bad debt *see also:* doubtful loan	créance irrécouvrable	deuda incobrable
B-11	BADEA, *see* Arab Bank for Economic Development in Africa		
B-12	Balance of Payments and External Debt Division I, II [IMF]	Division de la balance des paiements et de la dette extérieure I, II	División de Balanza de Pagos y Deuda Externa I, II
B-13	*Balance of Payments Compilation Guide* [IMF]	*Guide pour l'établissement des statistiques de balance des paiements*	*Guía para compilar estadísticas de balanza de pagos*
B-14	balance of payments constraint	contrainte extérieure contrainte de balance des paiements contrainte imposée par la balance des paiements	limitación impuesta por la balanza de pagos
B-15	*Balance of Payments Manual* [IMF] *BPM*	*Manuel de la balance des paiements*	*Manual de Balanza de Pagos*

B-16	balance of payments need [IMF]	besoin de balance des paiements besoin de financement de la balance des paiements besoin de soutien à la balance des paiements	necesidad de balanza de pagos necesidad de financiamiento de la balanza de pagos
B-17	balance of payments position payments position	position de la balance des paiements situation de la balance des paiements position des paiements situation des paiements	saldo de la balanza de pagos situación de la balanza de pagos situación de pagos externos
B-18	*Balance of Payments Statistics Yearbook* [IMF] *BOPSY*	*Balance of Payments Statistics Yearbook* Annuaire de statistiques de balance des paiements	*Balance of Payments Statistics Yearbook* Anuario de estadísticas de balanza de pagos
B-19	balance of payments surplus	excédent de la balance des paiements	superávit de la balanza de pagos superávit de pagos externos
B-20	balance of payments test [IMF]	critère de la situation de la balance des paiements	prueba de la situación de la balanza de pagos prueba de la necesidad de respaldo para la balanza de pagos
B-21	balance of risks	probabilité de révision des prévisions à la baisse ou à la hausse	balanza de riesgos
B-22	balance of trade trade balance	balance commerciale	balanza comercial saldo comercial
B-23	balance on current account, *see* current account balance		
B-24	balance sheet general balance sheet statement of financial position statement of financial condition statement of condition statement of assets and liabilities balance sheet statement	bilan état de la situation financière états des avoirs et engagements état des actifs et passifs compte de patrimoine situation patrimoniale	balance balance general estado de la condición financiera hoja de balance estado de pasivos y activos
B-25	balance sheet approach balance sheet approach to financial crisis	approche bilancielle approche patrimoniale méthode bilancielle analyse bilancielle	enfoque del balance análisis de las crisis financieras desde la óptica de los balances
B-26	balance sheet approach to financial crisis, *see* balance sheet approach		
B-27	balance sheet statement, *see* balance sheet		
B-28	balanced distribution of holdings [IMF]	répartition équilibrée des avoirs	distribución equilibrada de las tenencias
B-29	balanced positions [IMF]	positions en équilibre	posiciones equilibradas
B-30	balancing entry, *see* offsetting entry		

B-31	balancing item *see also:* counterpart entry; offsetting entry	solde comptable	partida equilibradora partida de resultado
B-32	balancing statement	tableau équilibré état comptable	estado contable equilibrado

B-33	balloon loan
	see also: bullet loan
		emprunt assorti d'un
		  remboursement forfaitaire
		prêt ballon
			préstamo *balloon*
			préstamo globo
			préstamo reembolsable en su
			  mayor parte al vencimiento

B-34	band, *see* fluctuation band		
B-35	bandwagon, *see* herd behavior		
B-36	bandwagon behavior, *see* herd behavior		
B-37	bandwagon effect, *see* herd behavior		
B-38	bank acceptance, *see* banker's acceptance		
B-39	bank advisory committee [London Club] *see also:* country advisory committee advisory committee steering committee	comité consultatif bancaire comité consultatif des banques comité de restructuration comité de coordination	comité consultivo de bancos comité consultivo bancario comité de coordinación
B-40	bank assessment	diagnostic des banques diagnostic de la situation bancaire	evaluación de la situación bancaria diagnóstico de la situación bancaria
B-41	bank call report, *see* call report		

B-42	bank call report form
	bank report form
	report form
		formulaire de communication des
		  données des banques
		formulaire de déclaration
		formulaire-navette
			formulario de declaración de datos
			  de los bancos
			formulario de declaración de datos

B-43	bank cash ratio
	see also: cash ratio
		ratio de liquidité immédiate (des
		  banques)
		coefficient de liquidité immédiate
		  (des banques)
			coeficiente bancario de caja
			índice de liquidez

B-44	bank check, *see* cashier's check		
B-45	bank debt, *see* commercial debt		
B-46	bank examination	inspection bancaire	inspección bancaria auditoría bancaria
B-47	Bank for International Settlements BIS	Banque des règlements internationaux BRI	Banco de Pagos Internacionales BPI
B-48	bank liquidity ratio	ratio de liquidité bancaire ratio de liquidité des banques coefficient de liquidité bancaire coefficient de liquidité des banques	coeficiente de liquidez bancaria
B-49	bank money	monnaie scripturale	dinero bancario dinero escritural

B-50	Bank of Central African States
	BEAC
		Banque des États de l'Afrique
		  centrale
		BEAC
			Banco de los Estados de África
			  Central
			BEAC

B-51	bank of issue currency issuing agency	banque d'émission institut d'émission	banco emisor banco de emisión entidad emisora de moneda
B-52	bank rate, *see* discount rate		
B-53	bank report form, *see* bank call report form		
B-54	bank run run on a bank	retraits massifs d'une banque ruée sur une banque	pánico bancario retirada masiva de los depósitos de un banco corrida bancaria
B-55	bank secrecy	secret bancaire	secreto bancario
B-56	bank supervision banking supervision	contrôle bancaire surveillance bancaire contrôle des banques	supervisión bancaria supervisión de bancos
B-57	bank supervisors	autorités de contrôle bancaire	autoridades de supervisión bancaria
B-58	banker's acceptance bank acceptance	acceptation de banque acceptation bancaire	aceptación bancaria
B-59	bankers' bank	banque des banques	banco de bancos

B-60	bankers' deposit
	[central bank]
		dépôt des banques
		dépôt à vue des banques
		  commerciales
			depósito a la vista de los bancos
			  comerciales en el banco central
			depósitos de encaje

B-61	bankers' reserves	réserves des banques
		  (commerciales)
			reservas de los bancos
			  (comerciales)

B-62	Bank/Fund Conferences Office
	[IMF]
	BFCO
		Service des conférences
		  Banque–FMI
			Oficina de Conferencias
			  del Banco y del Fondo

B-63	banking	activité bancaire activité des banques opérations bancaires	actividad bancaria operaciones bancarias banca
B-64	banking, *see* banking sector		
B-65	banking authorities	autorités bancaires	autoridades bancarias
B-66	banking sector banking	banque(s) système bancaire secteur bancaire	sector bancario sistema bancario banca bancos
B-67	banking soundness	solidité bancaire	solidez bancaria solidez del sistema bancario
B-68	banking supervision, *see* bank supervision		
B-69	banking survey	situation bancaire	panorama bancario

B-70	banklike institutions	institutions à caractère bancaire	instituciones afines a las bancarias instituciones parabancarias
B-71	banknotes and coins	billets et pièces	billetes y moneda metálica
B-72	bankruptcy *see also:* composition of creditors; default; insolvency; liquidation	faillite dépôt de bilan banqueroute	quiebra bancarrota concurso falencia
B-73	bar *see also:* ingot; small ingot	or en barres barre	barra barra de oro
B-74	bargaining power	pouvoir de négociation	poder de negociación
B-75	barren money	fonds improductifs	dinero improductivo barrera de entrada
B-76	barrier to entry	obstacle à l'entrée barrière à l'entrée	barrera a la entrada obstáculo al ingreso
B-77	barter	troc commerce par opérations compensées	trueque comercio de trueque
B-78	barter economy	économie de troc	economía de trueque
B-79	base lending rate, *see* prime rate		
B-80	base money monetary base reserve money central bank money high-powered money	monnaie centrale monnaie (de la) banque centrale base monétaire monnaie à grande puissance monnaie à haute puissance	base monetaria emisión primaria dinero primario dinero del banco central dinero de alta potencia dinero de gran potencia
B-81	base period	période de base période de référence	período base período de base
B-82	base year, *see* tax year		

B-83	Basel Committee on Banking
	    Supervision
	BCBS
	Basle Committee on Banking
	    Supervision
	Cooke Committee
	Basle Committee
		Comité de Bâle sur le contrôle
		    bancaire
		Comité de Bâle
		Comité Cooke
			Comité de Supervisión Bancaria
			    de Basilea
			Comité de Basilea
			Comité Cooke
			CSBB

B-84	Basel II [BIS]	Bâle II nouvel Accord de Bâle	Acuerdo de Basilea II
B-85	baseline scenario [IMF] reference scenario RS benchmark scenario trend scenario business-as-usual scenario nonintervention scenario	scénario de référence	escenario de referencia escenario de base

B-86	base-to-income elasticity	élasticité de l'assiette par rapport au revenu	elasticidad de la base tributaria con respecto al ingreso elasticidad base tributaria/ingreso
B-87	base-weighted index *see also:* current-weighted index base-weighted price index Laspeyres index	indice pondéré en fonction de l'année de base indice de Laspeyres	índice ponderado en función del período base índice de Laspeyres
B-88	base-weighted price index, *see* base-weighted index		
B-89	basic balance	solde de base balance de base	balanza básica
B-90	basic foodstuffs staples	denrées de première nécessité denrées de consommation courante	alimentos básicos alimentos de consumo corriente
B-91	basic period [IMF]	période de base	período básico
B-92	basic rate of charge [IMF]	taux de base des commissions	tasa de cargos básica
B-93	basic vote [IMF]	voix de base	voto básico
B-94	basis of assessment *see also:* tax base; tax incidence	base d'imposition	base imponible base de liquidación del impuesto
B-95	basis of reporting	base de communication des données	base para la declaración de datos
B-96	basis point BPS	point de base	punto básico centésimo de punto porcentual
B-97	basket of currencies, *see* currency basket		
B-98	basket peg basket pegging composite peg	détermination de la valeur (d'une monnaie) par référence à un panier rattachement à un panier parité par rapport à un groupe de monnaies rattachement à un groupe de monnaies	tipo de cambio fijo en relación con una canasta de monedas tipo de cambio vinculado a una cesta de monedas vinculación a una canasta
B-99	basket pegging, *see* basket peg		
B-100	Basle capital	fonds propres (définition Accord de Bâle)	capital según la definición de Basilea
B-101	Basle Capital Accord	Accord de Bâle sur les fonds propres	Acuerdo de Capital de Basilea
B-102	Basle Committee, *see* Basel Committee on Banking Supervision		
B-103	Basle Committee on Banking Supervision, *see* Basel Committee on Banking Supervision		
B-104	Basle Core Principles, *see* Core Principles for Effective Banking Supervision		
B-105	BCBS, *see* Basel Committee on Banking Supervision		

| B-106 | BCEAO, *see* Central Bank of West African States | | |

| B-107 | BEAC, *see* Bank of Central African States | | |

| B-108 | bear market
see also: bull market
bearish market | marché en baisse
marché baissier
marché orienté à la baisse | mercado bajista
mercado a la baja |

| B-109 | bearer instrument
see also: order instrument;
  registered instrument
bearer paper
bearer security | instrument au porteur
titre au porteur | instrumento al portador
título al portador |

| B-110 | bearer paper, *see* bearer instrument | | |

| B-111 | bearer security, *see* bearer instrument | | |

| B-112 | bearish market, *see* bear market | | |

| B-113 | before taxes
pretax | avant impôt(s)
brut d'impôt(s) | antes de impuestos
antes de deducir los impuestos |

| B-114 | beggar-my-neighbor policy
see also: Smoot-Hawley Tariff Act
  of 1930
beggar-thy-neighbor policy | politique du chacun pour soi
politique d'égoïsme sacré
politique d'appauvrissement du
  voisin | política de empobrecimiento del
  vecino
política de egoísmo nacional |

| B-115 | beggar-thy-neighbor policy, *see* beggar-my-neighbor policy | | |

| B-116 | behavior variable | variable de comportement | variable de comportamiento |

| B-117 | behavioral equation | équation de comportement | ecuación de comportamiento |

| B-118 | bell curve, *see* normal distribution curve | | |

| B-119 | bell-shaped curve, *see* normal distribution curve | | |

| B-120 | below the line | «au-dessous de la ligne»
«en dessous de la ligne» | por debajo de la línea |

| B-121 | below-the-line item | poste extraordinaire
poste «au-dessous de la ligne» | partida extraordinaria
partida que figura por debajo de la
  línea |

| B-122 | below-the-line item, *see* off-balance-sheet item | | |

| B-123 | benchmark
[IMF]
performance benchmark | repère
repère de réalisation | parámetro de referencia
punto de referencia
indicador de resultados
referente |

| B-124 | benchmark bond index
[IMF] | indice obligataire de référence | índice de bonos de referencia |

| B-125 | benchmark scenario, *see* baseline scenario | | |

| B-126 | benefit | avantage
prestation | beneficio
prestación
subsidio |

B-127	benefit principle of taxation	principe de l'imposition sur la base du service rendu	principio de la imposición basada en el servicio prestado
B-128	benign neglect	«douce insouciance» indifférence bienveillante	desatención benévola descuido benévolo indiferencia benévola
B-129	best-case scenario optimistic scenario	scénario optimiste scénario fondé sur les hypothèses les plus favorables	escenario optimista escenario óptimo marco hipotético optimista
B-130	best estimate	meilleure estimation	estimación óptima
B-131	best-policies scenario, *see* better-policies scenario		
B-132	better-policies scenario [*WEO*] best-policies scenario optimistic scenario	scénario fondé sur des politiques plus favorables scénario optimiste	escenario basado en la aplicación de políticas más favorables escenario optimista
B-133	BFCO, *see* Bank/Fund Conferences Office		
B-134	bias	biais erreur systématique	sesgo distorsión error sistemático
B-136	biased	biaisé non centré	sesgado
B-137	biased estimator	estimateur biaisé	estimador sesgado
B-138	bi-cycle [IMF] *see also:* biennial consultation; interim consultation bicyclic procedure	procédure de consultations à cycle double	ciclo bienal procedimiento de ciclo bienal de consultas
B-139	bicyclic procedure, *see* bi-cycle		
B-140	bid price	prix offert cours acheteur	cotización de compra precio ofrecido por el comprador
B-141	bid rate, *see* buying rate		
B-142	bid-ask spread	écart entre les cours acheteur et vendeur	diferencia entre el precio de compra y el precio de venta diferencial entre el precio de demanda y el precio de oferta
B-143	bidder tenderer	soumissionnaire	licitador licitante postor oferente concursante
B-144	bid-offer spread	écart entre les cours acheteur et vendeur	margen entre el tipo de cambio comprador y vendedor
B-145	biennial consultation [IMF] *see also:* bi-cycle; interim consultation	consultations biennales	consulta bienal

B-146	bilateral central rate	taux pivot (central) bilatéral cours pivot bilatéral	tipo de cambio central bilateral
B-147	bilateral creditor [HIPC Initiative]	créancier bilatéral créancier partie à un prêt bilatéral	acreedor bilateral
B-148	bilateral payments agreement bilateral payments arrangement	accord bilatéral de paiements	acuerdo bilateral de pagos convenio bilateral de pagos
B-149	bilateral payments arrangement, *see* bilateral payments agreement		
B-150	bilateral surveillance [IMF] Article IV surveillance	surveillance bilatérale surveillance au titre de l'article IV	supervisión bilateral supervisión en el marco de las consultas del Artículo IV
B-151	bilateral trade weight	pondération du commerce bilatéral coefficient de pondération du commerce bilatéral	ponderación del comercio bilateral
B-152	bill	effet effet à court terme	letra
B-153	billion [IMF-IBRD; USA]	milliard	mil millones
B-154	binding	exécutoire ayant force exécutoire obligatoire contraignant	obligatorio vinculante exigible
B-155	bipolar view	théorie bipolaire	enfoque bipolar
B-156	BIS, *see* Bank for International Settlements		
B-157	*blindaje*, *see* financial shield		

B-158	block grant
	[USA]
		don forfaitaire
		subvention globale
		subvention fonctionnelle
			subvención global para un fin
			  determinado
			subvención para determinadas
			  funciones
			subvención en bloque

B-159	blocked account	compte bloqué	cuenta bloqueada
B-160	BLR, *see* prime rate		
B-161	blue chip gilt-edged security [GBR]	valeur vedette valeur de premier ordre valeur sûre	valor de primera clase valor de primer orden acciones líderes valores punteros valores estrella
B-162	Board, *see* Executive Board		
B-163	Board of Governors [IMF]	Conseil des gouverneurs	Junta de Gobernadores
B-164	Board of Governors of the Federal Reserve System, *see* Federal Reserve Board		
B-165	bond *see also:* debenture	obligation bon	bono

B-166	bond market fixed-income market	marché obligataire marché des valeurs mobilières à revenu fixe	mercado de bonos mercado de títulos de renta fija
B-167	bond portfolio holdings of bonds	portefeuille d'obligations obligations en portefeuille	cartera de bonos bonos en cartera
B-168	bond swaps, *see* debt conversion		
B-169	bond warrant debt warrant	warrant obligataire droit de souscription obligataire	certificado para compra de bonos opción de compra de bonos
B-170	bonded good	marchandise non dédouanée marchandise en douane marchandise en entrepôt sous douane marchandise sous scellement	mercancía en depósito mercancía en almacén de aduana mercancía en aduana
B-171	bonded warehouse, *see* customs bonded warehouse		
B-172	bonus interest rate	taux d'intérêt à prime taux majoré prime d'intérêt	tasa de interés con prima
B-173	bonus share *see also:* stock dividend bonus stock	action gratuite	acción distribuida gratuitamente acción gratuita acción como gratificación bonificación
B-174	bonus stock, *see* bonus share		
B-175	book loss	perte comptable	pérdida contable
B-176	book profit	bénéfice comptable	ganancia contable beneficio contable
B-177	book rate, *see* accounting rate		
B-178	book value, *see* carrying value		
B-179	book-entry security paperless security	titre dématérialisé titre non matérialisé	título anotado en cuenta título escritural título desmaterializado
B-180	boom and bust, *see* business cycle		
B-181	*BOPSY, see Balance of Payments Statistics Yearbook*		
B-182	border tax adjustment	ajustement fiscal à la frontière	ajuste tributario en frontera
B-183	border trade *see also:* shuttle trade	commerce frontalier	comercio fronterizo compras transfronterizas para uso personal
B-184	border worker	frontalier travailleur frontalier	trabajador fronterizo
B-185	borrowed resources [IMF] *see also:* ordinary resources	ressources empruntées	recursos obtenidos en préstamo

B-186	Borrowed Resources Suspense Accounts [IMF] BRSA	comptes d'attente pour les ressources empruntées	Cuentas Suspensivas de Recursos Ajenos
B-187	borrower ownership, *see* ownership		
B-188	borrowing agreement, *see* borrowing arrangement		
B-189	borrowing arrangement [IMF] borrowing agreement	accord d'emprunt	acuerdo de obtención de préstamos
B-190	borrowing capacity *see also:* repayment capacity	capacité d'endettement capacité d'emprunt	capacidad de endeudamiento capacidad de obtención de préstamos
B-191	borrowing rate	taux créditeur taux des emprunts	tasa de interés de los empréstitos tasa pasiva
B-192	borrowing ratio [IMF]	coefficient d'emprunt	coeficiente de endeudamiento
B-193	borrowing requirement *see also:* net borrowing	besoin de financement besoin d'emprunt	necesidad de financiamiento necesidad de obtención de préstamos
B-194	borrowing-quota ratio [IMF]	ratio emprunts/quotes-parts	razón empréstitos/cuotas
B-195	bottleneck inflation	inflation causée par des goulets d'étranglement	inflación por estrangulamientos de la oferta inflación causada por limitaciones de la oferta inflación de demanda
B-196	*BPM, see Balance of Payments Manual*		
B-197	BPS, *see* basis point		
B-198	bracket creep [taxation] bracket progression	progression dans les tranches glissement d'une tranche d'imposition à l'autre (dû à l'effet de l'inflation)	progresión gradual a tasas impositivas más altas progresión escalonada
B-199	bracket progression, *see* bracket creep		
B-200	Brady bond Brady debt	obligations Brady	bono Brady deuda en bonos Brady
B-201	Brady debt, *see* Brady bond		
B-202	Brady Plan	Plan Brady	Plan Brady
B-203	branch	succursale	sucursal
B-204	Brazil Training Center, *see* Joint Regional Training Center for Latin America in Brazil		
B-205	break-even point	seuil de rentabilité point mort niveau d'équilibre	punto de equilibrio umbral de rentabilidad punto muerto
B-206	Bretton Woods Conference, *see* United Nations Monetary and Financial Conference		

B-207	bridge financing bridge loan bridging credit swing loan swing line	financement relais crédit de soudure crédit-relais prêt-relais crédit-relais crédit de soudure	financiamiento puente financiamiento de empalme préstamo puente préstamo de empalme préstamo transitorio descubierto recíproco margen de crédito recíproco
B-208	bridge loan, *see* bridge financing		
B-209	bridge table *see also:* reconciliation table	tableau de passage	cuadro puente cuadro de conciliación cuadro de empalme
B-210	bridging credit, *see* bridge financing		
B-211	briefing	mise au courant séance d'information remise des directives remise des instructions	sesión informativa sesión de orientación sesión de información instrucciones
B-212	broad financial market *see also:* deep financial market	marché financier développé marché financier diversifié	mercado financiero amplio
B-213	broad money broadly defined money supply	monnaie au sens large masse monétaire au sens large agrégat monétaire large	dinero en sentido amplio masa monetaria en sentido amplio disponibilidades líquidas oferta monetaria en sentido amplio base monetaria amplia dinero en su definición amplia
B-214	broadening of the capital market, *see* financial broadening		
B-215	broadening of the financial market, *see* financial broadening		
B-216	broadening of the tax base	élargissement de la base d'imposition	ampliación de la base imponible
B-217	broadly defined money supply, *see* broad money		
B-218	broker *see also:* dealer	courtier courtier en valeurs mobilières courtier en bourse maison de courtage maison de titres	*broker* agente de bolsa corredor de bolsa
B-219	brokerage, *see* brokerage fee		
B-220	brokerage fee brokerage	frais de courtage commission de courtage	comisión de corretaje
B-221	BRSA, *see* Borrowed Resources Suspense Accounts		
B-222	Brussels Nomenclature, *see* Nomenclature for the Classification of Goods in Customs Tariffs		
B-223	Brussels Office [IMF] EUO/BR	Bureau du FMI à Bruxelles Bureau de Bruxelles	Oficina del FMI en Bruselas
B-224	Brussels Tariff Nomenclature, *see* Nomenclature for the Classification of Goods in Customs Tariffs		
B-225	BSFF, *see* Buffer Stock Financing Facility		

B-226	BTC, *see* Joint Regional Training Center for Latin America in Brazil		
B-227	BTN, *see Nomenclature for the Classification of Goods in Customs Tariffs*		
B-228	BTO, *see* back-to-office report		
B-230	budget appropriation appropriation budget appropriation process budgetary appropriation budgetary appropriation process	ouverture d'un crédit affectation (d'une somme à ...) ouverture de crédit budgétaire	afectación presupuestaria autorización de crédito apropiación consignación presupuestaria
B-231	budget appropriation process, *see* budget appropriation		
B-232	budget bill, *see* budget proposal		
B-233	budget consolidation, *see* fiscal consolidation		
B-234	budget constraint *see also:* hard budget constraint; soft budget constraint	contrainte budgétaire	limitación presupuestaria
B-235	budget cut	compression budgétaire coupe budgétaire	reducción presupuestaria recorte presupuestario
B-236	budget deficit budget gap	déficit budgétaire impasse (budgétaire)	déficit presupuestario
B-237	budget estimate budget forecast	prévision budgétaire état prévisionnel des recettes et dépenses	previsión presupuestaria estimación presupuestaria
B-238	budget execution	exécution de la loi de finances exécution budgétaire exécution du budget	ejecución presupuestaria ejecución del presupuesto
B-239	budget forecast, *see* budget estimate		
B-240	budget framework law *see also:* budget law	loi relative aux lois de finances loi organique	ley de directrices presupuestarias
B-241	budget gap, *see* budget deficit		
B-242	budget law *see also:* budget framework law approved budget	loi de finances budget voté budget approuvé	ley de presupuesto presupuesto aprobado
B-243	budget outturn budget performance	résultats budgétaires résultat de l'exécution de la loi budgétaire	resultado presupuestario
B-244	budget performance, *see* budget outturn		
B-245	budget proposal draft budget budget bill	projet de loi de finances projet de budget	proyecto de ley de presupuesto proyecto de presupuesto
B-246	Budget Reform Division [IMF]	Division réforme budgétaire	División de Reforma Presupuestaria
B-247	budget savings	économies budgétaires	ahorro presupuestario

B-248	Budget Strategy Division [IMF]	Division stratégie budgétaire	División de Estrategia Presupuestaria
B-249	budget surplus/deficit, *see* fiscal balance		
B-250	budget year	exercice budgétaire	ejercicio presupuestario
B-251	budgetary appropriation, *see* budget appropriation		
B-252	budgetary appropriation process, *see* budget appropriation		
B-253	budgetary balance *see also:* fiscal equilibrium budgetary equilibrium	équilibre budgétaire	equilibrio presupuestario
B-254	budgetary balance, *see* fiscal balance		
B-255	budgetary central government budgetary central government accounts	opérations budgétaires de l'administration centrale administration publique centrale—comptes budgétaires comptes budgétaires de l'administration (publique) centrale	gobierno central presupuestario cuentas presupuestarias del gobierno central
B-256	budgetary central government accounts, *see* budgetary central government		
B-257	budgetary consolidation, *see* fiscal consolidation		
B-258	budgetary equilibrium, *see* budgetary balance		
B-259	budgetary expenditure budgetary outlay fiscal expenditure	dépense budgétaire	gasto presupuestario gasto fiscal
B-260	budgetary financing gap budgetary gap	écart de financement du budget	déficit de financiamiento del presupuesto brecha presupuestaria
B-261	budgetary gap, *see* budgetary financing gap		
B-262	budgetary outlay, *see* budgetary expenditure		
B-263	budgetary unit, *see* spending agency		
B-264	budgeted funds	crédits budgétisés fonds inscrits au budget	fondos presupuestados
B-265	budgeting	préparation du budget élaboration du budget établissement du budget	elaboración del presupuesto formulación del presupuesto
B-266	budgeting budgetization fiscalization	budgétisation inscription au budget	presupuestación incorporación al presupuesto inclusión en el presupuesto
B-267	budgetization, *see* budgeting		
B-268	BUFF, *see* Buff Document		
B-269	Buff, *see* Buff Document		

B-270 Buff Document [IMF] *see also:* buff (paper) BUFF	document BUFF	documento BUFF
B-271 buff (paper) [IMF] *see also:* BUFF Document; BUFF ED Document; Chairman's summing-up buff statement	intervention de M. X sur ... déclaration de M. X sur ... résumé du Président (Buff Paper) à l'issue de la discussion sur ...	intervención del Sr. X sobre ... exposición sumaria (del Presidente del Directorio Ejecutivo) al término de las deliberaciones sobre ...
B-272 buff statement, *see* buff (paper)		
B-273 BUFF/ED, *see* BUFF/ED Document		
B-274 BUFF/ED Document [IMF] BUFF/ED	document BUFF/ED	documento BUFF/ED
B-275 Buffer Stock Financing Facility BSFF	mécanisme de financement de stocks régulateurs	Servicio de Financiamiento de Existencias Reguladoras
B-276 building and loan association	organisme de crédit mutuel immobilier	asociación de préstamo y construcción asociación de crédito inmobiliario
B-277 building society [GBR]	société de crédit immobilier société mutuelle de crédit immobilier société de prêts à la construction	asociación de ahorro y préstamo sociedad hipotecaria sociedad de crédito inmobiliario
B-278 built-in elasticity of a tax system *see also:* elasticity of a tax system; tax buoyancy	élasticité intrinsèque d'un système fiscal	elasticidad intrínseca de un sistema tributario
B-279 built-in stabilizer automatic stabilizer	stabilisateur automatique stabilisateur incorporé stabilisateur intégré	estabilizador automático
B-280 bull market *see also:* bear market bullish market	marché en hausse marché haussier marché orienté à la hausse	mercado alcista mercado al alza
B-281 bullet loan *see also:* balloon loan	prêt remboursable *in fine* prêt remboursable en une fois à l'échéance prêt remboursable en un versement unique à l'échéance	préstamo reembolsable de una sola vez al vencimiento
B-282 bulletin board, *see* IMF Bulletin Board		
B-283 bullish market, *see* bull market		
B-284 bunching of maturities debt bunching	concentration des échéances	concentración de los plazos de vencimiento concentración de los vencimientos

B-285	buoyancy	dynamisme	dinamismo
		fermeté	auge
		vigueur	optimismo
			perspectivas favorables
			firmeza
			tendencia alcista de los precios

B-286   buoyancy of a tax system, *see* tax buoyancy

B-287   buoyancy of tax revenue, *see* tax buoyancy

B-288	burden sharing	répartition des charges	distribución de la carga
	[IMF]		distribución de los gastos
	see also: extended burden sharing		

| B-289 | burden-sharing mechanism | mécanisme de répartition des | mecanismo de distribución de la |
| | [IMF] | charges | carga |

B-290	business activity	activité industrielle et commerciale	actividad económica
		conjoncture	actividad empresarial
			actividad industrial y comercial

B-291	business community	milieux d'affaires	medios empresariales
		monde des affaires	círculos empresariales
			mundo de los negocios

B-292	business corporation	société	sociedad
	corporation	société industrielle ou commerciale	empresa
			sociedad anónima
			corporación
			empresa constituida en sociedad

B-293	business cycle	cycle économique	ciclo económico
	economic cycle	cycle conjoncturel	ciclo coyuntural
	trade cycle	conjoncture	coyuntura
	boom and bust	alternance d'expansion	auge y caída
		et de récession	

B-294	business expenses	frais professionnels	gastos de representación
	see also: operating costs	frais de représentation	gastos profesionales
	representation expenses		

B-295	business plan	plan d'entreprise	plan de operaciones
		plan d'action de l'entreprise	plan empresarial
		plan d'exploitation	

B-296	business profit tax	impôt sur les bénéfices industriels	impuesto sobre las utilidades
		et commerciaux	de las empresas
		BIC	impuesto sobre las ganancias
			de las empresas
			impuesto sobre los beneficios
			de las empresas

B-297	business profits	bénéfices industriels	utilidades de las empresas
	trading profits	et commerciaux	ganancias de las empresas
		BIC	beneficios de las empresas

| B-298 | business services | services aux entreprises | servicios empresariales |

| B-299 | business travel | voyages à titre professionnel | viaje por motivo de negocios |

B-300   business-as-usual scenario, *see* baseline scenario

B-301	buy long	acheter long	sobrecomprar especular al alza
B-302	buyback [WTO] buyback arrangement	achats en retour accord d'achats en retour règlement en produits accord de règlement en produits accord de reprise	pacto de recompra
B-303	buyback agreement debt buyback debt repurchase	accord de rachat rachat de créances rachat de dettes	acuerdo de recompra pacto de recompra recompra de deuda
B-304	buyback arrangement, *see* buyback		
B-305	buyer's credit [WTO]	crédit-acheteur	crédito al comprador
B-306	buyers' market	marché acheteur marché favorable à l'acheteur marché dominé par les acheteurs	mercado de compradores mercado favorable a los compradores
B-307	buyer's rate, *see* buying rate		
B-308	buying exchange rate, *see* buying rate		
B-309	buying member [IMF]	État membre acheteur	país miembro comprador país que efectúa una compra
B-310	buying rate buying exchange rate buyer's rate bid rate	cours acheteur cours d'achat taux acheteur taux d'achat	tipo comprador tipo de compra
B-311	By-Laws [IMF] *see also: By-Laws, Rules and* *Regulations* [IMF] by-laws	Réglementation générale réglementation interne règlement intérieur	Estatutos reglamento interno estatuto
B-312	by-laws, *see* By-Laws		
B-313	*By-Laws, Rules and Regulations* [IMF]	*Réglementation générale, Règles* *et Règlements*	*Estatutos y Reglamento*
B-314	byproduct *see also:* end product by-product	sous-produit	subproducto producto derivado
B-315	by-product, *see* byproduct		

C

C-1	c. & f., *see* cost & freight		
C-2	CAC, *see* collective action clause		
C-3	CACM, *see* Central American Common Market		
C-4	CAEMC, *see* Central African Economic and Monetary Community		

C-5	calculated market interest rate, *see* calculated market rate		
C-6	calculated market rate *see also:* combined market rate calculated market interest rate	taux calculé sur la base du marché taux d'intérêt calculé sur la base du marché	tasa de interés de mercado calculada
C-7	calculated quota share [IMF] share in calculated quotas	part (d'un pays) en pourcentage du total des quotes-parts calculées	cuota calculada relativa porcentaje que corresponde a un país en el total de cuotas calculadas
C-8	calendar year	année civile année calendaire	año civil año natural año calendario
C-9	call, *see* call for committed funds		
C-10	call, *see* call option		
C-11	call account	compte à vue	cuenta de depósitos a la vista cuenta a la vista
C-12	call for committed funds call	appel de capitaux appel de fonds	petición de fondos
C-13	call in debt	demander le remboursement anticipé de la dette rendre la dette exigible immédiatement	exigir el pago inmediato de la deuda exigir el pago anticipado de la deuda
C-14	call money	avances à vue argent à vue crédit interbancaire prêt au jour le jour	préstamo interbancario a un día dinero a la vista dinero a un día
C-15	call money rate, *see* cash rate		
C-16	call option call	option d'achat	opción de compra *call*
C-17	call option, *see* call option clause		
C-18	call option clause call option call provision	clause de remboursement anticipé option de remboursement anticipé faculté de remboursement par anticipation	cláusula de opción de renovación opción de renovación
C-19	call provision, *see* call option clause		
C-20	call rate, *see* cash rate		
C-21	call report bank call report	déclaration des transactions financières	informe financiero
C-22	callable bond	obligation remboursable avant l'échéance	bono rescatable antes del vencimiento bono amortizable antes del vencimiento bono redimible antes del vencimiento
C-23	CAM, *see* Committee on Executive Board Administrative Matters		

C-24	CAMU, *see* Central African Monetary Union		
C-25	cancellation of debt, *see* debt forgiveness		
C-26	cancellation of SDRs [IMF]	annulation (de DTS)	cancelación de DEG
C-27	cap, *see* interest rate cap		
C-28	cap option, *see* interest rate cap		
C-29	capacity building	renforcement des capacités	fortalecimiento de las capacidades

C-30	capacity constraint	contrainte de capacité
		insuffisance de (la) capacité
		  (de production)
		limites imposées par la capacité
		  de production
			limitación de la capacidad
			restricción de la capacidad
			  productiva

C-31	capacity output	capacité de production totale	producción a plena capacidad capacidad de producción total

C-32	capacity underutilization
	see also: capacity utilization
	underutilization
		sous-emploi de la capacité
		  de production
		sous-utilisation
			subutilización de la capacidad
			  productiva
			subutilización de la capacidad
			  de producción

C-33	capacity utilization
	see also: capacity underutilization
		emploi de la capacité
		emploi des capacités
		  de production
		utilisation de l'appareil productif
		utilisation de l'appareil
		  de production
			utilización de la capacidad
			  productiva
			utilización de la capacidad
			  de producción

C-34	capital, *see* net worth		
C-35	capital	capital	capital
C-36	capital own funds	fonds propres	capital fondos propios
C-37	capital account [budget]	compte de capital compte capital compte d'opérations en capital	cuenta de capital
C-38	capital account [balance of payments]	compte de capital compte des mouvements de capitaux	cuenta de capital balanza por cuenta de capital

C-39	capital account convertibility
	see also: freedom of capital
	  movements; liberalization of the
	  capital account
		convertibilité du compte de capital
		convertibilité de la monnaie
		  nationale aux fins des
		  mouvements de capitaux
			convertibilidad de la cuenta de
			  capital
			convertibilidad de los saldos de la
			  cuenta de capital
			convertibilidad de la moneda a los
			  efectos de las transacciones de
			  capital

C-40	capital adequacy	niveau suffisant de fonds propres adéquation du capital aux besoins	adecuación del capital capitalización adecuada suficiencia del capital

C-41	capital adequacy ratio *see also:* Basle capital adequacy ratio CAR	norme de fonds propres ratio de fonds propres	coeficiente de capitalización coeficiente de capital coeficiente mínimo de capital índice de adecuación de capital IAC coeficiente de suficiencia de capital
C-42	capital and financial account [balance of payments]	compte de capital et d'opérations financières	cuenta de capital y financiera
C-43	capital assets	immobilisations actifs en capital actifs financiers	activos de capital
C-44	capital assets pricing model CAPM	modèle d'équilibre des actifs financiers MEDAF modèle d'évaluation des actifs financiers modèle de détermination des prix des actifs en capital	modelo de determinación del precio de los activos de capital
C-45	capital base	assise financière fonds propres	base de capital capital base
C-46	capital budget [IMF] *see also:* administrative budget	budget d'équipement budget d'investissement budget des opérations en capital	presupuesto de capital
C-47	capital controls	contrôle des mouvements de capitaux	controles de capital
C-48	capital cost cost of capital	coût du capital	costo del capital costo de la inversión costo de instalación
C-49	capital deepening *see also:* capital widening; financial deepening	accroissement du ratio capital/travail accroissement du coefficient d'intensité du capital	aumento de la razón capital/trabajo intensificación del uso de capital intensificación del capital
C-50	capital, excluding reserves	capitaux autres que les réserves	capital, salvo activos de reserva
C-51	capital expenditure capital outlay	dépense(s) en capital dépense(s) d'équipement dépense(s) d'investissement	gasto de capital desembolso de capital
C-52	capital flight flight of funds	fuite de(s) capitaux exode de(s) capitaux	fuga de capitales
C-53	capital flow capital movements	flux de capitaux courant(s) de capitaux mouvements de capitaux	flujo de capital corriente de capital circulación del capital movimientos de capital
C-54	capital formation	formation de capital	formación de capital
C-55	capital gain	gain en capital gain de capital plus-value	ganancia de capital plusvalía

C-56	capital gains tax	taxe sur les plus-values taxe sur les gains en capital impôt sur les plus-values impôt sur les gains en capital	impuesto sobre las ganancias de capital
C-57	capital gearing ratio, *see* gearing ratio		
C-58	capital good producer good	bien d'équipement bien de capital bien de production	bien de capital bien de equipo bien de producción
C-59	capital income	revenu du capital	renta del capital
C-60	capital inflow, *see* inflow of capital		
C-61	capital intensity, *see* capital intensiveness		
C-62	capital intensiveness capital intensity	intensité du capital degré d'intensité du capital	intensidad de uso del capital
C-63	capital investment	investissement en capital	inversión de capital
C-64	capital loss	perte en capital moins-value	pérdida de capital
C-65	capital market	marché financier marché des capitaux	mercado de capital
C-66	Capital Market Development and Financial Infrastructure Division [IMF]	Division développement des marchés de capitaux et infrastructure financière	División de Desarrollo de Mercados de Capital e Infraestructura Financiera
C-67	capital movements, *see* capital flow		
C-68	capital outflow, *see* outflow of capital		
C-69	capital outlay, *see* capital expenditure		
C-70	capital ratio capital-asset ratio	ratio de fonds propres ratio fonds propres/actifs	coeficiente de capital razón capital/activo
C-71	capital revenue	recettes en capital	ingresos de capital
C-72	capital stock	stock de capital stock de biens de production équipements capital stock d'équipement	capital acervo de capital stock de capital masa de capital
C-73	capital stock, *see* share capital		
C-74	capital tier one, *see* tier 1 capital		
C-75	capital tier two, *see* tier 2 capital		
C-76	capital transaction *see also:* financial and capital transactions	transaction en capital	transacción de capital
C-77	capital transfer	transfert en capital	transferencia de capital

C-78	capital value	valeur de capital valeur en capital	valor de capital valor en capital valor capitalizado
C-79	capital widening *see also:* capital deepening widening of capital	investissement de capacité augmentation du stock de capital	ampliación del capital ampliación de la capacidad productiva del capital
C-80	capital-asset ratio, *see* capital ratio		
C-81	capital-debt ratio [corporations] equity-debt ratio	ratio capital/dettes ratio fonds propres/dettes	razón capital/deuda relación capital/deuda
C-82	capital-exporting country	pays exportateur de capitaux pays exportateur de capital	país exportador de capital
C-83	capital-importing country	pays importateur de capitaux pays importateur de capital	país importador de capital
C-84	capital-intensive	à forte intensité de capital à forte intensité capitalistique	con uso intensivo de capital que requiere mucho capital
C-85	capitalization bond *see also:* debt-equity swap	obligation de capitalisation	bono de capitalización
C-86	capitalization (of interest) [Paris Club]	capitalisation (des intérêts)	capitalización de los intereses
C-87	capitalized value	valeur capitalisée valeur calculée par capitalisation	valor capitalizado
C-88	capital-labor ratio	ratio capital/travail coefficient d'intensité de capital	razón capital/trabajo relación capital/trabajo
C-89	capital-loan ratio [banking]	ratio fonds propres/crédits	razón capital propio/préstamos relación capital propio/préstamos
C-90	capital-output ratio	coefficient de capital ratio capital/production	razón capital/producto relación capital/producto
C-91	CAPM, *see* capital assets pricing model		
C-92	CAR, *see* capital adequacy ratio		
C-93	CAR, *see* Committee on the Annual Report		
C-94	career pattern, *see* career stream		
C-95	career stream career pattern	profil de carrière	perfil de carrera escalafón
C-96	CARIBANK, *see* Caribbean Development Bank		
C-97	Caribbean Common Market, *see* Caribbean Community		
C-98	Caribbean Community CARICOM Caribbean Common Market	Communauté des Caraïbes CARICOM Marché commun des Caraïbes	Comunidad del Caribe CARICOM Mercado Común del Caribe

C-99	Caribbean Development Bank CARIBANK CDB	Banque de développement des Caraïbes CARIBANK BDC	Banco de Desarrollo del Caribe CARIBANK
C-100	Caribbean I, II Division [IMF]	Division Caraïbes I, II	División del Caribe I, II
C-101	Caribbean Regional Technical Assistance Center [IMF-CARICOM-UNDP] CARTAC	Centre régional d'assistance technique des Caraïbes	Centro de Asistencia Técnica Regional del Caribe CARTAC
C-102	CARICOM, *see* Caribbean Community		
C-103	carry trade	opération spéculative sur l'écart de rendement	arbitraje de tasas de interés entre divisas *carry trade*
C-104	carryback, *see* tax loss carryback		
C-105	carryforward carryover loss carryforward loss carryover tax loss carryforward tax loss carryover	report report sur les exercices ultérieurs report à nouveau report de perte sur les exercices ultérieurs report déficitaire report sur les exercices postérieurs	imputación al ejercicio siguiente traslado al ejercicio siguiente
C-106	carrying amount, *see* carrying value		
C-107	carrying cost (of inventories) *see also:* cost of carry	frais de détention (des stocks)	costo de mantener existencias
C-108	carrying value carrying amount written-down value book value	valeur comptable	valor contable valor en libros valor contabilizado en libros valor actual en libros
C-109	carryover, *see* carryforward		
C-110	CARTAC, *see* Caribbean Regional Technical Assistance Center		
C-111	Cartagena Agreement Andean Subregional Integration Agreement	Accord de Carthagène Accord d'intégration sous- régionale andine	Acuerdo de Cartagena Acuerdo de Integración Subregional Andina
C-112	cascade tax multistage cumulative tax	taxe en cascade taxe à cascade	impuesto en cascada
C-113	cascading [taxation]	effet de cascade	efecto de cascada efecto cascada
C-114	CASDB, *see* Central African States Development Bank		
C-115	case study	étude de cas	estudio de casos estudio de casos prácticos

C-116	cash [IMF] *see also:* cash payment	numéraire encaisse(s) disponibilités espèces	dinero efectivo contado metálico al contado disponibilidades caja
C-117	cash account [IMF]	compte espèces	cuenta de caja

C-118	cash accounting
	cash basis accounting
		comptabilité de caisse
		comptabilité sur la base des
		   encaissements et décaissements
		comptabilité encaissements–
		   décaissements
		comptabilité sur la base de caisse
		système de la gestion
			contabilidad base caja
			registro base caja
			contabilidad en valores de caja

C-119	cash balance	encaisse solde disponible solde de trésorerie	saldo de caja saldo en efectivo
C-120	cash basis accounting, *see* cash accounting		
C-121	cash bond	bon de caisse	bono de caja
C-122	cash budget cash flow budget cash plan	budget de trésorerie budget de gestion	presupuesto de caja presupuesto de flujo de fondos presupuesto de tesorería
C-123	cash buyback [debt]	rachat de la dette au comptant rachat au comptant	recompra de la deuda en efectivo
C-124	cash crop	culture de rapport culture commerciale	cultivo comercial cultivo de exportación

C-125	cash economy
	cash-based economy
		économie dont les opérations
		   sont fondées sur des règlements
		   en monnaie fiduciaire
		économie dont les opérations sont
		   fondées sur des règlements en
		   numéraire
			economía basada en el uso
			   de numerario

C-126	cash flow	cash-flow liquidité marge brute d'autofinancement MBA mouvements de fonds plan de trésorerie flux de trésorerie	flujo de caja flujo de efectivo flujo de fondos movimiento de caja
C-127	cash flow budget, *see* cash budget		

C-128	cash flow relief
	cash relief
		aide de trésorerie
		soutien de trésorerie
		amélioration de la situation de
		   liquidité
		déblocage de liquidités
			mejoramiento de la situación
			   de liquidez
			alivio en materia de liquidez

C-129	cash in bank	encaisse en banque avoir en banque disponible en banque disponibilité de trésorerie	efectivo en bancos fondos disponibles en bancos
C-130	cash in hand cash on hand	espèces en caisse espèces disponibles	efectivo disponible efectivo en caja
C-131	cash in rights [IMF]	utiliser les droits accumulés	canjear los derechos hacer efectivos los derechos
C-132	cash in vault, *see* vault cash		
C-133	cash loan financial loan	prêt en liquidités prêt au comptant	préstamo de dinero préstamo en efectivo préstamo financiero
C-134	cash loan disbursement	décaissement de prêt au comptant	desembolso de préstamo en efectivo
C-135	cash management	gestion de trésorerie gestion de liquidité gestion des fonds de roulement	administración de fondos gestión de caja gestión de tesorería
C-136	cash margin	volant de trésorerie marge de trésorerie	margen de caja margen de tesorería
C-137	cash market, *see* spot market		
C-138	cash on hand, *see* cash in hand		
C-139	cash outside banks, *see* currency outside banks		
C-140	cash payment	paiement au comptant paiement en numéraire paiement en espèces	pago al contado pago en efectivo
C-141	cash plan, *see* cash budget		
C-142	cash position	position de trésorerie situation de trésorerie	situación de liquidez saldo en efectivo
C-143	cash price, *see* spot price		
C-144	cash rate overnight rate call rate call money rate interbank call rate overnight call money rate	taux à un jour taux au jour le jour taux des avances à vue taux de l'argent au jour le jour	tasa de interés de los préstamos día a día tasa de interés de los préstamos a la vista tasa de interés del dinero a la vista tasa interbancaria
C-145	cash ratio *see also:* bank cash ratio liquidity ratio	ratio de liquidité immédiate ratio de liquidité coefficient de liquidité	coeficiente de liquidez coeficiente de liquidez inmediata
C-146	cash ratio requirement *see also:* reserve requirement [banking] minimum cash requirement	coefficient de trésorerie obligatoire encaisse obligatoire	coeficiente de liquidez obligatoria coeficiente mínimo de reservas en efectivo encaje en efectivo
C-147	cash relief, *see* cash flow relief		

C-148	cash settlement	règlement du différentiel de prix débouclement au comptant	pago al contado
C-149	cash voucher	bon de caisse	comprobante de caja
C-150	cash-based economy, *see* cash economy		
C-151	cashier's check *see also:* certified check; registered check official check treasurer's check bank check	chèque de caisse chèque de banque	cheque de caja cheque bancario cheque de gerencia
C-152	catalytic effect	effet catalyseur rôle d'agent catalyseur	efecto catalizador
C-153	catch-up demand	demande de rattrapage	demanda que recupera su nivel normal
C-154	categorical grant [public finance] special purpose grant	don à objectifs spécifiques subvention à objectifs spécifiques subvention affectée	subvención específica subvención para fines especiales subvención afectada a un fin determinado
C-155	CBA, *see* currency board arrangement		
C-156	CBO, *see* community-based organization		
C-157	*CCCN, see Nomenclature for the Classification of Goods in Customs Tariffs*		
C-158	CCFF, *see* Compensatory and Contingency Financing Facility		
C-159	CD, *see* time deposit		
C-160	CDB, *see* Caribbean Development Bank		
C-161	CEAO, *see* West African Economic Community		
C-162	ceiling price	prix plafond	precio tope precio máximo
C-163	CEMLA, *see* Center for Latin American Monetary Studies		
C-164	censure, *see* declaration of censure		

C-165	Center for Latin American
	  Monetary Studies
	CEMLA
		Centre d'études monétaires latino-
		  américaines
		CEMLA
			Centro de Estudios Monetarios
			  Latinoamericanos
			CEMLA

C-166	Central African Economic
	  and Monetary Community
	CAEMC
	Economic and Monetary
	  Community of Central Africa
		Communauté économique
		  et monétaire de l'Afrique centrale
		CEMAC
			Comunidad Económica
			  y Monetaria de África Central
			CEMAC

C-167	Central African Monetary Union CAMU	Union monétaire de l'Afrique centrale UMAC	Unión Monetaria de África Central UMAC

C-168	Central African States
	  Development Bank
	CASDB
		Banque de développement des
		  États de l'Afrique centrale
		BDEAC
			Banco de Desarrollo de los
			  Estados del África Central
			BDEAC

C-169	Central American Common Market CACM	Marché commun d'Amérique centrale MCAC	Mercado Común Centroamericano MCCA MERCOMUN
C-170	Central American Division [IMF]	Division Amérique centrale	División de América Central
C-171	central bank money, *see* fiat money		
C-172	central bank money, *see* base money		

C-173	Central Bank of West African
	   States
	BCEAO
		Banque centrale des États de
		   l'Afrique de l'Ouest
		BCEAO
			Banco Central de los Estados del
			   África Occidental
			BCEAO

C-174	central banking	activités des banques centrales	actividad de los bancos centrales operaciones de los bancos centrales banca central
C-175	Central Banking Division [IMF]	Division banques centrales	División de Banca Central
C-176	central government	administration centrale administration publique centrale	gobierno central administración central
C-177	Central I, II, III Division [IMF]	Division Europe centrale I, II, III	División de Europa Central I, II, III
C-178	central rate [IMF]	taux central	tipo de cambio central
C-179	centrally planned economy *see also:* command economy CPE	économie à planification centrale EPC économie centralisée économie planifiée	economía de planificación centralizada economía de planificación central economía planificada
C-180	cereal component, *see* compensatory financing of fluctuations in the cost of cereal imports		
C-181	cereal facility, *see* compensatory financing of fluctuations in the cost of cereal imports		
C-182	certificate of deposit, *see* time deposit		
C-183	certificate of indebtedness CI	reconnaissance de dette titre de créance	certificado de deuda
C-184	certified check *see also:* cashier's check; registered check marked check	chèque certifié chèque visé	cheque certificado

C-185	*ceteris paribus*
	all other things being equal
	other things equal
	other things being equal
		ceteris paribus
		toutes choses égales par ailleurs
		toutes choses étant égales par
		   ailleurs
			ceteris paribus
			siempre que las demás
			   condiciones no varíen
			en igualdad de circunstancias

C-186	CFA, *see* African Financial Community		
C-187	CFA Franc Zone franc zone franc area	zone franc	zona del franco CFA zona del franco

C-188	CFC, *see* fixed capital consumption	
C-189	CFF, *see* Compensatory Financing Facility	
C-190	CFP, *see* Pacific Financial Community	
C-191	CFR, *see* cost & freight	
C-192	CGER, *see* Consultative Group on Exchange Rate Issues	
C-193	chair, *see* constituency	
C-194	chair *see also:* constituency	Président Présidence	silla presidencia presidente
C-195	Chairman of the Executive Board [IMF]	Président du Conseil d'administration	Presidente del Directorio Ejecutivo
C-196	Chairman's Statement [IMF]	déclaration du Président	declaración del Presidente del Directorio Ejecutivo
C-197	Chairman's summing-up [IMF]	résumé du Président (du Conseil d'administration) résumé du Président	exposición sumaria del Presidente del Directorio Ejecutivo
C-198	change in holdings	variation des avoirs	variación de las tenencias
C-199	change of ownership	transfert de propriété	traspaso de propiedad cambio de propiedad transferencia de la propiedad
C-200	change point, *see* turning point		
C-201	character loan, *see* signature loan		
C-202	charge off, *see* write off (an asset)		
C-203	chargeback	rétrofacturation imputation des dépenses au service demandeur	facturación al solicitante del servicio cargo al usuario
C-204	charges [IMF]	commission(s)	cargos
C-205	charter [banking]	charte statuts acte constitutif	carta orgánica estatutos
C-206	cheap money policy easy money policy	politique d'argent à bon marché politique d'aisance monétaire	política de dinero barato política de dinero abundante política de expansión monetaria
C-207	checkable deposit	dépôt utilisable par chèque dépôt-compte chèques	depósito disponible mediante cheque
C-208	checkable savings account	compte d'épargne utilisable par chèque	cuenta de ahorro utilizable mediante cheques
C-209	checking account deposit, *see* demand deposit		

C-210	checks and balances system	système d'équilibre des pouvoirs système de poids et contrepoids	sistema de frenos y contrapesos sistema de equilibrio de poderes
C-211	Chief ..., *see* ..., Chief [IMF]		
C-212	chief of mission, *see* mission chief		
C-213	child allowance, *see* dependency allowance		
C-214	child allowance [IMF]	allocation pour enfant à charge	asignación por hijos a cargo
C-215	child benefit allowance, *see* dependency allowance		
C-216	Chinese, English, and Portuguese Division [IMF]	Division anglaise, chinoise et portugaise	División de Chino, Inglés y Portugués
C-217	CI, *see* certificate of indebtedness		
C-218	CIA, *see* covered interest rate arbitrage		
C-218a	c.i.f., *see* cost, insurance, and freight		
C-219	CIMA, *see* Inter-African Conference on Insurance Markets		
C-220	CIMA Code, *see* Insurance Code of the Inter-African Conference on Insurance Markets		
C-221	CIRR, *see* commercial interest reference rate		
C-222	CIS, *see* Country Information System		
C-223	civic society, *see* civil society		
C-224	civil service	fonction publique	función pública cuerpo de funcionarios públicos administración pública
C-225	civil society civic society	société civile	sociedad civil sociedad cívica
C-226	claim [finance]	créance droit	acreencia crédito derecho título de crédito activo frente a, sobre, contra crédito frente a, sobre, contra
C-227	claim, *see* insurance claim		
C-228	claims on central government	créances sur l'administration centrale	crédito al gobierno central crédito frente al gobierno central activos frente al gobierno central
C-229	claims on deposit money banks	créances sur les banques créatrices de monnaie	crédito a los bancos creadores de dinero
C-230	claims on general government	créances sur les administrations publiques	crédito al gobierno general crédito frente al gobierno general activos frente al gobierno general

C-231	claims on nonfinancial public enterprises	créances sur les entreprises publiques non financières	crédito a empresas públicas no financieras
C-232	claims on nonresidents	créances sur les non-résidents	activos frente a no residentes
C-233	claims on official entities	créances sur les organismes publics	crédito a entidades oficiales
C-234	claims on other financial institutions	créances sur les autres institutions financières	crédito a otras instituciones financieras
C-235	claims on private sector	créances sur le secteur privé	crédito al sector privado
C-236	claims on state and local governments	créances sur les administrations provinciales ou régionales et les administrations locales	crédito a gobiernos estatales y locales
C-237	classified asset, *see* classified loan		
C-238	classified credit, *see* classified loan		
C-239	classified loan *see also:* loan classification classified asset classified credit adversely classified asset scheduled item	prêt classé «à risque» prêt classé dans une catégorie spéciale	préstamo problemático préstamo de calidad inferior
C-240	clear the market	équilibrer l'offre et la demande équilibrer le marché ramener l'équilibre sur le marché ramener le marché à l'équilibre	equilibrar el mercado igualar la oferta y la demanda en el mercado
C-241	clearing account, *see* suspense account		
C-242	clearing account	compte de compensation	cuenta de compensación
C-243	clearing arrangement	accord de compensation accord de clearing	acuerdo de compensación
C-244	clearing bank	banque de compensation banque de virement banque commerciale	banco compensador banco de compensación banco afiliado a una cámara de compensación banco comercial [GBR]
C-245	clearing house, *see* clearinghouse		
C-246	clearing price market clearing price	prix d'équilibre prix d'équilibre du marché	precio de equilibrio precio de equilibrio del mercado
C-247	clearinghouse clearing house	chambre de compensation	cámara compensadora cámara de compensación
C-248	client due diligence customer due diligence know your clients KYC	règles de vigilance obligation(s) de vigilance devoir de vigilance devoir de diligence	procedimiento de debida diligencia con la clientela principio de conocimiento del cliente DDC
C-249	Client Services Division [IMF]	Division services clients	División de Servicios al Cliente

C-250	close substitute	substitut proche substitut facilement interchangeable	sustituto casi perfecto sucedáneo cercano buen sustituto
C-251	close the books	clore la comptabilité arrêter les comptes	cerrar la contabilidad
C-252	closed-end grant	don de montant déterminé subvention limitée	subvención limitada subvención de monto definido
C-253	closed-end investment company, *see* investment trust		
C-254	closed-end investment fund, *see* investment trust		
C-255	closed-end investment trust, *see* investment trust		
C-256	closing assets	actif(s) de clôture	activos al cierre del ejercicio activos de cierre
C-257	closing liabilities	passif(s) de clôture	pasivos al cierre del ejercicio pasivos de cierre
C-258	CMO, *see* collateralized mortgage obligation		
C-259	COB, *see* Committee on the Budget		
C-260	*Code of Good Practices on Fiscal Transparency, see Code of Good Practices on Fiscal Transparency-- Declaration on Principles*		

C-261	*Code of Good Practices on Fiscal
	  Transparency — Declaration on
	  Principles*
	[IMF]
	see also: *Manual on Fiscal
	  Transparency*
	*Code of Good Practices on Fiscal
	  Transparency*
		Code de bonnes pratiques en
		  matière de transparence des
		  finances publiques — Déclaration
		  de principes
		*Code révisé de bonnes pratiques
		  en matière de transparence des
		  finances publiques*
			Código de buenas prácticas de
			  transparencia fiscal: Declaración
			  de principios
			*Código de buenas prácticas de
			  transparencia fiscal*

C-262	Code of Good Practices on
	  Transparency in Monetary and
	  Financial Policies
	[IMF]
	MFP Code
		Code de bonnes pratiques pour la
		  transparence des politiques
		  monétaire et financière —
		  Déclaration de principes
			Código de buenas prácticas de
			  transparencia en las políticas
			  monetarias y financieras

C-263	coefficient of concentration, *see* Gini coefficient		
C-264	cofinancing arrangement [IBRD]	accord de cofinancement	acuerdo de cofinanciamiento

C-265	cofinancing trust account
	[IMF]
	CTA
		compte de fiducie pour
		  cofinancement
		CFC
			Cuenta Fiduciaria de
			  Cofinanciamiento
			CFC

C-266	COI, *see* Committee on Interpretation		
C-267	coinage minting	frappe de la monnaie monnayage	acuñación acuñación de moneda
C-268	coinage coin(s)	pièce (de monnaie) monnaie métallique	moneda metálica

C-269	coincident indicator *see also:* lagging indicator; leading indicator coincidental indicator	indicateur simultané indicateur coïncident	indicador coincidente indicador simultáneo
C-270	coincidental indicator, *see* coincident indicator		
C-271	coin(s), *see* coinage		
C-272	COLA, *see* cost of living adjustment		
C-273	co-lead manager, *see* co-manager		
C-274	collaboration with the World Bank [IMF] *see also:* avoidance of cross- conditionality; cross-conditionality	collaboration avec la Banque mondiale	colaboración con el Banco Mundial
C-275	collateral collateral security collateral guarantee	sûreté garantie garantie réelle nantissement gage	garantía real garantía de activos garantía prendaria garantía pignoraticia garantía colateral
C-276	collateral account [IMF]	compte de garantie	cuenta de garantía
C-277	collateral guarantee, *see* collateral		
C-278	collateral security, *see* collateral		
C-279	collateralize	constituer un nantissement (pour des paiements) gager sur adosser à des garanties garantir	garantizar otorgar una garantía real
C-280	collateralized bond	obligation garantie obligation cautionnée	bono con garantía bono con garantía real
C-281	collateralized mortgage obligation CMO	obligation hypothécaire obligation hypothécaire garantie	obligación hipotecaria obligación garantizada con hipoteca
C-282	collect tax *see also:* deposit withheld tax with government; withhold tax	percevoir un impôt	recaudar impuestos
C-283	collect withholding tax for the government, *see* withhold tax		
C-284	collection of data gathering of data	collecte de données rassemblement de données	recopilación de datos
C-285	collective action clause CAC	clause d'action collective	cláusula de acción colectiva CAC
C-286	collective bargaining	négociation(s) collective(s)	negociación colectiva

C-287	collective bargaining agreement	convention collective	convenio colectivo
	collective labor agreement		convenio colectivo de trabajo
	labor contract		
	union contract		
C-288	collective judgment	opinion générale	opinión colectiva
	sense of the meeting	appréciation générale	opinión general
		sentiment général	opinión de la mayoría
C-289	collective labor agreement, *see* collective bargaining agreement		
C-290	collective representation clause	clause de représentation collective	cláusula de representación colectiva
C-291	collusive bidding	soumission collusoire	oferta colusoria
		offre collusoire	puja colusoria
C-292	Cologne terms	conditions de Cologne	condiciones de Colonia
C-293	co-manager	cochef de file	codirector
	see also: lead manager		coadministrador
	co-lead manager		
C-294	combined market interest rate, *see* combined market rate		
C-295	combined market rate	taux composite du marché	tasa de interés de mercado combinada
	see also: calculated market rate	taux d'intérêt composite du marché	
	combined market interest rate		
C-296	comfort letter, *see* assessment letter		
C-297	command economy	économie dirigée	economía dirigida
	see also: centrally planned economy		
	controlled economy		
C-298	commercial arrears	arriérés envers les banques	atrasos en los pagos de la deuda frente a los bancos comerciales
	see also: trade arrears	arriérés envers les institutions financières	atrasos en los pagos de la deuda en condiciones de mercado
		arriérés aux taux du marché	
		arriérés de dettes contractées aux taux du marché	
C-299	commercial bank	banque commerciale	banco comercial
C-300	commercial credit, *see* commercial lending		
C-301	commercial credit, *see* trade credit		
C-302	commercial creditor	créancier bancaire	acreedor comercial
		créancier opérant aux conditions du marché	acreedor bancario
			acreedor de una deuda en condiciones de mercado
C-303	commercial debt	dette envers les banques	deuda frente a los bancos comerciales
	bank debt	dette bancaire	deuda frente a los bancos privados
		dette aux conditions du marché	deuda en condiciones de mercado
			deuda bancaria
C-304	commercial GDP	PIB marchand	PIB comercial
	commercialized GDP		

C-305	commercial interest reference rate CIRR	taux d'intérêt commercial de référence TICR	tasa de interés comercial de referencia
C-306	commercial lender	prêteur aux conditions du marché	prestamista comercial institución de crédito que opera en condiciones de mercado
C-307	commercial lending *see also:* trade credit commercial loan commercial credit [Paris Club] nonconcessional loan	prêt bancaire prêt aux conditions du marché crédit commercial créance commerciale	préstamo comercial crédito de bancos comerciales crédito en condiciones de mercado préstamo en condiciones no concesionarias
C-308	commercial loan, *see* commercial lending		
C-309	commercial paper	effet(s) financier(s) papier financier papier commercial billet(s) de trésorerie billet(s) à ordre	efectos comerciales papel comercial
C-310	commercial terms, *see* market terms		
C-311	commercialized GDP, *see* commercial GDP		
C-312	commitment, *see* expenditure commitment		
C-313	commitment basis accounting	comptabilité sur la base des engagements	contabilidad en base a compromisos
C-314	commitment basis, on a *see also:* accrual basis	sur la base des engagements base engagements	en base a compromisos
C-315	commitment charge, *see* commitment fee		
C-316	commitment fee *see also:* extended arrangement charge; stand-by charge commitment charge [IMF]	commission d'engagement	comisión por compromiso de recursos comisión de apertura de crédito comisión por inmovilización de fondos comisión de compromiso
C-317	commitment gap [IMF] *see also:* financing gap	écart entre engagements et lignes de crédit	déficit de recursos para atender compromisos contraídos
C-318	commitment period	période d'engagement	período de compromiso
C-319	commitments [IMF] committed resources	ressources engagées	recursos comprometidos compromisos
C-320	committed resources, *see* commitments		
C-321	Committee of the Whole for the Development Committee [IMF] CWDC	Comité plénier pour le Comité du développement	Comisión Plenaria sobre el Comité para el Desarrollo

C-322	Committee of the Whole on Review of Quotas [IMF] CQuota	Comité plénier chargé de la révision des quotes-parts	Comisión Plenaria sobre la Revisión de las Cuotas
C-323	Committee on Article XIV Consultations [IMF]	Comité des consultations au titre de l'article XIV	Comisión de Consultas del Artículo XIV
C-324	Committee on Executive Board Administrative Matters [IMF] CAM	Comité du Conseil d'administration chargé des questions administratives	Comisión de Asuntos Administrativos del Directorio Ejecutivo
C-325	Committee on Interpretation [IMF] COI	Comité d'interprétation	Comisión de Interpretación
C-326	Committee on Liaison with the WTO [IMF] CWTO	Comité de liaison avec l'OMC	Comisión de Enlace con la OMC
C-327	Committee on Membership — [country] [IMF] membership committee	Comité d'admission — [pays]	Comisión de Admisión — [país]
C-328	Committee on Rules for the [year] Regular Election of Executive Directors [IMF]	Comité des règles de procédure relatives à l'élection ordinaire d'administrateurs de [année]	Comisión de Reglas de Procedimiento para la Elección Ordinaria de [año] de Directores Ejecutivos
C-329	Committee on the Annual Report [IMF] CAR	Comité sur le Rapport annuel	Comisión sobre el Informe Anual
C-330	Committee on the Budget [IMF] COB	Comité du budget	Comisión de Presupuesto
C-331	commodities exchange, *see* commodity exchange		
C-332	commodity, *see* primary product		
C-333	commodity *see also:* primary product	marchandise produit de base produits marchands biens et services marchands	producto básico *commodity* producto mercancías
C-334	commodity bond commodity-indexed bond commodity-linked bond	obligation indexée sur (des) produits de base	bono indexado al precio de un producto básico
C-335	commodity composition of trade	ventilation des échanges (commerciaux) par catégories de produits	desglose del comercio por productos
C-336	commodity currency	monnaie-marchandise	dinero mercancía
C-337	commodity exchange commodities exchange exchange	bourse de commerce bourse de(s) marchandises	bolsa de comercio bolsa de productos mercado de productos

C-338	commodity future	contrat à terme sur marchandises	futuro de productos básicos futuro sobre productos contrato de futuros sobre productos básicos
C-339	commodity futures market	marché à terme de marchandises marché à terme de matières premières	mercado de futuros de productos bolsa de futuros de productos
C-340	commodity gold	or-marchandise	oro mercancía
C-341	commodity market	marché de produits marché des produits de base marché d'un produit	mercado de productos básicos
C-342	commodity-backed financing, *see* commodity-linked finance		
C-343	commodity-indexed bond, *see* commodity bond		
C-344	commodity-linked bond, *see* commodity bond		

C-345	commodity-linked finance
	commodity-backed financing
		financement lié aux prix des
		   produits de base
		financement indexé sur les prix
		   des produits de base
			financiamiento vinculado al precio
			   de productos básicos

C-346	common arrangement, *see* cooperative arrangement		
C-347	common currency area, *see* currency zone		
C-348	common currency zone, *see* currency zone		
C-349	common monetary arrangement, *see* cooperative arrangement		
C-350	common share *see also:* stocks common stock ordinary share	action ordinaire actions ordinaires part ordinaire	acción ordinaria
C-351	common stock, *see* common share		
C-352	commons	biens communautaires	patrimonio común
C-353	community charge, *see* head tax		
C-354	community-based organization CBO	organisation axée sur les collectivités association collective collectivité (privée)	organización de base entidad de base
C-355	comparable worth *see also:* pay parity	valeur équivalente	valor equivalente
C-356	comparative advantage *see also:* absolute advantage; fair trade; free trade	avantage comparatif	ventaja comparativa
C-357	compensation [SDR]	compensation	compensación

C-358	Compensation and Benefits Policy
	   Division
	[IMF]
		Division politique de rémunérations
		   et de prestations
			División de Política de
			   Remuneraciones y Prestaciones

C-359	compensation of employees	rémunération des salariés	remuneración de empleados remuneración de asalariados remuneración a los empleados remuneración de los asalariados
C-360	Compensatory and Contingency Financing Facility [IMF] CCFF	facilité de financement compensatoire et de financement pour imprévus FFCI	Servicio de Financiamiento Compensatorio y para Contingencias SFCC
C-361	compensatory drawing [IMF]	tirage compensatoire	giro compensatorio
C-362	Compensatory Financing Facility [IMF] CFF	facilité de financement compensatoire	Servicio de Financiamiento Compensatorio SFC
C-363	compensatory financing of export fluctuations	financement compensatoire des fluctuations des recettes d'exportation	financiamiento compensatorio de las fluctuaciones de los ingresos de exportación
C-364	compensatory financing of fluctuations in the cost of cereal imports [IMF] cereal facility cereal component	financement compensatoire des fluctuations du coût des importations de céréales mécanisme céréalier d'aide financière aux importations de céréales volet céréalier	financiamiento compensatorio de las fluctuaciones del costo de los cereales importados servicio financiero para las importaciones de cereales
C-365	competitive ability, *see* competitiveness		
C-366	competitive advantage	avantage concurrentiel avantage compétitif	ventaja competitiva
C-367	competitive bid	soumission concurrentielle offre compétitive	oferta competitiva
C-368	competitive depreciation	dépréciation concurrentielle	depreciación competitiva
C-369	competitive devaluation	surenchère dans la dévaluation dévaluation de surenchère dévaluation compétitive	devaluación competitiva
C-370	competitive disadvantage	situation de concurrence défavorable	desventaja competitiva
C-371	competitive good, *see* substitute		
C-372	competitiveness competitive ability	compétitivité capacité concurrentielle	competitividad capacidad competitiva
C-373	compilation of data	établissement de(s) données	compilación de datos
C-374	compiler	statisticien	compilador
C-375	compiling economy	économie déclarante	economía compiladora
C-376	completion point [IMF] *see also:* decision point [IMF, HIPC Initiative]	point d'achèvement fin du processus	punto de culminación

C-377	compliance (with performance criteria) [IMF]	observation respect	cumplimiento (de los criterios) observación de ejecución (de los criterios)
C-378	component currency [IMF]	monnaie entrant dans la composition (du panier du DTS)	moneda componente
C-379	composite of currencies, *see* currency composite		
C-380	composite peg, *see* basket peg		
C-381	composition agreement, *see* composition of creditors		
C-382	composition of creditors composition agreement creditors' arrangement	concordat accord avec les créanciers	concordato con los acreedores convenio con los acreedores
C-383	compound interest rate *see also:* simple interest rate compound rate	taux composé taux d'intérêt composé	tasa de interés compuesta tasa compuesta
C-384	compound rate, *see* compound interest rate		
C-385	compulsory intervention rate	cours d'intervention obligatoire	tipo de intervención obligatoria
C-386	compulsory reserve deposit	réserves obligatoires en compte	depósito de reserva obligatorio
C-387	compulsory withdrawal [IMF]	retrait obligatoire (d'un pays membre)	separación obligatoria
C-388	concealed subsidy, *see* hidden subsidy		
C-389	concertation of policies	concertation des politiques concertation des mesures mesures concertées	concertación de las medidas de política concertación de las políticas
C-390	concessional concessionary	concessionnel	concesionario de carácter concesionario en condiciones favorables
C-391	concessional aid, *see* concessional assistance		
C-392	concessional assistance concessional aid	assistance concessionnelle aide concessionnelle aide à des conditions concessionnelles	asistencia concesionaria asistencia de carácter concesionario ayuda en condiciones favorables
C-393	concessional element concessionary element	élément concessionnel élément de libéralité	elemento concesionario
C-394	concessional financing	financement concessionnel financement à des conditions concessionnelles	financiamiento concesionario financiamiento en condiciones concesionarias financiamiento en condiciones favorables
C-395	concessional flow concessionary flow	flux de capitaux concessionnels flux de capitaux assortis de conditions concessionnelles	flujo de capital concesionario
C-396	concessional interest rate	taux d'intérêt préférentiel taux d'intérêt concessionnel	tasa de interés concesionaria

C-397	concessional loan	prêt concessionnel prêt accordé à des conditions concessionnelles	préstamo en condiciones concesionarias
C-398	concessional terms concessionary terms	conditions concessionnelles	condiciones concesionarias
C-399	concessional treatment [Paris Club] concessionality	traitement concessionnel concessionnalité	tratamiento concesionario concesionalidad
C-400	concessionality	concessionnalité caractère concessionnel degré de libéralité	concesionalidad carácter concesionario
C-401	concessionality, *see* concessional treatment		
C-402	concessionary, *see* concessional		
C-403	concessionary element, *see* concessional element		
C-404	concessionary flow, *see* concessional flow		
C-405	concessionary terms, *see* concessional terms		
C-406	conciliation, *see* reconciliation		
C-407	concurrence of the member [IMF]	assentiment de l'État membre	asentimiento del país miembro
C-408	conditional grant [public finance]	don conditionnel subvention conditionnelle transfert conditionnel	subvención condicional transferencia condicional
C-409	conditional relief arrangement [customs]	régime suspensif des droits	régimen de suspensión condicional del impuesto
C-410	conditionality [IMF]	conditionnalité	condicionalidad
C-411	conditionality for the tranches [IMF]	conditionnalité des tirages dans les tranches de crédit	condicionalidad para el desembolso de cada tramo de crédito condicionalidad previa a los desembolsos
C-412	conduit	intermédiaire agent canal instrument de transmission	intermediario medio de transmisión
C-413	confidence interval	intervalle de confiance	intervalo de confianza
C-414	confidence level	niveau de confiance seuil de confiance	nivel de confianza
C-415	confiscation, *see* forfeit		
C-416	connected lending connected loan	prêt de faveur prêt entre parties liées	crédito a prestatarios relacionados con los bancos crédito a prestatarios relacionados préstamos vinculados

C-417	connected loan, *see* connected lending		
C-418	consent [IMF quotas] *see also:* act of consent	consentement acceptation	aceptación consentimiento asentimiento
C-419	conservator, *see* provisional administrator		
C-420	conservatorship, *see* provisional administration		
C-421	consistency	cohérence	consistencia coherencia
C-422	consistency check	test de cohérence vérification de la cohérence (des données)	verificación de la concordancia (de los datos)
C-423	consistency of valuation	uniformité d'évaluation cohérence dans l'évaluation	concordancia de la valoración
C-424	consistent estimator	estimateur convergent	estimador consistente estimador coherente
C-425	consol, *see* perpetual bond		
C-426	consolidated central government	opérations consolidées de l'administration centrale secteur consolidé de l'administration centrale administration publique centrale consolidée APUC	gobierno central consolidado operaciones consolidadas del gobierno central
C-427	consolidated general government]	opérations consolidées des administrations publiques administrations publiques consolidées APU	gobierno general consolidado operaciones consolidadas del gobierno general
C-428	consolidation *see also:* debt consolidation; fiscal consolidation; national consolidation	consolidation	consolidación
C-429	consolidation period	période de consolidation	período de consolidación
C-430	consortium, *see* syndicate		
C-431	consortium (for country X)	consortium (pour le ...)	consorcio (para ...) consorcio (de coordinación de la ayuda a ...)
C-432	conspicuous consumption	consommation ostentatoire	consumo suntuario consumo ostentoso consumo de ostentación
C-433	constant prices in constant prices	prix constants en prix constants	precios constantes a precios constantes
C-434	constant return	rendement constant	rendimiento constante

C-435	constituency
	[IMF]
	see also: chair [IMF Governance]
	chair
		pays représenté(s)
		groupe de pays (représentés
		  par ...)
		mandant(s)
		siège
			países representados
			grupo de países (que elige un
			  representante)
			jurisdicción
			representación

C-436	constraint	contrainte insuffisance obstacle entrave	restricción limitación
C-437	consultation cycle [IMF]	cycle de(s) consultations	ciclo de consultas
C-438	consultation discussions, *see* Article IV consultation discussions		

C-439	Consultative Group on Exchange
	  Rate Issues
	Consultative Group on Exchange
	  Rates
	CGER
		Groupe consultatif sur les taux
		  de change
			Grupo Consultivo sobre Tipos
			  de Cambio

C-440	Consultative Group on Exchange Rates, *see* Consultative Group on Exchange Rate Issues		

C-441	Consultative Group on
	  International Economic and
	  Monetary Affairs, Inc.
	Group of Thirty
		Groupe consultatif sur les
		  questions économiques et
		  monétaires internationales
		Groupe des Trente
			Grupo Consultivo sobre Asuntos
			  Económicos y Monetarios
			  Internacionales
			Grupo de los Treinta

C-442	consumer credit	crédit à la consommation	crédito al consumidor crédito a los consumidores crédito de consumo crédito personal
C-443	consumer durable *see also:* durable good hard good	bien de consommation durable bien d'équipement des ménages	bienes de consumo duraderos
C-444	consumer preferences, *see* consumer tastes		
C-445	consumer price index CPI	indice des prix à la consommation IPC	índice de precios al consumidor IPC
C-446	consumer saving, *see* household saving		
C-447	consumer spending, *see* household expenditure		
C-448	consumer surplus *see also:* producer surplus; social surplus	surplus du consommateur surplus des consommateurs	excedente del consumidor superávit del consumidor
C-449	consumer tastes consumer preferences	préférences des consommateurs	gustos de los consumidores preferencias de los consumidores
C-450	consumerism	consumérisme action des consommateurs	consumismo
C-451	consumption	consommation	consumo
C-452	consumption behavior, *see* consumption pattern		
C-453	consumption expenditure consumption spending	dépenses de consommation	gasto de consumo

C-454	consumption function	fonction de consommation	función de consumo
C-455	consumption of fixed capital, *see* fixed capital consumption		
C-456	consumption pattern consumption behavior	habitudes de consommation mode de consommation	preferencias de los consumidores hábitos de consumo estructura del consumo
C-457	consumption pattern consumption structure	structure de consommation	estructura del consumo patrón de consumo
C-458	consumption spending, *see* consumption expenditure		
C-459	consumption structure, *see* consumption pattern		
C-460	consumption tax *see also:* excise	impôt de consommation impôt sur la consommation taxe à la consommation	impuesto al consumo impuesto sobre el consumo
C-461	contemporaneous reserve accounting *see also:* lagged reserve accounting	comptabilisation non décalée des réserves obligatoires comptabilisation immédiate des réserves obligatoires	contabilización corriente de las reservas
C-462	contingencies	imprévus aléas	imprevistos contingencias riesgos
C-463	contingency clause [IMF]	clause de sauvegarde clause pour imprévus	cláusula para contingencias
C-464	contingency element [IMF]	composante pour imprévus volet pour imprévus	componente de financiamiento para contingencias
C-465	contingency financing contingent financing contingent credit line	financement pour imprévus financement conditionnel ligne de crédit préventive	financiamiento para contingencias línea de crédito contingente
C-466	contingency fund	fonds de prévoyance fonds de réserve fonds prévisionnel	fondo para contingencias fondo de reserva
C-467	contingency measure	mesure pour imprévus mesure pour faire face à des imprévus	medida para hacer frente a imprevistos medida contingente medida para contingencias
C-468	contingency mechanism contingency mechanism for the adjustment of targets	mécanisme d'ajustement automatique clause d'ajustement	mecanismo de contingencia para el ajuste de las metas
C-469	contingency mechanism for the adjustment of targets, *see* contingency mechanism		
C-470	contingent asset, *see* contingent claim		
C-471	contingent claim contingent asset	créance conditionnelle créance contingente actif conditionnel actif éventuel avoir conditionnel	crédito contingente crédito eventual activo contingente activo eventual
C-472	contingent credit line, *see* contingency financing		

C-473	contingent financing, *see* contingency financing		
C-474	contingent liability	passif conditionnel passif éventuel engagement éventuel engagement conditionnel	pasivo contingente pasivo eventual
C-475	continuous arrears (to the Fund) [IMF] *see also:* protracted arrears (to the Fund)	situation d'arriérés continuels envers le FMI	atrasos continuos en los pagos (al FMI)
C-476	continuous session [IMF]	session permanente	sesión permanente
C-477	contra entry, *see* offsetting entry		
C-478	contract price, *see* exercise price		
C-479	contracting out, *see* outsourcing		
C-480	contractionary impulse	impulsion restrictive	impulso contractivo impulso contraccionista
C-481	contractionary policy	politique restrictive politique d'austérité	política contractiva política contraccionista política restrictiva política de austeridad
C-482	contractual maturity	échéance contractuelle	vencimiento contractual plazo contractual
C-483	contrived scarcity	pénurie provoquée pénurie artificielle	escasez artificial
C-484	control *see also:* price control	réglementation encadrement contrôle maîtrise	control regulación
C-485	controlled economy, *see* command economy		
C-486	controlled price, *see* administered price		
C-487	conventional market terms, *see* market terms		
C-488	conventional terms, *see* market terms		
C-489	convergence criteria [EU] convergence goals Maastricht criteria Maastricht goals	critères de convergence critères de Maastricht	criterios de convergencia criterios de Maastricht
C-490	convergence goals, *see* convergence criteria		
C-491	conversion key, *see* correspondence table		
C-492	convertible debt instrument	instrument de dette convertible	instrumento de deuda convertible
C-493	Cooke Committee, *see* Basel Committee on Banking Supervision		

C-494	cooperation test [IMF]	test de coopération	prueba de cooperación
C-495	cooperative arrangement cooperative monetary arrangement common arrangement common monetary arrangement	mécanisme de coopération dispositif de coopération monétaire	régimen monetario cooperativo mecanismo de cooperación monetaria
C-496	cooperative arrangements (for maintenance of value of currencies) [IMF]	mécanisme de coopération (pour le maintien de la valeur des monnaies)	regímenes cooperativos (para mantener el valor de las monedas)
C-497	cooperative monetary arrangement, *see* cooperative arrangement		
C-498	cooperative savings association, *see* credit union		
C-499	cooperative sector	secteur mutualiste	sector de cooperativas
C-500	Coordinated Portfolio Investment Survey [IMF, OECD] CPIS	Enquête coordonnée sur les investissements de portefeuille	Encuesta coordinada sobre inversión de cartera ECIC
C-501	Coordination and Standards Division [IMF]	Division coordination et normes	División de Coordinación y Normas
C-502	core bank	banque commerciale principale	banco comercial principal
C-503	core capital, *see* tier 1 capital		
C-504	core data category [GDDS]	catégorie de(s) données de base catégorie de base	categoría de datos básicos
C-505	core inflation underlying inflation	inflation hors énergie et alimentation inflation sous-jacente inflation tendancielle	inflación subyacente inflación básica
C-506	core principles, *see* Core Principles for Effective Banking Supervision		
C-507	Core Principles for Effective Banking Supervision [BIS] Basle Core Principles core principles	Principes fondamentaux pour un contrôle bancaire efficace	Principios Básicos para una Supervisión Bancaria Efectiva
C-508	core statistical indicator [IMF]	indicateur statistique fondamental	indicador estadístico básico
C-509	corporate accounting standards	normes de comptabilité des sociétés	normas de contabilidad empresarial
C-510	corporate banking	services bancaires aux entreprises	servicios bancarios al sector empresarial
C-511	corporate body, *see* artificial person		
C-512	corporate bond	obligation (de société)	bono emitido por una empresa bono empresarial bono corporativo

C-513	corporate equity	capital social	patrimonio social
		capitaux propres d'une société	fondos propios
		fonds propres d'une société	

C-514	corporate governance	gouvernement de l'entreprise	gobierno societario
		gouvernement d'entreprise	gobierno corporativo
			gobierno empresarial
			gobierno de las sociedades

C-515	corporate income tax	impôt sur les sociétés	impuesto sobre la renta de las
		impôt sur les bénéfices des	sociedades
		sociétés	

| C-516 | corporate raider, *see* raider | | |

C-517	corporate sector workout	plan de redressement des	reestructuración de la deuda del
	see also: debt workout	entreprises en difficulté	sector empresarial
	corporate workout		
	workout		

| C-518 | corporate workout, *see* corporate sector workout | | |

| C-519 | corporation, *see* artificial person | | |

| C-520 | corporation, *see* business corporation | | |

| C-521 | corrective action, *see* remedial measure | | |

| C-522 | corrective measure, *see* remedial measure | | |

| C-523 | correlation coefficient | coefficient de corrélation | coeficiente de correlación |

| C-524 | correspondence table | tableau de correspondance | cuadro de correspondencia |
| | conversion key | clé de passage | clave de conversión |

| C-525 | correspondent bank | correspondant bancaire | banco corresponsal |

| C-526 | correspondent on statistical matters, *see* statistical correspondent | | |

C-527	cost & freight	coût et fret	costo y flete
	c. & f.	c. et f.	c. & f.
	CFR		

C-528	cost accounting	comptabilité de(s) prix de revient	contabilidad de costos
		comptabilité des coûts	contabilidad analítica
		comptabilité analytique	
		comptabilité analytique	
		d'exploitation	
		comptabilité industrielle	

C-529	cost effectiveness	rapport coût–efficacité	eficacia en función de los costos
		efficacité par rapport aux coûts	
		rentabilité	

C-530	cost inflation	inflation des coûts	inflación de costos
	see also: price inflation	inflation par les coûts	inflación ocasionada por los costos
	cost-push inflation	inflation due à la poussée des	
		coûts	

C-531	cost, insurance, and freight	coût, assurance, fret	costo, seguro y flete
	cost, insurance, freight	c.a.f.	c.i.f.
	c.i.f.		

C-532	cost, insurance, freight, *see* cost, insurance, and freight		
C-533	cost of capital, *see* capital cost		
C-534	cost of carry *see also:* carrying cost (of inventories)	coût de portage	costo de inmovilización del capital
C-535	cost of living adjustment COLA	ajustement (au titre du) coût de la vie ajustement en fonction du coût de la vie	ajuste por costo de vida
C-536	cost price	prix de revient	precio de costo
C-537	cost pricing	fixation du prix en fonction du coût détermination du prix en fonction du coût	determinación del precio en función del costo fijación del precio en función del costo
C-538	cost recovery	recouvrement des coûts récupération des coûts	recuperación de costos
C-539	cost-benefit analysis	analyse coûts–avantages	análisis de costo-beneficio
C-540	cost-push inflation, *see* cost inflation		
C-541	cottage industry, *see* artisanal industry		
C-542	Council [IMF]	Collège	Consejo
C-543	Counsel, Consulting [IMF]	Conseil juridique consultant	Consultor Jurídico
C-544	Counsellor (of the Fund) [IMF]	Conseiller (du FMI)	Consejero
C-545	countercyclical action anticyclical measure	mesure anticyclique mesure anticonjoncturelle mesure d'action conjoncturelle mesure de stabilisation conjoncturelle mesure de régulation de la conjoncture action anticyclique action contracyclique	medida anticíclica
C-546	counterpart entry *see also:* balancing item; offsetting entry	écriture de contrepartie inscription de contrepartie contre-inscription	asiento de contrapartida
C-547	counterpart fund	fonds de contrepartie	fondo de contrapartida
C-548	counterpart to allocation/cancellation [IMF]	contrepartie de l'allocation/annulation	contrapartida de asignación/cancelación
C-549	counterpart to monetization/demonetization	contrepartie de la monétisation/démonétisation	contrapartida de monetización/desmonetización
C-550	counterpart to valuation change, *see* counterpart to valuation changes		

C-551	counterpart to valuation changes revaluation counterpart counterpart to valuation change	contrepartie des réévaluations contrepartie des ajustements de valeur	contrapartida de las variaciones por revaloración contrapartida de variaciones de valoración contrapartida de variaciones por revalorización
C-552	counterparty risk, *see* credit risk		
C-553	counterpurchase [trade]	achats de compensation achats compensés	compras de contrapartida
C-554	countertrade	échanges compensés commerce de compensation exportations compensées	comercio de compensación
C-555	countervailing duty antibounty duty	droit compensateur	derecho compensatorio
C-556	country advisory committee *see also:* bank advisory committee	comité consultatif (pour un pays)	comité consultivo (para un país)
C-557	country coordinator [GDDS]	coordinateur national	coordinador nacional
C-558	Country Data Review Division [IMF]	Division examen des données par pays	División de Examen de las Estadísticas por Países
C-559	country desk, *see* desk economist (for ... [country])		
C-560	country in transition, *see* transition country		
C-561	Country Information System [IMF] CIS	système d'information sur les pays	Sistema de Información sobre los Países Miembros del FMI CIS
C-562	country ownership, *see* ownership		
C-563	country page	page-pays page par pays	página correspondiente a [país] páginas de países páginas por países
C-564	country rating country risk rating	cote de crédit (d'un pays) notation du risque-pays	clasificación crediticia de un país
C-565	country risk *see also:* sovereign risk	risque-pays	riesgo país
C-566	country risk rating, *see* country rating		
C-567	country strategy brief [IMF]	mémoire sur la stratégie-pays	documento de orientación sobre la estrategia para un país
C-568	country with payment arrears, *see* arrears country		
C-569	coupon bond	obligation à coupons	bono con cupones
C-570	coupon rate	taux d'intérêt nominal (d'une obligation à coupons)	tasa de interés nominal tasa de cupón
C-571	cover [export credit]	garantie de crédit à l'exportation	garantía de crédito a la exportación

C-572	cover letter, *see* letter of transmittal		
C-573	cover note, *see* letter of transmittal		
C-574	cover rate, *see* import capacity of exports		
C-575	coverage	couverture champ couvert champ d'application étendue articulation [indice]	cobertura campo específico de aplicación extensión amplitud

C-576	covered interest rate arbitrage
	CIA
		arbitrage de taux d'intérêt avec
		   couverture à terme
		arbitrage d'intérêts couvert
			arbitraje de tasas de interés con
			   cobertura

C-577	covered interest rate differential	écart entre les taux d'intérêt avec
		   couverture à terme
		différentiel d'intérêts couvert
			diferencial de tasas de interés con
			   cobertura
			diferencial de tasas de interés
			   cubierto

C-578	CPE, *see* centrally planned economy		
C-579	CPI, *see* consumer price index		
C-580	CPIS, *see* Coordinated Portfolio Investment Survey		
C-581	CQuota, *see* Committee of the Whole on Review of Quotas		
C-582	crawling peg	parité mobile parité ajustable parité à crémaillère parité glissante	tipo de cambio móvil paridad móvil paridad ajustable
C-583	credit	crédit	crédito abono
C-584	credit against (a) tax, *see* tax credit		
C-585	credit agency, *see* credit rating agency		
C-586	credit an account with an amount credit an amount to an account	créditer un compte d'un montant porter un montant au crédit d'un compte	acreditar una suma en una cuenta abonar en cuenta
C-587	credit an amount to an account, *see* credit an account with an amount		
C-588	credit balance	solde créditeur	saldo acreedor
C-589	credit bureau, *see* credit rating agency		
C-590	credit ceiling credit limit lending ceiling	plafond de crédit limite de crédit limite d'emprunt	tope de crédito límite de crédito
C-591	credit cooperative *see also:* credit union	coopérative de crédit	cooperativa de crédito
C-592	credit crunch credit squeeze tightening of credit	resserrement du crédit compression du crédit encadrement du crédit	compresión del crédito restricción pronunciada del crédito escasez de crédito

C-593	credit derivative [IMF]	dérivé de crédit	instrumento derivado sobre créditos
C-594	credit enhancement, *see* enhanced credit		
C-595	credit entry	inscription au crédit enregistrement au crédit	asiento de crédito abono
C-596	credit facility, *see* financing facility		
C-597	credit from monetary authorities	crédits des autorités monétaires	crédito de las autoridades monetarias
C-598	credit limit, *see* credit ceiling		
C-599	credit line, *see* line of credit		
C-600	credit monitoring agency, *see* credit rating agency		
C-601	credit policy	politique du crédit politique de crédit	política crediticia política de crédito
C-602	credit rating	notation	calificación crediticia
C-603	credit rating agency [consumers] credit bureau credit monitoring agency credit reporting agency credit reference agency	centrale des risques	central de riesgo organismo de verificación de antecedentes de crédito
C-604	credit rating agency [corporations] credit agency mercantile agency international rating agency rating agency rating services	agence de notation organisme de notation agence d'évaluation des sociétés agence de cotation	agencia calificadora del riesgo crediticio entidad de calificación del riesgo crediticio calificadora de riesgo
C-605	credit rationing	rationnement du crédit rationnement des crédits	racionamiento del crédito
C-606	credit reference agency, *see* credit rating agency		
C-607	credit reporting agency, *see* credit rating agency		
C-608	credit risk counterparty risk	risque de crédit risque de contrepartie risque d'insolvabilité	riesgo de crédito riesgo de contraparte riesgo de incumplimiento de la contraparte
C-609	credit squeeze, *see* credit crunch		
C-610	credit standing, *see* creditworthiness		
C-611	credit tranche [IMF]	tranche de crédit	tramo de crédito
C-612	credit tranche drawing [IMF]	tirage dans les tranches de crédit	giro en los tramos de crédito

C-613	credit tranche policies [IMF]	politique des tranches de crédit	política de tramos de crédito política relativa a los tramos de crédito
C-614	credit tranche purchase [IMF]	achat dans les tranches de crédit	compra en los tramos de crédito
C-615	credit union *see also:* credit cooperative cooperative savings association	association de crédit mutuel coopérative de crédit mutuelle de crédit caisse de crédit mutuel coopérative d'épargne et de crédit	cooperativa de crédito cooperativa de ahorro y crédito cooperativa de ahorro caja de crédito
C-616	creditor	créancier	acreedor
C-617	creditor bank	banque créancière	banco acreedor
C-618	creditor country	pays créancier	país acreedor
C-619	creditor position asset position	position d'encours à l'actif position d'actif position créditrice	saldo acreedor posición acreedora

C-620	creditor reporting system
	[OECD]
	CRS
		Système de notification des pays
		  créanciers
		SNPC
			Sistema de notificación (de la
			  deuda) por parte de los países
			  acreedores
			sistema de notificación de los
			  países acreedores de la OCDE
			sistema de notificación de la deuda
			  por el acreedor

C-621	creditors' arrangement, *see* composition of creditors		
C-622	creditworthiness credit standing	crédit solvabilité surface financière surface de l'emprunteur qualité de la signature	solvencia capacidad crediticia
C-623	creeping inflation (accelerating) *see also:* rampant inflation	inflation rampante	inflación progresiva inflación reptante
C-624	creeping inflation (steady)	inflation latente	inflación latente
C-625	CRI, *see* Crisis Resolution Issues Division		
C-626	Crisis Resolution Issues Division [IMF] CRI	Division résolution des crises	División de Asuntos relativos a la Resolución de Crisis
C-627	criticized asset *see also:* special mention	actifs classés à risque	activo de muy baja calificación
C-628	crony capitalism	capitalisme de connivence capitalisme de copinage «capitalisme des copains et des coquins»	capitalismo amiguista capitalismo prebendario capitalismo de camarilla capitalismo de compadrazgo
C-629	cronyism	connivence «copinage» népotisme	amiguismo

C-630	crop credit, *see* seasonal credit		
C-631	crop year	campagne campagne agricole	campaña campaña agrícola año agrícola
C-632	cross debts	dettes croisées	deudas cruzadas
C-633	cross elasticity	élasticité croisée	elasticidad cruzada
C-634	cross rate	taux croisé	tipo de cambio cruzado

C-635	cross-border claim
	transborder claim
	transborder interbank claim
		créance transfrontalière
		créance extérieure
		créance sur l'étranger
		créance extraterritoriale
		créance interbancaire
		  transfrontalière
			crédito externo
			crédito sobre el exterior
			crédito interbancario
			  transfronterizo
			crédito exterior

C-636	cross-border lending foreign lending	prêts extraterritoriaux prêts transfrontaliers prêts accordés à des non-résidents	préstamos al exterior préstamos a no residentes
C-637	cross-border risk	risque extérieur	riesgo externo riesgo exterior
C-638	cross-border trade, *see* trade		
C-639	cross-classification multiple classification	classification matricielle classification croisée classification à plusieurs entrées	clasificación cruzada clasificación múltiple clasificación de doble entrada

C-640	cross-conditionality
	[IMF-IBRD]
	see also: avoidance of cross-
	  conditionality; collaboration with
	  the World Bank
		conditionnalité croisée	condicionalidad cruzada

C-641	cross-country analysis cross-country review cross-country study	analyse comparative entre pays analyse portant sur plusieurs pays analyse multinationale étude internationale étude portant sur plusieurs pays étude dans plusieurs pays	análisis comparativo de países análisis multinacional estudio multinacional estudio de varios países
C-642	cross-country review, *see* cross-country analysis		
C-643	cross-country study, *see* cross-country analysis		
C-644	cross-currency swap, *see* reciprocal currency arrangement		
C-645	cross-currency warrant	droit d'option multidevises droit d'échange de devises droit d'option sur devises croisées bon d'option multidevises	certificado para compra indirecta de moneda

C-646	cross-default clause
	[London Club]
		clause de défaut croisé
		clause de généralisation de la
		  défaillance
		clause de réciprocité des défauts
		  de paiement
			cláusula de incumplimiento
			  cruzado

C-647	cross-section analysis cross-sectional study	analyse transversale analyse par coupe transversale analyse en coupe instantanée	análisis transversal análisis de corte transversal análisis de sección transversal
C-648	cross-sectional study, *see* cross-section analysis		
C-649	crowding out of private investment, *see* crowding-out effect		
C-650	crowding-in effect	effet d'attraction effet d'envahissement	efecto de atracción
C-651	crowding-out effect crowding out of private investment	effet d'éviction effet d'évincement	efecto de desplazamiento efecto de desplazamiento de la inversión privada efecto de expulsión efecto de exclusión
C-652	CRS, *see* creditor reporting system		
C-653	crude data, *see* raw data		
C-654	CSF, *see* foreign exchange equalization fund		
C-655	CTA, *see* cofinancing trust account		
C-656	CTP, *see* Joint China-IMF Training Program		
C-657	cumulative net drawings [IMF]	tirages nets cumulés	giros netos acumulados
C-658	currencies held by the Fund, *see* currency holdings		
C-659	currency	monnaie monnaie fiduciaire numéraire billets et pièces devise	dinero moneda circulante numerario dinero legal billetes y monedas en circulación billetes y monedas
C-660	currency acceptable to the Fund [IMF]	monnaie acceptable par le FMI	moneda aceptable para el FMI
C-661	currency alignment	alignement des monnaies	alineación de las monedas alineamiento de los tipos de cambio
C-662	currency area, *see* currency zone		
C-663	currency band, *see* fluctuation band		
C-664	currency basket *see also:* currency composite basket of currencies	panier de monnaies groupe de monnaies	cesta de monedas canasta de monedas
C-665	currency board, *see* currency board arrangement		

C-666	currency board arrangement [IMF exchange rate classification system, 2006] *see also:* foreign exchange equalization fund; monetary board CBA currency board	caisse d'émission office de stabilisation des changes	régimen de caja de conversión régimen de convertibilidad caja de conversión junta monetaria
C-667	currency component [IMF]	composante monétaire	componente monetario
C-668	currency composite *see also:* currency basket composite of currencies	unité monétaire composite	unidad monetaria compuesta
C-669	currency composition	composition par monnaies monnaies qui composent	composición monetaria composición por monedas
C-670	currency conversion	conversion en une autre monnaie conversion de la dette en une autre monnaie	cambio de la denominación monetaria de la deuda conversión de la deuda a otra moneda conversión de monedas
C-671	currency holdings [IMF] IMF holdings of currencies Fund holdings of currencies currencies held by the Fund	avoirs du FMI en monnaies avoirs du FMI en devises monnaies détenues par le FMI	tenencias de monedas tenencias del FMI de monedas monedas en poder del FMI
C-672	currency in circulation *see also:* currency outside banks	circulation fiduciaire billets et pièces en circulation monnaie en circulation (dans le public)	dinero en circulación billetes y monedas en circulación efectivo en circulación circulación fiduciaria numerario en circulación
C-673	currency issue	émission de monnaie	emisión monetaria
C-674	currency issuing agency, *see* bank of issue		
C-675	currency liabilities	passifs libellés en devises engagements libellés en devises passifs en monnaies étrangères engagements en devises	pasivos monetarios
C-676	currency liquidity, *see* foreign currency liquidity		
C-677	currency mismatch	déséquilibre entre les monnaies de libellé des actifs et passifs	descalce de monedas discordancia entre la moneda de denominación de los activos y pasivos
C-678	currency option bond	obligation avec option de change	bono con opción de cambio
C-679	currency outside banks *see also:* currency in circulation cash outside banks	circulation fiduciaire hors banques	billetes y monedas en circulación billetes en poder del público efectivo en circulación efectivo en manos del público dinero en circulación circulante
C-680	currency realignment, *see* exchange rate realignment		

C-681	currency redenomination	changement de l'unité monétaire	cambio de la unidad monetaria redenominación monetaria reexpresión monetaria
C-682	currency snake system, *see* European narrow margins arrangement		
C-683	currency stabilization fund, *see* foreign exchange equalization fund		
C-684	currency substitution	substitution entre monnaies substitution d'une monnaie à une autre	sustitución de monedas
C-685	currency swap	échange de devises *swap* de devises	swap de monedas canje de monedas
C-686	currency swap arrangement, *see* reciprocal currency arrangement		
C-687	currency unit	unité monétaire	unidad monetaria
C-688	currency valuation adjustment, *see* valuation adjustment		
C-689	currency warrant	bon mobilisable en devises droit d'achat de devises	certificado para compra de moneda
C-690	currency zone common currency area common currency zone currency area	zone d'unité monétaire zone monétaire	zona monetaria zona de moneda común
C-691	current account	compte courant compte des transactions courantes	cuenta corriente
C-692	current account balance balance on current account	solde des transactions courantes solde extérieur courant solde courant	saldo de la balanza de pagos en cuenta corriente saldo de la balanza en cuenta corriente saldo en cuenta corriente balanza corriente balanza en cuenta corriente saldo por cuenta corriente
C-693	current account convertibility	convertibilité aux fins des transactions courantes convertibilité de la monnaie nationale aux fins des transactions courantes convertibilité des transactions courantes	convertibilidad de la cuenta corriente convertibilidad de los saldos de la cuenta corriente convertibilidad de la moneda a los efectos de las transacciones corrientes
C-694	current asset *see also:* liquid asset; quick asset	actif à court terme actif réalisable à court terme actif disponible	activo corriente activo realizable a corto plazo
C-695	current budget	budget ordinaire budget de fonctionnement	presupuesto corriente presupuesto ordinario
C-696	current expenditure	dépenses courantes dépenses ordinaires dépenses de fonctionnement	gastos corrientes gasto corriente gasto ordinario
C-697	current grants	dons courants	donaciones corrientes subvenciones corrientes

C-698	current liability *see also:* liquid liability	passif à court terme engagement à court terme exigibilité à court terme dette à court terme	pasivo corriente pasivo disponible pasivo realizable a corto plazo

C-699	current maturities	échéances de la période en cours
		échéances de la période de
		  consolidation
		échéances de la période
		  considérée
			vencimientos corrientes
			deuda que vence durante el
			  período corriente

C-700	current prices in current prices	prix courants(, aux)	expresados en precios corrientes a precios corrientes
C-701	Current Publications Division [IMF]	Division publications périodiques	División de Publicaciones Periódicas
C-702	current replacement cost replacement cost	coût de remplacement	costo de reposición costo corriente de reposición
C-703	current revenue	recettes courantes recettes de fonctionnement	ingresos corrientes
C-704	current, to be [IMF]	être à jour	estar al día estar al corriente cumplir
C-705	current value present value	valeur actuelle	valor actual valor presente

C-706	current-weighted index
	see also: base-weighted index
	Paasche index
		indice pondéré en fonction de
		  l'année en cours
		indice de Paasche
			índice ponderado en función del
			  período corriente
			índice en magnitudes del período
			  corriente
			índice de Paasche

C-707	custodian account, *see* custody account		
C-708	custody account custodian account	compte de garde	cuenta en custodia
C-709	customary business practices	pratiques commerciales courantes usages commerciaux	prácticas comerciales habituales usos comerciales
C-710	customer due diligence, *see* client due diligence		
C-711	customs bond	caution en douane garantie de douane	fianza de aduanas garantía aduanera
C-712	customs bonded warehouse bonded warehouse	entrepôt sous douane entrepôt sous le contrôle de la douane entrepôt réel	almacén bajo control aduanero depósito bajo control aduanero recinto fiscal depósito de aduana
C-713	customs clearance	dédouanement formalités de douane	despacho de aduanas
C-714	*Customs Co-operation Council Nomenclature, see Nomenclature for the Classification of Goods in Customs Tariffs*		
C-715	customs duty	droit de douane	derecho aduanero derecho de aduanas

C-716	customs duty bill	obligation cautionnée traite douanière	letra de aduana garantizada
C-717	customs frontier	frontière douanière	frontera aduanera
C-718	customs tariff tariff	tarif douanier droit de douane	arancel aduanero arancel derechos de aduana
C-719	customs union tariff union	union douanière	unión aduanera unión arancelaria
C-720	customs valuation	valeur en douane	valoración en aduana aforo aduanero valoración aduanera
C-721	cutback(s) [fiscal policy]	compression des dépenses mesures d'austérité (budgétaire)	reducción del gasto público
C-722	cutoff date [Paris Club]	date butoir date limite	fecha límite fecha de corte
C-723	cut-off price, *see* minimum acceptable bid		
C-724	cutting edge technology, *see* frontier technology		
C-725	CVA, *see* valuation adjustment		
C-726	CWDC, *see* Committee of the Whole for the Development Committee		
C-727	CWTO, *see* Committee on Liaison with the WTO		
C-728	cyclical downswing, *see* downturn		
C-729	cyclical downturn, *see* downturn		
C-730	cyclical influence	impulsion conjoncturelle impulsion cyclique	influencia cíclica influencia del ciclo
C-731	cyclical unemployment	chômage cyclique chômage conjoncturel	desempleo cíclico
C-732	cyclically adjusted	corrigé des variations cycliques déconjoncturalisé	ajustado en función del ciclo ajustado en función de las variaciones cíclicas
C-733	cyclically neutral budget	budget cycliquement neutre	presupuesto neutro con respecto a la fase del ciclo presupuesto cíclicamente neutro

D

D-1	DAC, *see* Development Assistance Committee		
D-2	Data Dissemination Standards Division [IMF]	Division normes de diffusion des données	División de Normas para la Divulgación de Datos
D-3	data processing, *see* electronic data processing		

D-4	Data Quality Assessment Framework [IMF] DQAF	cadre d´évaluation de la qualité des données CEQD	Marco de Evaluación de la Calidad de los Datos MECAD
D-5	Data Quality Reference Site [IMF]	site de référence pour la qualité des données	sitio de referencia sobre la calidad de los datos
D-6	data reporting, *see* reporting		
D-7	dataset-specific framework, *see* dataset-specific quality assessment framework		
D-8	dataset-specific quality assessment framework *see also:* generic data quality assessment framework dataset-specific framework specific assessment framework	cadre d'évaluation de la qualité d'une catégorie spécifique de données cadre d'évaluation de la qualité d'un groupe de données spécifique cadre d'évaluation d'un ensemble de données spécifique cadre d'évaluation spécifique	marco específico de evaluación de la calidad de los datos
D-9	DC, *see* Office of Executive Secretary, Joint Development Committee		
D-10	DCB, *see* debt conversion bond		
D-11	DCE, *see* domestic credit expansion		
D-12	DDSR, *see* debt and debt service reduction		
D-13	*de minimis* clause [Paris Club]	clause *de minimis*	cláusula *de minimis*
D-14	deadweight loss, *see* excess tax burden		
D-15	deadweight loss efficiency loss	perte d'efficience	pérdida de eficiencia
D-16	dealer [USA] *see also:* broker jobber [GBR]	contrepartiste courtier en valeurs mobilières intermédiaire opérateur intervenant	operador de valores operador bursátil
D-17	death taxes, *see* inheritance tax		
D-18	debenture [GBR; USA]	obligation (garantie) [GBR] *debenture* [CAN] obligation (non garantie) [USA] bon	obligación *debenture* obligación sin garantía específica bono
D-19	debenture debt	dette obligataire	deuda en obligaciones deuda en bonos
D-20	debit	débit	débito cargo adeudo

D-21	debit an account with an amount debit an amount to an account	débiter un compte d'un montant porter un montant au débit d'un compte	debitar una suma en una cuenta adeudar en cuenta
D-22	debit an amount to an account, *see* debit an account with an amount		
D-23	debit balance	solde débiteur	saldo deudor
D-24	debit entry	inscription au débit enregistrement au débit	asiento de débito adeudo cargo
D-25	debrief, *see* back-to-office report		
D-26	debriefing [IMF]	compte rendu rapport de retour de mission rapport de mission	sesión informativa al regreso de una misión
D-27	debt and debt service reduction DDSR	réduction de l'encours et du service de la dette	reducción del saldo y el servicio de la deuda
D-28	debt bunching, *see* bunching of maturities		
D-29	debt burden	poids de la dette charge de la dette fardeau de la dette	carga de la deuda
D-30	debt buyback, *see* buyback agreement		
D-31	debt cancellation, *see* debt forgiveness		
D-32	debt capital loan capital	capitaux empruntés fonds empruntés	capital obtenido en préstamo recursos ajenos
D-33	debt ceiling	plafond d'endettement	tope de endeudamiento
D-34	debt consolidation debt funding	consolidation de la dette	consolidación de la deuda
D-35	debt conversion [Paris Club] debt swap debt-debt swap bond swaps	échange de créances échange de dettes conversion de créances conversion de dettes swap de dettes	conversión de la deuda canje de deudas canje de títulos de deuda swap de una deuda por otra
D-36	debt conversion bond DCB	obligation de conversion de la dette	bono de conversión de la deuda
D-37	debt disbursed and outstanding	crédits décaissés et non amortis encours de la dette	crédito desembolsado y pendiente de reembolso saldo de la deuda
D-38	debt distress *see also:* debt overhang debt-distressed situation	surendettement situation de surendettement	situación crítica causada por el sobreendeudamiento
D-39	debt fatigue	fatigue causée par la dette	fatiga causada por la deuda
D-40	debt financing *see also:* equity financing	financement par l'emprunt	financiamiento mediante deuda financiamiento mediante el endeudamiento

D-41	debt for aid swap [Paris Club]	échange de créances contre des programmes d'aide	canje de deuda por programas de asistencia
D-42	debt for development swap	échange de créances contre des programmes de développement conversion de dettes en programmes de développement	canje de la deuda por financiamiento para el desarrollo
D-43	debt for environment swap	échange de créances contre des programmes de protection de l'environnement remise de dettes en échange de programmes de protection de l'environnement	canje de la deuda por medidas de protección ambiental
D-44	debt for equity conversion, *see* debt-equity swap		
D-45	debt for equity swap, *see* debt-equity swap		
D-46	debt for nature swap [Paris Club]	échange dette(s)/nature conversion de créances en investissements écologiques conversion de dettes en programmes de protection de la nature	canje de la deuda por medidas de protección de la naturaleza canje de la deuda por medidas de protección de los recursos naturales
D-47	debt forgiveness debt cancellation cancellation of debt	remise de la dette annulation de la dette extinction de la dette annulation des créances	condonación de la deuda cancelación de la deuda remisión de la deuda anulación de deudas condonación de deudas
D-48	debt funding, *see* debt consolidation		
D-49	debt holder	créancier	tenedor de un instrumento de deuda acreedor
D-50	debt instrument, *see* debt security		
D-51	debt into equity, conversion of, *see* debt-equity swap		
D-52	debt management	gestion de la dette	gestión de la deuda
D-53	debt moratorium [London Club] debt standstill payments standstill	moratoire de la dette	moratoria de la deuda moratoria de pagos
D-54	debt overhang *see also:* debt distress	surendettement charge excessive de la dette poids excessif de la dette	sobreendeudamiento
D-55	debt prepayment, *see* prepayment of debt		
D-56	debt reconstruction, *see* debt restructuring		
D-57	Debt Reduction Facility for IDA-Only Countries [IBRD] IDA Debt Reduction Facility	Fonds de désendettement des pays exclusivement IDA	Fondo para la reducción de la deuda de países que solo pueden recibir financiamiento de la AIF

D-58	debt reduction fund [IBRD] multilateral debt facility MDF	fonds de désendettement mécanisme multilatéral de désendettement	fondo para la reducción de la deuda fondo multilateral para la reducción de la deuda
D-59	debt reduction operations DROPS	opérations de réduction de la dette	operaciones de reducción de la deuda
D-60	debt refinancing	refinancement de la dette	refinanciamiento de la deuda refinanciación de la deuda
D-61	debt relief	allégement de la dette allégement de dette	alivio de la deuda alivio de la carga de la deuda
D-62	*Debt Relief for Low-Income Countries: The Enhanced HIPC Initiative*	*Allégement de la dette des pays à faible revenu — L'Initiative renforcée en faveur des pays pauvres très endettés*	*Alivio de la deuda para los países de bajo ingreso: Iniciativa Reforzada para los Países Pobres Muy Endeudados*
D-63	debt renegotiation, *see* debt workout		
D-64	debt reporting system [IMF] *see also:* Debtor Reporting System, World Bank	système de communication des données sur la dette	sistema de notificación de la deuda por el deudor
D-65	debt repudiation	répudiation de la dette	repudio de la deuda
D-66	debt repurchase, *see* buyback agreement		
D-67	debt rescheduling *see also:* debt restructuring rescheduling	rééchelonnement de la dette	reprogramación de la deuda reprogramación
D-68	debt restructuring *see also:* debt rescheduling debt reconstruction restructuring	restructuration de la dette réaménagement de la dette reprofilage de la dette remodelage de la dette	reestructuración de la deuda
D-69	debt security debt instrument	titre de dette titre de créance instrument de la dette	título de deuda instrumento de deuda título de renta fija instrumento de deuda
D-70	debt service debt servicing	service de la dette	servicio de la deuda
D-71	debt service payment service payment	paiement du service de la dette paiement au titre du service de la dette obligation au titre du service de la dette	pago del servicio de la deuda pago por servicio de la deuda
D-72	debt service ratio	ratio du service de la dette	coeficiente del servicio de la deuda
D-73	debt service-to-export ratio debt service-to-exports ratio [HIPC Initiative]	ratio du service de la dette aux exportations ratio service de la dette/exportations	relación entre el servicio de la deuda y la exportación razón servicio de la deuda/exportación
D-74	debt service-to-exports ratio, *see* debt service-to-export ratio		
D-75	debt servicing, *see* debt service		

D-76	debt standstill, *see* debt moratorium		
D-77	debt stock agreement, *see* stock-of-debt operation		
D-78	debt sustainability	viabilité de la dette soutenabilité de la dette	sostenibilidad de la deuda viabilidad de la deuda sustentabilidad de la deuda

D-79	debt sustainability analysis
	[IMF]
	DSA
		analyse de viabilité de la dette
		analyse de soutenabilité
		  de la dette
			análisis de la sostenibilidad de la
			  deuda
			análisis de la viabilidad
			  de la deuda

D-80	debt sustainability threshold	seuil de viabilité de la dette	umbral de sostenibilidad de la deuda umbral de viabilidad de la deuda
D-81	debt swap, *see* debt conversion		
D-82	debt to exports ratio, *see* debt-export ratio		
D-83	debt warrant, *see* bond warrant		
D-84	debt workout *see also:* corporate sector workout debt renegotiation workout	renégociation de la dette	renegociación de la deuda

D-85	debt-bond exchange	conversion d'obligations
		  en créances
		échange créances contre
		  obligations
		conversion de créances
		  en obligations
			canje de deuda por bonos
			operación de intercambio de
			  deuda por bonos

D-86	debt-debt swap, *see* debt conversion		
D-87	debt-distressed country severely indebted country	pays surendetté pays accablé par la dette	país sobreendeudado país abrumado por la deuda país agobiado por la deuda
D-88	debt-distressed situation, *see* debt distress		
D-89	debt-equity ratio	ratio d'autonomie financière ratio dette(s)/fonds propres coefficient d'endettement	coeficiente de endeudamiento razón deuda/capital propio relación deuda/capital propio

D-90	debt-equity swap
	[Paris Club]
	see also: capitalization bond
	debt for equity swap
	debt for equity conversion
	debt into equity, conversion of
		échange de créances contre actifs
		conversion de créances en prises
		  de participation
		conversion de créances en fonds
		  propres
		conversion de dettes en actifs
		conversion de dettes en capital
			conversión de la deuda en capital
			capitalización de la deuda
			swap de deuda por capital
			conversión de la deuda externa en
			  capital accionario
			capitalización de la deuda externa

D-91	debt-export ratio debt to exports ratio	ratio de la dette aux exportations ratio dette/exportations	relación entre la deuda y la exportación razón deuda/exportación
D-92	debtor country	pays débiteur	país deudor

D-93	debtor position liability position	position d'encours au passif position de passif position débitrice	saldo deudor posición deudora posición de pasivo

D-94	Debtor Reporting System, World
	   Bank
	[IBRD]
	see also: debt reporting system
	   [IMF]
	DRS
		Système de notification de la dette
		   à la Banque mondiale
			Sistema de Notificación de la
			   Deuda al Banco Mundial

D-95	debt-servicing capacity	capacité de service de la dette
		aptitude à assurer le service de la
		   dette
			capacidad de servicio de la deuda
			capacidad para atender el servicio
			   de la deuda

D-96	decentralized agency	unité autonome des administrations publiques	organismo descentralizado
D-97	decision maker	décideur responsable responsable des décisions	autoridad decisoria responsable de adoptar decisiones
D-98	decision making (process)	processus de décision processus décisionnel	proceso decisorio proceso de toma de decisiones
D-99	decision point [IMF; HIPC Initiative] *see also:* completion point	point de décision prise de décision	punto de decisión
D-100	declaration of BOP-related need, *see* representation of balance of payments financing need		
D-101	declaration of censure [IMF] censure	déclaration de censure	declaración de censura censura
D-102	declaration of ineligibility [IMF]	déclaration d'irrecevabilité	declaración de inhabilitación
D-103	declaration of need, *see* representation of balance of payments financing need		

D-104	declaration of noncooperation
	[IMF]
		déclaration de non-coopération
		déclaration de manque de
		   coopération
			declaración de no cooperación
			declaración de falta de
			   cooperación

D-105	decontrol, *see* deregulation		

D-106	deep-discount bond
	see also: discount bond
	deep-discounted bond
		obligation à prime d'émission
		   élevée
		obligation à forte prime d'émission
		obligation émise très au-dessous
		   du pair
		obligation à forte décote
			bono con fuerte descuento
			bonos de alta tasa de descuento

D-107	deep financial market *see also:* broad financial market	marché financier actif	mercado financiero profundo
D-108	deep-discounted bond, *see* deep-discount bond		
D-109	deepening of the capital market, *see* financial deepening		
D-110	deepening of the financial market, *see* financial deepening		

D-111	default *see also:* bankruptcy; insolvency default on payment	défaut de paiement cessation des paiements dépôt de bilan	cesación de pagos incumplimiento de pagos incumplimiento suspensión de pagos falta de pago
D-112	default on obligations	manquement aux obligations inexécution des obligations	incumplimiento de obligaciones
D-113	default on payment, *see* default		
D-114	deferred charges [IMF]	commissions comptabilisées comme recettes différées commission différée	cargos diferidos
D-115	deferred credit	crédit reporté	crédito diferido
D-116	deferred income [IMF]	recettes différées	ingreso diferido

D-117	deficit financing
	deficit spending
	pump priming
		financement par le déficit
		  (budgétaire)
		financement par l'impasse
		  budgétaire
		déficit systématique
		dépenses financées par un déficit
		  systématique
		politique de déficit budgétaire
		relance de l'activité par le déficit
			financiamiento de la economía
			  mediante déficit presupuestario
			gasto financiado mediante déficit
			financiamiento de gastos mediante
			  déficit

D-118	deficit reduction package	plan de réduction du déficit	plan de reducción del déficit
D-119	deficit spending, *see* deficit financing		
D-120	defined benefit plan	régime à prestations prédéfinies régime de pension à prestations prédéfinies	plan de prestaciones definidas
D-121	defined contribution plan money purchase plan	régime à cotisations déterminées	plan de aportes definidos plan de cotizaciones definidas
D-122	deflate (an economy)	abaisser le niveau des prix	deflactar (la economía)
D-123	deflate (prices)	déflater exprimer en prix constants	deflactar convertir a precios constantes
D-124	deflation *see also:* disinflation	déflation	deflación
D-125	deflationary *see also:* disinflationary	déflationniste	deflacionario deflacionista

D-126	deflationary demand measure	mesure de compression de la
		  demande
			medida de compresión de la
			  demanda

D-127	deflationary gap	écart déflationniste	brecha deflacionaria
D-128	deflationary pressure	pression déflationniste	presión deflacionaria
D-129	deflator	déflateur indice d'ajustement des prix	deflactor

D-130	delegation of authority [IMF]	délégation de pouvoir(s)	delegación de poderes
D-131	delinquent borrower	emprunteur défaillant	deudor moroso prestatario en mora
D-132	delinquent tax	arriéré d'impôt(s)	impuesto en mora impuesto atrasado
D-133	demand curve	courbe de demande	curva de demanda
D-134	demand deposit checking account deposit sight deposit	dépôt à vue	depósito a la vista
D-135	demand elasticity elasticity of demand	élasticité de la demande	elasticidad de la demanda
D-136	demand for money	demande de monnaie	demanda de dinero
D-137	demand function	fonction de demande	función de demanda
D-138	demand management	gestion de la demande régulation de la demande	gestión de la demanda regulación de la demanda
D-139	demand, payable on [banking]	payable à vue	pagadero a la vista
D-140	demand restraint	modération de la demande	contención de la demanda restricción de la demanda limitación de la demanda moderación de la demanda
D-141	demand schedule	tableau de la demande	tabla de demanda
D-142	demand shift, *see* shift in the demand curve		
D-143	demand-pull inflation	inflation par la demande	inflación de demanda inflación producida por la presión de la demanda
D-144	demographic pressure, *see* population pressure		
D-145	demonetization	démonétisation	desmonetización
D-146	demonstration effect	effet de démonstration effet d'entraînement effet d'émulation	efecto de demostración
D-147	denomination [banknotes]	coupure valeur nominale	denominación serie
D-148	denomination [currency]	dénomination unité monétaire dans laquelle ... est exprimé unité monétaire de libellé	denominación
D-149	denomination, *see* nominal value		
D-150	Department Head [IMF]	directeur de département	Director de Departamento

D-151	departmental agency	organisme ministériel	organismo ministerial
D-152	departmental enterprise *see also:* ancillary departmental enterprise	unité de production marchande des administrations publiques	empresa adscrita
D-153	dependency allowance [IMF] *see also:* child allowance [IMF]; spouse allowance family allowance child allowance [UN] child benefit allowance	allocations familiales indemnité pour enfant à charge indemnité pour charge de famille	asignación por familiares a cargo asignación familiar asignación por hijos a cargo subvención por hijos a cargo subsidio familiar
D-154	dependency ratio *see also:* support ratio	ratio inactifs/actifs ratio de dépendance rapport de dépendance charge supportée par la population active poids des inactifs	tasa de dependencia razón población inactiva/población activa
D-155	depletion allowance	provision pour épuisement (de ressources, de stock) déduction pour épuisement (de ressources, de stock)	reserva por agotamiento de los recursos depreciación por agotamiento de los recursos amortización del agotamiento de los recursos
D-156	depletion of natural resources, *see* environmental depletion		
D-157	deposit bank	institution de dépôts banque de dépôt(s)	banco de depósito
D-158	deposit claims	créances sous forme de dépôts dépôts (qui constituent des créances pour les banques) actifs sous forme de dépôts	activos por depósitos activos por concepto de depósitos
D-159	deposit insurance	garantie des dépôts assurance des dépôts	garantía de depósitos seguro de depósitos
D-160	deposit liabilities	dépôts (qui constituent des engagements pour les banques) engagements sous forme de dépôts	pasivos por depósitos pasivos por concepto de depósitos
D-161	deposit money bank	banque créatrice de monnaie	banco creador de dinero banco de depósito
D-162	deposit rate	taux de rémunération des dépôts taux d'intérêt créditeur taux des intérêts servis sur les dépôts	tasa de interés de los depósitos tasa de los depósitos tasa pasiva interés pasivo
D-163	deposit taking attracting deposits	collecte de dépôts	captación de depósitos
D-164	deposit withheld tax with government *see also:* collect tax; withhold tax	verser au Trésor les impôts recouvrés à la source	ingresar en el Tesoro los impuestos retenidos depositar los impuestos retenidos

D-165	deposit/loan ratio	taux de couverture des crédits par les dépôts	relación depósitos/préstamos razón depósitos/préstamos
D-166	depository [IMF] *see also:* fiscal agency	dépositaire	depositaría
D-167	depository corporation	institution de dépôts	sociedad de depósito
D-168	depository institution	institution de dépôts établissement de dépôts	institución de depósito
D-169	depreciation *see also:* amortization	amortissement dépréciation amortissement (des immobilisations corporelles) dotation aux amortissements	depreciación amortización
D-170	depreciation allowance *see also:* provision; reserve allowance for depreciation allowance depreciation provision	dépréciation réduction de valeur provision pour amortissement	provisión para depreciación provisión para amortización reserva para amortización
D-171	depreciation provision, *see* depreciation allowance		
D-172	depressed area	zone défavorisée zone déshéritée zone déprimée	zona desfavorecida zona deprimida zona de depresión económica
D-173	depth of the market market depth	profondeur du marché capacité d'absorption du marché	profundidad del mercado
D-174	Deputy ..., *see* ..., Deputy [IMF]		
D-175	Deputy Managing Director [IMF] *see also:* First Deputy Managing Director DMD	Directeur général adjoint	Subdirector Gerente
D-176	deregulation decontrol	déréglementation dérégulation libéralisation libération levée du contrôle	desregulación desreglamentación liberalización
D-177	derivation table	tableau de calcul	cuadro de derivación tabla de cálculo
D-178	derivative	dérivée	derivada
D-179	derivative, *see* derivative instrument		
D-180	derivative instrument financial derivative derivative	dérivé dérivé financier instrument financier dérivé produit financier dérivé produit dérivé	instrumento derivado instrumento financiero derivado producto derivado derivado

D-181	designated depository [IMF]	dépositaire désigné	depositaría designada
D-182	designated transaction, *see* transaction with designation		
D-183	designation [IMF; SDR]	désignation	designación
D-184	designation plan [IMF]	plan de désignation	plan de designación
D-185	desk audit, *see* office audit		
D-186	desk economist (for ... [country]) [IMF] desk officer for (... [country]) country desk	économiste chargé de ... [pays]	Economista encargado (de ...)
D-187	desk officer for (... [country]), *see* desk economist (for ... [country])		
D-188	destabilizing disequilibrating	déstabilisateur déséquilibrant	desestabilizador desequilibrador
D-189	deterrence [IMF] deterrence measure deterrent measure	dissuasion mesure dissuasive	disuasión medida disuasoria medida de disuasión
D-190	deterrence measure, *see* deterrence		
D-191	deterrent	facteur de dissuasion facteur dissuasif facteur préventif	elemento disuasivo factor disuasivo factor disuasorio
D-192	deterrent measure, *see* deterrence		
D-193	devaluation	dévaluation	devaluación
D-194	developing country	pays en développement	país en desarrollo
D-195	development aid development assistance	aide au développement assistance au développement	ayuda para el desarrollo asistencia para el desarrollo
D-196	development assistance, *see* development aid		
D-197	Development Assistance Committee [OECD] DAC	Comité d'aide au développement CAD	Comité de Asistencia para el Desarrollo CAD
D-198	Development Committee Joint Development Committee Joint Ministerial Committee of the Boards of Governors of the Bank and the Fund on the Transfer of Real Resources to Developing Countries	Comité ministériel conjoint des Conseils des gouverneurs de la Banque et du Fonds sur le transfert de ressources réelles aux pays en développement Comité du développement	Comité Ministerial Conjunto de las Juntas de Gobernadores del Banco y del Fondo para la Transferencia de Recursos Reales a los Países en Desarrollo Comité para el Desarrollo
D-199	development contract, *see* performance contract		
D-200	Development Issues Division [IMF] DID	Division développement	División de Cuestiones de Desarrollo

D-201	development partner	partenaire pour le développement	socio en el desarrollo
D-202	development round, *see* Doha Round		
D-203	DFI, *see* foreign direct investment		
D-204	DID, *see* Development Issues Division		
D-205	difference [calculus]	différence	diferencia
D-206	difference equation	équation aux différences (finies)	ecuación en diferencias
D-207	differential equation [calculus]	équation différentielle	ecuación diferencial
D-208	differential (first, second, ...)	différentiel (premier, second, ...)	diferencial (primer, segundo, ...)
D-209	differential in inflation rates, *see* inflation differential		
D-210	differential pricing, *see* split pricing		
D-211	diminishing returns	rendements décroissants	rendimientos decrecientes
D-212	direct foreign investment, *see* foreign direct investment		
D-213	direct inflation targeting, *see* inflation-targeting framework		
D-214	direct investment	investissement direct	inversión directa
D-215	direct investment income	revenu des investissements directs	renta de la inversión directa
D-216	directed credit	crédit orienté crédit dirigé orientation du crédit	crédito dirigido
D-217	direction of trade geographical direction of trade	répartition géographique du commerce extérieur répartition géographique des échanges	distribución geográfica del comercio exterior
D-218	*Direction of Trade Statistics* [IMF] *DOTS*	*Direction of Trade Statistics* *DOTS*	*Direction of Trade Statistics* *DOTS*
D-219	*Direction of Trade Statistics Yearbook* [IMF] *DOTS Yearbook* *DOTSY*	*Direction of Trade Statistics Yearbook* *DOTS Yearbook* Annuaire de *DOTS*	*Direction of Trade Statistics Yearbook* *DOTS Yearbook* anuario de DOTS
D-220	Director [IMF]	Directeur	Director
D-221	Director and Special Representative to the United Nations [IMF]	Directeur et Représentant spécial auprès des Nations Unies	Director y Representante Especial ante las Naciones Unidas
D-222	Director, Assistant [IMF]	Sous-Directeur	Director Adjunto

D-223	Director, Associate [IMF]	Directeur associé	Director Asociado
D-224	Director, Deputy [IMF]	Directeur adjoint	Subdirector
D-225	Director for Special Operations	Directeur des opérations spéciales	Director de Operaciones Especiales
D-226	Director, Offices in Europe [IMF]	Directeur des bureaux du FMI en Europe	Director de las Oficinas en Europa
D-227	directorship [IMF]	poste d'administrateur	cargo de director ejecutivo puesto de director ejecutivo
D-228	dirty float, *see* managed floating		
D-229	disaggregated data	données désagrégées	datos desagregados
D-230	disbursed debt	crédits versés crédits décaissés montant effectivement reçu (par l'emprunteur) prêt décaissé	préstamos desembolsados
D-231	disbursement	décaissement versement déboursement	desembolso gasto
D-232	discharge an obligation [IMF] *see also:* fulfill an obligation	s'acquitter d'une obligation régler une obligation	cumplir una obligación
D-233	discount	réduction rabais	rebaja descuento
D-234	discount [securities]	prime d'émission décote	descuento desagio
D-235	discount, at a	au-dessous du pair	bajo la par con descuento por debajo del valor nominal
D-236	discount bond *see also:* deep discount bond discount note	obligation émise au-dessous du pair obligation émise à prime bon à prime d'émission obligation à intérêts précomptés obligation émise avec une décote	bono emitido bajo la par bono con descuento pagaré con descuento
D-237	discount note, *see* discount bond		
D-238	discount rate [central banking] *see also:* rediscount rate minimum lending rate [GBR] MLR bank rate [GBR]	taux d'escompte	tasa de descuento tasa de redescuento tasa de descuento oficial tasa de redescuento oficial

D-239	discount rate [finance]	taux d'actualisation	tasa de actualización tasa de descuento
D-240	discount window [central banking]	guichet du réescompte service du réescompte	ventanilla de descuento ventanilla de redescuento servicio de redescuento
D-241	discountable eligible for discounting eligible for rediscounting	escomptable réescomptable éligible au réescompte admis au réescompte mobilisable bancable	descontable redescontable
D-242	discrete [mathematics]	discret discontinu	discreto
D-243	discrete depreciation, *see* step depreciation		
D-244	discrete devaluation *see also:* incremental devaluation step devaluation	dévaluation ponctuelle	devaluación discreta
D-245	discrete step depreciation, *see* step depreciation		
D-246	discretionary policy, *see* activist policy		
D-247	discriminating monopoly	monopole discriminant	monopolio discriminatorio
D-248	discriminatory currency practice [IMF]	pratique monétaire discriminatoire	práctica monetaria discriminatoria
D-249	discriminatory pricing, *see* price discrimination		
D-250	discriminatory tariff preference	préférence tarifaire discriminatoire	preferencia arancelaria discriminatoria
D-251	diseconomy	déséconomie	deseconomía
D-252	disequilibrating, *see* destabilizing		
D-253	disguised inflation, *see* hidden inflation		
D-254	disguised unemployment, *see* hidden unemployment		
D-255	dishoarding	déthésaurisation	desatesoramiento
D-256	disincentive	désincitation frein incitation à ne pas ... obstacle mesure de dissuasion mesure de freinage mesure décourageant ...	desincentivo elemento disuasivo
D-257	disinflation *see also:* deflation	désinflation	desinflación
D-258	disinflationary *see also:* deflationary	désinflationniste	desinflacionario desinflacionista
D-259	disintermediation	désintermédiation	desintermediación

D-260	disinvestment	désinvestissement réduction (des investissements) décapitalisation liquidation (des investissements)	desinversión descapitalización liquidación de los activos de inversión
D-261	disorderly exchange market conditions	désordre sur le marché des changes conditions désordonnées sur le marché des changes	condiciones anormales en el mercado cambiario desorden en el mercado de cambios
D-262	disposable income	revenu disponible	ingreso disponible renta disponible
D-263	disposition (of assets)	cession transfert aliénation vente	enajenación cesión venta disposición
D-264	disruption	désorganisation perturbation dislocation dérèglement	perturbación desorden desorganización
D-265	dissave	désépargner	desahorrar
D-266	dissaving negative saving	désépargne épargne négative	desahorro ahorro negativo
D-267	Dissemination Standards Bulletin Board [IMF] DSBB	tableau d'affichage des normes de diffusion des données TAND	Cartelera Electrónica de Divulgación de Datos CEDD
D-268	distortion	distorsion	distorsión
D-269	distributed earnings	bénéfices distribués	utilidades distribuidas beneficios distribuidos
D-270	distribution channel	circuit de distribution	canal de distribución cauce de distribución
D-271	distribution function	fonction de distribution	función de distribución
D-272	distribution of income income distribution	distribution/répartition du/des revenu(s)	distribución del ingreso
D-273	distributional effect distributive effect	effet de répartition effet sur la répartition	efecto distributivo efecto sobre la distribución del ingreso
D-274	distributive effect, *see* distributional effect		
D-275	disturbance	turbulence perturbation	perturbación
D-276	divergence indicator *see also:* European Monetary System; Exchange Rate Mechanism; intervention point; parity grid	indicateur de divergence	indicador de divergencia
D-277	divergence threshold, *see* intervention point		

D-278	diversified borrower	emprunteur à diverses sources	prestatario en fuentes diversificadas
D-279	divestiture (of assets)	cession désengagement dessaisissement vente déssaisissement du débiteur	enajenación privatización desincorporación cesión traspaso
D-280	divestiture (of enterprises) *see also:* privatization	cession désengagement (de l'État) déssaisissement	cesión (de empresas del Estado) venta traspaso desincorporación privatización
D-281	Division 1, 2, 3, ... [IMF]	Division 1, 2, 3, ...	División 1, 2, 3, ...
D-282	Division Chief [IMF]	Chef de division	Jefe de División
D-283	Division Chief, Deputy [IMF]	Chef de division adjoint	Subjefe de División
D-284	DMD, *see* Deputy Managing Director		
D-285	doctored data	données altérées données manipulées données maquillées	datos manipulados datos adulterados datos retocados
D-286	documentary audit, *see* office audit		
D-287	Doha Round development round	Cycle de négociations commerciales de Doha Programme de Doha Cycle de Doha Programme de Doha pour le développement Programme du développement de Doha	Ronda de Doha ronda del desarrollo
D-288	dollar balances	soldes en dollars balances dollar	saldos en dólares
D-289	domestic content [imports]	contenu en produits nationaux teneur en produits nationaux	contenido nacional elementos nacionales contenido de origen nacional proporción de productos nacionales
D-290	domestic credit expansion DCE	expansion du crédit intérieur	expansión del crédito interno expansión del crédito interior
D-291	domestic currency local currency	monnaie nationale unité monétaire nationale	moneda nacional
D-292	domestic currency unit value	valeur unitaire en monnaie nationale	valor unitario en moneda nacional
D-293	domestic financing	financement intérieur	financiamiento interno
D-294	domestic liabilities	engagements intérieurs	pasivos internos obligaciones internas

D-295	domestic liquidity	liquidité intérieure	liquidez interna
D-296	domestic market home market	marché intérieur marché national	mercado interno mercado nacional
D-297	domestic resource cost DRC	coût en ressources intérieures CRI	costo en recursos internos
D-298	domestic saving	épargne intérieure	ahorro interno
D-299	domestic securities	titres nationaux	títulos nacionales títulos del país
D-300	domestic taxes on goods and services	impôts intérieurs sur les biens et services	impuestos internos sobre bienes y servicios
D-301	donor	donateur donneur	donante
D-302	donor country	pays donateur pays donneur	país donante
D-303	donors and creditors donors and lenders	donateurs et créanciers bailleurs de fonds	donantes y acreedores donantes y prestamistas
D-304	donors and lenders, *see* donors and creditors		
D-305	dormant debt	dette dormante	deuda inactiva
D-306	*DOTS, see Direction of Trade Statistics*		
D-307	*DOTS Yearbook, see Direction of Trade Statistics Yearbook*		
D-308	*DOTSY, see Direction of Trade Statistics Yearbook*		
D-309	double counting	duplication d'écritures double comptage double emploi	doble contabilización doble cómputo doble cálculo doble registro
D-310	double taxation dual taxation	double imposition	doble imposición doble tributación
D-311	double-entry system	système d'enregistrement en partie double comptabilité en partie double	método de contabilidad por partida doble
D-312	doubtful credit, *see* doubtful loan		
D-313	doubtful loan *see also:* loss doubtful credit	prêt douteux prêt problème	préstamo de cobro dudoso préstamo problemático
D-314	down payment	acompte versement initial apport personnel	cuota inicial anticipo pago a cuenta entrada

D-315	downgrading	déclassement	bajar la calificación
			reclasificación en una categoría
			  inferior
			reclasificación en una categoría
			  más baja

D-316	downside risk
	see also: upside risk
		risque de révision à la baisse des
		  prévisions
		risque de dégradation de la
		  situation
			riesgo de que los resultados sean
			  inferiores a lo previsto
			probabilidad de que las cifras
			  reales sean menores de las que
			  indican las proyecciones
			riesgo de que no se cumpla lo
			  previsto
			riesgo de deterioro de la situación
			riesgo a la baja

D-317	downstream integration	intégration en aval	integración vertical hacia abajo
D-318	downswing, *see* downturn		
D-319	downtrend, *see* downward trend		

D-320	downturn
	cyclical downturn
	downswing
	cyclical downswing
		phase descendante (du cycle
		  économique/conjoncturel)
		phase de contraction
		ralentissement
			desaceleración
			iniciación de la fase descendente
			cambio desfavorable de la
			  coyuntura
			fase descendente
			movimiento descendente
			fase de contracción
			fase descendente del ciclo

D-321	downward adjustment	ajustement en baisse ajustement à la baisse	ajuste a la baja
D-322	downward bias negative bias	erreur systématique par défaut biais par défaut distorsion par défaut	sesgo a la baja
D-323	downward pressure	pression à la baisse	presión a la baja
D-324	downward rigidity, *see* stickiness		
D-325	downward trend falling trend downtrend	tendance à la baisse tendance descendante évolution à la baisse	tendencia descendente tendencia a la baja
D-326	downward-sloping curve	courbe descendante courbe décroissante	curva descendente curva de pendiente descendente
D-327	DQAF, *see* Data Quality Assessment Framework		
D-328	draft amendment [IMF] *see also:* proposed amendment	projet d'amendement projet de modification	proyecto de enmienda proyecto de modificación proyecto de reforma
D-329	draft budget, *see* budget proposal		
D-330	draft resolution [IMF] *see also:* proposed resolution	projet de résolution	proyecto de resolución
D-331	draw on the IMF	tirer sur le FMI	girar contra el FMI efectuar un giro contra el FMI

D-332	drawback
	[customs]
		ristourne des droits de douane
		drawback
		rembours (des droits de douane)
			reintegro de los derechos de
			  aduana
			devolución de los impuestos
			drawback
			desgravación fiscal a la
			  exportación

D-333	drawdown period	période de tirage	período de giro
D-334	drawer [IMF] drawing country	tireur État tireur pays tireur	girador país girador
D-335	drawing country, *see* drawer		
D-336	drawing down	déstockage utilisation (des stocks) réduction (des stocks)	disminución de las existencias uso de las existencias
D-337	drawing facility [IMF]	mécanisme de tirage	servicio de giro
D-338	drawing on loans extended	tirage sur prêts accordés	giro contra préstamos concedidos
D-339	drawing right [IMF]	droit de tirage	derecho de giro
D-340	DRC, *see* domestic resource cost		
D-341	DROPS, *see* debt reduction operations		
D-342	DRS, *see* Debtor Reporting System, World Bank		
D-343	DSA, *see* debt sustainability analysis		
D-344	DSBB, *see* Dissemination Standards Bulletin Board		
D-345	dual economy	économie duale économie à deux vitesses économie à double secteur	economía dual economía dualista
D-346	dual exchange market	double marché des changes	mercado de cambios dual
D-347	dual pricing	régime du double prix régime des prix doubles système de prix doubles	sistema dual de precios régimen de precios dobles
D-348	dual rate system	régime de taux de change double double marché des changes	régimen cambiario dual régimen de cambios doble
D-349	dual taxation, *see* double taxation		
D-350	due and payable	échu et exigible	vencido y exigible vencido y pagadero
D-351	due date	date d'exigibilité échéance date limite	fecha de vencimiento plazo de vencimiento
D-352	due diligence	processus de «due diligence» audits préalables	diligencia debida

D-353	dummy out	éliminer par le recours à une variable muette	sustituir por una variable ficticia
D-354	dummy variable	variable muette variable fictive	variable ficticia
D-355	dumping	dumping	*dumping*
D-356	durable good *see also:* consumer durable	bien durable	bienes duraderos
D-357	duration	duration	duración
D-358	Durbin-Watson statistic DW	coefficient de Durbin–Watson DW fonction des observations de Durbin-Watson DW	estadístico Durbin-Watson coeficiente de Durbin-Watson DW
D-359	Dutch auction	adjudication à la hollandaise adjudication à la baisse enchère dégressive adjudication au prix marginal décroissant	subasta a la baja
D-360	duty-free	en franchise détaxé exempt de droits	exento de derechos libre de impuestos
D-361	DW, *see* Durbin-Watson statistic		
D-362	dynamic multiplier	multiplicateur dynamique	multiplicador dinámico

E

E-1	EA, *see* Extended Arrangement		
E-2	EAP, *see* policy on enlarged access to the Fund's resources		
E-3	EAP, *see* labor force		
E-4	EAR, *see* enlarged access to the Fund's resources		
E-5	EAR, *see* enlarged access resources		
E-6	early repurchase [IMF] advance repurchase	rachat par anticipation rachat anticipé rachat effectué avant l'échéance	recompra anticipada
E-7	early repurchase expectation [IMF] prompt repurchase expectation	principe du rachat par anticipation	expectativa de recompra anticipada
E-8	early repurchase of accelerated set-aside amounts [IMF] *see also:* repurchase of accelerated set-aside amounts	rachat anticipé au titre d'achats accélérés de montants mis en réserve rachat anticipé au titre d'achats accélérés de montants préaffectés	recompra anticipada de montos consignados adquiridos de manera acelerada
E-9	early retirement [IMF]	retraite anticipée	jubilación anticipada

E-10	early stabilizer *see also:* mature stabilizer	pays en phase initiale de stabilisation	país en fase inicial de estabilización
E-11	early warning system EWS	système d'alerte avancée système d'alerte rapide clignotants d'alarme	sistema de alerta anticipada
E-12	earmark	affecter réserver	afectar a un fin determinado reservar para un fin específico destinar a un fin específico consignar
E-13	earmarked account	compte affecté compte d'affectation	cuenta consignada
E-14	earmarked tax	impôts d'affectation spéciale	impuesto afectado a un fin específico
E-15	earned income	revenu du travail revenu d'une activité professionnelle	ingreso realizado renta ganada renta derivada del trabajo ingreso derivado del trabajo renta salarial ingreso salarial
E-16	earning asset income-earning asset productive asset	avoir productif actif productif	activo rentable activo productivo
E-17	earning power, *see* profitability		
E-18	earnings [corporations]	bénéfices profits résultat revenus	utilidades ganancias beneficios
E-19	earnings [individuals]	revenu(s) bénéfices gain(s) rémunération	renta ingresos remuneración
E-20	easing softening	détente desserrement relâchement fléchissement baisse glissement	baja distensión
E-21	easing, *see* accommodative monetary policy		
E-22	easing of monetary policy, *see* accommodative monetary policy		
E-23	Eastern Caribbean Central Bank ECCB	Banque centrale des Caraïbes orientales ECCB	Banco Central del Caribe Oriental
E-24	easy monetary policy, *see* accommodative monetary policy		
E-25	easy money policy, *see* cheap money policy		
E-26	easy rider, *see* easy rider bank		

E-27	easy rider bank *see also:* free rider bank easy rider	banque qui ne participe que partiellement	banco que solo participa parcialmente
E-28	EBF, *see* extrabudgetary account		
E-29	EBRD, *see* European Bank for Reconstruction and Development		
E-30	EC, *see* European Commission		
E-31	ECA, *see* Economic Commission for Africa		
E-32	ECB, *see* European Central Bank		
E-33	ECCAS, *see* Economic Community of Central African States		
E-34	ECCB, *see* Eastern Caribbean Central Bank		
E-35	ECE, *see* Economic Commission for Europe		
E-36	ECLAC, *see* Economic Commission for Latin America and the Caribbean		
E-37	economic agent *see also:* transactor economic entity economic unit	agent économique entité économique unité économique cellule économique	agente económico entidad económica unidad económica
E-38	Economic and Monetary Community of Central Africa, *see* Central African Economic and Monetary Community		
E-39	Economic and Monetary Union [EU] EMU	Union économique et monétaire européenne Union économique et monétaire UEM	Unión Económica y Monetaria UEM
E-40	Economic and Social Commission for Asia and the Pacific [UN-ECOSOC] ESCAP	Commission économique et sociale pour l'Asie et le Pacifique CESAP	Comisión Económica y Social para Asia y el Pacífico CESPAP
E-41	Economic and Social Commission for Western Asia [UN-ECOSOC] ESCWA	Commission économique et sociale pour l'Asie occidentale CESAO	Comisión Económica y Social para Asia Occidental CESPAO
E-42	Economic and Social Council, United Nations [UN] ECOSOC	Conseil économique et social des Nations Unies ECOSOC	Consejo Económico y Social de las Naciones Unidas ECOSOC
E-43	Economic Commission for Africa [UN-ECOSOC] ECA	Commission économique pour l'Afrique CEA	Comisión Económica para África CEPA
E-44	Economic Commission for Europe [UN-ECOSOC] ECE	Commission économique pour l'Europe CEE	Comisión Económica para Europa CEPE
E-45	Economic Commission for Latin America and the Caribbean ECLAC	Commission économique pour l'Amérique latine et les Caraïbes CEPAL	Comisión Económica para América Latina y el Caribe CEPAL

E-46	Economic Community of Central African States ECCAS	Communauté économique des États de l'Afrique centrale CEEAC	Comunidad Económica del África Central CEAC
E-47	Economic Community of West African States ECOWAS	Communauté économique des États de l'Afrique de l'Ouest CEDEAO	Comunidad Económica de los Estados de África Occidental CEDEAO
E-48	Economic Counsellor [IMF]	Conseiller économique	Consejero Económico
E-49	economic cycle, *see* business cycle		
E-50	Economic Data Sharing System [IMF] EDSS	système électronique d'échange de données	Sistema de Intercambio de Datos Económicos
E-51	economic entity, *see* economic agent		
E-52	economic fundamentals, *see* fundamentals		
E-53	Economic Information System [IMF] EIS	système d'information économique SIE	Sistema de Información Económica SIE
E-54	Economic Issues [IMF]	série des «Dossiers économiques»	Temas de economía
E-55	economic life useful life service life	durée de vie économique durée utile durée de vie utile	vida útil duración vida económica
E-56	Economic Modeling Division [IMF]	Division modèles économiques	División de Modelos Económicos
E-57	economic performance	résultats économiques performance(s) économique(s)	resultados económicos trayectoria económica evolución de la economía
E-58	economic price efficiency price	prix économique	precio económico precio de eficiencia económica
E-59	economic recovery recovery	redressement reprise	recuperación económica reactivación repunte de la economía
E-60	economic rent *see also:* rent seeking rent	rente économique	renta económica renta
E-61	Economic Systems Division [IMF]	Division systèmes économiques	División de Sistemas Económicos
E-62	economic unit, *see* economic agent		
E-63	economic welfare welfare	bien-être économique conditions de vie	bienestar económico bienestar
E-64	economically active population, *see* labor force		
E-65	economics	aspects économiques	aspectos económicos

E-66	economics	science(s) économique(s) économie	economía ciencias económicas
E-67	economies of scale	économies d'échelle	economías de escala
E-68	Economist Program [IMF] EP	Programme-économistes PE	Programa para Economistas PE
E-69	ECOSOC, *see* Economic and Social Council, United Nations		
E-70	ECOWAS, *see* Economic Community of West African States		
E-71	ECP, *see* Eurocommercial paper		
E-72	ECU, *see* European currency unit		
E-73	ED, *see* Executive Director (Mr./Ms. ...)		
E-74	EDF, *see* European Development Fund		
E-75	Editor, Chief [IMF]	Directeur des publications	Director Editorial
E-76	Editorial and Publications Division [IMF]	Division rédaction et publication	División de Redacción y Publicaciones
E-77	EDP, *see* electronic data processing		
E-78	EDSS, *see* Economic Data Sharing System		
E-79	educated guess	estimation raisonnée estimation fondée	estimación razonada
E-80	education	enseignement	educación
E-81	EEA, *see* European Economic Area		
E-82	EER, *see* effective exchange rate		
E-83	EFF, *see* Extended Fund Facility		
E-84	effective date	date d'entrée en vigueur date de prise d'effet	fecha de entrada en vigor
E-85	effective exchange rate *see also:* real effective exchange rate index EER	taux de change effectif	tipo de cambio efectivo
E-86	effective rate of protection ERP	taux de (la) protection effective	tasa de protección efectiva
E-87	effective yield, *see* actual interest yield		
E-88	efficiency loss, *see* excess tax burden		
E-89	efficiency loss, *see* deadweight loss		
E-90	efficiency price, *see* economic price		
E-91	EFT, *see* electronic funds transfer		

E-92	EFTA, *see* European Free Trade Association		
E-93	EIB, *see* European Investment Bank		
E-94	EIS, *see* Economic Information System		
E-95	elasticity of a tax system *see also:* built-in elasticity of a tax system; tax buoyancy	élasticité d'un système fiscal	elasticidad de un sistema tributario
E-96	elasticity of demand, *see* demand elasticity		
E-97	elasticity of expectations	élasticité des anticipations	elasticidad de las expectativas
E-98	elasticity of supply supply elasticity	élasticité de l'offre	elasticidad de la oferta
E-99	elected Executive Director [IMF]	administrateur élu	Director Ejecutivo Elegido
E-100	elective Executive Director [IMF]	administrateur électif	Director Ejecutivo Electivo
E-101	electronic data processing EDP data processing informatics	traitement électronique des données traitement informatique	procesamiento electrónico de datos informática procesamiento de datos elaboración electrónica de datos
E-102	electronic funds transfer EFT	transfert électronique de fonds	transferencia electrónica de fondos
E-103	eligibility	admissibilité	habilitación elegibilidad
E-104	eligible *see also:* qualified	recevable admis à bénéficier de pouvant être admis à bénéficier de admissible habilité à ayant droit éligible	habilitado capacitado admisible que reúne los requisitos
E-105	eligible asset [banking]	actif pris en considération	activo computable
E-106	eligible debt [Paris Club]	dette restructurable dette admissible	deuda reestructurable deuda admisible
E-107	eligible for discounting, *see* discountable		
E-108	eligible for rediscounting, *see* discountable		
E-109	eligible vote [IMF]	voix prise en compte pour l'élection	voto computable voto que cuenta para la elección
E-110	ELRIC, *see* external audit mechanism, legal structure and independence of the central bank, financial reporting practices, internal audit mechanism, and the system of internal controls		
E-111	embodied cost	coût incorporé	costos incurridos
E-112	EME, *see* emerging market economy		

E-113	emergency and post-conflict assistance, *see* emergency post-conflict assistance		
E-114	emergency assistance [IMF]	aide d'urgence secours d'urgence	asistencia de emergencia
E-115	Emergency Assistance for Natural Disasters ENDA	aide d'urgence à la suite de catastrophes naturelles	Asistencia de Emergencia para Catástrofes Naturales
E-116	Emergency Facility for Natural Disasters [IMF Facilities]	facilité d'urgence pour les catastrophes naturelles	Servicio Financiero de Emergencia para Catástrofes Naturales
E-117	emergency financing mechanism [IMF]	mécanisme de financement d'urgence	mecanismo de financiamiento de emergencia
E-118	emergency post-conflict assistance [IMF] EPCA emergency and post-conflict assistance policy of emergency assistance to post-conflict countries	assistance d'urgence après un conflit aide d'urgence postconflit AUPC aide d'urgence aux pays sortant d'un conflit	asistencia de emergencia a países en situación de posconflicto
E-119	emergency provisions [IMF]	dispositions d'exception	disposiciones de emergencia
E-120	emergency purchase [IMF]	achat d'urgence	compra de emergencia
E-121	emerging market	marché émergent pays émergent	mercado emergente
E-122	emerging market economy EME	pays émergent économie de marché émergente	economía de mercado emergente
E-123	emigration of the tax base	nomadisme fiscal	emigración de la base imponible nomadismo fiscal
E-124	empirical evidence	données empiriques	datos empíricos evidencia empírica
E-125	empirical study	étude empirique étude concrète travail empirique	estudio empírico
E-126	employee attrition rate	taux de diminution naturelle des effectifs taux d'attrition	tasa de reducción natural del personal
E-127	employee benefits, *see* fringe benefits		
E-128	employee contribution *see also:* fringe benefits employee's social contribution	cotisation salariale cotisations sociales	aporte del empleado cotización a cargo del empleado
E-129	employee's social contribution, *see* employee contribution		

E-130	employer contribution employer's social contributions	cotisations sociales à la charge des employeurs cotisation patronale part patronale	aporte patronal cuota patronal cuota del empleador cotización patronal cotización del empleador cotización a cargo del empleador cotización empresarial
E-131	employer's social contributions, *see* employer contribution		
E-132	employment slack	volant de main-d'œuvre inutilisé	subempleo del factor trabajo mano de obra no utilizada
E-133	empowerment	démarginalisation autonomisation	empoderamiento potenciación promoción de la autonomía plena participación en la sociedad pleno ejercicio de los derechos realización del potencial
E-134	EMS, *see* European Monetary System		
E-135	EMU, *see* Economic and Monetary Union		
E-136	enabling environment	environnement propice climat favorable	entorno propicio clima propicio
E-137	encash [IMF]	mobiliser réaliser convertir en liquidités	hacer efectivo convertir en efectivo
E-138	encashable	mobilisable réalisable convertible en un moyen de paiement	convertible en efectivo
E-139	encashable loan claim	créance sur prêt mobilisable	crédito convertible crédito realizable
E-140	encashment	encaissement mobilisation réalisation conversion en liquidités	realización conversión en efectivo presentación de valores al cobro cobro
E-141	encashment of rights [IMF] *see also:* rights approach	utilisation des droits (cumulés)	utilización de los derechos acumulados
E-142	encashment right [IMF]	droit de conversion en liquidités	derecho de conversión en efectivo
E-143	encumbered	grevé	gravado sujeto a carga o gravamen
E-144	end consumer	consommateur final	consumidor final
E-145	end product final product	produit fini produit final	producto final producto terminado
E-146	end product *see also:* byproduct	produit dérivé	producto derivado

E-147	end use	emploi final	uso final
E-148	end user final user	utilisateur final	usuario final
E-149	ENDA, *see* Emergency Assistance for Natural Disasters		
E-150	endogenous shock	perturbation endogène choc endogène	*shock* endógeno perturbación endógena
E-151	endogenous variable	variable endogène	variable endógena
E-152	energy-intensive	à forte consommation d'énergie grand consommateur d'énergie	de alto consumo energético con uso intensivo de energía
E-153	energy-saving technology	techniques d'utilisation rationnelle de l'énergie techniques permettant d'économiser l'énergie	tecnología con bajo consumo de energía
E-154	enforceable [IMF]	exécutoire	exigible
E-155	enforced collection, *see* tax enforcement		
E-156	enforcement of security realization of collateral	réalisation d'une sûreté réalisation d'un gage	ejecución de garantías ejecución de bienes en garantía
E-157	enforcement power [IMF]	pouvoir de sanctionner le non- respect de ... pouvoir d'appliquer des mesures coercitives	potestad fiscalizadora poder de sanción por incumplimiento
E-158	engagement, *see* engagement of the IMF in a country		
E-159	engagement of the IMF in a country IMF engagement Fund involvement Fund engagement engagement	présence (active) du FMI (dans un pays) relations (actives) du FMI (avec un pays) engagement du FMI (envers un pays, aux côtés d'un pays) activités du FMI (dans un pays) participation du FMI action du FMI (dans un pays)	la labor del FMI las actividades del FMI el trabajo que realiza el FMI trabajo del FMI con el país labor que desempeña el FMI en el país relación entre el FMI y el país relación del FMI con el país
E-160	enhanced collaborative approach, *see* intensified collaboration		
E-161	enhanced cooperative approach, *see* intensified cooperative approach		
E-162	enhanced cooperative strategy, *see* intensified cooperative approach		
E-163	enhanced credit credit enhancement	amélioration de la cote du crédit amélioration du crédit amélioration de la signature amélioration de la qualité des créances amélioration des conditions du crédit revalorisation des créances	crédito reforzado refuerzo del crédito
E-164	Enhanced Heavily Indebted Poor Countries Initiative, *see* enhanced Initiative for Heavily Indebted Poor Countries		

E-165	enhanced HIPC Initiative, *see* enhanced Initiative for Heavily Indebted Poor Countries		
E-166	enhanced Initiative for Heavily Indebted Poor Countries [IMF] enhanced HIPC Initiative Enhanced Heavily Indebted Poor Countries Initiative	initiative renforcée en faveur des pays pauvres très endettés initiative PPTE renforcée	Iniciativa Reforzada para los Países Pobres Muy Endeudados Iniciativa Reforzada para los PPME Iniciativa PPME Reforzada
E-167	enhanced obligation [securities]	amélioration de la qualité d'une obligation créance revalorisée	obligación reforzada
E-168	Enhanced Structural Adjustment Facility Trust [IMF] *see also:* ESAF-HIPC Trust [IMF]; HIPC Trust Fund [World Bank] ESAF Trust	Compte de fiducie de la facilité d'ajustement structurel renforcé Compte de fiducie de la FASR	Cuenta Fiduciaria del Servicio Reforzado de Ajuste Estructural Cuenta Fiduciaria del SRAE
E-169	enhanced surveillance, *see* enhanced surveillance procedure		
E-170	enhanced surveillance procedure [IMF] enhanced surveillance	surveillance renforcée surveillance accentuée	procedimiento de supervisión reforzada supervisión reforzada
E-171	enhancement money	contribution destinée à améliorer la qualité des créances	refuerzo monetario de los activos
E-172	enhancement of resources	augmentation des ressources disponibles	aumento de los recursos refuerzo de los recursos financieros
E-173	enhancement of SDRs	amélioration de la qualité du DTS renforcement du DTS	refuerzo del DEG
E-174	enlarged access policy, *see* policy on enlarged access to the Fund's resources		
E-175	enlarged access resources [IMF] *see also:* enlarged access to the Fund's resources EAR	ressources disponibles en vertu de la politique d'accès élargi	recursos disponibles en el marco de la política de mayor acceso
E-176	enlarged access to Fund resources, *see* enlarged access to the Fund's resources		
E-177	enlarged access to the Fund's resources [IMF] *see also:* enlarged access resources EAR enlarged access to Fund resources	accès élargi aux ressources du FMI AER	mayor acceso a los recursos del FMI
E-178	enterprise	entreprise	empresa
E-179	enterprise economy *see also:* free enterprise economy; market economy	économie d'entreprise	economía de empresa economía de libre empresa
E-180	entitlement program [USA]	programme de protection sociale programme de droits à prestations	programa de prestaciones estatales programa de subsidios sociales establecido por ley

E-181	entrepreneur	chef d'entreprise entrepreneur créateur d'entreprise	empresario
E-182	entrepreneurial and property income	revenu de l'entreprise et de la propriété	ingresos empresariales y de la propiedad
E-183	entrepreneurial income	revenu de l'entreprise	renta empresarial renta de la empresa ingreso empresarial
E-184	entrepreneurship	esprit d'entreprise entreprenariat	capacidad empresarial espíritu de empresa espíritu empresarial organización empresarial
E-185	entry [accounting]	écriture écriture comptable inscription enregistrement	asiento partida registro entrada
E-186	entry duty, *see* import duty		
E-187	entry tax, *see* import duty		
E-188	environmental accounting green accounting	comptabilité de l'environnement	contabilidad ambiental
E-189	environmental action plan [IBRD]	plan pour la protection de l'environnement	plan de acción ambiental
E-190	environmental depletion depletion of natural resources	épuisement des ressources naturelles épuisement du patrimoine de l'environnement épuisement des actifs naturels	agotamiento de los recursos naturales
E-191	environmental impact	effet écologique effet sur l'environnement impact sur l'environnement	impacto ambiental efecto sobre el medio ambiente
E-192	environmental tax green tax	écotaxe taxe écologique taxe à finalité écologique taxe verte	impuesto para protección del medio ambiente impuesto ambiental
E-193	E&O, net, *see* errors and omissions, net		
E-194	EP, *see* Economist Program		
E-195	EPA, *see* ex post assessment of Fund-supported programs		
E-196	EPCA, *see* emergency post-conflict assistance		
E-197	EPE, *see* ex post evaluation		
E-198	EPZ, *see* export processing zone		
E-199	equal value exchange rate [SDR]	taux de change donnant valeur égale taux de change fondé sur le principe de la valeur égale	tipo de cambio de igual valor tipo de cambio basado en el principio de igual valor

E-200	equal value principle [SDR]	principe de la valeur égale	principio de igual valor principio de igualdad de valor
E-201	equalization fund	caisse de péréquation caisse de compensation caisse de stabilisation fonds de péréquation fonds de compensation fonds de stabilisation	fondo de equiparación
E-202	equalization grant	transfert de péréquation subvention de péréquation	subvención de equiparación subvención de nivelación subvención de igualación
E-203	equation of exchange Fisher equation	équation des échanges équation de Fisher	ecuación de cambio ecuación de Fisher
E-204	equilibrating capital flow equilibrating capital movement	mouvement de capitaux stabilisateur mouvement de capitaux équilibrant flux de capitaux stabilisateur flux de capitaux équilibrant	flujo de capital que contribuye al equilibrio corriente de capital que contribuye al equilibrio movimiento de capital que contribuye al equilibrio
E-205	equilibrating capital movement, *see* equilibrating capital flow		
E-206	equilibrium effects	effets d'équilibre	efectos de equilibrio
E-207	equilibrium exchange rate	taux de change d'équilibre	tipo de cambio de equilibrio
E-208	equilibrium path	trajectoire d'équilibre sentier d'équilibre	trayectoria de equilibrio
E-209	equiproportional increase in quotas, *see* general increase in quotas		
E-210	equiproportionality [SDR]	équiproportionnalité	equiproporcionalidad
E-211	equity, *see* net worth		
E-212	equity, *see* equity capital		
E-213	equity allocation of SDRs, *see* special one-time allocation of SDRs		
E-214	equity capital equity	capital social fonds propres capital sous forme d'actions financement sur fonds propres participations	capital social capital accionario capital propio acciones y otras participaciones de capital participación de capital
E-215	equity capital inflow	entrée de capitaux sous forme de prises de participation	entrada de capital para la compra de acciones
E-216	equity credit line, *see* home equity loan		
E-217	equity financing *see also:* debt financing	financement par émission d'actions ou de parts participation au capital prise de participation au capital social financement sur fonds propres	financiamiento mediante venta de acciones

E-218	equity income	revenu du capital dividendes	renta de la inversión en acciones
E-219	equity investment	prise de participation apport de fonds propres participation au capital	inversión en participaciones de capital inversión de capital

E-220	equity issue
	[IMF]
	see also: special one-time
	  allocation of SDRs
		question de l'équité des allocations
		  de DTS
			cuestión de la equidad de las
			  asignaciones de DEG

E-221	equity loan	prêt participatif (sur capital)
		prêt sous forme de prise de
		  participation
			préstamo en forma de
			  participación en el capital

E-222	equity loan, *see* home equity loan		
E-223	equity market	marché des actions marché boursier marché des fonds propres marché des valeurs mobilières à revenu variable	mercado de acciones mercado accionario
E-224	equity ownership equity participation	titres de participation (au capital) parts du capital social prise de participation au capital	participación accionaria participación en el capital social propiedad del capital social
E-225	equity participation, *see* equity ownership		
E-226	equity portfolio	portefeuille d'actions et de participations	cartera de acciones
E-227	equity security	titre de participation	título de participación en el capital título participativo

E-228	equity transaction	transaction sur titres
		transaction sur titres de
		  participation au capital
		transaction sur valeurs mobilières
		  à revenu variable
			transacción de capital
			transacción relativa a
			  participaciones de capital

E-229	equity warrant, *see* warrant		
E-230	equity-debt ratio, *see* capital-debt ratio		
E-231	equity-like instrument	instrument participatif	instrumento financiero con características patrimoniales
E-232	ERM, *see* Exchange Rate Mechanism		
E-233	ERM II, *see* Exchange Rate Mechanism II		
E-234	ERP, *see* effective rate of protection		
E-235	error of the first kind, *see* type I error		
E-236	error of the second kind, *see* type II error		
E-237	errors and omissions, net E&O, net	erreurs et omissions nettes	errores y omisiones netos
E-238	ESAF Trust, *see* Enhanced Structural Adjustment Facility Trust		

E-239	ESAF-HIPC Trust [IMF] *see also:* ESAF Trust [IMF]; HIPC Trust Fund [World Bank] Trust for Special ESAF Operations for the Heavily Indebted Poor Countries and Interim ESAF Subsidy Operations	fonds fiduciaire FASR–PPTE fonds fiduciaire pour les opérations spéciales de la FASR en faveur des pays pauvres très endettés et pour les opérations de bonification aux fins de la FASR intérimaire	Fondo Fiduciario SRAE–PPME Fondo Fiduciario para las operaciones especiales en el marco del SRAE a favor de los países pobres muy endeudados y las operaciones de subvención en el marco del SRAE transitorio
E-240	ESAF-HIPC Trust Account [IMF] *see also:* ESAF-HIPC Trust; HIPC Trust Fund	compte du fonds fiduciaire FASR– PPTE	Cuenta Fiduciaria SRAE–PPME
E-241	escalation clause, *see* escalator clause		
E-242	escalator clause escalation clause	clause d'indexation clause de révision clause d'échelle mobile	cláusula de reajuste cláusula de corrección monetaria cláusula de escala móvil cláusula de ajuste automático
E-243	ESCAP, *see* Economic and Social Commission for Asia and the Pacific		
E-244	escape clause	clause de sauvegarde	cláusula liberatoria cláusula de salvaguardia cláusula de excepción
E-245	escrow account [IMF/World Bank; HIPC]	compte de garantie bloqué compte-séquestre compte spécial	cuenta de depósito en garantía cuenta de fondos en custodia cuenta de garantía bloqueada
E-246	escrowed grant [HIPC]	don en dépôt	donación en custodia
E-247	escrowed loan [HIPC]	prêt en dépôt	préstamo en custodia
E-248	ESCWA, *see* Economic and Social Commission for Western Asia		
E-249	ESF, *see* European Social Fund		
E-250	ESF, *see* Exogenous Shocks Facility		
E-251	ESF Subsidy Account [IMF]	compte de bonification FCE	Cuenta de Subvención del SSE
E-252	ESF-PRGF Subsidy Account [IMF]	compte de bonification FCE-FRPC	Cuenta de Subvención SCLP-SSE
E-253	essential goods *see also:* staples	produits de première nécessité	artículos de primera necesidad productos de primera necesidad
E-254	establishment of provisions, *see* provisioning		
E-255	estate duty *see also:* inheritance tax; estate, inheritance, and gift taxes estate tax	droit(s) sur la masse successorale droit(s) sur la succession droit(s) de succession	impuesto sucesorio impuesto de sucesión impuesto sobre la masa hereditaria

E-256	estate, inheritance, and gift taxes *see also:* estate duty; gift tax; inheritance tax	impôts sur les mutations par décès, les successions et les donations entre vifs et legs impôts sur les mutations par décès, les successions et les donations droits de succession, de mutation par décès et de donation	impuestos sobre sucesiones, herencias y regalos
E-257	estate tax, *see* estate duty		
E-258	estimated expenditure	estimation de dépenses prévision de dépenses	estimación de gastos gasto estimado gasto previsto
E-259	Ethics Office [IMF]	Bureau de la déontologie	Oficina de Ética
E-260	EU, *see* European Union		
E-261	EU Policies Division [IMF]	Division politiques de l'Union européenne	División de Políticas de la UE
E-262	EUO, *see* Offices in Europe		
E-263	EUO/BR, *see* Brussels Office		
E-264	EUO/GE, *see* Geneva Office		
E-265	EUO/PA, *see* Paris Office		
E-266	EUR, *see* euro		
E-267	EUR, *see* European Department		
E-268	euro EUR	euro	euro
E-269	Eurobond	euro-obligation	eurobono
E-270	Eurobond market	marché euro-obligataire marché des euro-obligations marché des euro-émissions obligataires	mercado de eurobonos
E-271	Eurocommercial paper ECP Euro-CP	effet(s) de commerce en eurodevises eurobillet(s) de trésorerie europapier commercial	efectos comerciales en eurodivisas
E-272	Euro-CP, *see* Eurocommercial paper		
E-273	Eurocredit Eurocurrency loan	eurocrédit	eurocrédito
E-274	Eurocurrency loan, *see* Eurocredit		
E-275	euroization	euroïsation	eurización euroización
E-276	Euromarket	euromarché	euromercado
E-277	Euronote	euronote	europagaré

E-278	Europe Regional Division [IMF]	Division Europe	División de la Región de Europa
E-279	European Bank for Reconstruction and Development EBRD	Banque européenne pour la reconstruction et le développement BERD	Banco Europeo de Reconstrucción y Desarrollo BERD
E-280	European Central Bank ECB	Banque centrale européenne BCE	Banco Central Europeo BCE
E-281	European Commission EC	Commission européenne	Comisión Europea
E-282	European currency unit ECU	unité monétaire européenne écu	unidad de cuenta europea ecu
E-283	European Department [IMF] EUR	Département Europe	Departamento de Europa
E-284	European Development Fund EDF	Fonds européen de développement FED	Fondo Europeo de Desarrollo FED
E-285	European Division [IMF]	Division Europe	División de Europa
E-286	European Economic Area EEA European Economic Space	Espace économique européen EEE	Espacio Económico Europeo EEE Zona Económica Europea
E-287	European Economic Space, *see* European Economic Area		
E-288	European Free Trade Association EFTA	Association européenne de libre-échange AELE	Asociación Europea de Libre Comercio AELC
E-289	European Investment Bank EIB	Banque européenne d'investissement BEI	Banco Europeo de Inversiones BEI
E-290	European Monetary System EMS	Système monétaire européen SME	Sistema Monetario Europeo SME
E-291	European narrow margins arrangement snake in the tunnel snake system currency snake system multicurrency intervention system	accord européen sur le maintien de marges étroites serpent (dans le tunnel) intervention en plusieurs monnaies	acuerdo europeo de márgenes estrechos serpiente (en el túnel) intervención en múltiples monedas
E-292	European Social Fund [EU] ESF	Fonds social européen FSE	Fondo Social Europeo FSE
E-293	European Union EU	Union européenne UE	Unión Europea UE
E-294	Evaluation Committee [IMF] EVC	Comité d'évaluation	Comisión de Evaluación

E-295	EVC, *see* Evaluation Committee		
E-296	even par swap	échange de titres de valeur nominale égale	canje de valores de igual valor nominal
E-297	event of default [London Club]	déchéance du terme	causal de incumplimiento caso de incumplimiento
E-298	EVO, *see* Independent Evaluation Office		
E-299	EWS, *see* early warning system		
E-300	ex ante	*ex ante*	*ex ante* a priori
E-301	ex factory price, *see* ex works price		
E-302	ex post [economics]	*ex post*	*ex post* a posteriori
E-303	Ex Post Assessment, *see* ex post assessment of Fund-supported programs		
E-304	ex post assessment of Fund-supported programs Ex Post Assessment EPA	analyse rétrospective et prospective des programmes soutenus par le FMI analyse rétrospective et prospective évaluation *ex post*	análisis *ex post* de los programas respaldados por el FMI análisis *ex post*
E-305	ex post evaluation [IMF] *see also:* ex post assessment of Fund-supported programs EPE	examen rétrospectif examen *ex post*	evaluación *ex post*
E-306	ex works price ex factory price factory (gate) price	prix départ-usine prix usine	precio de fábrica
E-307	exceptional circumstances clause [IMF, access limit]	clause de circonstances exceptionnelles	cláusula de circunstancias excepcionales
E-308	excess burden, *see* excess tax burden		
E-309	excess capital accumulation, *see* excess capital formation		
E-310	excess capital formation excess capital accumulation	surcapitalisation suraccumulation de capital	formación excesiva de capital sobreacumulación de capital sobrecapitalización
E-311	excess demand	excès de (la) demande demande excédentaire	exceso de demanda demanda excedentaria
E-312	excess employment	suremploi	sobreempleo
E-313	excess holding ratio [SDR]	rapport des avoirs excédentaires	proporción de tenencias en exceso
E-314	excess liquidity, *see* liquidity overhang		

E-315	excess profit *see also:* windfall profit	superbénéfice bénéfice excédentaire bénéfice exceptionnel bénéfice extraordinaire	utilidades extraordinarias ganancias extraordinarias beneficios extraordinarios
E-316	excess purchasing power	pouvoir d'achat excédentaire	exceso de poder adquisitivo
E-317	excess reserves	réserves excédentaires	sobreencaje excedente de reservas exceso de reservas
E-318	excess supply, *see* oversupply		
E-319	excess tax burden excess burden deadweight loss efficiency loss	perte d'efficacité fardeau excédentaire poids excédentaire	presión fiscal excesiva tributación excesiva pérdida de eficiencia debida a los impuestos
E-320	exchange, *see* foreign currency		
E-321	exchange, *see* commodity exchange		
E-322	exchange allocation	allocation de devises	asignación de divisas
E-323	exchange arrangements exchange rate arrangement exchange rate regime exchange system	régime de change régime des changes régime de taux de change dispositions de change	régimen cambiario régimen de tipos de cambio régimen de cambio
E-324	exchange arrangements with no separate legal tender [IMF exchange rate classification system, 2006]	régime des pays n'ayant pas de monnaie officielle distincte	regímenes de cambio sin una moneda nacional de curso legal
E-325	exchange bureau, *see* exchange house		
E-326	exchange contract	contrat de change	contrato de cambio
E-327	exchange control exchange restriction	contrôle des changes réglementation des changes restriction de change	control de cambios regulación cambiaria restricción cambiaria
E-328	exchange cost	coût en devises	costo en divisas
E-329	exchange house exchange bureau	bureau de change	casa de cambio
E-330	exchange market, *see* foreign exchange market		
E-331	exchange policy, *see* exchange rate policy		
E-332	exchange profits	bénéfices de change	utilidades cambiarias utilidades de operaciones cambiarias
E-333	exchange rate anchor [IMF]	ancrage du taux de change taux de change comme point d'ancrage	uso del tipo de cambio como ancla ancla cambiaria
E-334	exchange rate arrangement, *see* exchange arrangements		
E-335	exchange rate corridor, *see* fluctuation band		

E-336	exchange rate differential	écart de taux de change différentiel de taux de change	diferencial de tipos de cambio diferencial cambiario diferencia entre los tipos de cambio
E-337	exchange rate future	contrat de taux de change à terme	futuro sobre tipos de cambio contrato de tipo de cambio a término contrato de tipo de cambio a plazo
E-338	exchange rate management	gestion du taux de change	regulación del tipo de cambio gestión del tipo de cambio

E-339	Exchange Rate Mechanism
	  [EMS]
	see also: Exchange Rate
	  Mechanism II
	  ERM
		mécanisme de change européen
		MCE
		mécanisme de taux de change
		mécanisme de change du Système
		  monétaire européen
			mecanismo de tipos de cambio
			MTC

E-340	Exchange Rate Mechanism II ERM II	mécanisme de change européen II MCE II MCE bis	mecanismo de tipos de cambio 2 MTC 2
E-341	exchange rate policy exchange policy foreign exchange policy	politique de change politique du taux de change politique de taux de change	política cambiaria política de tipos de cambio
E-342	exchange rate realignment currency realignment	réalignement du taux de change réalignement monétaire réalignement des monnaies alignement monétaire	realineamiento de los tipos de cambio realineamiento de las paridades realineamiento de las monedas
E-343	exchange rate regime, *see* exchange arrangements		

E-344	exchange rate targeting
	exchange rate targeting strategy
		ciblage du taux de change
		stratégie fondée sur une cible de
		  taux de change
			estrategia de objetivos de tipo de
			  cambio
			estrategia basada en objetivos de
			  tipo de cambio

E-345	exchange rate targeting strategy, *see* exchange rate targeting		

E-346	exchange rates within crawling
	  bands
	  [IMF exchange rate classification
	  system, 2006]
		système de bandes de fluctuation
		  mobiles
			tipos de cambio dentro de bandas
			  de fluctuación

E-347	exchange record, *see* foreign exchange record		
E-348	exchange reserves, *see* foreign exchange reserves		
E-349	exchange restriction, *see* exchange control		
E-350	exchange risk	risque de change	riesgo cambiario riesgo de cambio
E-351	exchange risk insurance	assurance contre les risques de change	seguro de cambio
E-352	exchange stability	stabilité des taux de change stabilité des changes	estabilidad de los tipos de cambio estabilidad cambiaria
E-353	exchange stabilization fund, *see* foreign exchange equalization fund		

E-354	exchange system, *see* exchange arrangements		
E-355	exchange taxes	taxes sur les opérations de change taxes sur les opérations en devises	impuestos sobre las operaciones cambiarias impuestos sobre las operaciones de cambio
E-356	exchange valuation adjustment	ajustement pour tenir compte des variations (de taux) de change	ajuste por revaloración de divisas ajuste por revaloración cambiaria
E-357	excise *see also:* consumption tax excise tax	accise droit d'accise impôt indirect sur la consommation accises	impuesto selectivo al consumo impuesto selectivo impuesto específico sobre el consumo impuestos específicos impuestos selectivos a la producción y al consumo de bienes
E-358	excise tax, *see* excise		
E-359	excluded holdings [IMF]	avoirs exclus principe de l'exclusion	tenencias excluidas
E-360	Executive Board [IMF] Board	Conseil d'administration	Directorio Ejecutivo Directorio
E-361	Executive Director, Alternate [IMF]	administrateur suppléant	Director Ejecutivo Suplente
E-362	Executive Director (Mr./Ms. ...) [IMF] ED	administrateur	Director Ejecutivo
E-363	Executive Secretary [IMF-IBRD, Development Committee]	Secrétaire exécutif	Secretario Ejecutivo
E-364	executive session [IMF] *see also:* restricted session	séance à huis clos	sesión a puerta cerrada
E-365	exercise an option [securities]	exercer une option	ejercer una opción
E-366	exercise price striking price strike price contract price	prix d'exercice prix d'exécution	precio de ejercicio precio de ejecución
E-367	exhaustible resource	ressource épuisable ressource non renouvelable	recurso no renovable recurso agotable
E-368	exit agreement *see also:* exit consent	accord de sortie accord final accord définitif	acuerdo de salida acuerdo final acuerdo definitivo
E-369	exit bank	banque sortante	banco saliente banco que opta por la exclusión
E-370	exit bond exit instrument	bon de sortie	bono de salida

E-371	exit consent *see also:* exit agreement	accord de sortie	cláusula de consentimiento de salida
E-372	exit instrument, *see* exit bond		
E-373	exit policy	politique de sortie (du marché, du système)	política de salida (del mercado)
E-374	exit rescheduling [Paris Club]	rééchelonnement final rééchelonnement de sortie	reprogramación definitiva
E-375	exogenous shock	perturbation exogène choc exogène	shock exógeno perturbación exógena
E-376	Exogenous Shocks Facility ESF shocks facility	facilité de protection contre les chocs exogènes FCE facilité de protection contre les chocs facilité d'amortissement des chocs facilité antichocs	Servicio para Shocks Exógenos
E-377	exogenous variable	variable exogène	variable exógena
E-378	expansionary impulse	impulsion expansionniste	impulso expansivo impulso expansionista
E-379	expansionary policy	politique expansionniste politique économique expansionniste politique d'expansion	política expansiva política expansionista política de expansión
E-380	expected economic life expected economic lifetime	durée de vie escomptée	vida económica probable vida económica esperada
E-381	expected economic lifetime, *see* expected economic life		
E-382	expected rate	taux attendu taux escompté taux prévu	tasa prevista tasa esperada
E-383	expected utility	utilité attendue utilité escomptée	utilidad prevista utilidad esperada
E-384	expected value mathematical expectation	espérance mathématique valeur probable	valor esperado esperanza matemática
E-385	expenditure authorization	autorisation de dépenses	autorización de gastos
E-386	expenditure by function	classification fonctionnelle des dépenses	gastos por funciones
E-387	expenditure commitment commitment	engagement engagement comptable de dépenses	compromiso de gastos compromiso de autorización de gastos
E-388	expenditure item expense item	poste de dépenses poste de charges	partida de gastos rubro de gastos rúbrica de gastos
E-389	Expenditure Policy Division [IMF]	Division politique des dépenses publiques	División de Políticas de Gasto

E-390	expenditure switching policy switching policy	politique de réorientation des dépenses politique de modification de la composition des dépenses	política de reorientación del gasto política de modificación de la composición del gasto
E-391	expenditure tax	impôt sur la dépense taxe sur la dépense	impuesto sobre el gasto impuesto al gasto
E-392	expenditure validation *see also:* expenditure verification validation	liquidation	liquidación validación
E-393	expenditure verification *see also:* expenditure validation verification	liquidation	verificación
E-394	expense	charges	gasto desembolso
E-395	expense item, *see* expenditure item		
E-396	expert panel, *see* panel		
E-397	explanatory variable	variable explicative	variable explicativa
E-398	exploratory mission, *see* acquaintance mission		
E-399	export capacity	capacité d'exportation	capacidad exportadora capacidad de exportación
E-400	export credit	crédit à l'exportation crédit-export	crédito de exportación crédito a la exportación
E-401	export duty	droit d'exportation droit de sortie taxe à l'exportation	derecho de exportación
E-402	export earnings export proceeds	recettes d'exportation produit des exportations	ingresos de exportación ingresos provenientes de la exportación
E-403	export performance	résultats des exportations comportement à l'exportation (d'un secteur)	resultado de las exportaciones evolución de la exportación trayectoria de las exportaciones situación de las exportaciones comportamiento de las exportaciones
E-404	export proceeds, *see* export earnings		
E-405	export processing zone *see also:* free trade zone EPZ industrial free trade zone industrial free trade area	zone franche industrielle ZFI	zona franca para la industria de exportación zona de procesamiento para la exportación zona maquiladora zona franca industrial
E-406	export promotion	encouragement à l'exportation promotion des exportations	fomento de la exportación promoción de las exportaciones

E-407	export retention scheme foreign exchange retention scheme foreign exchange retention	régime permettant (aux exportateurs) de conserver (une partie) des recettes d'exportation	sistema de retención de los ingresos de exportación
E-408	export shortfall *see also:* shortfall	insuffisance des recettes d'exportation déficit d'exportation déficit des recettes d'exportation écart (en moins) par rapport à la tendance des recettes d'exportation	insuficiencia de las exportaciones insuficiencia de los ingresos de exportación
E-409	export surplus	excédent de la balance commerciale	superávit de exportación superávit de la balanza comercial
E-410	exporting industry	industrie exportatrice industrie à vocation exportatrice industrie orientée vers l'exportation secteur exportateur secteur à vocation exportatrice secteur orienté vers l'exportation	industria exportadora sector de exportación
E-411	export-led recovery	reprise par les exportations reprise entraînée par les exportations reprise tirée par les exportations	recuperación económica basada en la exportación recuperación inducida por la exportación recuperación impulsada por las exportaciones
E-412	exposure, *see* risk exposure		
E-413	EXR, *see* External Relations Department		
E-414	Extended Arrangement [IMF] *see also:* Extended Fund Facility EA	accord élargi de crédit accord élargi AE	Acuerdo Ampliado del FMI AA acuerdo en virtud del Servicio Ampliado del FMI
E-415	extended arrangement charge [IMF] *see also:* commitment fee [IMF]	commission d'engagement afférente à un accord (au titre du mécanisme) élargi	comisión por inmovilización de fondos para acuerdos en virtud del Servicio Ampliado del FMI
E-416	extended burden sharing [IMF] *see also:* burden sharing extension of burden sharing	élargissement du mécanisme de répartition des charges répartition élargie des charges	distribución ampliada de la carga ampliación de la distribución de la carga
E-417	Extended Facility, *see* Extended Fund Facility		
E-418	Extended Fund Facility [IMF] *see also:* Extended Arrangement EFF Extended Facility	mécanisme élargi de crédit MEDC	Servicio Ampliado del FMI SAF
E-419	extension of burden sharing, *see* extended burden sharing		
E-420	extension of Toronto terms *see also:* Trinidad terms	élargissement du champ d'application des dispositions de Toronto	ampliación del campo de aplicación de las condiciones de Toronto
E-421	extension services, *see* agricultural extension		

E-422	external account	compte des opérations avec l'étranger compte extérieur	cuenta externa balanza de pagos cuenta de transacciones con el exterior
E-423	external asset (assets owned abroad by residents) foreign asset]	avoir extérieur avoir sur l'extérieur	activo externo activo frente al exterior
E-424	External Audit Committee [IMF]	Comité de vérification externe des comptes	Comité de Auditoría Externa
E-425	external audit mechanism, legal structure and independence of the central bank, financial reporting practices, internal audit mechanism, and the system of internal controls [IMF] ELRIC	mécanisme d'audit externe, structure juridique et indépendance (de la banque centrale), pratiques d'information financière, mécanisme d'audit interne et système des contrôles internes ELRIC	mecanismo ELRIC de evaluación de las salvaguardias mecanismo de auditoría externa; estructura e independencia jurídicas (del banco central); presentación de información financiera; mecanismo de auditoría interna y sistema de controles internos ELRIC
E-426	external auditor	auditeur externe commissaire aux comptes vérificateur externe des comptes	auditor externo
E-427	external bond see also: foreign bond	obligation externe	bono externo
E-428	external claim foreign claim	créance sur l'extérieur créance sur l'étranger créance sur les non-résidents	crédito frente al exterior activo externo activo sobre el exterior
E-429	external debt	dette extérieure	deuda externa
E-430	external diseconomy, see negative externality		
E-431	external disturbance	perturbation d'origine externe perturbation exogène	perturbación externa perturbación de origen externo
E-432	external economy, see positive externality		
E-433	external imbalance	déséquilibre extérieur déséquilibre des paiements extérieurs déséquilibre des comptes extérieurs	desequilibrio externo desequilibrio de la balanza de pagos desequilibrio de los pagos exteriores desequilibrio de pagos externos
E-434	External Relations Department [IMF] EXR	Département des relations extérieures	Departamento de Relaciones Externas
E-435	external reserves, see international reserves		
E-436	externality see also: negative externality; positive externality	externalité	externalidad

117

E-437	extrabudgetary account *see also:* off-budget transaction extrabudgetary fund EBF extra-budgetary account	compte extrabudgétaire fonds extrabudgétaire	cuenta extrapresupuestaria fondo extrapresupuestario
E-438	extra-budgetary account, *see* extrabudgetary account		
E-439	extrabudgetary fund, *see* extrabudgetary account		

F

F-1	face value, *see* nominal value		
F-2	Facilities Management Division [IMF]	Division gestion des installations	División de Administración de Instalaciones
F-3	facility, *see* financing facility		
F-4	factor, *see* production factor		
F-5	factor cost, at	au coût des facteurs	al costo de los factores
F-6	factor endowment	dotation en facteurs de production	dotación de factores dotación de factores de producción
F-7	factor income	revenu des facteurs	renta de los factores de producción ingreso de los factores ingreso de factores
F-8	factor of production, *see* production factor		
F-9	factor payments	rémunération des facteurs de production	remuneración de los factores de producción pago por factores de producción
F-10	factor shares income share	parts des facteurs parts des divers facteurs de production parts des groupes de facteurs de production parts des groupes de facteurs dans le revenu national part des différents groupes de facteurs dans le revenu national part du revenu national part de revenu	participación de los factores de producción participación en el ingreso nacional
F-11	factoring *see also:* forfaiting	société d'affacturage affacturage	*factoring* descuento de facturas factoraje
F-12	factor-price distortion	distorsion entre les prix des facteurs désajustement des prix des facteurs	distorsión de los precios de los factores distorsión de los precios de los factores de producción
F-13	factory (gate) price, *see* ex works price		
F-14	FAD, *see* Fiscal Affairs Department		
F-15	fair market price, *see* fair price		

F-16	fair market value, *see* market value		

F-17	fair price	juste prix	precio justo
	see also: market value fair market price	prix équitable	precio justo de mercado

F-18	fair trade	commerce équitable	comercio justo
	see also: comparative advantage; free trade		comercio equitativo

F-19	falling trend, *see* downward trend		

F-20	false negative, *see* type II error		

F-21	family allowance, *see* dependency allowance		

F-22	family living expenses	frais de subsistance de la famille	gasto de subsistencia familiar gasto de subsistencia de una familia

F-23	FAO, *see* Food and Agriculture Organization of the United Nations		

F-24	farm gate price	prix à la production agricole	precio del productor agrícola precio al productor agrícola

F-25	FATF, *see* Financial Action Task Force on Money Laundering		

F-26	*F&D, see Finance & Development*		

F-27	FDI, *see* foreign direct investment		

F-28	FDIC, *see* Federal Deposit Insurance Corporation		

F-29	FDMD, *see* First Deputy Managing Director		

F-30	feasibility study	étude de faisabilité étude de rentabilité étude de viabilité	estudio de factibilidad estudio de viabilidad

F-31	Fed, *see* Federal Reserve System		

F-32	Federal Deposit Insurance
	  Corporation
	[USA]
	FDIC
		Federal Deposit Insurance
		  Corporation
		Institut fédéral de garantie des
		  dépôts
			Corporación Federal de Seguros
			  de Depósitos
			FDIC

F-33	federal funds market
	[USA]
		marché des fonds fédéraux
		marché des *federal funds*
		marché monétaire interbancaire au
		  jour le jour
			mercado de fondos federales
			mercado monetario interbancario
			mercado de préstamos
			  interbancarios a un día
			mercado de préstamos
			  interbancarios día a día

F-34	Federal Open Market Committee
	[USA]
	Federal Reserve Open Market
	  Committee
	FOMC
	Open Market Committee
		Comité de l'open-market du
		  Système fédéral de réserve
			Comité de Operaciones de
			  Mercado Abierto de la Reserva
			  Federal
			Comité de Mercado Abierto

F-35	Federal Reserve, *see* Federal Reserve System		

F-36	Federal Reserve Bank [USA]	Banque fédérale de réserve	Banco de la Reserva Federal
F-37	Federal Reserve Board [USA] FRB Board of Governors of the Federal Reserve System	Conseil des gouverneurs du Système fédéral de réserve	Junta de Gobernadores del Sistema de la Reserva Federal Junta de la Reserva Federal
F-38	Federal Reserve Open Market Committee, *see* Federal Open Market Committee		
F-39	Federal Reserve System [USA] Fed Federal Reserve	Système fédéral de réserve Réserve fédérale FED Fed	Sistema de la Reserva Federal Reserva Federal
F-40	fiat money fiduciary money central bank money	monnaie fiduciaire monnaie à cours forcé	moneda fiduciaria dinero de curso forzoso
F-41	fiduciary account, *see* trust account		
F-42	fiduciary money, *see* fiat money		
F-43	field audit *see also:* office audit on-site supervision on-site inspection	contrôle sur place contrôle dans l'entreprise vérification sur place vérification dans l'entreprise audit sur place audit dans l'entreprise inspection sur place inspection sur le terrain	inspección auditoría in situ
F-44	FIFO, *see* first in, first out		
F-45	file a tax return	souscrire une déclaration de revenu	presentar una declaración de impuestos presentar una declaración de rentas
F-46	filled market, *see* saturated market		
F-47	FILO, *see* first in, last out		
F-48	FIN, *see* Finance Department		
F-49	final consumption	consommation finale	consumo final
F-50	final product, *see* end product		
F-51	final user, *see* end user		
F-52	*Finance & Development* [IMF] *F&D*	*Finances & Développement* *F&D*	*Finanzas & Desarrollo* F&D
F-53	finance company finance house [GBR]	société de crédit à la consommation société de financement	compañía financiera financiera

F-54	Finance Department [IMF] FIN	Département financier	Departamento Financiero
F-55	finance house, *see* finance company		
F-56	financial account	compte d'opérations financières	cuenta financiera
F-57	Financial Action Task Force, *see* Financial Action Task Force on Money Laundering		
F-58	Financial Action Task Force on Money Laundering FATF Financial Action Task Force	Groupe d'action financière sur le blanchiment de capitaux GAFI Groupe d'action financière	Grupo de Acción Financiera Internacional sobre el Blanqueo de Capitales GAFI Grupo de Acción Financiera Internacional
F-59	Financial and Administrative Systems Division [IMF]	Division systèmes financiers et administratifs	División de Sistemas Financieros y Administrativos
F-60	financial and capital transactions	opérations financières et opérations en capital transactions mobilières et immobilières	transacciones financieras y de capital
F-61	financial armor plating, *see* financial shield		
F-62	financial assurances, *see* financing assurances		
F-63	financial broadening broadening of the financial market broadening of the capital market	élargissement de la gamme de services financiers accroissement de l'offre de services financiers diversification des services financiers	ampliación del mercado financiero diversificación del mercado de capitales
F-64	financial center	place financière centre financier	centro financiero plaza financiera
F-65	financial channels	circuits financiers	circuitos financieros
F-66	financial condition, *see* financial position		
F-67	financial credit, *see* financial loan		
F-68	financial crowding out	éviction du secteur privé (du marché des capitaux)	desplazamiento del sector privado en el mercado de capitales
F-69	financial deepening *see also:* capital deepening deepening of the financial market deepening of the capital market	expansion des circuits financiers augmentation de l'importance des circuits financiers financiarisation de l'économie fourniture de services financiers à un plus grand nombre densification des circuits financiers diversification des circuits financiers	profundización financiera profundización del mercado financiero intensificación de la intermediación financiera desarrollo de los circuitos financieros
F-70	financial derivative, *see* derivative instrument		

F-71	*Financial Derivatives: A Supplement to the Fifth Edition (1993) of the Balance of Payments Manual*	*Dérivés financiers : Supplément à la cinquième édition (1993) du Manuel de la balance des paiements*	*Instrumentos financieros derivados: Suplemento a la quinta edición (1993) del Manual de Balanza de Pagos*
F-72	financial economy *see also:* real economy	économie financière	economía financiera sector financiero de la economía sector financiero
F-73	financial future	contrat à terme d'instruments financiers CATIF contrat à terme (sur actif) financier contrat à terme sur instrument financier	futuro financiero contrato de futuros financieros
F-74	financial futures exchange, *see* financial futures market		
F-75	financial futures market financial futures exchange	marché à terme d'instruments financiers MATIF bourse de contrats à terme d'instruments financiers	mercado de futuros financieros bolsa de futuros financieros
F-76	financial gearing, *see* gearing ratio		
F-77	Financial Institutions Division I, II [IMF]	Division institutions financières I, II	División de Instituciones Financieras I, II
F-78	financial institutions sector	secteur des institutions financières	sector de instituciones financieras
F-79	financial intermediation services indirectly measured FISIM	services d'intermédiation financière indirectement mesurés SIFIM	servicios de intermediación financiera medidos indirectamente SIFMI
F-80	financial leasing leasing	crédit-bail [FRA] location-financement leasing leasing financier bail financier [FRA]	arrendamiento financiero arrendamiento con opción a compra *leasing*
F-81	financial liabilities	engagements financiers	pasivos financieros
F-82	financial loan, *see* cash loan		
F-83	financial loan financial credit	crédit financier	préstamo financiero crédito financiero
F-84	Financial Operations and Reporting Division [IMF]	Division opérations et déclarations financières	División de Operaciones y Declaración de Datos Financieros
F-85	*Financial Organization and Operations of the IMF* [IMF]	*Organisation et opérations financières du FMI*	Organización y operaciones financieras del FMI
F-86	financial package, *see* financing package		

F-87	financial pooling financial pooling arrangement	mise en commun de ressources financières	fondo común de recursos financieros fondo común mancomunación de recursos
F-88	financial pooling arrangement, *see* financial pooling		
F-89	financial position financial condition	situation financière information financière	situación financiera
F-90	financial reporting	information financière communication des situations financières	declaración de datos financieros información financiera
F-91	financial repression financial restriction	dispositions financières contraignantes répression financière	represión financiera restricción financiera
F-92	financial restriction, *see* financial repression		
F-93	Financial Sector Assessment Program [IMF-World Bank] FSAP	Programme d'évaluation du secteur financier PESF	Programa de Evaluación del Sector Financiero PESF
F-94	Financial Sector Policy Division [IMF]	Division politique du secteur financier	División de Políticas del Sector Financiero
F-95	Financial Sector Review Group [IMF]	Groupe chargé d'examiner le secteur financier	Grupo de Examen del Sector Financiero
F-96	Financial Sector Stability Assessment [IMF-World Bank] FSSA	évaluation de la stabilité du secteur financier	Evaluación de la Estabilidad del Sector Financiero EESF
F-97	financial shield financial armor plating loan package shield package *blindaje*	«blindage financier» montage de protection financière	blindaje blindaje financiero
F-98	financial soundness	solidité financière	solidez financiera
F-99	financial soundness indicator FSI	indicateur de solidité financière ISF	indicador de solidez financiera ISF
F-100	Financial Stability Forum [G-7] FSF	Forum de stabilité financière	Foro sobre Estabilidad Financiera
F-101	financial statement	état financier relevé comptable état comptable	estado financiero estado contable
F-102	Financial Studies Division [IMF]	Division études financières	División de Estudios Financieros
F-103	financial survey [IMF]	situation financière	panorama financiero

F-104	financial transactions plan [IMF] transactions plan	programme de transactions financières programme de transactions	plan de transacciones financieras plan de transacciones
F-105	financial year, *see* fiscal year		
F-106	financial year of the Fund	exercice du FMI	ejercicio del FMI
F-107	financing	financement	financiamiento financiación
F-108	financing abroad	financement extérieur	financiamiento externo
F-109	financing assurances [IMF] financial assurances	assurance de financement assurances en matière de financement assurances financières	seguridades de financiamiento
F-110	financing facility credit facility facility	facilité mécanisme mécanisme de financement ligne de crédit ligne de tirage	servicio financiero línea de crédito mecanismo de financiamiento mecanismo financiero
F-111	financing gap *see also:* commitment gap; gap financing	besoin de financement non couvert besoin de financement résiduel écart de financement déficit de financement	déficit de financiamiento insuficiencia de financiamiento brecha financiera
F-112	financing package *see also:* package financial package	montage financier	plan de financiamiento paquete de financiamiento paquete financiero
F-113	financing requirements	besoin de financement	necesidades de financiamiento
F-114	fine gold	or fin	oro fino
F-115	fine ounce fine troy ounce troy ounce of fine gold	once d'or fin once troy d'or fin	onza de oro fino onza troy de oro fino
F-116	fine troy ounce, *see* fine ounce		
F-117	fine tuning	réglage de précision réglage au plus près réglage minutieux réglage micrométrique modulation	afinación ajuste ajuste preciso
F-118	fineness of gold	titre de l'or	ley del oro
F-119	finished good	produit fini	producto terminado producto acabado
F-120	first credit tranche conditionality [IMF]	conditionnalité de la première tranche de crédit	condicionalidad del primer tramo de crédito
F-121	first credit tranche purchase [IMF]	achat dans la première tranche de crédit	compra en el primer tramo de crédito

F-122	First Deputy Managing Director [IMF] *see also:* Deputy Managing Director FDMD	Premier Directeur général adjoint Première Directrice générale adjointe	Primer Subdirector Gerente
F-123	first in, first out FIFO	premier entré, premier sorti PEPS	método de primeras entradas, primeras salidas método PEPS método FIFO
F-124	first in, last out FILO	premier entré, dernier sorti PEDS	método de primeras entradas, últimas salidas método PEUS método FILO
F-125	First Special Contingent Account, *see* Special Contingent Account 1		
F-126	fiscal adjustment, *see* fiscal consolidation		
F-127	Fiscal Affairs Department [IMF] FAD	Département des finances publiques	Departamento de Finanzas Públicas
F-128	fiscal agency [IMF] *see also:* depository [IMF]	agent financier organisme financier	agente fiscal organismo fiscal
F-129	fiscal balance, *see* fiscal equilibrium		
F-130	fiscal balance *see also:* fiscal equilibrium budgetary balance budget surplus/deficit	solde des finances publiques excédent/déficit des finances publiques solde budgétaire excédent/déficit budgétaire	saldo fiscal saldo presupuestario saldo del presupuesto superávit/déficit fiscal superávit/déficit presupuestario
F-131	fiscal capacity *see also:* fiscal effort	capacité budgétaire	capacidad fiscal
F-132	fiscal consolidation fiscal adjustment fiscal tightening budget consolidation budgetary consolidation fiscal retrenchment fiscal containment	rééquilibrage budgétaire rééquilibrage des finances publiques assainissement des finances publiques	consolidación fiscal reordenamiento de las finanzas públicas saneamiento de las finanzas públicas ajuste fiscal ajuste presupuestario contención del gasto público
F-133	fiscal containment, *see* fiscal consolidation		
F-134	fiscal deficit	déficit budgétaire déficit des finances publiques	déficit fiscal déficit de las finanzas públicas
F-135	fiscal discipline fiscal restraint	discipline budgétaire rigueur budgétaire austérité budgétaire politique budgétaire restrictive	disciplina fiscal restricción fiscal austeridad fiscal restricción del gasto público compresión fiscal compresión del gasto público reducción de gastos

F-136	fiscal dominance *see also:* monetary dominance	domination de la politique budgétaire (sur la politique monétaire)	predominio fiscal dominancia fiscal
F-137	fiscal drag	frein fiscal freinage fiscal	lastre fiscal freno fiscal rémora fiscal
F-138	fiscal effort *see also:* fiscal capacity tax effort	effort budgétaire effort fiscal	esfuerzo fiscal esfuerzo tributario
F-139	fiscal equilibrium *see also:* budgetary balance fiscal balance	équilibre des finances publiques équilibre budgétaire	equilibrio fiscal equilibrio del presupuesto equilibrio de las finanzas públicas
F-140	fiscal expenditure, *see* budgetary expenditure		
F-141	fiscal federalism	fédéralisme budgétaire	federalismo fiscal
F-142	fiscal illusion	illusion fiscale	ilusión fiscal
F-143	fiscal impulse fiscal stimulus	relance budgétaire relance par le budget stimulant budgétaire mesure budgétaire de stimulation de l'économie impulsion budgétaire	impulso fiscal estímulo fiscal
F-144	fiscal monopoly revenue-producing monopoly	monopole fiscal	monopolio fiscal
F-145	Fiscal Operations Division 1, 2, 3 [IMF] FOD1, FOD2, FOD3	Division opérations de finances publiques I, II, III	División de Operaciones Fiscales 1, 2, 3
F-146	fiscal panel [IMF *see also:* panel expert	fichier d'experts (consultants en finances publiques)	grupo de expertos consultores en finanzas públicas
F-147	fiscal policy	politique de finances publiques politique budgétaire	política fiscal
F-148	Fiscal Policy and Surveillance Division [IMF]	Division de la politique et de la surveillance des finances publiques	División de Política y Supervisión Fiscales
F-149	fiscal position	situation des finances publiques situation budgétaire position budgétaire position des finances publiques	situación fiscal situación de las finanzas públicas
F-150	fiscal restraint, *see* fiscal discipline		
F-151	fiscal retrenchment, *see* fiscal consolidation		
F-152	fiscal revenue	recettes budgétaires	ingreso fiscal
F-153	fiscal skeleton "skeleton"	dettes implicites	esqueleto fiscal

F-154	fiscal stabilization	stabilisation budgétaire stabilisation par voie budgétaire	estabilización fiscal estabilización mediante la política fiscal
F-155	fiscal stance	orientation de la politique budgétaire orientation de la politique de finances publiques orientation de l'action budgétaire	orientación fiscal orientación de la política fiscal
F-156	fiscal stimulus, *see* fiscal impulse		
F-157	fiscal sustainability	viabilité des finances publiques viabilité du budget	sostenibilidad fiscal viabilidad fiscal viabilidad de las finanzas públicas sustentabilidad fiscal
F-158	fiscal tariff [customs] revenue tariff	tarif fiscal tarif à but fiscal droit à caractère fiscal	arancel fiscal
F-159	fiscal tightening, *see* fiscal consolidation		
F-160	fiscal transparency	transparence en matière de finances publiques transparence budgétaire	transparencia fiscal
F-161	fiscal withdrawal	retrait de l'impulsion budgétaire compression budgétaire	retiro del estímulo fiscal retracción del estímulo fiscal
F-162	fiscal year financial year FY	exercice année financière année budgétaire exercice financier	ejercicio año fiscal
F-163	fiscal year, *see* tax year		
F-164	fiscalization, *see* budgeting		
F-165	Fisher equation, *see* equation of exchange		
F-166	FISIM, *see* financial intermediation services indirectly measured		
F-167	fit	ajustement	ajuste
F-168	fit a trend [econometrics]	ajuster une tendance	determinar una tendencia
F-169	five-year review of quotas, *see* General Review of Quotas		
F-170	fixed assets fixed capital	actifs fixes capital fixe biens de capital fixe immobilisations actif immobilisé corporel	activo fijo capital fijo activos fijos
F-171	fixed but adjustable exchange rate, *see* adjustable peg		
F-172	fixed capital, *see* fixed assets		

F-173	fixed capital consumption consumption of fixed capital CFC	consommation de capital fixe	consumo de capital fijo CCF
F-174	fixed capital formation	formation de capital fixe	formación de capital fijo
F-175	fixed cost	coûts fixes frais fixes	costo fijo
F-176	fixed exchange rate parity fixed par value fixed parity fixed rate parity	parité fixe pair fixe	paridad fija
F-177	fixed expenditure	dépenses fixes frais fixes	gasto fijo
F-178	fixed par value, *see* fixed exchange rate parity		
F-179	fixed parity, *see* fixed exchange rate parity		
F-180	fixed rate parity, *see* fixed exchange rate parity		
F-181	fixed-income market, *see* bond market		
F-182	fixed-term deposit, *see* time deposit		
F-183	fixed-weight price index	indice des prix à pondération fixe	índice de precios con ponderación fija
F-184	fixing	*fixing* cotation	cotización base cambio base *fixing* fijación del precio del oro cotización cotización fijada
F-185	flash estimate	estimation instantanée estimation préliminaire estimation rapide	cifra preliminar estimación preliminar
F-186	flat rate *see also:* lump sum	taux forfaitaire taux fixe taux proportionnel tarif forfaitaire	tasa única tasa fija tarifa única
F-187	flat-loading [IMF] *see also:* back-loading; front-loading	distribution uniforme (des tirages, mesures, etc.) sur la période distribution uniforme (des tirages, mesures, etc.) pendant la durée du programme répartition uniforme sur la période répartition uniforme pendant la durée du programme	distribución uniforme (de medidas, gastos, etc.) durante el período distribución uniforme (de medidas, gastos, etc.) durante el programa
F-188	flight into quality, *see* flight to quality		
F-189	flight money, *see* hot money		
F-190	flight of funds, *see* capital flight		

F-191	flight to quality flight into quality	recherche de la qualité	fuga hacia activos de calidad desplazamiento hacia inversiones de alta calidad huida hacia la calidad búsqueda de calidad
F-192	FLIRB, *see* front-loaded interest reduction bond		
F-193	float [banking] *see also:* items in transit	moyens de paiement en cours d'encaissement fonds en route chèques en cours d'encaissement flottant bancaire valeurs en recouvrement chèques en route effets en cours de recouvrement	cheques no canjeados cheques pendientes de cobro efectos en cobro efectos en cobranza
F-194	floating completion point [HIPC Initiative]	point d'achèvement flottant	punto de culminación flotante
F-195	floating currency	monnaie flottante	moneda flotante moneda de tipo de cambio flotante
F-196	floating debt	impayés dette flottante	deuda flotante

F-197	floating facility
	[IMF]
		facilité dissociée
		mécanisme «dissocié»
		  (des tranches de crédit)
		mécanisme exclu du calcul
		  des tranches de crédit
			servicio financiero flotante

F-198	floating interest rate floating rate variable rate adjustable rate	taux d'intérêt variable taux variable taux ajustable	tasa de interés variable tasa variable tasa ajustable tasa flotante
F-199	floating rate, *see* floating interest rate		
F-200	flotation *see also:* initial public offering	émission lancement offre de titres	emisión lanzamiento
F-201	flow *see also:* stock	flux	flujo corriente
F-202	flow data *see also:* stock data	données de flux	datos de flujos datos sobre flujos
F-203	flow of funds	opérations financières flux financiers apport financier mouvements de fonds	flujo de fondos corrientes financieras
F-204	flow of funds table	tableau des opérations financières TOF	cuadro de flujo de fondos
F-205	flow variable	variable de flux	variable de flujo

F-206	fluctuation band	bande de fluctuation	banda de fluctuación
	fluctuation margin	marge de fluctuation	margen de fluctuación
	band	limite de fluctuation	banda cambiaria
	exchange rate corridor		corredor cambiario
	currency band		corredor

F-207   fluctuation margin, *see* fluctuation band

F-207a f.o.b., *see* free on board

F-208   FOD1, *see* Fiscal Operations Division 1, 2, 3

F-209   FOD2, *see* Fiscal Operations Division 1, 2, 3

F-210   FOD3, *see* Fiscal Operations Division 1, 2, 3

| F-211 | follow-up mission | mission de suivi | misión de seguimiento |
| | [IMF] | | misión complementaria |

F-212   FOMC, *see* Federal Open Market Committee

| F-213 | Food and Agriculture Organization of the United Nations | Organisation des Nations Unies pour l'alimentation et l'agriculture | Organización de las Naciones Unidas para la Agricultura y la Alimentación |
| | FAO | OAA, FAO | FAO |

| F-214 | food crop | culture vivrière | cultivo alimentario |
| | | | cultivo comestible |

| F-215 | force majeure | cas de force majeure | fuerza mayor |
| | *see also:* act of God | | |

| F-216 | forced saving | épargne forcée | ahorro forzoso |

F-217   foreign asset, *see* external asset (assets owned abroad by residents)

| F-218 | foreign bond | obligation étrangère | bono extranjero |
| | *see also:* external bond | | |

| F-219 | foreign borrowing | emprunt(s) à l'étranger | préstamo del exterior |
| | | | empréstito externo |

| F-220 | foreign capital | capitaux étrangers | capital extranjero |

F-221   foreign claim, *see* external claim

F-222	foreign currency	devise	moneda extranjera
	foreign exchange	monnaie étrangère	divisa
	forex		divisas
	exchange		cambio

| F-223 | foreign currency liquidity | liquidités en devises | liquidez en moneda extranjera |
| | currency liquidity | liquidité en devises | liquidez en divisas |

F-224   foreign currency swap, *see* reciprocal currency arrangement

F-225	foreign direct investment	investissement direct étranger	inversión extranjera directa
	FDI	IDE	IED
	direct foreign investment		
	DFI		

F-226   foreign exchange, *see* foreign currency

F-227	foreign exchange assets	avoirs en devises	activos en divisas
F-228	foreign exchange auction	adjudication de(s) devises enchères de(s) devises	subasta de divisas subasta de moneda extranjera
F-229	foreign exchange dealer foreign exchange trading officer trading officer	agent de change cambiste	cambista agente de cambios

F-230	foreign exchange equalization fund
	see also: currency board
	  arrangement; monetary board
	exchange stabilization fund
	currency stabilization fund
	CSF
		fonds de stabilisation des changes
		fonds de stabilisation de la
		  monnaie
			fondo de estabilización cambiaria
			fondo de estabilización monetaria

F-231	foreign exchange market exchange market	marché des changes marché des devises	mercado de divisas mercado de cambios mercado cambiario
F-232	foreign exchange policy, *see* exchange rate policy		
F-233	foreign exchange position	position de change	nivel de divisas situación cambiaria posición en moneda extranjera posición cambiaria
F-234	foreign exchange record exchange record	relevé des opérations de change relevé des opérations en devises	registro de operaciones cambiarias registro de cambios
F-235	foreign exchange reserves *see also:* international reserves exchange reserves	réserves de change réserves en devises	reservas de divisas reservas en moneda extranjera
F-236	foreign exchange retention, *see* export retention scheme		
F-237	foreign exchange retention scheme, *see* export retention scheme		
F-238	foreign exchange speculation	spéculation sur devises spéculation sur les changes	especulación cambiaria especulación en divisas
F-239	foreign exchange trading officer, *see* foreign exchange dealer		
F-240	foreign lending, *see* cross-border lending		
F-241	foreign liabilities	engagements extérieurs	pasivos externos pasivos exteriores pasivos frente al exterior pasivos sobre el exterior
F-242	foreign official sector	secteurs officiels étrangers	sector oficial extranjero

F-243	foreign tax credit	déduction pour impôt payé à
		  l'étranger
		dégrèvement pour impôt étranger
			crédito tributario por impuestos
			  pagados en el exterior

F-244	foreign trade, *see* trade		
F-245	foreign trade multiplier	multiplicateur du commerce extérieur	multiplicador del comercio exterior
F-246	foreign trade zone, *see* free trade zone		

F-247	foreign-held balances	soldes extérieurs soldes débiteurs extérieurs avoirs nets détenus par des non- résidents	saldos en manos de no residentes saldos en el exterior saldos deudores en el exterior
F-248	foreign-owned corporation	société à capital étranger société sous contrôle étranger	empresa de propiedad extranjera
F-249	forex, *see* foreign currency		
F-250	forfaiting *see also:* factoring	affacturage à forfait	*forfaiting* forfetización descuento de pagarés
F-251	forfeit *see also:* fines and forfeits forfeiture confiscation	confiscation	confiscación decomiso
F-252	forfeiture, *see* forfeit		
F-253	forgone earnings, *see* forgone revenue		
F-254	forgone income, *see* forgone revenue		
F-255	forgone revenue *see also:* tax expenditure forgone income forgone earnings	manque à gagner	ingreso sacrificado ingreso fiscal no percibido
F-256	formal consultation [IMF] *see also:* periodic consultation regular consultation	consultations régulières consultations ordinaires	consulta ordinaria
F-257	formal ineligibility [IMF]	non-admissibilité formelle irrecevabilité formelle	inhabilitación oficial
F-258	formal sector	secteur formel secteur structuré	sector formal
F-259	formal vote [IMF]	vote formel	votación formal
F-260	formally convertible currency [IMF]	monnaie officiellement convertible	moneda oficialmente convertible
F-261	formula grant, *see* formula-based grant		
F-262	formula-based grant [public finance] formula grant	subvention calculée sur la base d'une formule	subvención basada en fórmulas
F-263	forty-eight-hour report, *see* back-to-office report		
F-264	forward contract *see also:* future	contrat à terme (de gré à gré) contrat à livraison différée	contrato a término contrato a plazo
F-265	forward cover	couverture à terme	cobertura a término cobertura a plazo

F-266	forward discount	déport décote à terme	descuento a término descuento a plazo descuento
F-267	forward exchange transaction	opération de change à terme	operación de cambio a término operación cambiaria a plazo
F-268	forward foreign exchange contract	opération de change à terme	contrato de cambio a plazo contrato de cambio a término contrato a futuro sobre divisas
F-269	forward-looking expectations	anticipations prospectives	expectativas basadas en la evolución prevista expectativas basadas en las previsiones
F-270	forward market	marché à terme	mercado a término mercado a plazo
F-271	forward operation	opération à terme	operación a término operación a plazo
F-272	forward premium	report report à terme	prima a término prima a plazo prima a futuro
F-273	forward rate agreement FRA future rate agreement [BIS]	accord de taux futur ATF contrat de garantie de taux contrat de garantie de taux d'intérêt contrat de change à terme	contrato a futuro sobre tasas de interés acuerdo a futuro sobre tasas de interés AFTI acuerdo de tasa de interés a término acuerdo a plazo sobre tasas de interés
F-274	forward shifting see also: backward shifting	répercussion en aval	traslación hacia adelante traslación del impuesto hacia adelante
F-275	forwarding	transit expédition	expedición
F-276	forward-looking indicator, see leading indicator		
F-277	FRA, see forward rate agreement		
F-278	Framework Administered Account for Technical Assistance Activities [IMF]	Compte-cadre administré pour le financement d'activités d'assistance technique Compte-cadre administré pour les activités d'assistance technique	Cuenta Administrada General para las Actividades de Asistencia Técnica
F-279	framework agreement	accord-cadre	acuerdo marco
F-280	franc area, see CFA Franc Zone		
F-281	franc zone, see CFA Franc Zone		
F-282	franchising	franchisage	franquicia franquicia comercial concesión de franquicias

F-283	FRB, *see* Federal Reserve Board		
F-284	free enterprise economy *see also:* enterprise economy; market economy	économie de libre entreprise	economía de libre empresa
F-285	free entry (into a market)	libre accès (au marché)	libre ingreso al mercado
F-286	free floating	flottement libre	libre flotación flotación libre
F-287	free good [economics]	bien gratuit bien non marchand	bien gratuito
F-288	free good [customs]	bien non taxé bien libre produit exonéré produit en franchise	producto libre de impuestos producto exento de impuestos
F-289	free market pricing	libre fixation des prix	libertad de precios determinación de precios en un mercado libre
F-290	free movement of capital, *see* freedom of capital movements		
F-290a	free on board f.o.b.	franco à bord f.à.b.	franco a bordo f.o.b.
F-291	free port, *see* free trade zone		
F-292	free reserves	réserves disponibles réserves libres	reservas libres reservas disponibles
F-293	free rider, *see* free rider bank		
F-294	free rider bank [London Club] *see also:* easy rider bank free rider	banque opportuniste banque abstentionniste resquilleur	banco abstencionista

F-295	free trade
	see also: comparative advantage;
	   fair trade; globalization; liberal
	   trade; new trade theory
	open trade
		libre-échange	libre comercio
			libre cambio

F-296	free trade area	zone de libre-échange	zona de libre comercio zona franca
F-297	free trade zone *see also:* export processing zone free zone free port free warehouse foreign trade zone	zone franche	zona franca
F-298	free warehouse, *see* free trade zone		
F-299	free zone, *see* free trade zone		

F-300	freedom of capital movements
	see also: capital account
	  convertibility; liberalization of the
	  capital account
	free movement of capital
		libre circulation des capitaux	libre circulación del capital

F-301	freely usable currency [IMF]	monnaie librement utilisable	moneda de libre uso moneda de libre disponibilidad
F-302	French Division [IMF]	Division française	División de Francés

F-303	French international financial
	  futures market
	[FRA]
	MATIF
		marché à terme international de
		  France
		MATIF
			mercado francés de futuros
			  financieros
			MATIF

F-304	frequency *see also:* periodicity	fréquence	frecuencia
F-305	frequency distribution	distribution de fréquences	distribución de frecuencias
F-306	fresh money, *see* new money		
F-307	frictional unemployment transitional unemployment search unemployment	chômage frictionnel chômage transitionnel taux de chômage transitionnel	desempleo friccional tasa friccional de desempleo
F-308	fringe benefits *see also:* employee contribution employee benefits	avantages sociaux avantages indirects indemnités et avantages divers	prestaciones suplementarias prestaciones accesorias beneficios y prestaciones no salariales prestaciones sociales
F-309	Front Office [IMF] *see also:* Immediate Office	Direction (d'un département)	Dirección (de un departamento)
F-310	front office	front office	*front office*
F-311	front-end fee	commission initiale commission versée à la signature	comisión inicial comisión abonada al firmar comisión pagadera a la firma
F-312	front-end loading, *see* front-loading		
F-313	frontier technology *see also:* high technology industry; pioneer industry leading technology leading edge technology cutting edge technology	technologie d'avant-garde techniques d'avant-garde technologie de pointe techniques de pointe	tecnología de vanguardia tecnología avanzada

F-314	front-loaded interest reduction
	  bond
	FLIRB
		obligation à taux d'intérêt réduit
		  en début de période
			bono a tasa de interés reducida
			  al comienzo del período con
			  capitalización

F-315	front-loading [IMF] *see also:* back-loading; flat-loading front-end loading	concentration des décaissements en début de période concentration (des tirages, mesures, etc.) en début de programme	concentración de desembolsos al comienzo del período del acuerdo concentración (de medidas, gastos, etc.) al comienzo del período concentración al comienzo del programa
F-316	FSAP, *see* Financial Sector Assessment Program		
F-317	FSF, *see* Financial Stability Forum		
F-318	FSI, *see* financial soundness indicator		
F-319	FSSA, *see* Financial Sector Stability Assessment		
F-320	fuel exporters	pays exportateurs de combustibles exportateurs de combustibles	exportadores de combustibles
F-321	fulfill an obligation [IMF] *see also:* discharge an obligation	remplir une obligation exécuter une obligation honorer une obligation	cumplir una obligación
F-322	full asset settlement	règlement intégral en actifs	liquidación total en activos liquidación integral en activos
F-323	full capacity level	niveau de pleine capacité	nivel de plena capacidad
F-324	full cost pass-through	répercussion intégrale du coût	traslado íntegro de los costos
F-325	full currency convertibility	pleine convertibilité de la monnaie pleine convertibilité des monnaies	plena convertibilidad de las monedas
F-326	full employment	plein emploi	pleno empleo
F-327	full employment balance	solde de plein emploi solde budgétaire de plein emploi	equilibrio de pleno empleo
F-328	full employment budget surplus	excédent budgétaire de plein emploi	superávit presupuestario de pleno empleo
F-329	full employment multiplier	multiplicateur de plein emploi	multiplicador de pleno empleo
F-330	full participatory PRSP, *see* participatory PRSP		
F-331	full PRSP *see also:* interim PRSP full-fledged Poverty Reduction Strategy Paper full-fledged PRSP	DSRP complet document complet de stratégie pour la réduction de la pauvreté	DELP definitivo Documento Definitivo de Estrategia de Lucha contra la Pobreza
F-332	full-employment unemployment rate, *see* natural rate of unemployment		
F-333	full-fledged Poverty Reduction Strategy Paper, *see* full PRSP		
F-334	full-fledged PRSP, *see* full PRSP		
F-335	fully funded pension plan, *see* funded system		
F-336	fully funded plan, *see* funded system		
F-337	fully funded system, *see* funded system		

F-338	fully owned subsidiary, *see* wholly owned subsidiary		
F-339	full-year basis, on a, *see* annual basis, on an		
F-340	functional and special services departments [IMF]	départements fonctionnels et services spéciaux	departamentos funcionales y de servicios especiales
F-341	functional classification of expenditure	classification fonctionnelle des dépenses	clasificación funcional del gasto
F-342	Fund Agreement, *see Articles of Agreement of the International Monetary Fund*		
F-343	Fund engagement, *see* engagement of the IMF in a country		
F-344	Fund holdings of currencies, *see* currency holdings		
F-345	Fund involvement, *see* engagement of the IMF in a country		
F-346	Fund liquidity	liquidité du FMI	liquidez del FMI
F-347	Fund Office in the United Nations [IMF] UN	Bureau du FMI aux Nations Unies	Oficina del FMI en las Naciones Unidas
F-348	Fund quota	quote-part au FMI	cuota en el FMI
F-349	Fund staff, *see* staff		
F-350	fundamental determinants, *see* fundamentals		
F-351	fundamentals economic fundamentals fundamental determinants	paramètres fondamentaux aspects fondamentaux données fondamentales (de l'économie) facteurs économiques de base	fundamentos económicos parámetros fundamentales de la economía elementos económicos fundamentales variables fundamentales de la economía
F-352	Fund-Bank mission	mission mixte FMI–Banque mondiale mission conjointe FMI–Banque mondiale	misión conjunta del FMI y el Banco Mundial
F-353	funded debt	dette consolidée dette émise dette à long terme	deuda consolidada deuda perpetua deuda financiada
F-354	funded system *see also:* pay-as-you-go system fully funded system fully funded plan fully funded pension plan	régime avec constitution de réserves régime de retraite par capitalisation régime financé par capitalisation	sistema de capitalización régimen de capitalización régimen de plena capitalización
F-355	funding [debt]	consolidation	consolidación
F-356	funding [finance]	financement	financiamiento provisión de fondos provisión de recursos financieros fondeo

F-357	funding of deferred charges [IMF]	financement requis par le non-paiement des commissions financement des commissions comptabilisées en recettes différées	financiamiento de cargos diferidos financiamiento para cubrir cargos diferidos
F-358	Fund-monitored program, *see* staff-monitored program		
F-359	Fund-related accounts	comptes d'un pays avec le FMI comptes du FMI	cuentas relacionadas con el FMI
F-360	Fund-related assets	avoirs en compte au FMI	activos relacionados con el FMI
F-361	Fund-supported program	programme appuyé par le FMI programme bénéficiant de l'appui du FMI	programa respaldado por el FMI
F-362	future, *see* futures contract		
F-363	future rate agreement, *see* forward rate agreement		
F-364	futures contract *see also:* forward contract future	contrat à terme normalisé contrat à terme standardisé contrat à terme contrat à terme sur marché organisé futur opération à terme instrument à terme	contrato de futuros futuro contrato a término contrato a plazo operación a término operación a plazo contrato a futuro
F-365	futures option	option sur contrat à terme option sur futur	opción sobre futuros
F-366	FY, *see* fiscal year		

G

G-1	G-10, *see* Group of Ten		
G-2	G-20, *see* Group of Twenty		
G-3	G-24, *see* Group of Twenty-Four		
G-4	G-24, *see* Intergovernmental Group of Twenty-Four on International Monetary Affairs and Development		
G-5	G-7, *see* Group of Seven		
G-6	GAAP, *see* generally accepted accounting principles		
G-7	GAAS, *see* generally accepted auditing standards		
G-8	GAB, *see* General Arrangements to Borrow		
G-9	galloping inflation, *see* rampant inflation		
G-10	game theory *see also:* Nash equilibrium; prisoner's dilemma; zero-sum game	théorie des jeux	teoría de los juegos
G-11	GAO, *see* General Administrative Order		

G-12	gap financing *see also:* financing gap	couverture du besoin de financement couverture de l'impasse	financiamiento del déficit
G-13	gathering of data, *see* collection of data		
G-14	GATS, *see* General Agreement on Trade in Services		
G-15	GATT, *see* General Agreement on Tariffs and Trade		
G-16	GCA, *see* Guidelines on Corrective Action		
G-17	GDDS, *see* General Data Dissemination System		
G-18	GDP, *see* gross domestic product		
G-19	GDP deflator, *see* implicit price deflator		
G-20	gearing, *see* gearing ratio		

G-21	gearing ratio
	capital gearing ratio
	leverage
	gearing
	financial gearing
		ratio fonds propres/total du bilan
		coefficient emprunts/fonds propres
		rapport encours des prêts/fonds
		  propres
		[BIRD]
		coefficient d'utilisation des fonds
		  propres
		[BIRD]
		ratio d'autonomie financière
		levier
		effet de levier
			razón deuda/capital
			relación préstamos
			  desembolsados y pendientes-
			  capital y reservas
			[BIRD]
			nivel de endeudamiento en
			  relación con el capital propio
			razón préstamos obtenidos/capital
			coeficiente de apalancamiento
			apalancamiento
			poder multiplicador
			capacidad de palanqueo

G-22	GEF, *see* Global Environment Facility		
G-23	General Administrative Order [IMF] GAO	instruction administrative générale	Orden Administrativa General

G-24	General Agreement on Tariffs
	  and Trade
	GATT
		Accord général sur les tarifs
		  douaniers et le commerce
		GATT
			Acuerdo General sobre Aranceles
			  Aduaneros y Comercio
			GATT

G-25	General Agreement on Trade
	  in Services
	[WTO]
	GATS
		Accord général sur le commerce
		  des services
			Acuerdo General sobre el
			  Comercio de Servicios

G-26	general allocation of SDRs, *see* general SDR allocation		
G-27	General Arrangements to Borrow [IMF] GAB	Accords généraux d'emprunt AGE	Acuerdos Generales para la Obtención de Préstamos AGP
G-28	general balance sheet, *see* balance sheet		

G-29	general budget rule	principe de l'universalité
		  budgétaire
		règle de l'universalité budgétaire
			principio de universalidad
			  presupuestaria

G-30	General Counsel [IMF]	Conseiller juridique	Consejero Jurídico

G-31	General Counsel, Assistant [IMF]	Conseiller juridique assistant	Consejero Jurídico Adjunto
G-32	General Counsel, Deputy [IMF]	Conseiller juridique adjoint (du FMI)	Subconsejero Jurídico
G-33	General Data Dissemination System [IMF] *see also:* Special Data Dissemination Standard GDDS	système général de diffusion des données SGDD	Sistema General de Divulgación de Datos SGDD
G-34	General Department [IMF]	Département général	Departamento General
G-35	general exchange arrangements [IMF]	dispositions générales des régimes de change	regímenes generales de cambios
G-36	general government *see also:* government general government sector	secteur des administrations publiques ensemble des administrations publiques administrations publiques	gobierno general sector gobierno general
G-37	general government sector, *see* general government		
G-38	general increase in quotas equiproportional increase in quotas	augmentation générale des quotes-parts augmentation équiproportionnelle des quotes-parts	aumento general de las cuotas aumento equiproporcional de las cuotas
G-39	general public services	services généraux des administrations publiques	servicios públicos generales servicios generales de la administración pública
G-40	General Resources Account [IMF] GRA	compte des ressources générales	Cuenta de Recursos Generales CRG
G-41	General Resources and SDR Policy Division [IMF]	Division politique des ressources générales et des DTS	División de Política sobre Recursos Generales y DEG
G-42	General Review of Quotas [IMF] *see also:* quota review five-year review of quotas quinquennial review of quotas	révision générale des quotes-parts révision quinquennale des quotes-parts	revisión general de cuotas revisión quinquenal de cuotas
G-43	general sales tax GST	taxe générale sur les ventes	impuesto general sobre las ventas
G-44	general SDR allocation general allocation of SDRs	allocation générale de DTS	asignación general de DEG
G-45	General Services Division [IMF]	Division services généraux	División de Servicios Generales
G-46	Generalized System of Preferences [WTO] GSP	Système généralisé de préférences SGP	Sistema Generalizado de Preferencias SGP

G-47	generally accepted accounting principles GAAP	principes comptables généralement reconnus	principios de contabilidad generalmente aceptados
G-48	generally accepted auditing standards GAAS	normes de vérification généralement reconnues	normas de auditoría generalmente aceptadas
G-49	generation of savings	formation de l'épargne	formación del ahorro
G-50	generational accounting	comptabilité générationnelle	contabilidad generacional
G-51	generic assessment framework, *see* generic data quality assessment framework		
G-52	generic data quality assessment framework [IMF] *see also:* dataset-specific quality assessment framework generic assessment framework generic framework	cadre générique d'évaluation de la qualité des données cadre d'évaluation générique cadre générique	marco general para el análisis de la calidad de los datos
G-53	generic framework, *see* generic data quality assessment framework		
G-54	Geneva Office [IMF] EUO/GE	Bureau du FMI à Genève Bureau de Genève	Oficina del FMI en Ginebra
G-55	geographical direction of trade, *see* direction of trade		
G-56	GFCF, *see* gross fixed capital formation		
G-57	*GFS Yearbook*, *see* *Government Finance Statistics Yearbook*		
G-58	*GFSM*, *see* *Government Finance Statistics Manual 2001*		
G-59	*GFSM 2001*, *see* *Government Finance Statistics Manual 2001*		
G-60	*GFSY*, *see* *Government Finance Statistics Yearbook*		
G-61	gift element, *see* grant element of a loan		
G-62	gift tax *see also:* estate, inheritance, and gift taxes	impôts sur les donations entre vifs et les legs droits sur les donations (entre vifs et les legs)	impuesto sobre donaciones y legados impuesto sobre la transmisión gratuita de bienes
G-63	gilt-edged security, *see* blue chip		
G-64	Gini coefficient Gini inequality index coefficient of concentration	coefficient de Gini indice d'inégalité de Gini indice de concentration de Gini	coeficiente de Gini índice de desigualdad de Gini índice de concentración de Gini
G-65	Gini inequality index, *see* Gini coefficient		
G-66	gliding parity sliding parity	parité glissante parité mobile	paridad móvil paridad ajustable
G-67	global world universal	planétaire mondial universel	mundial universal
G-68	global balance of payments	balance mondiale des paiements	balanza de pagos mundial

G-69	global bond	obligation multimarchés	bono global
G-70	global commons	patrimoine commun de l'humanité patrimoine planétaire patrimoine universel ressources communes à l'humanité	patrimonio común de la humanidad patrimonio universal
G-71	global consolidation *see also:* consolidation	consolidation globale	consolidación mundial
G-72	global current account balance	balance mondiale des transactions courantes	balanza mundial en cuenta corriente
G-73	Global Environment Facility [IBRD-UNEP-UNDP] GEF	Fonds pour l'environnement mondial FEM	Fondo para el Medio Ambiente Mundial FMAM GEF
G-74	Global Environment Facility Trust Fund [IBRD-UNEP-UNDP]	Caisse du FEM	Fondo Fiduciario para el Medio Ambiente Mundial
G-75	Global Financial Stability Division [IMF]	Division stabilité financière mondiale	División de Estabilidad Financiera Mundial
G-76	global imbalances	déséquilibres mondiaux déséquilibres de l'économie mondiale	desequilibrios mundiales
G-77	Global Markets Monitoring and Analysis Division [IMF]	Division surveillance et analyse des marchés mondiaux	División de Monitoreo y Análisis de los Mercados Mundiales
G-78	global need to supplement reserve assets [IMF]	besoin global d'ajouter aux instruments de réserve	necesidad global de complementar los activos de reserva
G-79	global public goods *see also:* public good	biens publics mondiaux	bienes públicos mundiales
G-80	global stewardship [environment]	intendance planétaire	custodia del medio ambiente mundial
G-81	globalization *see also:* free trade; hot money	mondialisation	globalización mundialización
G-82	GNDI, *see* gross national disposable income		
G-83	GNDY, *see* gross national disposable income		
G-84	GNE, *see* gross national expenditure		
G-85	GNI, *see* gross national income		
G-86	GNP, *see* gross national product		
G-87	GNY, *see* gross national income		
G-88	going concern	entreprise en exploitation entreprise viable	empresa en marcha empresa en funcionamiento

G-89	going price	prix courant cours du jour	precio corriente
G-90	going rate, *see* prevailing market rate		
G-91	gold bullion	or en lingots lingots d'or	oro no amonedado oro en lingotes
G-92	gold coin	or en pièces	oro amonedado
G-93	gold exchange standard gold standard	étalon de change or étalon or	patrón de cambio oro patrón oro
G-94	gold parity	parité or	paridad oro
G-95	gold pledge [IMF]	nantissement de l'or	garantía de oro
G-96	gold standard, *see* gold exchange standard		
G-97	gold subscription [IMF]	souscription or	suscripción en oro
G-98	gold valuation	calcul de la valeur de l'or	valoración del oro
G-99	gold-backed	gagé sur l'or gagé par l'or avec garantie or	con garantía oro con respaldo en oro con respaldo oro
G-100	golden rule of accumulation golden rule of capital accumulation golden rule of growth	règle d'or (de l'accumulation)	regla de oro de acumulación de capital
G-101	golden rule of capital accumulation, *see* golden rule of accumulation		
G-102	golden rule of growth, *see* golden rule of accumulation		
G-103	good governance	bonne gestion des affaires publiques bonne gestion de la chose publique bonne gouvernance bonne gestion publique	buen gobierno
G-104	goodness of fit	degré d'ajustement précision de l'ajustement	precisión del ajuste bondad del ajuste
G-105	goods on consignment	marchandises en consignation biens en consignation	mercancías en consignación bienes en consignación
G-106	goods, services, and income	biens, services et revenus	bienes, servicios y renta
G-107	goodwill	fonds de commerce éléments incorporels du fonds de commerce valeur de la clientèle survaleur pas de porte achalandage écart d'acquisition	fondo de comercio buen nombre derecho de llave [Am. Lat.] valor llave plusvalía adquirida plusvalía mercantil renombre comercial

G-108	goodwill clause *see also:* improved goodwill clause	clause de bonne volonté	cláusula de buena voluntad
G-109	government *see also:* general government government sector	secteur public secteur des administrations publiques administrations publiques État gouvernement	gobierno sector gobierno
G-110	government agency government department	organisme public ministère service direction département ministériel unité administrative	organismo público organismo estatal organismo gubernamental dependencia del Estado entidad pública
G-111	government bond	obligation publique obligation d'État	bono público bono del Estado bono del gobierno
G-112	government borrowing	emprunt public emprunt d'État	empréstito público empréstito del Estado deuda pública
G-113	government corporation, *see* public enterprise		
G-114	government department, *see* government agency		
G-115	government enterprise, *see* public enterprise		
G-116	government expenditure	dépenses publiques dépenses des administrations publiques	gasto público
G-117	Government Finance Division [IMF]	Division finances publiques	División de Finanzas Públicas
G-118	government finance statistics	statistiques de finances publiques	estadísticas de finanzas públicas

G-119	*Government Finance Statistics
	  Manual 2001*
	GFSM 2001
	GFSM
		*Manuel de statistiques de finances
		  publiques 2001*
		Manuel SFP
			*Manual de estadísticas de finanzas
			  públicas 2001*
			MEFP

G-120	*Government Finance Statistics
	  Yearbook*
	[IMF]
	GFS Yearbook
	GFSY
		*Government Finance Statistics
		  Yearbook*
		Annuaire de statistiques de
		  finances publiques
			*Government Finance Statistics
			  Yearbook*
			anuario de estadísticas de
			  finanzas públicas

G-121	government or government-guaranteed debt, *see* public or publicly guaranteed debt		
G-122	government paper, *see* government security		
G-123	government receipts government revenue	recettes publiques recettes des administrations publiques	ingresos fiscales ingresos públicos rentas públicas
G-124	government revenue, *see* government receipts		
G-125	government sector, *see* government		

G-126	government security government paper	effets publics fonds d'État	valor público valor gubernamental valor emitido por el Estado título público
G-127	Governor [IMF, World Bank]	gouverneur	Gobernador
G-128	Governor, Alternate [IMF, World Bank]	gouverneur suppléant	Gobernador Suplente
G-129	Governor of the Fund for [country] [IMF]	Gouverneur du FMI pour [pays]	Gobernador del FMI por [país]
G-130	Governor, Temporary Alternate [IMF]	gouverneur suppléant temporaire	Gobernador Suplente Interino
G-131	GRA, see General Resources Account		
G-132	grace period	différé d'amortissement délai de grâce délai de remboursement	período de gracia
G-133	grade creep, see grade drift		
G-134	grade drift see also: wage drift grade creep	glissement catégoriel inflation hiérarchique reclassements abusifs	aceleración de la escala de grados reclasificación ascendente de los puestos de trabajo
G-135	gradual devaluation, see incremental devaluation		
G-136	graduate [IDA]	être reclassé ne plus avoir besoin de faire appel aux ressources de l'IDA être intégré dans un régime normal être exclu (d'un régime privilégié)	pasar de las condiciones de asistencia de la AIF a las del Banco dejar de reunir las condiciones para recibir financiamiento del Banco "graduarse"
G-137	graduated tax	impôt par tranches impôt progressif	impuesto escalonado
G-138	graduation [World Bank] see also: maturation	reclassement cessation des crédits (de l'IDA)	"graduación"
G-139	grandfather clause, see acquired rights clause		
G-140	grant	don subvention transfert concours financier aide financière dotation	donación subvención subsidio transferencia
G-141	grant element, see grant element of a loan		
G-142	grant element of a loan grant element gift element	élément de libéralité élément de don	nivel de concesionalidad

G-143	gray area measure [trade] grey area measure	mesure de la zone grise mesure tangente mesure floue	medida de zona gris
G-144	GRAY Document [IMF]	document GRAY	documento GRAY
G-145	gray economy, *see* shadow economy		
G-146	gray market	marché gris	mercado gris
G-147	green accounting, *see* environmental accounting		
G-148	green conditionality	conditionnalité verte	condicionalidad verde condicionalidad de carácter ecológico
G-149	green tax, *see* environmental tax		
G-150	grey area measure, *see* gray area measure		
G-151	grid, *see* parity grid		
G-152	grid of parities, *see* parity grid		
G-153	Grievance Committee [IMF]	Comité d'appel interne	Comité de Apelación Interna
G-154	gross accumulation	accumulation brute variation brute du patrimoine	acumulación bruta
G-155	gross domestic expenditure	dépenses intérieures brutes	gasto interno bruto
G-156	gross domestic product GDP	produit intérieur brut PIB	producto interno bruto PIB producto geográfico bruto [*a veces*] PGB
G-157	gross fixed capital formation GFCF	formation brute de capital fixe FBCF	formación bruta de capital fijo FBCF formación bruta de capital fijo

G-158	gross Fund position (of a member)
	[IMF]
		position brute (d'un pays membre)
		  au FMI
			posición bruta (de un país
			  miembro) en el FMI

G-159	gross national disposable income GNDY GNDI	revenu national disponible brut RNDB	ingreso nacional disponible bruto
G-160	gross national expenditure GNE	dépense(s) nationale(s) brute(s)	gasto nacional bruto
G-161	gross national income GNI GNY	revenu national brut	ingreso nacional bruto renta nacional bruta
G-162	gross national product GNP	produit national brut PNB	producto nacional bruto PNB

G-163	gross operating balance gross operating profit or loss	bénéfices ou pertes brutes d'exploitation résultat brut d'exploitation RBE solde brut de gestion	resultado operativo bruto resultado bruto de explotación pérdidas o beneficios brutos de explotación
G-164	gross operating profit or loss, *see* gross operating balance		
G-165	gross output	production brute sortie brute	producto bruto producción bruta
G-166	gross recording	enregistrement brut comptabilisation sur une base brute	registro bruto registro en cifras brutas
G-167	gross reserve position [IMF]	situation des réserves brutes	nivel de las reservas brutas situación de las reservas brutas
G-168	gross social product [centrally planned economies] GSP	produit social brut PSB	producto social bruto PSB
G-169	gross up	calculer le montant brut (à partir du montant net) majorer	calcular el valor bruto (a partir del valor neto)
G-170	group lending	prêts collectifs	préstamos a grupos solidarios préstamos colectivos préstamos de grupo préstamos a grupos
G-171	Group of 10, *see* Group of Ten		
G-172	Group of 24, *see* Group of Twenty-Four		
G-173	Group of 7, *see* Group of Seven		
G-174	Group of African Governors, *see* African Group		
G-175	Group of Seven Group of 7 G-7	Groupe des Sept G-7	Grupo de los Siete G-7
G-176	Group of Ten Group of 10 G-10	Groupe des Dix G-10	Grupo de los Diez G-10
G-177	Group of Thirty, *see* Consultative Group on International Economic and Monetary Affairs, Inc.		
G-178	Group of Twenty G-20	Groupe des Vingt G-20	Grupo de los Veinte G-20
G-179	Group of Twenty-Four Group of 24 G-24	Groupe des Vingt-Quatre G-24	Grupo de los 24 G-24
G-180	Group of Twenty-Four, *see* Intergovernmental Group of Twenty-Four on International Monetary Affairs and Development		
G-181	growth accounting framework	analyse explicative de la croissance	método de análisis del crecimiento análisis explicativo del crecimiento

G-182	growth path	sentier de croissance trajectoire de croissance	trayectoria de crecimiento
G-183	growth-oriented adjustment	ajustement axé sur la croissance	ajuste orientado al crecimiento
G-184	GSP, *see* Generalized System of Preferences		
G-185	GSP, *see* gross social product		
G-186	GST, *see* general sales tax		
G-187	guarantee	garantie cautionnement aval sûreté	garantía aval fianza
G-188	guaranteed loan backed loan	prêt avalisé prêt garanti prêt cautionné prêt gagé	préstamo garantizado préstamo avalado
G-189	*Guide on Resource Revenue* *Transparency*	*Guide sur la transparence* *des recettes des ressources* *naturelles*	*Guía sobre la transparencia* *del ingreso proveniente de los* *recursos naturales*
G-190	guidelines for borrowing by the Fund [IMF]	directives concernant les emprunts du FMI	directrices sobre empréstitos del FMI
G-191	*Guidelines for Public Expenditure* *Management*	*Directives pour la gestion des* *dépenses publiques*	Directrices para la gestión del gasto público
G-192	Guidelines on Conditionality (2002)	directives sur la conditionnalité (2002) orientations en matière de conditionnalité	directrices sobre condicionalidad
G-193	Guidelines on Corrective Action [IMF] GCA Guidelines on Remedial Action	directives relatives aux mesures correctrices	directrices sobre medidas correctivas
G-194	Guidelines on Remedial Action, *see* Guidelines on Corrective Action		

H

H-1	hard budget constraint *see also:* budget constraint; soft budget constraint HBC	contrainte budgétaire rigoureuse	limitación presupuestaria estricta
H-2	hard currency	monnaie forte	moneda fuerte moneda dura divisas
H-3	hard good, *see* consumer durable		
H-4	hard loan	prêt aux conditions (commerciales) du marché prêt assorti de conditions rigoureuses	préstamo en condiciones de mercado préstamo en condiciones rigurosas

H-5	hard terms, *see* market terms		
H-6	hardening (of currency)	hausse affermissement	alza fortalecimiento
H-7	hardening of policy, *see* tightening of policy		
H-8	hardship [IMF]	difficultés exceptionnelles	dificultades extraordinarias dificultades excepcionalmente gravosas

H-9	Harmonized System of Customs
	  Classification
	[WTO]
		Système harmonisé de
		  nomenclature douanière
			Sistema Armonizado de
			  Clasificación Aduanera

H-10	HBC, *see* hard budget constraint		
H-11	HDI, *see* human development index		
H-12	head of mission, *see* mission chief		
H-13	head tax *see also:* rates [GBR] community charge [GBR] poll tax	impôt de capitation impôt personnel impôt sur la personne taxe civique	impuesto de capitación

H-14	headline inflation
	overall inflation
		inflation non corrigée
		inflation mesurée par l'indice
		  général des prix à la
		  consommation
		inflation publiée
		inflation globale
			inflación global
			nivel general de inflación

H-15	headquarters principal office of the Fund HQ	siège du FMI	sede del FMI
H-16	health	santé	salud sanidad
H-17	heavily indebted country	pays lourdement endetté	país muy endeudado

H-18	Heavily Indebted Poor Countries
	  Debt Initiative
	[IMF]
	HIPC Initiative
	HIPC Debt Initiative
		initiative en faveur des pays
		  pauvres très endettés
		initiative en faveur des PPTE
		initiative PPTE
			Iniciativa para la Reducción de la
			  Deuda de los Países Pobres muy
			  Endeudados
			Iniciativa para los PPME
			Iniciativa PPME
			Iniciativa HIPC

H-19	heavily indebted poor country HIPC highly indebted poor country	pays pauvre très endetté PPTE	país pobre muy endeudado PPME
H-20	hedge, *see* hedging		
H-21	hedge clause	clause de sauvegarde clause de couverture	cláusula de salvaguardia cláusula de protección
H-22	hedge currency	monnaie de couverture	moneda de cobertura

H-23	hedge fund	fonds d'arbitrage	*hedge fund*
	see also: vulture fund	fonds spéculatif	fondo de cobertura
	absolute return fund	fonds de placement à haut risque	fondo de inversión especulativo
		fonds de couverture	fondo especulativo de cobertura
			fondo de inversión de alto riesgo
			fondo de retorno absoluto
H-24	hedge ratio	ratio de couverture	coeficiente de cobertura
		taux de couverture	
H-25	hedging	couverture	cobertura de riesgos
	hedge	couverture à terme	cobertura
		opération de couverture	
H-26	herd behavior	instinct grégaire	comportamiento de rebaño
	herd effect	effet d'entraînement	comportamiento gregario
	bandwagon	effet de ralliement	comportamiento mimético
	bandwagon behavior	effet de Panurge	efecto de manada
	bandwagon effect	comportement moutonnier	efecto de arrastre
	lemming-like behavior	mimétisme	
H-27	herd effect, *see* herd behavior		
H-28	hidden inflation	inflation larvée	inflación encubierta
	disguised inflation	inflation masquée	inflación oculta
			inflación latente
H-29	hidden subsidy	subvention déguisée	subvención encubierta
	concealed subsidy		subsidio encubierto
H-30	hidden unemployment	chômage latent	desempleo encubierto
	disguised unemployment	chômage occulte	paro oculto
		chômage déguisé	[ESP]
		chômage invisible	desempleo latente
		chômage non déclaré	
H-31	high official, *see* senior official		
H-32	high technology industry	industrie de haute technicité	industria de alta tecnología
	see also: frontier technology;	industrie de haute technologie	industria de tecnología avanzada
	pioneer industry		
H-33	higher-middle-income country	pays à revenu intermédiaire	país de ingreso mediano alto
	HMIC	(tranche supérieure)	
	upper-middle-income countries		
	UMICS		
H-34	high-inflation country	pays à forte inflation	país de alta inflación
			país con alta tasa de inflación
H-35	highly indebted poor country, *see* heavily indebted poor country		
H-36	highly leveraged institution	institution financière à fort effet	institución fuertemente apalancada
	HLI	de levier	
		IFFEL	
H-37	high-powered money, *see* base money		
H-38	HIPC, *see* heavily indebted poor country		
H-39	HIPC Debt Initiative, *see* Heavily Indebted Poor Countries Debt Initiative		

H-40	HIPC Initiative, *see* Heavily Indebted Poor Countries Debt Initiative		
H-41	HIPC Trust Fund [World Bank] *see also:* PRGF-HIPC Trust	Fonds fiduciaire PPTE	Fondo Fiduciario para los PPME
H-42	historical cost original cost	coût historique coût initial coût rétrospectif coût d'origine valeur d'origine	costo histórico costo inicial costo original
H-43	historical trend	tendance historique tendance rétrospective	tendencia histórica
H-44	HLI, *see* highly leveraged institution		
H-45	HMIC, *see* higher-middle-income country		
H-46	hoarding [goods]	accaparement rétention accumulation de réserves achats de précaution	acaparamiento de provisiones retención de existencias acumulación de reservas acaparamiento
H-47	hoarding [money]	thésaurisation	atesoramiento
H-48	holder of record	détenteur titulaire	tenedor titular
H-49	holder of SDRs	détenteur de DTS	tenedor de DEG
H-50	holding company holding corporation	société holding société de portefeuille société de contrôle compagnie financière	sociedad tenedora de acciones de otras empresas *holding* sociedad *holding* empresa *holding* sociedad de control
H-51	holding corporation, *see* holding company		
H-52	holdings below allocations [SDR]	avoirs inférieurs aux allocations	tenencias de DEG inferiores a las asignaciones
H-53	holdings of bonds, *see* bond portfolio		
H-54	holdings rate [IMF]	taux des avoirs cours de trésorerie taux de comptabilisation des avoirs du FMI	tipo de cambio de las tenencias tipo de cambio de ajuste de las tenencias
H-55	home country *see also:* host country	pays d'origine	país de origen
H-56	home equity credit, *see* home equity loan		
H-57	home equity loan equity loan home equity credit equity credit line	prêt gagé sur (la valeur acquise d')un bien immobilier ligne de crédit garantie par (la valeur acquise d')un bien immobilier	préstamo con garantía hipotecaria préstamo respaldado por capital inmobiliario línea de crédito garantizada por el capital inmobiliario

H-58	home goods	biens d'origine intérieur	bienes nacionales productos nacionales
H-59	home market, *see* domestic market		
H-60	home production household production	production domestique	producción doméstica producción casera producción en el hogar
H-61	host country *see also:* home country	pays hôte pays d'accueil	país receptor país sede país anfitrión
H-62	hostile takeover *see also:* takeover	offre publique d'achat hostile offre publique d'achat inamicale OPA hostile	compra hostil opa hostil
H-63	hot money *see also:* globalization flight money	capitaux fébriles capitaux spéculatifs	capital especulativo
H-64	household, *see* household sector		
H-65	household expenditure consumer spending	dépenses des ménages dépenses des consommateurs	gasto de los hogares gasto de los particulares gasto de los consumidores
H-66	household production, *see* home production		
H-67	household saving consumer saving	épargne des ménages épargne des consommateurs	ahorro de los hogares ahorro de los particulares ahorro de los consumidores
H-68	household sector household	secteur des ménages ménage cellule familiale	sector de hogares sector de unidades familiares particulares hogares unidades familiares
H-69	housing and community amenities	logements et équipements collectifs	vivienda y servicios comunitarios
H-70	HQ, *see* headquarters		
H-71	HR Services, *see* Human Resources Services Division		
H-72	HRD, *see* Human Resources Department		
H-73	human development index [UN] HDI	indicateur du développement humain IDH	índice de desarrollo humano IDH
H-74	Human Resources Department [IMF] HRD	Département des ressources humaines	Departamento de Recursos Humanos
H-75	Human Resources Services Division [IMF] HR Services	Division services de ressources humaines	División de Servicios de Recursos Humanos
H-76	hyperinflation	hyperinflation	hiperinflación

H-77	hypothesis testing	test d'hypothèse vérification des hypothèses	verificación de hipótesis contraste de hipótesis contrastación de hipótesis
H-78	hysteresis effect	effet d'hystérèse	efecto de histéresis

I

I-1	IA, *see* Investment Account		
I-2	IADB, *see* Inter-American Development Bank		
I-3	IBOR, *see* interbank offered rate		
I-4	IBRD, *see* International Bank for Reconstruction and Development		
I-5	IBS, *see* international banking statistics		
I-6	*ICGS, see International Standard Classification of all Goods and Services*		
I-7	ICM, *see* international capital markets		
I-8	ICOR, *see* incremental capital-output ratio		
I-9	ICR, *see* import-consumption ratio		
I-10	ICS, *see* Integrated Correspondence System		
I-11	ICSID, *see* International Centre for Settlement of Investment Disputes		
I-12	IDA, *see* International Development Association		
I-13	IDA Debt Reduction Facility, *see* Debt Reduction Facility for IDA-Only Countries		
I-14	IDA-only country [IBRD]	pays exclusivement IDA	país que solo puede recibir financiamiento de la AIF
I-15	IDB, *see* Inter-American Development Bank		
I-16	IDB, *see* Islamic Development Bank		
I-17	IDGs, *see* International Development Goals		
I-18	idle balances	encaisses oisives soldes inactifs	saldos inactivos
I-19	idle capacity, *see* slack capacity		
I-20	idle money	fonds inactifs capitaux inactifs monnaie oisive	dinero inactivo dinero ocioso
I-21	idle resources	ressources inemployées	recursos inactivos recursos no utilizados recursos ociosos
I-22	IEA, *see* International Energy Agency		
I-23	IEG, *see* Independent Evaluation Group		
I-23a	IEO, *see* Independent Evaluation Office		

I-24	IFC, *see* International Finance Corporation		
I-25	*IFS, see International Financial Statistics*		
I-26	*IFS Yearbook, see International Financial Statistics Yearbook*		
I-27	IIF, *see* Institute of International Finance		
I-28	IIP, *see* international investment position		
I-29	illiquidity	illiquidité pénurie de liquidité(s)	iliquidez falta de liquidez
I-30	illiquidity risk risk of illiquidity	risque de pénurie de liquidité(s) risque d'illiquidité	riesgo de iliquidez riesgo de insuficiencia de liquidez
I-31	illustrative quota [IMF]	quote-part indicative quote-part illustrative quote-part calculée à titre indicatif	cuota ilustrativa
I-32	ILO, *see* International Labour Office		
I-33	ILO, *see* International Labour Organisation		
I-34	IMF, *see* International Monetary Fund		
I-35	IMF accounts in member countries, *see* accounts of the IMF in member countries		
I-36	IMF Bulletin Board IMF Electronic Bulletin Board bulletin board	tableau d'affichage électronique du FMI	cartelera electrónica del FMI
I-37	IMF Committee on Balance of Payments Statistics	Comité d'experts de la balance des paiements créé sous les auspices du FMI	Comité del FMI sobre Estadísticas de Balanza de Pagos
I-38	IMF Electronic Bulletin Board, *see* IMF Bulletin Board		
I-39	IMF engagement, *see* engagement of the IMF in a country		
I-40	IMF holdings of currencies, *see* currency holdings		
I-41	IMF Institute [IMF] Institute	Institut du FMI	Instituto del FMI
I-42	IMF No. 1 Account	compte n° 1 (du FMI)	Cuenta No. 1 del FMI
I-43	IMF No. 2 Account	compte n° 2 (du FMI)	Cuenta No. 2 del FMI
I-44	*IMF Survey*	*Bulletin du FMI*	*Boletín del FMI*
I-45	IMF Terminology Working Group TWG	Groupe de recherche terminologique du FMI	Grupo de Trabajo de Terminología del FMI
I-46	IMF Working Paper, *see* Working Paper		
I-47	IMF-AMF Regional Training Program [IMF] RTP	Programme régional de formation FMI–FMA	Programa Regional de Capacitación del FMI y el FMA

I-48	IMFC, *see* International Monetary and Financial Committee		
I-49	IMF-Singapore Regional Training Institute [IMF] STI	Institut régional de Singapour IRS	Instituto Regional de Capacitación del FMI en Singapur
I-50	IMF-supported or other monetary program	programme soutenu par le FMI ou autre programme monétaire	programa monetario respaldado por el FMI u otro programa monetario
I-51	Immediate Office [IMF] *see also:* Front Office .../AI	Bureau du Directeur	Oficina del Director
I-52	immunity from judicial process [IMF]	immunité judiciaire	inmunidad judicial
I-53	immunity from taxation [IMF]	immunité fiscale	inmunidad tributaria
I-54	immunity of archives [IMF]	inviolabilité des archives	inviolabilidad de los archivos
I-55	immunity of assets [IMF]	insaisissabilité des avoirs	inmunidad de los activos indisponibilidad de los activos
I-56	implicit cost *see also:* shadow price imputed cost	coût implicite coût imputé	costo implícito costo virtual precio de cuenta
I-57	implicit price deflator GDP deflator	déflateur implicite des prix déflateur du PIB	deflactor implícito de los precios deflactor del PIB
I-58	import absorption	absorption des importations	absorción de las importaciones
I-59	import bill	facture d'importation facture des importations coût global des importations	costo total de las importaciones
I-60	import capacity importing power	capacité d'importation	capacidad de importación
I-61	import capacity of exports import coverage cover rate	taux de couverture des importations couverture des importations par les exportations pouvoir d'importation des exportations	poder de importación de las exportaciones proporción de las importaciones cubierta por las exportaciones tasa de cobertura (de importaciones con exportaciones)
I-62	import content (of domestic products)	contenu en importations (dans les produits d'origine nationale) composante importations (des produits nationaux)	contenido de importaciones (en los productos nacionales) proporción de insumos importados (en los productos nacionales)
I-63	import coverage, *see* import capacity of exports		
I-64	import deposit, *see* advance deposit		

I-65	import duty	droit de douane	derecho de importación
	entry duty	droit d'importation	derecho de aduana
	entry tax	droit d'entrée	impuesto a las importaciones
		droit de porte	
		taxe à l'importation	
I-66	import penetration ratio	taux de pénétration des importations (dans une économie)	coeficiente de penetración de las importaciones (en una economía)
	IPR	TPI	CPI
		taux de pénétration des importations sur le marché intérieur	
		TPI	
I-67	import price	prix à l'importation	precio de importación
I-68	import substitute	substitut des importations	sustituto de las importaciones
		produit de substitution aux importations	
		produit de remplacement des importations	
I-69	import substitution	substitution de produits nationaux aux importations	sustitución de importaciones
		remplacement des importations	
		activités réductrices d'importations	
I-70	import surcharge	surtaxe à l'importation	recargo a la importación
I-71	import-consumption ratio	ratio importations/consommation	relación importaciones/consumo
	ICR		razón importación/consumo
I-72	imported inflation	inflation importée	inflación importada
		inflation d'origine externe	inflación de origen externo
I-73	imported unemployment	chômage importé	desempleo importado
		chômage d'origine externe	desempleo de origen externo
I-74	importing power, *see* import capacity		
I-75	import-intensive	à forte intensité d'importations	con gran intensidad de importaciones
		à forte composante d'importations	con un fuerte componente de importaciones
I-76	impound appropriations	bloquer des crédits	bloquear partidas presupuestarias
	sequester appropriations		
I-77	improved goodwill clause [Paris Club] *see also:* goodwill clause	clause de bonne volonté améliorée	cláusula mejorada de buena voluntad
I-78	imputed cost, *see* implicit cost		
I-79	imputed social contributions	cotisations sociales imputées	contribuciones sociales imputadas
I-80	imputed value	valeur fictive	valor implícito
		valeur imputée	valor imputado
I-81	in constant prices, *see* constant prices		
I-82	in current prices, *see* current prices		

I-83	in real terms, *see* real terms		
I-84	inactive market, *see* narrow market		
I-85	inadequacy of reserves	insuffisance des réserves	insuficiencia de las reservas
I-86	in-bond industry *see also:* offshore processing industry	industrie manufacturière sous douane industrie sous douane	industria en zona franca maquiladora industria maquiladora
I-87	incidence of taxation, *see* tax incidence		
I-88	incidental costs or charges	frais accessoires	costos o gastos conexos
I-89	incidental unemployment	chômage ponctuel	desempleo coyuntural desempleo circunstancial
I-90	income account *see also:* operating account revenue and expense account	compte de résultat compte de profits et pertes	cuenta de pérdidas y ganancias cuenta de resultados cuenta de ingresos y gastos
I-91	income and outlay account	compte des revenus et dépenses	cuenta de ingresos y desembolsos cuenta de ingresos y gastos
I-92	income bracket	tranche de revenu	categoría de ingreso tramo de renta
I-93	income distribution, *see* distribution of income		
I-94	income effect *see also:* substitution effect	effet de revenu	efecto ingreso efecto renta
I-95	income elasticity	élasticité par rapport au revenu élasticité-revenu	elasticidad con respecto al ingreso elasticidad-ingreso elasticidad-renta
I-96	income multiplier	multiplicateur du revenu	multiplicador del ingreso
I-97	income policy incomes policy	politique des revenus	política de ingresos
I-98	income share, *see* factor shares		
I-99	income statement statement of income statement of income and expenses profit and loss statement	compte de résultat état des résultats compte de profits et pertes état de bénéfices	estado de resultados cuenta de resultados estado de pérdidas y ganancias estado de ingresos y gastos
I-100	income target [IMF] target income	objectif de revenu	meta de ingresos meta de ingreso ingreso fijado como meta
I-101	income tax	impôt sur le revenu	impuesto sobre la renta impuesto a la renta impuesto a las ganancias [ARG]
I-102	income value	valeur de revenu valeur sous forme de revenu	valor locativo valor en renta

I-103	income velocity of money	vitesse-revenu de la monnaie vitesse de circulation-revenu de la monnaie vitesse de transformation de la monnaie en revenu(s)	velocidad-ingreso del dinero velocidad-renta del dinero
I-104	income-earning asset, *see* earning asset		
I-105	incomes policy, *see* income policy		
I-106	income-spending lag	décalage revenu–dépense	desfase ingreso-gasto
I-107	income-split tax system split system	régime fiscal du quotient familial système des parts	sistema de división de la renta de la unidad familiar a efectos tributarios
I-108	income-tested assistance *see also:* means-tested assistance	assistance sous conditions de revenu (du bénéficiaire) système de prestations modulées en fonction des ressources (du bénéficiaire)	asistencia condicionada al nivel de ingresos del beneficiario
I-109	incomings	entrées recettes encaissements	entradas ingresos
I-110	incorporated branch, *see* subsidiary		
I-111	incorporated enterprise	entreprise constituée en société	empresa constituida en sociedad
I-112	increase in quotas [IMF] *see also:* General Review of Quotas	augmentation des quotes-parts relèvement des quotes-parts	aumento de cuotas
I-113	increasing marginal return	rendement marginal croissant	rendimiento marginal creciente
I-114	incremental approach [IMF quota calculations] *see also:* selective increase in quotas	méthode d'augmentation sélective	método de aumento selectivo
I-115	incremental capital-output ratio ICOR	coefficient marginal de capital ratio marginal capital–production	relación marginal capital–producto
I-116	incremental devaluation *see also:* discrete devaluation gradual devaluation	dévaluation progressive	devaluación gradual
I-117	incremental labor-output ratio	ratio marginal travail-production	relación marginal trabajo-producto
I-118	incurrence of liabilities	souscription d'engagements accroissement des passifs	contraer obligaciones asumir pasivos acto de contraer obligaciones acto de contraer pasivos incurrimiento de pasivos pasivos incurridos emisión de pasivos
I-119	indebtedness	dette endettement montant de la dette	deuda endeudamiento monto de la deuda

I-120	Independent Evaluation Group [World Bank] IEG	Groupe d'Évaluation Indépendante GEI	Grupo de Evaluación Independiente GEI
I-120a	Independent Evaluation Office [IMF] *see also:* Independent Evaluation Group [World Bank] IEO EVO	Bureau indépendant d'évaluation BIE	Oficina de Evaluación Independiente OEI
I-121	independent float arrangement, *see* independent floating		
I-122	independent floating [IMF exchange rate classification system, 2006] independent float arrangement	flottement indépendant régime de flottement indépendant flottement autonome	flotación independiente régimen de flotación independiente
I-123	independent labor force, *see* self-employed		
I-124	index future, *see* securities index future		
I-125	indexation index-linking	indexation	indexación indización [ESP] corrección monetaria ajuste monetario
I-126	indexed index-linked index-tied	indexé	indexado indizado reajustable en función de un índice vinculado a un índice
I-127	indexed bonds	obligations indexées	bonos indexados
I-128	index-linked, *see* indexed		
I-129	index-linking, *see* indexation		
I-130	index-tied, *see* indexed		
I-131	individual, *see* natural person		
I-132	industrial classification	classification des branches d'activité marchande classification par activité nomenclature des activités	clasificación de las industrias clasificación de los ramos de actividad económica
I-133	industrial country	pays industrialisé	país industrial
I-134	industrial estate [GBR] industrial park [USA]	zone industrielle parc industriel domaine industriel complexe industriel	complejo industrial polígono industrial parque industrial
I-135	industrial free trade area, *see* export processing zone		
I-136	industrial free trade zone, *see* export processing zone		
I-137	industrial park, *see* industrial estate		

I-138	industry	branche d'activité branche d'activités marchandes branche d'industrie	industria
I-139	industry	secteur d'activité secteur industriel	industria sector actividad ramo de actividad
I-140	ineligibility to use the Fund's resources, automatic [IMF]	irrecevabilité automatique d'une demande d'utilisation des ressources du FMI	inhabilitación automática para usar los recursos del FMI
I-141	inertial inflation	inflation inertielle	inflación inercial
I-142	infant industry	industrie naissante industrie de création récente	industria incipiente industria naciente
I-143	inflation	inflation	inflación
I-144	inflation accounting	comptabilité prenant en compte l'inflation comptabilité d'inflation	contabilidad de la inflación contabilidad ajustada en función de la inflación contabilidad ajustada por inflación
I-145	inflation differential differential in inflation rates	écart entre (les) taux d'inflation différence de taux d'inflation disparité (de taux) d'inflation différentiel (de taux) d'inflation	diferencial de inflación diferencial de las tasas de inflación
I-146	inflation gap	écart d'inflation différentiel d'inflation	brecha de inflación brecha inflacionaria diferencial inflacionario
I-147	inflation targeting, *see* inflation-targeting framework		
I-148	inflation targeting framework, *see* inflation-targeting framework		
I-149	inflation targeting strategy, *see* inflation-targeting framework		
I-150	inflation tax seignorage	impôt prélevé par l'inflation	impuesto inflacionario inflación como impuesto
I-151	inflationary expectations	anticipations inflationnistes	expectativas inflacionarias expectativas inflacionistas
I-152	inflationary finance	financement inflationniste financement par création monétaire financement «par la planche à billets»	financiamiento inflacionario financiamiento por la vía de la inflación
I-153	inflation-targeting framework [IMF monetary policy framework classification system, 2006] inflation targeting IT direct inflation targeting inflation targeting strategy inflation targeting framework	ciblage de l'inflation cible d'inflation stratégie fondée sur une cible d'inflation stratégie fondée sur une cible directe d'inflation objectif d'inflation	régimen de metas de inflación sistema de metas de inflación marco basado en la adopción de objetivos de inflación estrategia de objetivos explícitos de inflación esquema de objetivos directos de inflación fijación de metas de inflación

I-154	inflow of capital capital inflow	entrée(s) de capitaux apport(s) de capitaux	entrada de capital afluencia de capital
I-155	informal financial sector, *see* noninstitutional financial sector		
I-156	informal meeting [IMF Executive Board]	séance informelle	reunión informal reunión oficiosa
I-157	informal savings	épargne informelle	ahorro informal
I-158	informal sector	secteur non structuré secteur informel	sector informal
I-159	informatics, *see* electronic data processing		
I-160	information cost	coût de l'information	costo de la información
I-161	information notice system [IMF] *see also:* notification system INS system of information notices	système des avis d'information	sistema de notificaciones
I-162	Information Officer, Senior [IMF]	agent principal de la Division de l'information	Oficial Principal de Información
I-163	Information Services Division [IMF] *see also:* Joint Library	Division services d'information	División de Servicios de Información
I-164	information technology IT	technologie(s) de l'information	tecnología de la información informática
I-165	Information Technology Services [IMF] IT Services	Services des technologies de l'information	Servicios de Tecnología de la Información
I-166	Infrastructure Division [IMF]	Division infrastructure	División de Infraestructura
I-167	ingot *see also:* bar; small ingot	lingot	lingote
I-168	inheritance tax *see also:* estate duty; estate, inheritance, and gift taxes death taxes	droits de succession impôt de succession impôt de mutation taxe successorale	impuesto a la herencia impuesto sobre sucesiones impuesto sucesorio
I-169	initial capital, *see* seed capital		
I-170	initial margin margin	dépôt de garantie marge marge initiale	margen inicial depósito inicial de garantía garantía inicial depósito de garantía
I-171	initial maturity, *see* original maturity		
I-172	initial public offering *see also:* flotation IPO	premier appel public à l'épargne	oferta pública inicial

I-173	initiative clause [Paris Club]	clause d'initiative	cláusula de iniciativa
I-174	input *see also:* production factor	intrant consommations intermédiaires composant moyen de production	insumo
I-175	input, *see* production factor		
I-176	input-output matrix, *see* input-output table		
I-177	input-output table IOT input-output matrix	tableau entrées–sorties TES tableau d'échanges interindustriels TEI matrice entrées–sorties	matriz de insumo–producto tabla de insumo-producto TIP
I-178	INS, *see* information notice system		
I-179	INS, *see* IMF Institute		
I-180	in-service training *see also:* on-the-job training	formation en cours d'emploi stage de perfectionnement	capacitación interna capacitación en el servicio perfeccionamiento laboral
I-181	insider	initié	persona que tiene acceso a información privilegiada especulador que aprovecha información interna
I-182	insider dealing insider trading	délit d'initié transaction d'initié	operaciones basadas en información privilegiada transacciones basadas en información privilegiada especulación aprovechando información interna
I-183	insider loan	prêt interne	préstamo interno préstamo a personas o entidades vinculadas con el prestamista préstamo vinculado autopréstamo
I-184	insider trading, *see* insider dealing		
I-185	insolvency *see also:* bankruptcy; default; unsoundness	insolvabilité	insolvencia
I-186	insolvency risk risk of insolvency	risque d'insolvabilité	riesgo de insolvencia
I-187	installed capacity plant capacity	puissance installée capacité de production installée capacité installée	capacidad instalada capacidad productiva capacidad instalada de producción
I-188	installment installment payment	versement partiel versement périodique remboursement échelonné	cuota pago parcial plazo

I-189	installment credit	crédit à tempérament prêt à tempérament	crédito de consumo crédito al consumidor crédito para compras a plazos
I-190	installment loan	prêt à remboursements échelonnés	préstamo reembolsable a plazos préstamo en cuotas
I-191	installment payment, *see* installment		
I-192	Institute, *see* IMF Institute		
I-193	Institute of International Finance IIF	Institut de finance internationale IFI	Instituto de Finanzas Internacionales IIF
I-194	institutional investor	investisseur institutionnel	inversionista institucional
I-195	institutional table	tableau institutionnel	cuadro institucional
I-196	institutionalization [financial sector]	institutionnalisation	institucionalización
I-197	insurance claim claim	sinistre d'assurance déclaration de sinistre	indemnización indemnización de seguros
I-198	Insurance Code of the Inter-African Conference on Insurance Markets [WAEMU] CIMA Code	Code des assurances de la Conférence interafricaine des marchés d'assurances Code CIMA	Código de Seguros de la Conferencia Interafricana de Mercados de Seguros Código de la CIMA
I-199	insurance technical reserves	réserves techniques d'assurance	reservas técnicas de seguros
I-200	intangible assets	actifs incorporels avoirs incorporels	activos intangibles activos inmateriales
I-201	Integrated Correspondence System [IMF] ICS	système de correspondance intégré	Sistema Integrado de Correspondencia SIC
I-202	intensified collaboration [IMF] intensified collaborative element intensified collaborative approach enhanced collaborative approach	collaboration intensifiée stratégie de collaboration renforcée approche de collaboration renforcée	colaboración intensificada intensificación de la colaboración enfoque de colaboración intensificada enfoque de colaboración reforzada
I-203	intensified collaborative approach, *see* intensified collaboration		
I-204	intensified collaborative element, *see* intensified collaboration		
I-205	intensified cooperative approach [IMF] intensified cooperative strategy enhanced cooperative approach enhanced cooperative strategy strengthened cooperative strategy strengthened cooperative strategy on overdue financial obligations strengthened cooperative strategy on arrears arrears strategy	approche fondée sur une coopération intensifiée approche fondée sur une coopération renforcée stratégie fondée sur une coopération intensifiée stratégie fondée sur une coopération renforcée stratégie de coopération renforcée stratégie de coopération renforcée en matière d'arriérés	estrategia de cooperación intensificada enfoque de cooperación reforzada estrategia de cooperación reforzada estrategia de cooperación reforzada frente a los atrasos en los pagos

I-206	intensified cooperative strategy, *see* intensified cooperative approach		
I-207	intensified surveillance [IMF]	surveillance renforcée	supervisión reforzada intensificación de la supervisión
I-208	Inter-African Conference on Insurance Markets CIMA	Conférence interafricaine des marchés d'assurances CIMA	Conferencia Interafricana de Mercados de Seguros CIMA
I-209	Inter-American Development Bank IDB IADB	Banque interaméricaine de développement BID	Banco Interamericano de Desarrollo BID
I-210	interbank call rate, *see* cash rate		
I-211	interbank offered rate IBOR	taux interbancaire offert TIO IBOR	tasa interbancaria de oferta IBOR
I-212	interbank rate	taux interbancaire	tasa de interés interbancaria
I-213	interenterprise arrears	arriérés interentreprises	atrasos en los pagos entre empresas atrasos entre empresas
I-214	interest differential interest rate differential	écart d'intérêt écart de taux d'intérêt différentiel d'intérêt différentiel de taux d'intérêt	diferencial de tasas de interés diferencia entre las tasas de interés
I-215	interest due but not paid	intérêts échus mais non payés	interés devengado pero no pagado
I-216	interest elasticity	élasticité par rapport aux taux d'intérêt élasticité-intérêt	elasticidad con respecto a la tasa de interés elasticidad-interés
I-217	interest equalization tax, *see* interest rate equalization tax		
I-218	interest mismatch	asymétrie des taux d'intérêt	descalce de las tasas de interés
I-219	interest payable	intérêts à payer	intereses por pagar
I-220	interest payment	paiement d'intérêts	pago de intereses pago por concepto de intereses
I-221	interest rate anchor	taux d'intérêt comme point d'ancrage	uso de la tasa de interés como ancla
I-222	interest rate cap cap option cap	taux plafond taux plafonné taux d'intérêt maximum	tasa de interés máxima tope de la tasa de interés
I-223	interest rate capping	plafonnement des taux d'intérêt	limitación de las tasas de interés
I-224	interest rate differential, *see* interest differential		
I-225	interest rate equalization tax interest equalization tax	taxe de péréquation des taux d'intérêt	impuesto de equiparación de intereses impuesto de igualación de intereses

I-226	interest rate future	contrat financier à terme sur taux d'intérêt contrat à terme (normalisé) sur taux d'intérêt	futuro sobre tasas de interés contrato de tasas de interés a término contrato de tasas de interés a plazo
I-227	interest rate sensitivity, *see* interest sensitivity		
I-228	interest rate structure, *see* yield curve		
I-229	interest rate swap	échange de taux d'intérêt	swap de tasas de interés canje de tasas de interés
I-230	interest recapture clause	clause de recouvrement clause de récupération des intérêts	cláusula de recuperación de los intereses
I-231	interest receivable	intérêts à recevoir	intereses por cobrar
I-232	interest reduction bond	obligation à intérêts réduits obligation assortie d'intérêts réduits	bono a tasa de interés reducida
I-233	interest rescheduling interest retiming	rééchelonnement des paiements d'intérêts modification de l'échéancier des intérêts	reprogramación de los pagos de interés modificación del calendario de pago de intereses
I-234	interest retiming, *see* interest rescheduling		
I-235	interest sensitivity interest rate sensitivity	sensibilité-intérêt sensibilité aux taux d'intérêt	sensibilidad a la tasa de interés
I-236	interest subsidy	bonification d'intérêts bonification du taux d'intérêt	subvención de la tasa de interés
I-237	interest-bearing	rémunéré portant intérêts productif d'intérêts	con interés que devenga interés remunerado
I-238	interest-free loan	prêt sans intérêts prêt à taux zéro prêt non rémunéré	préstamo sin interés préstamo que no devenga interés préstamo no remunerado
I-239	intergovernmental grants or transfers	dons et transferts interadministrations	donaciones o transferencias intergubernamentales subvenciones o transferencias intergubernamentales
I-240	Intergovernmental Group of Twenty-Four on International Monetary Affairs and Development Group of Twenty-Four G-24	Groupe intergouvernemental des Vingt-Quatre pour les questions monétaires internationales et le développement Groupe des Vingt-Quatre G-24	Grupo Intergubernamental de los Veinticuatro para Asuntos Monetarios Internacionales y Desarrollo Grupo de los Veinticuatro G-24
I-241	intergovernmental transaction intragovernmental transaction	opérations interadministrations opération intra-administration	transacción intergubernamental transacción intragubernamental
I-242	interim assistance [IMF; PRGF]	assistance intérimaire assistance transitoire	asistencia transitoria asistencia durante el período intermedio

I-243	interim consultation	consultations intermédiaires	consulta intermedia
	[IMF]	consultations intermédiaires	consulta intermedia simplificada
	see also: bi-cycle; biennial consultation	simplifiées	
	interim simplified consultation		

| I-244 | interim disbursement | versement provisionnel | desembolso provisional |

| I-245 | interim Poverty Reduction Strategy Paper, *see* interim PRSP |

I-246	interim PRSP	DSRP intérimaire	DELP provisional
	[PRGF]	document intérimaire de stratégie	Documento Provisional de
	see also: full PRSP	pour la réduction de la pauvreté	Estrategia de Lucha contra la
	interim Poverty Reduction Strategy Paper		Pobreza
	I-PRSP		

| I-247 | interim simplified consultation, *see* interim consultation |

| I-248 | intermediate consumption | consommation intermédiaire | consumo intermedio |

| I-249 | intermediation | intermédiation | intermediación |

I-250	internal auditor	auditeur interne	auditor interno
		vérificateur interne des comptes	
		auditeur bancaire	
		contrôleur interne	
		commissaire aux comptes	

I-251	internal rate of return	taux interne de rentabilité	tasa interna de rentabilidad
	IRR	TIR	TIR
		rentabilité interne	tasa interna de retorno
			TIR

I-252	International Bank for Reconstruction and Development	Banque internationale pour la reconstruction et le	Banco Internacional de Reconstrucción y Fomento
	[World Bank Group]	développement	BIRF
	see also: World Bank	BIRD	
	IBRD		

| I-253 | International Banking Statistics, *see* international banking statistics |

I-254	international banking statistics	statistiques bancaires	estadísticas bancarias
	[IMF]	internationales	internacionales
	IBS	SBI	EBI
	International Banking Statistics		

| I-255 | international bond | obligation internationale | bono internacional |

I-256	international capital markets	marchés internationaux	mercados internacionales
	ICM	des capitaux	de capital
		marchés des capitaux	
		internationaux	

I-257	International Centre for Settlement of Investment Disputes	Centre international pour le règlement des différends relatifs	Centro Internacional de Arreglo de Diferencias Relativas
	[World Bank Group]	aux investissements	a Inversiones
	ICSID	CIRDI	CIADI

| I-258 | International Compilers Working Group on External Debt Statistics | Groupe de travail international des statisticiens spécialisés dans la | Grupo de Trabajo Internacional de Compiladores de Estadísticas |
| | [IMF, IBRD, OECD, BIS, Berne Union] | collecte des données sur la dette extérieure | sobre la Deuda Externa |

I-259	International Conference on National Poverty Reduction Strategies International Conference on Poverty Reduction Strategies	Conférence internationale sur les stratégies nationales de réduction de la pauvreté Conférence internationale sur les stratégies de réduction de la pauvreté	Conferencia Internacional sobre Estrategias de Lucha contra la Pobreza
I-260	International Conference on Poverty Reduction Strategies, *see* International Conference on National Poverty Reduction Strategies		
I-261	International Development Association [World Bank Group] IDA	Association internationale de développement AID IDA	Asociación Internacional de Fomento AIF
I-262	International Development Goals [OECD] *see also:* Millennium Development Goals IDGs 2015 targets	objectifs internationaux de développement objectifs de développement international objectifs pour l'an 2015	objetivos de desarrollo internacionales objetivos para el año 2015
I-263	International Energy Agency IEA	Agence internationale de l'énergie AIE	Agencia Internacional de Energía AIE
I-264	International Finance Corporation [World Bank Group] IFC	Société financière internationale SFI	Corporación Financiera Internacional CFI
I-265	*International Financial Statistics* [IMF] *IFS*	*Statistiques financières internationales* *SFI*	*International Financial Statistics* Estadísticas financieras internacionales [título no oficial]
I-266	*International Financial Statistics Yearbook* [IMF] *IFS Yearbook*	*Statistiques financières internationales — Annuaire* *Annuaire SFI*	*International Financial Statistics Yearbook* anuario de estadísticas financieras internacionales
I-267	international investment net position net external asset position	position extérieure globale nette	posición neta de inversión internacional posición neta de activos externos
I-268	international investment position [balance of payments] IIP	position extérieure globale PEG	posición de inversión internacional PII
I-269	International Labour Office ILO	Bureau international du travail BIT	Oficina Internacional del Trabajo OIT
I-270	International Labour Organisation ILO	Organisation internationale du travail OIT	Organización Internacional del Trabajo OIT
I-271	international lending process	apports financiers internationaux flux de financements internationaux opérations internationales de prêt	operaciones internacionales de préstamo transacciones internacionales de concesión de crédito
I-272	International Monetary and Financial Committee [IMF] IMFC	Comité monétaire et financier international CMFI	Comité Monetario y Financiero Internacional CMFI

I-273	International Monetary Fund IMF	Fonds monétaire international FMI	Fondo Monetario Internacional FMI
I-274	international rating agency, *see* credit rating agency		
I-275	international reserves [IMF] *see also:* foreign exchange reserves external reserves	réserves internationales réserves de change réserves officielles de change réserves publiques de change	reservas internacionales reservas externas reservas exteriores

I-276	*International Reserves and Foreign
	  Currency Liquidity: Guidelines for
	  a Data Template*
	[IMF]
		*Réserves internationales
		  et liquidité internationale —
		  Directives de déclaration des
		  données*
			*Reservas internacionales
			  y liquidez en moneda extranjera:
			  Pautas para una planilla de datos*

I-277	*International Standard
	  Classification of all Goods and
	  Services*
	[UN]
	ICGS
		Classification internationale type
		  de tous les biens et services
		ICGS
			Clasificación Internacional
			  Uniforme de todos los Bienes
			  y Servicios
			CIBS

I-278	*International Standard Industrial
	  Classification of all Economic
	  Activities*
	[UN]
	ISIC
		Classification internationale type,
		  par industrie, de toutes les
		  branches d'activité économique
		CITI
			Clasificación Industrial
			  Internacional Uniforme de todas
			  las Actividades Económicas
			CIIU

I-279	international trade, *see* trade		
I-280	interofficial transaction	transaction entre secteurs officiels	transacción interoficial
I-281	Interpreter, Chief [IMF]	Chef interprète	Jefe de Intérpretes
I-282	interrelated entries	inscriptions corrélatives	asientos relacionados asientos correlativos asientos interrelacionados entre sí
I-283	intervention	intervention	intervención administración provisional
I-284	intervention currency	monnaie d'intervention	moneda de intervención

I-285	intervention point
	see also: divergence indicator;
	  European Monetary System;
	  Exchange Rate Mechanism;
	  parity grid
	divergence threshold
	maximum fluctuation limit
		point d'intervention	punto de intervención

I-286	intragovernmental transaction, *see* intergovernmental transaction		
I-287	INV, *see* Investment Office		
I-288	inventory stock	stock	existencias inventario bienes de cambio
I-289	inventory accumulation	accumulation de stocks reconstitution des stocks	acumulación de existencias

I-290	inventory cycle, *see* stock cycle		
I-291	inventory investment	investissement en stocks constitution de stocks	inversión en existencias inversión en mercancías
I-292	inventory rundown rundown on inventories	déstockage	disminución de existencias liquidación de las existencias desacumulación de existencias
I-293	inverse term structure, *see* inverse yield curve		
I-294	inverse yield curve *see also:* yield curve inverse term structure	courbe inverse de rendements structure de taux d'intérêt décroissants	curva de rendimientos invertida
I-295	investment [finance]	investissement placement mise de fonds	inversión
I-296	Investment Account [IMF] IA	compte d'investissement	Cuenta de Inversiones
I-297	investment bank [USA merchant bank [GBR]	banque d'investissement banque d'affaires	banco de inversiones
I-298	investment budget	budget d'équipement budget d'investissement	presupuesto de inversiones presupuesto de capital
I-299	investment company *see also:* investment trust; mutual fund	société de placement société d'investissement	compañía de inversiones fondo de inversión
I-300	investment expenditure investment spending	dépenses d'investissement dépenses d'équipement	gasto de inversión
I-301	investment income	revenu(s) des investissements	renta de la inversión
I-302	Investment Office [IMF] INV	Bureau des placements	Oficina de Inversiones
I-303	investment spending, *see* investment expenditure		
I-304	investment trust *see also:* mutual fund closed-end investment company closed-end investment trust closed-end investment fund	société d'investissement à capital fixe SICAF société d'investissement fermée SIF fonds de placement à capital fixe	fondo de inversiones cerrado sociedad de inversión cerrada sociedad de inversión
I-305	invisible item, *see* invisibles		
I-306	invisible transaction [balance of payments]	transaction invisible transaction sur invisibles	transacción invisible transacción de invisibles
I-307	invisibles invisible item	invisible(s)	partida invisible invisibles

I-308	invitation to bid [procurement] *see also:* request for proposal ITB	appel d'offres avis de mise en adjudication avis d'appel d'offres	llamada a licitación apertura de concurso [*a veces*] convocatoria de ofertas anuncio de subasta
I-309	invoice value	valeur facturée prix de facture	valor facturado

I-310	inward investment	investissements étrangers dans le
		  pays
		investissements étrangers dans le
		  pays déclarant
			inversiones del exterior
			inversiones de no residentes en la
			  economía

I-311	inward-oriented economy	économie repliée sur elle-même
		économie fonctionnant en autarcie
			economía autárquica
			economía orientada al mercado
			  interno
			economía orientada hacia el
			  interior

I-312	IOT, *see* input-output table		
I-313	IPO, *see* initial public offering		
I-314	IPR, *see* import penetration ratio		
I-315	I-PRSP, *see* interim PRSP		
I-316	IRR, *see* internal rate of return		
I-317	IsDB, *see* Islamic Development Bank		
I-318	*ISIC, see International Standard Industrial Classification of all Economic Activities*		
I-319	Islamic Development Bank IsDB IDB	Banque islamique de développement BIsD BID	Banco Islámico de Desarrollo BIsD BID
I-320	isocost	isocoût	isocosto
I-321	isoquant	isoquant courbe isoquante	isocuanta
I-322	issuance cost, *see* issue cost		

I-323	issue a complaint (against a
	  member)
	[IMF]
		formuler une plainte (à l'encontre
		  d'un pays membre)
			formular una queja (contra un país
			  miembro)

I-324	issue cost issuance cost	coût d'émission	costo de emisión
I-325	issue syndicate, *see* underwriters		
I-326	issuer [BIS]	organisme d'émission émetteur	entidad emisora emisor
I-327	IT, *see* information technology		
I-328	IT, *see* inflation-targeting framework		
I-329	IT Services, *see* Information Technology Services		

I-330	ITB, *see* invitation to bid		
I-331	items in transit *see also:* float [banking]	éléments en transit éléments en route	partidas en tránsito

J

J-1	JAI, *see* Joint Africa Institute		
J-2	JCAAM, *see* Joint Ad Hoc Committee of Arrangements for the Annual Meetings of the Boards of Governors of the Bank and the Fund		
J-3	J-curve	courbe en J	curva en J curva en forma de J curva J
J-4	JDC, *see* Office of Executive Secretary, Joint Development Committee		
J-5	JL, *see* Joint Library		
J-6	job opening, *see* vacancy		
J-7	job seeker	demandeur d'emploi personne apte et disponible à la recherche d'un emploi PADRE	persona en busca de empleo persona que busca empleo
J-8	job vacancy, *see* vacancy		
J-9	jobber, *see* dealer		

J-10	Joint Ad Hoc Committee of
	  Arrangements for the Annual
	  Meetings of the Boards of
	  Governors of the Bank and the
	  Fund
	[IMF/World Bank]
	JCAAM
		Comité mixte *ad hoc* chargé des
		  dispositions pour l'Assemblée
		  annuelle des Conseils des
		  gouverneurs de la Banque et du
		  Fonds
		JCAAM
			Comité Conjunto Ad Hoc para la
			  Organización de las Reuniones
			  Anuales de las Juntas de
			  Gobernadores del Banco y del
			  Fondo
			JCAAM

J-11	Joint Africa Institute [IMF, AfDB, IBRD] JAI	Institut multilatéral d'Afrique IMA Institut conjoint pour l'Afrique	Instituto Multilateral Africano IMA
J-12	Joint Bank-Fund Library, *see* Joint Library		

J-13	Joint China-IMF Training Program
	[IMF]
	CTP
		Programme de formation conjoint
		  Chine–FMI
			Programa Conjunto de
			  Capacitación de China y el FMI
			PCC

J-14	Joint Development Committee, *see* Development Committee		
J-15	Joint External Debt Hub	site conjoint sur la dette extérieure	Central de Información sobre la Deuda Externa
J-16	joint Fund/World Bank AML Methodology Document, *see* AML Methodology Document		

J-17	Joint IMF-Arab Monetary Fund
	  Regional Training Program
		Programme régional de formation
		  FMI-Fonds monétaire arabe
			Programa Regional Conjunto de
			  Capacitación del FMI y el Fondo
			  Monetario Árabe

J-18	joint intervention	intervention conjointe intervention concertée	intervención conjunta

J-19	Joint Library
	[IMF]
	see also: Information Services
	  Division
	JL
	Joint Bank-Fund Library
		Bibliothèque commune
		  (de la Banque et du FMI)
			Biblioteca Conjunta
			  (del Banco y el Fondo)

J-20	Joint Ministerial Committee of the Boards of Governors of the Bank and the Fund on the Transfer of Real Resources to Developing Countries, *see* Development Committee		
J-21	Joint Procedures Committee [IMF/World Bank] JPC	Comité mixte de la procédure	Comisión Conjunta de Procedimiento CCP

J-22	Joint Regional Training Center
	  for Latin America in Brazil
	Brazil Training Center
	[IMF]
	BTC
		Centre régional multilatéral
		  pour l'Amérique latine au Brésil
			Centro Regional Conjunto
			  de Capacitación para América
			  Latina en Brasil
			Centro de Capacitación en Brasil
			CCB

J-23	Joint Secretariat [IMF/World Bank]	Secrétariat commun	Secretaría Conjunta
J-24	joint stock company	société par actions société de capitaux société à responsabilité limitée SARL société par actions à responsabilité illimitée [USA] société anonyme	sociedad por acciones
J-25	joint venture	coentreprise société en participation entreprise commune entreprise à risques communs opération conjointe	empresa conjunta asociación de empresas en participación operación conjunta sociedad en participación [ESP] sociedad accidental [ESP] unión transitoria de empresas [ARG]
J-26	Joint Vienna Institute [IMF] JVI	Institut multilatéral de Vienne IMV	Instituto Multilateral de Viena IMV
J-27	JPC, *see* Joint Procedures Committee		

J-28	judgmental forecast	prévision fondée sur une
		  appréciation
		prévision faisant intervenir un
		  élément d'appréciation
			pronóstico discrecional
			previsión discrecional
			pronóstico basado en una
			  evaluación discrecional de la
			  situación
			previsión basada en apreciaciones

J-29	junior debt, *see* subordinated debt		
J-30	junk bond	obligation à haut risque obligation de pacotille obligation déclassée	bono basura bono chatarra bono de alto riesgo
J-31	JVI, *see* Joint Vienna Institute		

K

K-1 kinked curve   courbe coudée   curva quebrada

K-2 know your clients, *see* client due diligence

K-3 know-how   savoir-faire   conocimientos técnicos
                                        connaissances techniques   conocimientos tecnológicos
                                        technologie   conocimientos especializados
                                                                               pericia
                                                                               know-how

K-4 KYC, *see* client due diligence

L

L-1 labor   travail   trabajo
                                        main-d'œuvre   mano de obra

L-2 labor contract, *see* collective bargaining agreement

L-3 labor cost   coût de main-d'œuvre   costo de la mano de obra
                                        coût du travail   costo laboral

L-4 labor force   population active   fuerza de trabajo
         workforce   main-d'œuvre disponible   fuerza laboral
         economically active population   población activa
         EAP   población económicamente activa
                                                                               PEA

L-5 labor force participation rate, *see* participation rate

L-6 labor hoarding   rétention de main-d'œuvre   mantenimiento preventivo de
                                        maintien d'effectifs surnuméraires   personal

L-7 labor income   revenu du travail   renta del trabajo

L-8 labor input   facteur travail   insumo de trabajo
                                        utilisation du facteur travail   insumo de mano de obra
                                        apport de travail   factor trabajo
                                        apport de main-d'œuvre   trabajo
                                        quantité de travail

L-9 labor intensity, *see* labor intensiveness

L-10 labor intensiveness   intensité du travail   uso intensivo de mano de obra
         labor intensity   degré d'intensité du travail
                                        proportion de main-d'œuvre

L-11 labor market   marché du travail   mercado de trabajo
                                        marché de l'emploi   mercado laboral

L-12 labor participation rate, *see* participation rate

L-13 labor productivity   productivité de la main-d'œuvre   productividad de la mano de obra
         productivity of labor   productivité du travail   productividad del trabajo

L-14 labor supply   offre de travail   oferta de mano de obra
                                        offre de main-d'œuvre   oferta de trabajo
                                        main-d'œuvre disponible   mano de obra disponible

L-15	labor-intensive	à forte intensité de main-d'œuvre à forte intensité de travail à coefficient élevé de main- d'œuvre	con uso intensivo de mano de obra que requiere mucha mano de obra
L-16	labor-output ratio	coefficient de travail rapport travail–production	razón trabajo/producto relación trabajo/producto
L-17	LACs, *see* least advanced countries		
L-18	lag time lag	décalage délai retard	retraso desfase retardo plazo de adaptación
L-19	lagged reserve accounting *see also:* contemporaneous reserve accounting	comptabilisation décalée des réserves obligatoires comptabilisation différée des réserves obligatoires	contabilización diferida de las reservas
L-20	lagged variable	variable décalée	variable desfasada variable rezagada variable retardada
L-21	lagging indicator *see also:* coincident indicator; leading indicator	indicateur retardé	indicador retrospectivo indicador desfasado indicador retardado indicador retrasado
L-22	land	terre	tierras terrenos
L-23	land development [agriculture] land improvement land reclamation	aménagement agricole aménagement foncier aménagement du territoire mise en culture mise en valeur des terres	aprovechamiento de tierras adecuación de tierras mejoramiento de tierras y terrenos mejora de tierras y terrenos
L-24	land development [urbanism]	viabilisation lotissement	urbanización
L-25	land improvement, *see* land development		
L-26	land reclamation, *see* land development		
L-27	land reform agrarian reform	réforme agraire réforme foncière	reforma agraria
L-28	landed cost landed price	prix au débarquement prix débarqué prix à quai	precio al desembarque precio en muelle
L-29	landed price, *see* landed cost		
L-30	landlocked country	pays enclavé pays sans littoral	país sin litoral país mediterráneo [Am. Lat.]
L-31	Language Services [IMF] LS	Services linguistiques	Servicios Lingüísticos

L-32	lapse of time completion of Article IV consultation [IMF]	achèvement des consultations de l'article IV par défaut d'opposition achèvement des consultations de l'article IV selon la procédure du défaut d'opposition	conclusión tácita de las consultas del Artículo IV
L-33	lapse of time decision [IMF] LOT	décision (adoptée) par défaut d'opposition	decisión tácita por vencimiento del plazo
L-34	Laspeyres index, *see* base-weighted index		
L-35	last in, first out [inventory accounting] LIFO	dernier entré, premier sorti DEPS	método de últimas entradas, primeras salidas método UEPS método LIFO
L-36	late filer [taxation]	contribuable retardataire	contribuyente moroso
L-37	late payment [IMF]	retard de paiement paiement en retard paiement tardif	pago atrasado pago en mora pago con retraso
L-38	Latin American Economic System SELA	Système économique latino-américain SELA	Sistema Económico Latinoamericano SELA
L-39	layoff pay, *see* severance pay		
L-40	LBO, *see* leveraged buyout		
L-41	LDCs, *see* less developed countries		
L-42	LDCs, *see* least advanced countries		
L-43	lead bank, *see* lead manager		
L-44	lead manager *see also:* co-manager lead bank lead underwriter syndicate leader	chef de file banque chef de file	banco director
L-45	lead underwriter, *see* lead manager		
L-46	leader market	marché pilote marché principal	mercado principal mercado líder
L-47	leading edge technology, *see* frontier technology		
L-48	leading indicator *see also:* coincident indicator; lagging indicator forward-looking indicator	indicateur avancé indicateur précurseur indicateur prospectif	indicador anticipado indicador adelantado indicador de pronóstico indicador prospectivo
L-49	leading sector	secteur pilote	sector líder sector que fija las pautas
L-50	leading technology, *see* frontier technology		

L-51	leakage [economics]	fuite déperdition détournement (de ressources)	filtración
L-52	leaseback	cession-bail	venta con pacto de arrendamiento retrocesión en arriendo
L-53	leased goods	matériel loué	bienes arrendados
L-54	leasing, *see* financial leasing		
L-55	least advanced countries LACs least developed countries LDCs	pays les moins avancés PMA	países menos adelantados PMA
L-56	least developed countries, *see* least advanced countries		
L-57	least-squares estimate LSE	estimation par les moindres carrés estimation des moindres carrés estimation obtenue par la méthode des moindres carrés	estimación por mínimos cuadrados estimación minimocuadrática
L-58	LEG, *see* Legal Department		
L-59	legal and regulatory framework	cadre légal et réglementaire	régimen legal y reglamentario marco legal y reglamentario marco legal y regulatorio ordenamiento jurídico
L-60	Legal Department [IMF] LEG	Département juridique	Departamento Jurídico
L-61	legal entity, *see* artificial person		
L-62	legal reserve, *see* statutory reserve		
L-63	legal reserve ratio, *see* required reserve ratio		
L-64	legal reserves, *see* statutory reserve		
L-65	lemming-like behavior, *see* herd behavior		
L-66	lender	prêteur	prestamista acreedor
L-67	lender of last resort LOLR LLR	prêteur de dernier ressort prêteur en dernier ressort	prestamista de última instancia prestamista de último recurso
L-68	lending capacity	capacité de prêt	capacidad prestable capacidad de concesión de préstamos capacidad de préstamo
L-69	lending ceiling, *see* credit ceiling		
L-70	lending funds loanable funds	fonds prêtables	fondos prestables

L-71	lending into arrears policy [IMF]	politique de prêt aux pays en situation d'arriérés	política de concesión de préstamos a países con atrasos
L-72	lending minus repayment	prêts moins recouvrements	concesión de préstamos menos reembolsos concesión de préstamos menos recuperaciones
L-73	lending rate loan rate	taux prêteur taux débiteur taux d'intérêt des prêts	tasa de interés de los préstamos tasa de los préstamos tasa activa
L-74	less developed countries LDCs	pays en voie de développement PVD pays économiquement peu développés	países menos desarrollados PMD
L-75	lessor	bailleur	arrendador arrendador(a)
L-76	letter of appointment [IMF]	lettre d'engagement	carta de nombramiento
L-77	letter of credit, commercial	lettre de crédit commercial	carta de crédito comercial
L-78	Letter of Intent [IMF] LOI	lettre d'intention	carta de intención
L-79	letter of transmittal cover letter cover note	lettre d'accompagnement	carta de remisión nota de envío carta de presentación
L-80	level playing field	conditions d'égalité uniformité de traitement concurrence sur un pied d'égalité concurrence sur les mêmes bases	condiciones igualitarias igualdad de condiciones condiciones equitativas tratamiento igualitario terreno neutral
L-81	level-based interest surcharge, *see* level-based surcharge		
L-82	level-based surcharge [IMF] *see also:* surcharge to the basic rate of charge level-based interest surcharge	commission additionnelle proportionnelle à l'encours des crédits commission additionnelle majoration des commissions de base	sobretasa basada en el nivel de uso de recursos sobretasa basada en el nivel del crédito pendiente de reembolso
L-83	leveling off	plafonnement stabilisation tassement	nivelación estabilización
L-84	leverage, *see* gearing ratio		
L-85	leverage	influence moyens d'action prise sur pouvoir	influencia poder ventaja

L-86	leveraged buyout LBO leveraged takeover	rachat par l'emprunt prise de contrôle par l'emprunt leveraged buy out offre publique d'achat à crédit OPA à crédit rachat par recours à des crédits gagés	adquisición apalancada

L-87	leveraged, highly	à fort effet de levier
		fortement endetté
		caractérisé par un fort degré
		  d'endettement
			con un elevado nivel de
			  endeudamiento
			con alto apalancamiento
			con un alto grado de
			  apalancamiento

L-88	leveraged management buyout LMBO	rachat d'entreprise par les salariés reprise d'entreprise par les salariés RES	adquisición de una empresa por parte de sus empleados
L-89	leveraged takeover, *see* leveraged buyout		
L-90	levy	prélèvement	gravamen
L-91	liabilities	passif(s) engagements dettes obligations ensemble des engagements	pasivos pasivo obligaciones
L-92	liability	passif élément du passif total des engagements	pasivo elemento del pasivo rubro del pasivo
L-93	liability insurance	assurance responsabilité civile	seguro de responsabilidad civil
L-94	liability operation	opération sur passif transaction sur passif	operación pasiva
L-95	liability position, *see* debtor position		
L-96	liberal trade *see also:* free trade	commerce libéral	comercio liberal
L-97	liberalization	libéralisation ouverture libération	liberalización apertura liberación

L-98	liberalization of the capital account
	[IMF]
	see also: capital account
	  convertibility; freedom of capital
	  movements; open capital account
		libéralisation des mouvements
		  de capitaux
			liberalización de la cuenta
			  de capital

L-99	Libor, *see* London Interbank Offered Rate		
L-100	Librarian, Chief [IMF]	Bibliothécaire en chef	Jefe de Biblioteca
L-101	LIC, *see* low-income country		
L-102	life, *see* term of maturity		

L-103	life annuity *see also:* lifetime income; reverse mortgage	rente viagère	renta vitalicia contrato de renta vitalicia
L-104	life cycle hypothesis life cycle theory	théorie du cycle de vie	teoría del ciclo de vida teoría del ciclo vital
L-105	life cycle theory, *see* life cycle hypothesis		
L-106	life expectancy	durée utile probable	vida útil prevista vida útil probable
L-107	lifetime income *see also:* life annuity	revenu d'une vie entière revenu engendré pendant une vie revenu viager	ingreso vitalicio
L-108	LIFO, *see* last in, first out		
L-109	likelihood function	fonction de vraisemblance	función de verosimilitud
L-110	limited recourse financing	financement avec possibilité de recours limité	financiamiento con posibilidad de recurso limitado
L-111	line of credit credit line	ligne de crédit	línea de crédito
L-112	linear programming	programmation linéaire	programación lineal
L-113	liquid asset portfolio, *see* liquidity portfolio		
L-114	liquid asset(s) *see also:* current asset(s); quick asset(s)	liquidités avoirs liquides actifs liquides disponibilités	activo(s) líquido(s)
L-115	liquid liability *see also:* current liability	engagement exigible engagement à court terme engagement à très court terme exigibilité	pasivo líquido pasivo a muy corto plazo pasivo exigible a corto plazo
L-116	liquidation winding up winding down	liquidation	liquidación
L-117	liquidation of the Fund [IMF]	liquidation du FMI	disolución del FMI
L-118	liquidity control, *see* liquidity management		
L-119	liquidity crisis, *see* liquidity squeeze		
L-120	liquidity loan	prêt de liquidités	préstamo de liquidez préstamo de recursos líquidos
L-121	liquidity management liquidity control	régulation de la liquidité	regulación de la liquidez control de la liquidez gestión de la liquidez
L-122	liquidity of Fund resources [IMF]	liquidité des ressources du FMI	liquidez de los recursos del FMI

L-123	liquidity overhang excess liquidity monetary overhang	excès de liquidité liquidité(s) excédentaire(s) surliquidité	exceso de liquidez excedente de liquidez
L-124	liquidity portfolio liquid asset portfolio	portefeuille liquide	cartera líquida cartera de activos líquidos
L-125	liquidity position [IMF]	position de liquidité	nivel de liquidez posición de liquidez
L-126	liquidity preference	préférence pour la liquidité	preferencia por la liquidez
L-127	liquidity ratio, *see* cash ratio		
L-128	liquidity ratio [IMF]	ratio de liquidité coefficient de liquidité	coeficiente de liquidez índice de liquidez
L-129	liquidity requirement	liquidité obligatoire	liquidez obligatoria requisito de liquidez
L-130	liquidity squeeze liquidity crisis	crise de liquidité compression des liquidités	contracción de la liquidez restricción de la liquidez crisis de liquidez
L-131	liquidity trap money trap	trappe de liquidité(s) trappe monétaire	trampa de liquidez trampa monetaria
L-132	liquidity-asset ratio	ratio liquidité/actif	razón liquidez/activo
L-133	listed security quoted security	titre officiellement coté titre inscrit à la cote officielle valeur (mobilière) cotée en bourse	título cotizado en bolsa valor admitido a cotización oficial
L-134	listing of securities	inscription à la cote cotation en bourse admission de titres à la cote officielle	inscripción de valores en la bolsa admisión de valores en bolsa cotización de títulos en bolsa
L-135	LLR, *see* lender of last resort		
L-136	LMBO, *see* leveraged management buyout		
L-137	LMIC, *see* lower-middle-income country		
L-138	loan	prêt emprunt avance	préstamo
L-139	Loan Account, *see* PRGF Trust Loan Account		
L-140	loan agreement	accord de prêt	convenio de préstamo contrato de préstamo acuerdo de préstamo
L-141	loan capital, *see* debt capital		
L-142	loan claim	créance (au titre de prêts)	créditos por préstamos activos por concepto de préstamos
L-143	loan classification *see also:* classified loan	classement des prêts	clasificación de préstamos

L-144	loan commitment	engagement de prêt	compromiso de préstamo
			oferta de préstamo
L-145	loan loss	créance irrécouvrable	deuda incobrable
	see also: doubtful loan	créance perdue	pérdida por préstamos incobrables
	loss	perte sur prêt	
L-146	loan loss provision	provision pour créances	previsión para deudas incobrables
	allowance for loan losses	irrécouvrables	
	allowance for bad debts	réserves pour créances douteuses	
		provision pour pertes sur prêts	
L-147	loan loss reserve	réserve pour pertes sur prêts	reservas para préstamos incobrables
			reservas para pérdidas por concepto de préstamos
L-148	loan mix	composition d'un prêt	composición de un préstamo
		dosage des crédits	
L-149	loan package, *see* financial shield		
L-150	loan portfolio	portefeuille de prêts	cartera de préstamos
			cartera crediticia
L-151	loan rate, *see* lending rate		
L-152	loan resources	ressources de prêt	recursos para préstamos
	see also: subsidy resources		recursos prestables
L-153	loan swap	échange de créances	swap de préstamos
			canje de préstamos
L-154	loanable funds, *see* lending funds		
L-155	loans extended	prêts accordés	préstamos concedidos
L-156	local currency, *see* domestic currency		
L-157	local currency clause	clause de paiements de	cláusula de pagos de contrapartida
	[Paris Club]	contrepartie en monnaie nationale	en moneda nacional
L-158	local government	administration locale	gobierno local
		administration publique locale	
		collectivité locale	
		collectivité territoriale	
		administration territoriale	
L-159	LOI, *see* Letter of Intent		
L-160	LOLR, *see* lender of last resort		
L-161	Lombard facility	guichet Lombard	servicio de crédito Lombard
L-162	Lombard rate	taux des avances sur titres	tasa Lombard
		taux Lombard	
		taux des crédits Lombard	

L-163 Lomé Convention, *see* ACP-EEC Convention (between the African, Caribbean and Pacific States and the European Economic Community)

L-164	London interbank offered rate Libor	taux interbancaire offert à Londres taux de l'euromarché interbancaire de Londres Libor	tasa interbancaria de oferta de Londres Libor
L-165	long position	position longue position acheteur	posición sobrecomprada posición larga
L-166	long-term interest rate, *see* long-term rate		
L-167	long-term rate long-term interest rate	taux d'intérêt à long terme taux à long terme	tasa a largo plazo tasa de interés a largo plazo
L-168	long-term trend	tendance à long terme tendance de longue période	tendencia a largo plazo
L-169	loophole *see also:* tax loophole	échappatoire lacune (de la loi) faille	laguna de la ley laguna de la legislación escapatoria vacío legislativo
L-170	loss, *see* loan loss		
L-171	loss carryback, *see* tax loss carryback		
L-172	loss carryforward, *see* carryforward		
L-173	loss carryover, *see* carryforward		
L-174	LOT, *see* lapse of time decision		
L-175	lower-middle-income country LMIC	pays à revenu intermédiaire (tranche inférieure) PRITI tranche inférieure de la catégorie des pays à revenu intermédiaire	país de ingreso mediano bajo PIMB
L-176	low-income country LIC	pays à faible revenu	país de bajo ingreso
L-177	low-inflation country	pays à faible inflation	país de baja inflación país con baja tasa de inflación
L-178	LS, *see* Language Services		
L-179	LSE, *see* least-squares estimate		
L-180	lump sum lump sum payment	forfait somme forfaitaire paiement unique paiement en capital versement unique versement global	tanto alzado cantidad alzada pago de una suma fija suma fija monto global suma global
L-181	lump sum payment, *see* lump sum		
L-182	lumpiness	concentration	concentración indivisibilidad
L-183	Lyon terms Lyons terms	conditions de Lyon dispositions de Lyon	condiciones de Lyon

M-7	macro-critical issue	question essentielle pour la situation macroéconomique	cuestión esencial para la situación macroeconómica
M-8	macroeconomic balance exchange rate MBER	taux de change d'équilibre macroéconomique	tipo de cambio de equilibrio macroeconómico
M-9	Macroeconomic Studies Division [IMF]	Division des études macroéconomiques	División de Estudios Macroeconómicos
M-10	macroprudential indicator MPI	indicateur macroprudentiel IMP	indicador macroprudencial IMP
M-11	macroprudential policy	politique macroprudentielle	política macroprudencial
M-12	maintenance of value [IMF] *see also:* valuation adjustment	maintien de la valeur	mantenimiento de valor
M-13	maintenance of value obligation [IMF]	obligation de maintien de la valeur	obligación de mantenimiento del valor (de las tenencias de DEG) obligación de mantener el valor
M-14	major borrowers	principaux pays emprunteurs	principales países prestatarios
M-15	major industrial countries	principaux pays industrialisés	principales países industriales
M-16	majority action clause [debt restructuring]	clause de décision à la majorité clause d'action majoritaire	cláusula de decisión por mayoría

M-19	majority ownership majority interest majority control	participation majoritaire détention de la majorité des actions	participación mayoritaria control accionario
M-20	maladjustment	désajustement déséquilibre	desajuste desequilibrio

M-21	managed floating dirty float	flottement contrôlé flottement dirigé flottement assisté flottement soutenu flottement impur	flotación regulada flotación controlada flotación dirigida flotación impura flotación sucia
M-22	managed floating with no predetermined path for the exchange rate [IMF exchange rate classification system, 2006]	flottement dirigé sans annonce préalable de la trajectoire du taux de change	flotación dirigida sin una trayectoria predeterminada del tipo de cambio
M-23	managed rate	taux dirigé taux orienté	tipo de cambio regulado tipo de cambio controlado tipo de cambio dirigido
M-24	managed trade	commerce organisé commerce réglementé organisation des échanges (commerciaux)	comercio dirigido comercio regulado comercio controlado
M-25	Management [IMF]	Direction	Gerencia, la
M-26	management contract, *see* performance contract		
M-27	management fee [securities]	commission de gérance commission de direction commission de gestion	comisión de gestión comisión por administración
M-28	management letter [IMF]	lettre de recommandations	carta de recomendaciones
M-29	Managing Director [IMF] MD	Directeur général	Director Gerente
M-30	Managing Director, Acting [IMF]	Directeur général par intérim	Director Gerente Interino
M-31	Managing Director, Temporary Acting [IMF]	Directeur général par intérim à titre provisoire	Director Gerente Interino temporal
M-32	mandatory prepayment clause [London Club]	clause de paiement anticipé obligatoire	cláusula de pago anticipado obligatorio
M-33	mandatory repurchase [IMF]	rachat obligatoire	recompra obligatoria
M-34	*Manual on Fiscal Transparency* [IMF] *see also: Code of Good Practices on Fiscal Transparency-- Declaration on Principles*	*Manuel sur la transparence des finances publiques*	*Manual de Transparencia Fiscal*
M-35	manufactured goods, *see* manufactures		
M-36	manufactures manufactured goods	produits manufacturés biens manufacturés	manufacturas productos manufacturados productos elaborados

M-37	manufacturing manufacturing industry	industrie manufacturière industrie de transformation	industria manufacturera industria fabril manufacturas
M-38	manufacturing industry, *see* manufacturing		
M-39	margin	dépôt de garantie	margen depósito de garantía
M-40	margin, *see* initial margin		
M-41	margin account	compte d'avances (à découvert) compte sur marge	cuenta de margen cuenta para comprar al margen cuenta para operaciones en descubierto
M-42	marginal borrower	emprunteur marginal	prestatario marginal

M-43	marginal cost pricing	détermination du prix en fonction
		  du coût marginal
			determinación del precio en
			  función del costo marginal

M-44	marginal propensity to consume	propension marginale à consommer	propensión marginal al consumo propensión marginal a consumir
M-45	marginal propensity to save	propension marginale à épargner	propensión marginal al ahorro propensión marginal a ahorrar
M-46	marginal rate [taxation]	taux marginal	tasa marginal

M-47	marginal reserve requirement	coefficient marginal de réserves
		  obligatoires
			coeficiente marginal de encaje
			coeficiente marginal de reserva
			  obligatoria
			encaje marginal

M-48	mark a position to market, *see* mark to market		

M-49	mark to market
	mark a position to market
	mark to the market
	MTM
		réévaluer ses avoirs au(x) cours
		  du marché
			revaluar una posición a precios
			  de mercado
			actualizar la valoración de una
			  posición

M-50	mark to the market, *see* mark to market		
M-51	marked check, *see* certified check		
M-52	market borrowers	pays emprunteurs sur les marchés	prestatarios en los mercados
M-53	market breadth	étendue du marché diversification du marché	amplitud del mercado diversificación del mercado
M-54	market capitalization	capitalisation boursière valeur en bourse	capitalización bursátil capitalización de mercado capitalización en el mercado
M-55	market clearing price, *see* clearing price		
M-56	market depth, *see* depth of the market		

M-57	market economy *see also:* enterprise economy; free enterprise economy market-oriented economy	économie de marché	economía de mercado economía orientada al mercado
M-58	market failure	défaillance du marché marché inopérant inefficacité du marché	falla de mercado fallo del mercado mal funcionamiento del mercado ineficacia del mercado imperfección del mercado deficiencia del mercado
M-59	market financing	financement sur le marché financement obtenu sur le marché	financiamiento de mercado
M-60	market glut	offre excédentaire engorgement du marché	saturación del mercado sobreoferta
M-61	market maker	teneur de marché mainteneur de marché contrepartiste	agente creador de mercado creador de mercado formador de mercado
M-62	market power	pouvoir de marché puissance de marché puissance sur le marché puissance commerciale influence économique	poder de mercado influencia en el mercado
M-63	market price equivalent	valeur comparable au prix du marché	equivalente de precios de mercado
M-64	market rate *see also:* prevailing market rate	taux du marché taux pratiqué sur le marché	tasa del mercado tasa de mercado tasa de interés de mercado
M-65	market risk, *see* systematic risk		
M-66	market share	part de marché	participación en el mercado cuota de mercado

M-67	market sharing arrangement	accord de partage des marchés	acuerdo de repartición de
			  mercados
			acuerdo de distribución del
			  mercado

M-68	market size	taille du marché grandeur du marché	dimensión del mercado magnitud del mercado tamaño del mercado
M-69	market terms commercial terms hard terms conventional terms conventional market terms	conditions du marché conditions ordinaires conditions bancaires conditions classiques	condiciones del mercado condiciones ordinarias condiciones corrientes
M-70	market value *see also:* fair price fair market value sale value	valeur marchande valeur loyale et marchande valeur de marché valeur vénale valeur boursière valeur en bourse	valor de mercado valor venal cotización del mercado valor de venta

M-71	market yield	rendement du marché rendement sur le marché	rentabilidad de mercado rendimiento de mercado
M-72	marketable good	bien marchand bien commercialisable	bien comerciable bien comercializable
M-73	marketable security, *see* negotiable security		
M-74	market-based approach	techniques inspirées du marché techniques faisant appel au jeu de l'offre et de la demande	enfoque basado en el mercado enfoque basado en técnicas de mercado
M-75	market-based debt reduction	opérations de réduction de la dette qui s'inspirent du marché opérations de réduction de la dette fondées sur le marché	operaciones de reducción de la deuda basadas en el mercado
M-76	market-friendly policy market-oriented policy	politique favorable à l'économie de marché politique favorable à la mise en place de l'économie de marché	política favorable a la economía de mercado política orientada al mercado
M-77	marketing board	office de commercialisation	junta de comercialización
M-78	marketing channels, *see* marketing facilities		
M-79	marketing facilities marketing channels	circuits commerciaux	circuitos de comercialización medios de comercialización
M-80	market-oriented economy, *see* market economy		
M-81	market-oriented policy, *see* market-friendly policy		
M-82	market-related terms	conditions du marché	condiciones de mercado
M-83	markup *see also:* profit margin	taux de marque marge brute marge bénéficiaire brute majoration de prix	margen de beneficio margen de utilidad margen de comercialización
M-84	matched sale-purchase agreement, *see* reverse operation		
M-85	matching grant	don proportionnel don de contrepartie subvention proportionnelle subvention de contrepartie	subvención de contrapartida subvención proporcional subvención compensatoria
M-86	mathematical expectation, *see* expected value		
M-87	MATIF, *see* French international financial futures market		
M-88	maturation [USA Treasury] *see also:* graduation	reclassement cessation des crédits (de l'IDA)	maduración
M-89	mature [finance]	arriver à échéance	vencer
M-90	mature stabilizer *see also:* early stabilizer	pays en phase de stabilisation avancée	país ya estabilizado país en una etapa avanzada del proceso de estabilización

M-91	mature technology	technologie mise au point technologie qui a fait ses preuves technologie établie	tecnología madura tecnología establecida
M-92	maturity, *see* term of maturity		
M-93	maturity, *see* maturity date		
M-94	maturity date maturity	échéance date d'échéance	vencimiento fecha de vencimiento
M-95	maturity gap, *see* maturity mismatch		
M-96	maturity mismatch *see also:* maturity transformation maturity gap	asymétrie des échéances non-concordance des échéances	desfase de vencimientos descalce de vencimientos
M-97	maturity period [Paris Club]	période d'amortissement	período de vencimiento
M-98	maturity profile maturity structure repayment profile	calendrier d'échéances structure des échéances échéancier (de remboursement)	perfil de vencimientos estructura de vencimientos estructura de los reembolsos perfil de reembolsos calendario de vencimientos
M-99	maturity structure, *see* maturity profile		
M-100	maturity transformation *see also:* maturity mismatch	transformation des échéances	transformación de los vencimientos

M-101	maximum access entitlement
	[IMF]
		plafond d'accès aux ressources du
		    FMI
			límite máximo de acceso
			límite máximo de acceso a los
			    recursos del FMI

M-102	maximum fluctuation limit, *see* intervention point		
M-103	MBER, *see* macroeconomic balance exchange rate		
M-104	MCD, *see* Middle East and Central Asia Department		
M-105	MCM, *see* Monetary and Capital Markets Department		
M-106	MD, *see* Managing Director		
M-107	MDF, *see* debt reduction fund		
M-108	MDGs, *see* Millennium Development Goals		
M-109	MDRI, *see* Multilateral Debt Relief Initiative		

M-110	MDRI-I Trust
	see also: Multilateral Debt Relief
	Initiative
		Compte de fiducie de l'initiative
		    d'allégement de la dette
		    multilatérale-I
		Compte IADM-I
			Cuenta Fiduciaria de la IADM-I

M-111	MDRI-II Trust
	see also: Multilateral Debt Relief
	Initiative
		Compte de fiducie de l'initiative
		    d'allégement de la dette
		    multilatérale-II
		Compte IADM-II
			Cuenta Fiduciaria de la IADM-II

M-112	mean, *see* arithmetic mean		

M-113	means of payment	moyen de paiement	medio de pago
M-114	means-tested assistance *see also:* income-tested assistance	assistance subordonnée au niveau des ressources assistance sous conditions de ressources	asistencia condicionada al nivel de recursos del beneficiario asistencia condicionada al patrimonio
M-115	Media Relations Division [IMF]	Division relations avec les médias	División de Relaciones con los Medios
M-116	median	médiane	mediana
M-117	medium of exchange	moyen d'échange intermédiaire d'échanges	medio de cambio instrumento de cambio
M-118	medium-term instrument [IMF]	instrument à moyen terme	instrumento a mediano plazo
M-119	medium-term interest rate, *see* medium-term rate		
M-120	medium-term loan	prêt à moyen terme	préstamo a mediano plazo préstamo a plazo medio
M-121	medium-term rate medium-term interest rate	taux d'intérêt à moyen terme	tasa a mediano plazo tasa a plazo medio tasa de interés a mediano plazo
M-122	MEFP, *see* Memorandum on Economic and Financial Policies		
M-123	member [IMF] member country	État membre pays membre	país miembro país
M-124	member country, *see* member		
M-125	membership [IMF]	États membres pays membres qualité de membre	países miembros calidad de miembro
M-126	membership committee, *see* Committee on Membership -- [country]		
M-127	membership quota quota in the Fund quota	quote-part au FMI quote-part	cuota en el FMI cuota
M-128	membership resolution [IMF]	résolution d'admission	resolución de admisión
M-129	memorandum account *see also:* suspense account	compte d'ordre	cuenta de orden
M-130	memorandum entry memorandum item	pour mémoire poste pour mémoire	partida informativa *pro memoria* cuentas de orden
M-131	memorandum item, *see* memorandum entry		

M-132	memorandum of understanding [IMF] *see also:* Memorandum on Economic and Financial Policies [IMF] MOU	protocole d'accord	memorando de entendimiento
M-133	Memorandum on Economic and Financial Policies [IMF] *see also:* memorandum of understanding MEFP	mémorandum de politique économique et financière	Memorando de Política Económica y Financiera
M-134	menu approach [debt restructuring]	approche à la carte approche du menu méthode du menu	método de la lista de opciones menú de opciones enfoque del menú
M-135	menu item [debt restructuring]	option option du menu	opción del menú
M-136	mercantile agency, *see* credit rating agency		
M-137	merchant bank, *see* investment bank		
M-138	MERCOSUR, *see* Southern Common Market		
M-139	merit good *see also:* public good	bien d'intérêt social bien tutélaire bien sous tutelle	bien de interés social
M-140	merit increase	augmentation au mérite	aumento por mérito
M-141	MERM, *see* Multilateral Exchange Rate Model		
M-142	metadata [IMF]	métadonnées	metadatos
M-143	Mexico/Latin Caribbean Division [IMF]	Division Mexique et pays latins des Caraïbes	División de México y los Países Latinos del Caribe
M-144	MFN clause, *see* most favored nation clause		
M-145	MFP Code, *see* Code of Good Practices on Transparency in Monetary and Financial Policies		
M-146	*MFSM, see Monetary and Financial Statistics Manual*		
M-147	Middle East and Central Asia Department [IMF] MCD	Département Moyen-Orient et Asie centrale	Departamento del Oriente Medio y Asia Central
M-148	Middle East and Central Asia Regional Division [IMF]	Division Moyen-Orient et Asie centrale	División de la Región de Oriente Medio y Asia Central
M-149	Middle Eastern Division [IMF]	Division Moyen-Orient	División de Oriente Medio
M-150	middle rate midpoint rate	taux médian	tipo de cambio intermedio tipo intermedio
M-151	midpoint rate, *see* middle rate		

M-152	midterm review [IMF programs]	revue de mi-période examen à mi-parcours	examen de mitad de período revisión de mitad de período
M-153	midyear review [IMF]	réexamen en milieu d'exercice examen en milieu d'exercice examen en milieu d'année	examen de mitad de ejercicio examen de mitad de año revisión de medio ejercicio
M-154	MIGA, *see* Multilateral Investment Guarantee Agency		
M-155	migrant labor, *see* seasonal labor		
M-156	migrants' remittances *see also:* migrants' transfers	envois de fonds des travailleurs émigrés	remesas de emigrantes remesas de migrantes
M-157	migrants' transfers *see also:* migrants' remittances	transferts des migrants	transferencias de emigrantes
M-158	Millennium Development Goals MDGs	objectifs du Millénaire pour le développement OMD	Objetivos de Desarrollo del Milenio ODM
M-159	mineral rights	droits tréfonciers droits d'exploitation du sous-sol	derechos de explotación minera derechos mineros derechos sobre yacimientos de minerales
M-160	minimum acceptable bid stop-out price cut-off price	prix minimum demandé	precio de oferta mínimo aceptable oferta mínima aceptable precio de corte
M-161	minimum cash requirement, *see* cash ratio requirement		
M-162	minimum lending rate, *see* discount rate		
M-163	minimum living wage	salaire minimum vital	salario mínimo vital
M-164	minimum reserve ratio, *see* required reserve ratio		
M-165	minimum reserve requirement, *see* reserve requirement		
M-166	mining	industries extractives	industria minera minería
M-167	mining and mineral resources, manufacturing, and construction	industries extractives et ressources minérales, industries de transformation, bâtiment et travaux publics	minería y recursos minerales, manufacturas y construcción
M-168	minting, *see* coinage		
M-169	misallocation of resources	mauvaise affectation de(s) ressources	asignación ineficiente de los recursos asignación desacertada de los recursos
M-170	misreporting [IMF]	communication d'informations inexactes communication d'informations erronées	declaración de datos inexactos

M-171	mission chief [IMF] mission head head of mission chief of mission	chef de mission	jefe de misión jefe de la misión
M-172	mission head, *see* mission chief		
M-173	mission report [IMF]	rapport de mission	informe de la misión
M-174	mixed enterprise, *see* semipublic enterprise		
M-175	MLR, *see* discount rate		
M-176	mode	mode	moda
M-177	monetary accommodation, *see* accommodative monetary policy		
M-178	monetary aggregate *see also:* money supply M1, M2, etc.	agrégat monétaire	agregado monetario
M-179	monetary aggregate anchor [IMF monetary policy framework classification system, 2006]	ancrage des agrégats monétaires	uso de un agregado monetario como ancla
M-180	Monetary and Capital Markets Department MCM	Département des marchés monétaires et de capitaux	Departamento de Mercados Monetarios y de Capital
M-181	Monetary and Exchange Regimes Division [IMF]	Division régimes monétaires et régimes de change	División de Regímenes Monetarios y Cambiarios
M-182	*Monetary and Financial Statistics Manual* MFSM	*Manuel de statistiques monétaires et financières* MSMF	*Manual de estadísticas monetarias y financieras* MEMF
M-183	monetary asset	avoir monétaire actif monétaire	activo monetario
M-184	monetary authorities	autorités monétaires	autoridades monetarias
M-185	monetary base, *see* base money		
M-186	monetary board *see also:* currency board arrangement; foreign exchange equalization fund	conseil monétaire comité monétaire	junta monetaria comisión monetaria
M-187	monetary control *see also:* monetary management	régulation monétaire	control monetario
M-188	monetary dominance *see also:* fiscal dominance	domination de la politique monétaire (sur la politique budgétaire)	predominio de la política monetaria dominio de la política monetaria
M-189	monetary easing, *see* accommodative monetary policy		
M-190	monetary economics	économie monétaire	economía monetaria

M-191	monetary economy monetized economy	économie monétaire économie monétisée	economía monetizada economía monetaria
M-192	monetary flow	flux monétaire	flujo monetario
M-193	monetary gold	or monétaire	oro monetario
M-194	monetary management *see also:* monetary control	régulation monétaire conduite de la politique monétaire	gestión monetaria regulación monetaria
M-195	monetary overhang, *see* liquidity overhang		
M-196	monetary policy framework	cadre de politique monétaire	marco de política monetaria régimen de política monetaria
M-197	monetary restraint, *see* monetary tightening		
M-198	monetary stringency, *see* monetary tightening		
M-199	monetary survey	situation monétaire	panorama monetario

M-200	monetary tightening
	tight monetary policy
	tightening
	monetary restraint
	monetary stringency
	tight money
	tight money policy
		resserrement de la politique
		  monétaire
		durcissement de la politique
		  monétaire
		politique de resserrement du crédit
			austeridad monetaria
			restricción monetaria
			contracción monetaria
			aplicación de una política
			  monetaria restrictiva
			política monetaria restrictiva

M-201	monetization	monétisation	monetización
M-202	monetization of government debt monetization of the deficit	monétisation de la dette publique	monetización de la deuda pública monetización del déficit
M-203	monetization of the deficit, *see* monetization of government debt		
M-204	monetization of the economy	monétisation (de l'économie) passage à l'économie monétaire	monetización de la economía
M-205	monetized economy, *see* monetary economy		
M-206	money	monnaie argent espèces fonds	dinero moneda
M-207	money creation	création de monnaie création monétaire	creación de dinero creación monetaria
M-208	money GDP, *see* nominal GDP		
M-209	money illusion	illusion monétaire	ilusión monetaria
M-210	money income	revenu nominal	ingreso nominal ingreso monetario
M-211	money market	marché monétaire marché de l'argent	mercado monetario mercado de dinero mercado del dinero
M-212	money multiplier	multiplicateur monétaire coefficient d'expansion monétaire	multiplicador monetario multiplicador del dinero

M-213	money purchase plan, *see* defined contribution plan		
M-214	money rate	taux de l'argent loyer de l'argent	tasa de interés a corto plazo costo del dinero
M-215	money stock, *see* money supply		
M-216	money supply *ee also*: monetary aggregate supply of money M money stock stock of money	masse monétaire stock de monnaie	oferta de dinero oferta monetaria masa monetaria cantidad de dinero
M-217	money trap, *see* liquidity trap		
M-218	money value, *see* nominal value		
M-219	money wage nominal wage	salaire nominal	salario nominal
M-220	monocurrency loan, *see* single currency loan		
M-221	moonlighting *see also:* undeclared employment	cumul d'emplois travail au noir	segundo empleo pluriempleo
M-222	moral hazard	aléa moral risque d'abus risque d'excès risque moral risque d'effet pervers risque de négligence aléa de moralité	riesgo moral
M-223	moral suasion	persuasion pression morale influence morale	presión moral persuasión moral disuasión moral
M-224	moratorium interest, *see* moratory interest		
M-225	moratory interest [Paris Club] *see also:* penalty interest moratorium interest	intérêts moratoires intérêts de retard	interés por mora interés por atraso en el pago interés moratorio
M-226	more demanding standard, *see* Special Data Dissemination Standard		
M-227	mortgage	prêt hypothécaire	hipoteca
M-228	mortgage bank mortgage credit institution	banque de crédit hypothécaire institution de crédit hypothécaire	banco hipotecario institución de crédito hipotecario
M-229	mortgage credit institution, *see* mortgage bank		
M-230	mortgage redemption	extinction remboursement (intégral) purge	cancelación de hipoteca extinción

M-231	most favored nation clause
	[Paris Club]
	MFN clause
		clause de la nation la plus
		  favorisée
		clause NPF
			cláusula de la nación más
			  favorecida
			cláusula NMF

M-232	MOU, *see* memorandum of understanding		
M-233	moving average	moyenne mobile	media móvil promedio móvil
M-234	MPI, *see* macroprudential indicator		
M-235	MSP, *see* reverse operation		
M-236	MTM, *see* mark to market		
M-237	MTN, *see* multilateral trade negotiations		
M-238	multicurrency intervention system, *see* European narrow margins arrangement		
M-239	multicurrency loan	prêt à plusieurs devises prêt multidevises	préstamo en varias monedas préstamo multidivisa

M-240	multicurrency peg
	multicurrency pegging
		détermination du taux de change
		  par référence à plusieurs
		  monnaies
		rattachement à plusieurs monnaies
			tipo de cambio fijo frente a varias
			  monedas
			determinación del tipo de cambio
			  en relación con varias monedas
			vinculación a múltiples monedas

M-241	multicurrency pegging, *see* multicurrency peg		
M-242	multilateral creditor	créancier multilatéral	acreedor multilateral
M-243	multilateral debt facility, *see* debt reduction fund		

M-244	Multilateral Debt Relief Initiative
	MDRI
		initiative d'allégement de la dette
		  multilatérale
		IADM
			Iniciativa para el Alivio de la Deuda
			  Multilateral
			IADM

M-245	Multilateral Exchange Rate Model
	[IMF]
	MERM
		modèle multilatéral de taux de
		  change
		MMTC
			modelo multilateral de tipos de
			  cambio
			modelo MERM

M-246	Multilateral Investment Guarantee
	  Agency
	[World Bank Group]
	MIGA
		Agence multilatérale de garantie
		  des investissements
		MIGA
		AMGI
			Organismo Multilateral de Garantía
			  de Inversiones
			OMGI

M-247	multilateral system of payments	système multilatéral de paiements	sistema multilateral de pagos

M-248	multilateral trade negotiations
	MTN
		négociations commerciales
		  multilatérales
		NCM
			negociaciones comerciales
			  multilaterales
			NCM

M-249	Multimedia Services Division [IMF]	Division services multimédias	División de Servicios Multimedia
M-250	MULTIMOD, *see* multiregion econometric model		
M-251	multinational enterprise transnational enterprise	firme multinationale FMN entreprise multinationale entreprise transnationale multinationale	empresa multinacional empresa transnacional
M-252	multiple bank, *see* multipurpose bank		
M-253	multiple classification, *see* cross-classification		

M-254	multiple exchange rate system	système de taux de change multiples	sistema de tipos de cambio múltiples
M-255	multiple exchange rates split exchange rates	taux de change multiples	tipos de cambio múltiples
M-256	multiple regression	régression multiple	regresión múltiple
M-257	multipurpose bank multiservice bank multiple bank all-purpose bank universal bank	banque à vocation générale banque multiservices banque à vocation universelle banque polyvalente	banco universal multibanco banco de operaciones generales
M-258	multiregion econometric model [IMF] MULTIMOD	modèle économétrique multirégional MULTIMOD	modelo econométrico multirregional modelo MULTIMOD
M-259	multiservice bank, *see* multipurpose bank		
M-260	multistage cumulative tax, *see* cascade tax		
M-261	multiyear debt rescheduling, *see* multiyear rescheduling arrangement		
M-262	multiyear debt rescheduling agreement, *see* multiyear rescheduling arrangement		
M-263	multiyear debt rescheduling arrangement, *see* multiyear rescheduling arrangement		
M-264	multiyear rescheduling agreement, *see* multiyear rescheduling arrangement		
M-265	multiyear rescheduling arrangement [Paris Club] MYRA multiyear debt rescheduling arrangement multiyear debt rescheduling agreement multiyear debt rescheduling multiyear rescheduling agreement	rééchelonnement pluriannuel de la dette	acuerdo de reprogramación multianual de la deuda ARMD
M-266	mutual fund *see also:* investment trust open-end mutual fund unit trust [GBR] open-end investment company open-end investment trust open-end investment fund	organisme de placement collectif en valeurs mobilières OPCVM société d'investissement à capital variable SICAV fonds commun de placement FCP fonds d'investissement	fondo común de inversión fondo de inversión colectiva fondo de inversiones abierto sociedad de inversión mobiliaria (con capital variable) fondo común de inversión
M-267	mutual savings bank	caisse de crédit mutuel banque mutuelle d'épargne	banco mutualista de ahorro
M-268	MYRA, *see* multiyear rescheduling arrangement		

N

N-1	n.a., *see* not available		
N-2	n.a., *see* not applicable		

N-3	NAB, *see* New Arrangements to Borrow		
N-4	NAFTA, *see* North American Free Trade Agreement		
N-5	NAIRU, *see* natural rate of unemployment		
N-6	naive model	modèle élémentaire modèle naïf modèle simpliste	modelo simplista
N-7	Naples terms	conditions de Naples dispositions de Naples	condiciones de Nápoles
N-8	narrow market thin market tight market inactive market	marché peu actif marché étroit	mercado poco activo mercado de poco movimiento mercado limitado mercado restringido
N-9	narrow money narrowly defined money supply transaction money	monnaie au sens étroit monnaie au sens strict masse monétaire au sens étroit masse monétaire au sens strict disponibilité monétaire	dinero en sentido estricto oferta monetaria en sentido estricto base monetaria reducida medio circulante [Am. Lat.]
N-10	narrowly defined money supply, *see* narrow money		
N-11	Nash equilibrium *see also:* game theory; prisoner's dilemma; zero-sum game	équilibre de Nash	equilibrio de Nash
N-12	national accounting national accounts	comptabilité nationale comptes de la nation comptes nationaux	contabilidad nacional cuentas nacionales
N-13	national accounts, *see* national accounting		
N-14	national consolidation *see also:* consolidation	consolidation au niveau national	consolidación nacional consolidación a nivel nacional

N-15	national estimates	estimations des autorités
		  nationales
		estimations communiquées par les
		  autorités nationales
			estimaciones de las autoridades
			  nacionales
			estimaciones proporcionadas por
			  las autoridades nacionales

N-16	national income *see also:* net material product	revenu national	ingreso nacional renta nacional
N-17	national product	produit national	producto nacional
N-18	national wealth	patrimoine national richesse nationale	patrimonio nacional riqueza nacional
N-19	natural disaster, *see* act of God		
N-20	natural person *see also:* artificial person individual	personne physique particulier	persona física particular

N-21	natural rate of unemployment	taux de chômage naturel	tasa natural de desempleo
	nonaccelerating inflation rate of unemployment	taux de chômage résiduel	tasa de desempleo no aceleradora de los precios
	NAIRU	taux de chômage incompressible	nivel de desempleo no inflacionario
	normal unemployment rate	taux de chômage non inflationniste	nivel de desempleo no inflacionista
	full-employment unemployment rate	taux de chômage compatible avec une inflation stable	
	warranted unemployment rate		

N-22   NB, *see* News Brief

N-23   NBFI, *see* nonbank financial institution

N-24   NDA, *see* net domestic assets

N-25   NDP, *see* net domestic product

N-26   near bank, *see* nonbank bank

N-27   near cash instrument, *see* quasi-money instrument

N-28   near-money, *see* quasi-money

N-29   n.e.c., *see* not elsewhere classified

N-30   NEER index, *see* nominal effective exchange rate index

N-31   negative bias, *see* downward bias

N-32	negative externality	déséconomie externe	externalidad negativa
	external diseconomy	coût externe	deseconomía externa

N-33	negative pledge clause [London Club]	clause de non-préférence de tiers	cláusula de obligación negativa
			cláusula de abstención
			cláusula de pignoración negativa

N-34   negative saving, *see* dissaving

N-35	negotiable security	titre négociable	valor negociable
	marketable security		título negociable

N-36   NEPAD, *see* New Partnership for Africa's Development

N-37   n.e.s., *see* not elsewhere specified

N-38   net assets, *see* net worth

N-39	net borrowing	besoin de financement	endeudamiento neto
	see also: borrowing requirement	besoin net de financement	obtención neta de préstamos
		emprunt(s) net(s)	empréstitos netos
			préstamos netos recibidos

N-40	net capital formation	formation nette de capital	formación neta de capital

N-41	net cash basis	sur une base nette encaissements–décaissements	en valores netos de caja
		sur base caisse nette	

N-42	net cash income	revenu monétaire net	ingreso líquido neto
			ingreso neto de caja

N-43	net creditor country	pays créancier (en termes nets)	acreedor neto

N-44	net creditor position	position créditrice nette	saldo acreedor neto
N-45	net cumulative allocation	allocation cumulative nette	asignación acumulativa neta
N-46	net debtor country	pays débiteur (en termes nets) pays débiteurs (net)	deudor neto
N-47	net debtor position	position débitrice nette	saldo deudor neto
N-48	net domestic assets NDA	avoirs intérieurs nets	activos internos netos AIN
N-49	net domestic product NDP	produit intérieur net PIN	producto interno neto PIN
N-50	net earnings	résultat	resultados resultado neto
N-51	net errors and omissions, *see* errors and omissions, net		
N-52	net external asset position, *see* international investment net position		
N-53	net factor income	revenu net des facteurs rémunération nette des facteurs	renta neta de los factores de producción ingreso neto de los factores de producción
N-54	net foreign assets NFA	avoirs extérieurs nets position extérieure nette	activos externos netos AEN
N-55	net Fund position, *see* position in the Fund		
N-56	net interest income	revenu d'intérêts (net)	renta neta por concepto de intereses ingreso financiero neto
N-57	net international reserves NIR	réserves internationales nettes	reservas internacionales netas RIN
N-58	net lending	capacité de financement capacité nette de financement prêts nets	préstamo neto préstamo neto concedido concesión neta de préstamos financiamiento neto
N-59	net material product [centrally planned economies] *see also:* national income NMP	produit matériel net PMN	producto material neto
N-60	net national product NNP	produit national net PNN	producto nacional neto PNN
N-61	net official holdings	avoirs officiels nets	tenencias oficiales netas
N-62	net operating balance	solde de fonctionnement net solde net de gestion	resultado operativo neto
N-63	net operational income [IMF]	recettes d'exploitation nettes recettes nettes des opérations et transactions	ingreso neto por operaciones
N-64	net position	position nette	posición neta

N-65	net present value NPV	valeur actualisée nette VAN valeur actuelle nette valeur actuarielle	valor presente neto VPN valor neto actualizado VNA valor actual neto
N-66	net present value of debt-to-export ratio net present value of debt-to-exports ratio [HIPC Initiative] NPV of debt-to-export ratio NPV of debt-to-exports ratio	ratio valeur actualisée nette de la dette/exportations ratio VAN de la dette/exportations ratio VAN de la dette aux exportations	razón valor presente neto de la deuda/exportación relación entre el valor presente neto de la deuda y la exportación relación entre el VPN de la deuda y la exportación
N-67	net present value of debt-to-exports ratio, *see* net present value of debt-to-export ratio		
N-68	net present value of debt-to-fiscal revenue target [HIPC Initiative] NPV of debt-to-fiscal revenue target	ratio VAN de la dette/recettes budgétaires retenu comme objectif	meta para la relación entre el VPN de la deuda y el ingreso fiscal
N-69	net recording	comptabilisation sur une base nette enregistrement sur une base nette	contabilización en valores netos registro en cifras netas registro neto
N-70	net reserves indicator	indicateur des réserves nettes	indicador de reservas netas
N-71	net SDR charges [IMF]	commissions nettes sur DTS commissions nettes des intérêts à recevoir sur les avoirs en DTS	cargos netos sobre las tenencias de DEG
N-72	net social benefit of production, *see* social surplus		
N-73	net taker of funds	emprunteur net de fonds	prestatario neto de fondos
N-74	net worth *see also:* equity capital net assets owner equity owners' equity stockholder equity equity	valeur nette actif net fonds propres situation nette patrimoine	patrimonio valor neto patrimonio neto
N-75	net yield	rendement net	rendimiento neto
N-76	netting	enregistrement net	registro neto neteo
N-77	New Arrangements to Borrow [IMF] NAB	Nouveaux Accords d'emprunt NAE	Nuevos Acuerdos para la Obtención de Préstamos NAP
N-78	new credit, *see* new money		
N-79	new money [London Club] new credit fresh money	apport d'argent frais crédit(s) additionnel(s) crédit de restructuration (de la dette) nouveaux prêts financement(s) additionnel(s)	nuevos fondos nuevos recursos nuevos créditos nuevos préstamos recursos frescos

200

N-80	new money bond NMB	obligation de restructuration	bono de fondos nuevos

N-81	New Partnership for Africa's
	  Development
	NEPAD
		Nouveau Partenariat pour le
		  développement de l'Afrique
		NOPADA
		NEPAD
			Nueva Alianza para el Desarrollo
			  de África
			NEPAD .

N-82	new trade theory
	see also: free trade; North
	  American Free Trade Agreement
		nouvelle théorie du commerce	nueva teoría del comercio
			  internacional

N-83	newly industrialized economy
	[IMF]
	NIE
		nouvelle économie industrielle
		NEI
		économie d'industrialisation
		  récente
		EIR
			economía de reciente
			  industrialización
			ERI

N-84	newly industrializing country [IMF, OECD] NIC	nouveau pays industriel NPI	país de reciente industrialización PRI
N-85	News Brief [IMF] NB	note d'information	nota informativa
N-86	NFA, *see* net foreign assets		
N-87	NFPS, *see* nonfinancial public sector		
N-88	NGO, *see* nongovernmental organization		
N-89	NIC, *see* newly industrializing country		
N-90	NIE, *see* newly industrialized economy		
N-91	n.i.e., *see* not included elsewhere		
N-92	NIF, *see* note issuance facility		
N-93	NIR, *see* net international reserves		
N-94	NMB, *see* new money bond		
N-95	NMP, *see* net material product		
N-96	NNP, *see* net national product		
N-97	NODC, *see* non-oil developing country		

N-98	*Nomenclature for the Classification*
	  of Goods in Customs Tariffs
	Customs Co-operation Council
	  Nomenclature
	CCCN
	Brussels Tariff Nomenclature
	BTN
	Brussels Nomenclature
		Nomenclature pour la classification
		  des marchandises dans les tarifs
		  douaniers
		Nomenclature du Conseil de
		  coopération douanière
		NCCD
		Nomenclature douanière de
		  Bruxelles
		NDB
		Nomenclature de Bruxelles
			Nomenclatura para la Clasificación
			  de Mercancías en los Aranceles
			  de Aduanas
			Nomenclatura del Consejo de
			  Cooperación Aduanera
			NCCA
			Nomenclatura Arancelaria de
			  Bruselas
			NAB
			Nomenclatura de Bruselas

N-99	nominal anchor	point d'ancrage nominal	anclaje nominal ancla nominal

N-100	nominal effective exchange rate index NEER index	indice du taux de change effectif nominal	índice del tipo de cambio efectivo nominal
N-101	nominal GDP money GDP	PIB nominal	PIB nominal
N-102	nominal interest rate *see also:* actual interest yield stated interest rate	taux d'intérêt nominal taux d'intérêt facial	tasa de interés nominal
N-103	nominal interest rate	taux d'intérêt nominal	tasa de interés nominal
N-104	nominal value money value par value face value denomination	valeur nominale valeur faciale montant nominal	valor nominal valor facial denominación
N-105	nominal wage, *see* money wage		
N-106	nonaccelerating inflation rate of unemployment, *see* natural rate of unemployment		
N-107	nonacceleration clause *see also:* acceleration clause	clause de non-accélération	cláusula de no caducidad de plazos
N-108	nonaccrual asset, *see* nonaccrual loan		
N-109	nonaccrual country, *see* nonaccrual status, country on		
N-110	nonaccrual credit, *see* nonaccrual loan		
N-111	nonaccrual loan problem loan nonaccrual asset nonaccrual credit	dont les intérêts impayés ne sont pas comptabilisés improductif classé improductif	préstamo improductivo activo improductivo crédito improductivo
N-112	nonaccrual status, country on nonaccrual country	pays dont la dette est improductive	país cuyos préstamos son declarados improductivos (y no devengan intereses)
N-113	nonbank bank near bank	quasi-banque institution parabancaire société parabancaire	institución cuasibancaria
N-114	nonbank financial institution NBFI	institution financière non bancaire	institución financiera no bancaria
N-115	nonbank financing	financement par le secteur non bancaire financement non bancaire	financiamiento no bancario
N-116	nonbanks	secteur non bancaire	entidades no bancarias instituciones no bancarias sector no bancario
N-117	nonborrowed reserves own reserves owned reserves	réserves propres réserves non empruntées	reservas propias

N-118	noncapital goods	biens autres que les biens d'équipement	bienes, excluidos los bienes de capital
			bienes que no son de capital
N-119	noncash economy	économie non monétarisée	economía desmonetizada
N-120	noncash issuance (of government securities)	émission (d'effets publics) sans contrepartie monétaire	emisión (de valores públicos) sin contrapartida monetaria
N-121	noncompetitive bid	soumission non concurrentielle	oferta sin cotización de precio
		offre non compétitive	oferta no competitiva
		ONC	oferta fuera de concurso
		soumission hors concours	
		soumission sans enchères	
N-122	noncompliance, *see* nonobservance		
N-123	noncomplying purchase [IMF]	achat non conforme	compra improcedente
N-124	nonconcessional flow, *see* nonconcessionary flow		
N-125	nonconcessional loan, *see* commercial lending		
N-126	nonconcessionary flow	flux de capitaux non concessionnels	flujo de capital no concesionario
	nonconcessional flow	flux de capitaux assortis de conditions non concessionnelles	flujo de capital de carácter no concesionario
			corriente no concesionaria
			corriente de capital no concesionaria
N-127	nonconditional grant	don inconditionnel	subvención incondicional
	unconditional grant	subvention inconditionnelle	transferencia incondicional
		subvention sans condition	
		transfert inconditionnel	
N-128	noncooperation	non-coopération	no cooperación
			falta de cooperación
N-129	noncore bank	banque commerciale secondaire	banco secundario
N-130	nondebt flow, *see* non-debt-generating flow		
N-131	non-debt-creating flow, *see* non-debt-generating flow		
N-132	non-debt-generating flow	flux non générateur d'endettement	flujo de capital no generador de deuda
	non-debt-creating flow	flux non lié à la dette	corriente de capital que no crea deuda
	nondebt flow		flujo de capital no relacionado con la deuda
			corriente de capital no relacionada con la deuda
N-133	nondurable good	bien non durable	bien no duradero
		bien consomptible	bien consumible
N-134	nonearning asset	avoir non productif	activo improductivo
		actif improductif	

N-135	nonequity financial flow	flux financier non participatif	flujo financiero no destinado a inversión en participaciones de capital
			flujo financiero no destinado a inversión en acciones
N-136	nonequity security	titre non participatif	valores que no constituyen una participación de capital
			título que no constituye una participación de capital
N-137	nonfactor inputs	intrants non factoriels	insumos no factoriales
			insumos no atribuibles a factores
N-138	nonfactor payments	paiements autres que la rémunération des facteurs	pagos no destinados a los factores de producción
N-139	nonfactor services	services, non compris les revenus des facteurs	servicios no factoriales
			servicios no atribuibles a factores
N-140	nonfiler [taxation]	non-déclarant	contribuyente omiso
			no declarante
N-141	nonfinancial corporate and quasi-corporate enterprise sector	secteur des sociétés et quasi-sociétés non financières	sector de empresas no financieras constituidas en sociedades y cuasisociedades de capital
N-142	nonfinancial intangible assets	avoirs incorporels non financiers	activos intangibles no financieros
N-143	nonfinancial public sector NFPS	secteur public non financier SPNF	sector público no financiero SPNF
N-144	nonfranc country	pays n'appartenant pas à la zone franc	país que no pertenece a la zona del franco
N-145	nonfuel exporters	(pays) exportateurs de produits autres que les combustibles	exportadores de productos no combustibles
N-146	nongold reserves	réserves, or exclu	reservas, excluido el oro
N-147	nongovernmental organization NGO	organisation non gouvernementale ONG	organización no gubernamental ONG
N-148	nongovernmental sector	secteur hors administrations publiques	sector no gubernamental
N-149	noninstitutional financial sector informal financial sector	secteur financier non structuré secteur financier informel secteur financier inorganisé	sector financiero informal sector financiero paralelo sector financiero no estructurado
N-150	noninterest expenditure	dépenses hors intérêts	gasto no correspondiente a intereses
			gasto, excluidos los intereses
N-151	non-interest-bearing	non rémunéré ne portant pas intérêts non productif d'intérêts	que no devenga interés no remunerado improductivo no generador de interés sin intereses
N-152	nonintervention scenario, see baseline scenario		
N-153	nonlabor cost	coûts non salariaux coûts autres que ceux du travail	costos no salariales costos no laborales

N-154	nonmarket activity	activité hors marché activité non marchande	actividad ajena al mercado
N-155	nonmarket economy	économie non marchande	economía no basada en principios de mercado economía controlada economía dirigida
N-156	nonmarketable security, *see* nonnegotiable security		
N-157	nonmatching grant	don sans contrepartie subvention sans contrepartie	subvención sin contrapartida subvención no compensatoria
N-158	nonmaturing bond, *see* perpetual bond		
N-159	nonmonetary capital	capitaux non monétaires immobilisations	capital no monetario
N-160	nonmonetary financial institution	institution financière non monétaire	institución financiera no monetaria
N-161	nonmonetary gold	or non monétaire	oro no monetario
N-162	nonnegotiable security nonmarketable security	titre non négociable	valor no negociable título no negociable
N-163	nonobservance [IMF] noncompliance	manquement non-respect inobservation	inobservancia incumplimiento
N-164	non-oil developing country NODC	pays en développement non pétrolier PDNP	país en desarrollo no petrolero PDNP
N-165	non-oil GDP	PIB non pétrolier PIB, pétrole exclu PIB, pétrole non compris	PIB no petrolero PIB, excluido el petróleo
N-166	non-oil primary producing country	pays non pétrolier de production primaire	país no petrolero de producción primaria
N-167	nonperformance [contracts]	inexécution	incumplimiento
N-168	nonperforming asset, *see* nonperforming loan		
N-169	nonperforming credit, *see* nonperforming loan		
N-170	nonperforming loan NPL nonperforming asset nonperforming credit	prêt improductif créance improductive créance immobilisée créance gelée prêt déclassé prêt inexécuté	préstamo en mora préstamo moroso préstamo en situación de incumplimiento préstamo en situación irregular cartera irregular préstamo no redituable cartera vencida préstamo no rentable préstamo improductivo activo improductivo
N-171	nonprofit body, *see* nonprofit institution		

N-172	nonprofit institution NPI nonprofit organization NPO nonprofit body	institution sans but lucratif ISBL association sans but lucratif ASBL organisme sans but lucratif OSBL	institución sin fines de lucro sociedad sin fines lucrativos institución sin ánimo de lucro
N-174	non-profit institutions serving households [UN] NPISH	institutions sans but lucratif au service des ménages ISBLSM	instituciones sin fines de lucro que sirven a los hogares ISFLSH
N-175	nonprofit organization, *see* nonprofit institution		
N-176	nonpublic sector	secteur non public	sector no público
N-177	nonpublic utilities	services publics assurés par des entreprises privées	servicios públicos prestados por empresas privadas
N-178	nonrecurrent expenditure nonrecurrent expense nonrecurrent outlay	dépense non récurrente dépense exceptionnelle dépense non renouvelable	gasto extraordinario
N-179	nonrecurrent expense, *see* nonrecurrent expenditure		
N-180	nonrecurrent income, *see* nonrecurrent revenue		
N-181	nonrecurrent outlay, *see* nonrecurrent expenditure		
N-182	nonrecurrent receipt, *see* nonrecurrent revenue		
N-183	nonrecurrent revenue nonrecurrent receipt nonrecurrent income	recette extraordinaire recette exceptionnelle	ingreso extraordinario
N-184	nonrecurrent taxes on property	impôts non périodiques sur le patrimoine	impuestos no permanentes sobre la propiedad
N-185	nonredeemable bond, *see* perpetual bond		
N-186	nonreserve capital	capitaux ne constituant pas des réserves	capital que no constituye reservas capital que no es de reserva
N-187	nonreserve claim	créance non incluse dans les réserves	activo que no constituye reservas activo no incluido en las reservas
N-188	nonreserve currencies	monnaies autres que les monnaies de réserve	monedas que no constituyen monedas de reserva monedas no utilizadas como reserva
N-189	nonresponse	sans réponse	sin respuesta falta de respuestas
N-190	nonsalary earner	non-salarié	no asalariado
N-191	nontariff nontariff measure NTM nontariff barrier NTB	mesure non tarifaire barrière non tarifaire obstacle non tarifaire	medida no arancelaria barrera no arancelaria obstáculo no arancelario
N-192	nontariff barrier, *see* nontariff		

N-193 nontariff measure, *see* nontariff		
N-194 nontax revenue	recettes non fiscales	ingreso no tributario

N-195 nontradable goods
nontradables
	biens non échangeables
	biens non exportables
	biens ne pouvant faire l'objet
	  d'échanges internationaux
		bienes no transables
		bienes no comerciables
		bienes no exportables
		  o importables
		bienes no comercializables

N-196 nontradables, *see* nontradable goods		

N-197 nontraded good	bien non échangé
	bien non commercialisé
	bien non exporté
	bien ne faisant pas l'objet
	  d'échanges internationaux
		bien no comerciado
		bien no comercializado
		bien que no es objeto de comercio
		  exterior

N-198 nonwage awards	octroi d'avantages indirects	prestaciones no salariales prestaciones complementarias
N-199 nonwage income	revenu non salarial	ingreso no salarial

N-200 nonwage labor costs	coûts salariaux indirects
	coûts sociaux
		costos no salariales de la mano
		  de obra
		costos laborales indirectos
		costos indirectos de la mano
		  de obra

N-201 norm for remuneration [IMF]	norme de rémunération	norma de remuneración
N-202 normal distribution curve bell curve bell-shaped curve	courbe de distribution normale courbe normale courbe en cloche	curva de distribución normal curva campaniforme curva acampanada
N-203 normal unemployment rate, *see* natural rate of unemployment		

N-204 normal variable	variable normale
	variable aléatoire à distribution
	  normale
	variable aléatoire suivant une loi
	  normale
		variable normal

N-205 normalize	normaliser ramener à une même échelle translater [courbe] rapporter [ratio]	normalizar

N-206 normalized unit labor cost	coût unitaire normalisé de (la)
	  main-d'œuvre
		costo unitario normalizado de la
		  mano de obra
		costo unitario normalizado del
		  trabajo

N-207 North American Division [IMF]	Division Amérique du Nord	División de América del Norte

N-208 North American Free Trade
  Agreement
see also: new trade theory
NAFTA
	Accord de libre-échange nord-
	  américain
	ALENA
		Tratado de Libre Comercio de
		  América del Norte
		TLCAN
		NAFTA

N-209	Northeastern Division [IMF]	Division Europe du Nord-Est	División de Europa Nororiental
N-210	Northern Division [IMF]	Division Europe du Nord	División de Europa Septentrional
N-211	not applicable n.a.	sans objet s.o. néant	no se aplica n.a. no aplicable
N-212	not available n.a.	non disponible n.d. données non disponibles	no disponible n.d. dato no disponible
N-213	not elsewhere classified n.e.c.	non classé ailleurs n.c.a.	no clasificado en otra parte n.c.o.p. no clasificado separadamente n.c.s.
N-214	not elsewhere specified n.e.s.	non dénommé ailleurs n.d.a. non spécifié ailleurs n.s.a.	no especificado en otra parte n.e.o.p. no especificado separadamente n.e.s.
N-215	not included elsewhere n.i.e.	non inclus ailleurs n.i.a.	no incluido en otra parte n.i.o.p. no incluido separadamente n.i.s.
N-216	not separately recorded n.s.r.	non inscrit séparément n.i.s.	no registrado separadamente n.r.s.
N-217	note	billet effet bon obligation	pagaré
N-218	note issuance facility *see also:* revolving underwriting facility NIF note purchase facility	facilité d'émission d'effets NIF facilité d'émission de notes	servicio de emisión de pagarés SEP
N-219	note purchase facility, *see* note issuance facility		
N-220	notice of failure to fulfill obligations [IMF]	notification de manquement aux obligations	notificación de incumplimiento de las obligaciones
N-221	notification system [IMF] *see also:* information notice system	système de notification	sistema de notificación
N-222	notional	fictif hypothétique théorique notionnel	ficticio hipotético teórico imaginario nocional
N-223	notional bond	emprunt notionnel	bono ficticio bono hipotético bono nocional

N-224	notional drawing right [IMF] see also: rights approach	droit de tirage de principe	derecho de giro hipotético
N-225	notional unit	unité hypothétique unité théorique	unidad hipotética unidad teórica unidad ficticia
N-226	NPI, see nonprofit institution		
N-227	NPISH, see nonprofit institutions serving households		
N-228	NPL, see nonperforming loan		
N-229	NPO, see nonprofit institution		
N-230	NPV, see net present value		
N-231	NPV of debt-to-export ratio, see net present value of debt-to-export ratio		
N-232	NPV of debt-to-exports ratio, see net present value of debt-to-export ratio		
N-233	NPV of debt-to-fiscal revenue target, see net present value of debt-to-fiscal revenue target		
N-234	n.s.r., see not separately recorded		
N-235	NTB, see nontariff		
N-236	NTM, see nontariff		
N-237	null hypothesis null, the	hypothèse nulle	hipótesis nula
N-238	null, the, see null hypothesis		

O

O-1	OAP, see Regional Office for Asia and the Pacific		
O-2	OAS, see Organization of American States		
O-3	obligation	obligation	obligación
O-4	OBP, see Office of Budget and Planning		
O-5	obsolescence	obsolescence	obsolescencia desuso
O-6	OBU, see offshore banking unit		
O-7	OCA, see optimal currency area		
O-8	Occasional Paper [IMF]	Étude spéciale (de la série des «Occasional Papers»)	estudio de la serie «Occasional Papers»
O-9	ODA, see official development assistance		
O-10	ODF, see Official Development Finance		
O-11	OECD, see Organisation for Economic Co-operation and Development		

O-12	OED, *see* Office of Executive Directors		
O-14	OFC, *see* offshore financial center		
O-15	OFC assessment report, *see* offshore financial center assessment report		
O-16	off-balance-sheet account, *see* off-balance-sheet item		
O-17	off-balance-sheet item below-the-line item off-balance-sheet account	poste hors bilan	partida complementaria partida extraordinaria partida no incluida en el balance general partida por debajo de la línea
O-18	off-budget activity, *see* off-budget transaction		
O-19	off-budget transaction *see also:* extra-budgetary account off-budget activity	opération hors budget	operación extrapresupuestaria
O-20	offer rate, *see* selling rate		
O-21	office audit *see also:* field audit desk audit documentary audit off-site supervision off-site inspection	contrôle sur pièces contrôle sur dossiers vérification sur pièces vérification sur dossiers inspection sur pièces	auditoría basada en archivos verificación documental verificación de documentos
O-22	Office of Budget and Planning [IMF] OBP	Bureau du budget et de la planification	Oficina de Presupuesto y Planificación
O-23	Office of Executive Directors [IMF] OED	Bureaux des administrateurs	Oficinas de los Directores Ejecutivos
O-24	Office of Executive Secretary, Joint Development Committee [IMF-OED] DC JDC	Bureau du Secrétaire exécutif du Comité du développement	Oficina del Secretario Ejecutivo del Comité Ministerial Conjunto para el Desarrollo
O-25	Office of Internal Audit and Inspection [IMF] OIA	Bureau de la vérification et de l'inspection internes	Oficina de Auditoría e Inspección Internas
O-26	Office of Technical Assistance Management [IMF] OTM	Bureau de la gestion de l'assistance technique	Oficina de Gestión de la Asistencia Técnica
O-27	Office of the Deputy Managing Director [IMF]	Bureau du Directeur général adjoint Bureau de la Directrice générale adjointe	Oficina del Subdirector Gerente
O-28	Office of the Managing Director [IMF] OMD	Bureau du Directeur général	Oficina del Director Gerente

O-29	Offices in Europe [IMF] EUO	Bureaux du FMI en Europe Bureaux européens	Oficinas del FMI en Europa
O-30	official borrowers	pays emprunteurs à des créanciers officiels	prestatarios en fuentes oficiales
O-31	official capital flows, *see* official flows		
O-32	official check, *see* cashier's check		
O-33	official community	institutions officielles	instituciones oficiales
O-34	official creditor	créancier officiel créancier public	acreedor oficial
O-35	official debt	dette officielle dette envers des créanciers officiels	deuda oficial deuda frente a acreedores oficiales
O-36	official development assistance ODA	aide publique au développement APD	asistencia oficial para el desarrollo AOD
O-37	official development bank	banque publique de développement	banco oficial de desarrollo
O-38	Official Development Finance ODF	financement public du développement	financiamiento oficial para el desarrollo
O-39	official exchange rate	taux de change officiel	tipo de cambio oficial
O-40	Official Financing Operations Division [IMF] OFOD	Division opérations de financement officiel	División de Operaciones de Financiamiento Público
O-41	official flows official capital flows	flux officiels flux de capitaux publics flux de capitaux de sources publiques apport de fonds publics	flujos oficiales de capital flujo de capital oficial
O-42	official holdings	avoirs officiels	tenencias oficiales
O-43	official multilateral debt renegotiation	renégociation multilatérale de la dette officielle	renegociación multilateral de la deuda oficial
O-44	official sector	secteur officiel	sector oficial
O-45	official settlement balance	solde (établi) sur la base des règlements officiels	saldo según liquidaciones oficiales
O-46	official traveler	voyageur en mission officielle	viajero en misión oficial
O-47	official value [customs] posted value administrative value standard value	valeur du barème valeur mercuriale	valor fijado por la aduana aforo aduanero aforo fijado por la aduana valuación oficial
O-48	officially guaranteed trade-related claims	crédits bénéficiant d'une garantie publique et liés au commerce extérieur	créditos con garantía oficial relacionados con el comercio exterior

O-49	officially supported export credit	crédit(s) à l'exportation bénéficiant d'un soutien public	crédito a la exportación con respaldo oficial
O-50	offset, *see* offset agreement		
O-51	offset agreement [trade] offset	accord de compensation	acuerdo de compensación
O-52	offsetting entry balancing entry contra entry	écriture de contrepartie écriture compensatoire poste de contrepartie inscription de contrepartie poste d'ajustement inscription compensatoire contre-écriture	asiento compensatorio asiento de contrapartida
O-53	offshore assembly, *see* offshore processing		
O-54	offshore bank offshore deposit taker	banque extraterritoriale banque offshore	banco extraterritorial banco *offshore* institución de depósito *offshore*
O-55	offshore banking center	centre bancaire extraterritorial centre bancaire offshore	centro bancario extraterritorial centro bancario *offshore*
O-56	offshore banking unit OBU	unité bancaire extraterritoriale unité bancaire offshore	unidad bancaria *offshore* unidad bancaria extraterritorial UBE
O-57	offshore deposit taker, *see* offshore bank		
O-58	offshore enterprise, *see* offshore processing industry		
O-59	offshore financial center OFC	centre financier offshore place financière offshore	centro financiero extraterritorial centro financiero *offshore*
O-60	offshore financial center assessment report OFC assessment report	rapport d'évaluation des centres financiers offshore	informe de evaluación de centros financieros *offshore*
O-61	offshore processing offshore assembly	opérations d'assemblage hors du pays opérations de montage à l'étranger délocalisation des opérations de montage	maquila montaje de material fabricado en otro país ensamblaje en el extranjero ensamblado en el extranjero
O-62	offshore processing industry *see also:* in-bond industry offshore enterprise	entreprise de montage à l'étranger entreprise délocalisée	maquiladora empresa maquiladora
O-63	off-site inspection, *see* office audit		
O-64	off-site supervision, *see* office audit		
O-65	off-track	mal engagé déraillé dérapé dont l'exécution s'écarte des objectifs	descarrilado mal encaminado desviado de sus metas desviado de su curso
O-66	OFOD, *see* Official Financing Operations Division		

O-67	OIA, *see* Office of Internal Audit and Inspection		
O-68	oil bill	facture pétrolière coût des importations de pétrole	costo total del petróleo importado costo de las importaciones de petróleo
O-69	Oil Facility [IMF]	mécanisme pétrolier	Servicio Financiero del Petróleo servicio del petróleo
O-70	oil-exporting country	pays exportateur de pétrole	país exportador de petróleo
O-71	OJT, *see* on-the-job training		
O-72	OLS, *see* ordinary least squares		
O-73	OMA, *see* orderly marketing arrangement		
O-74	OMA, *see* orderly marketing arrangement		
O-75	Ombudsman [IMF] Ombudsperson	Médiateur	*Ombudsman*
O-76	Ombudsperson, *see* Ombudsman		
O-77	OMD, *see* Office of the Managing Director		
O-78	one-crop economy single crop economy	économie de monoculture	economía de monocultivo
O-79	one-off depreciation, *see* step depreciation		
O-80	one-sided test, *see* one-tailed test		
O-81	one-stop shop one-stop window	guichet unique	ventanilla única oficina centralizadora
O-82	one-stop window, *see* one-stop shop		
O-83	one-tailed test one-sided test single-tailed test	test unilatéral test à une queue	prueba a un extremo prueba unilateral
O-84	one-time special SDR allocation, *see* special one-time allocation of SDRs		
O-85	onlending *see also:* relending	rétrocession de fonds empruntés rétrocession de prêts	represtamo
O-86	onlending cost	coût d'intermédiation coût de rétrocession	costo de los represtamos costo de intermediación
O-87	online access	accès direct accès en ligne	acceso *on-line* acceso en línea acceso directo
O-88	online course [IMF]	cours en ligne	curso en línea

O-89	online information network	réseau donnant un accès direct à l'information réseau d'information en ligne	red de información de acceso *online* red de información de acceso en línea red de información de acceso directo
O-90	onshore bank	banque soumise à la réglementation nationale	banco sujeto a la reglamentación nacional
O-91	on-site inspection, *see* field audit		
O-92	on-site supervision, *see* field audit		
O-93	on-the-job training *see also:* in-service training OJT	formation sur le tas formation en cours d'emploi formation dans l'entreprise	capacitación práctica en el empleo capacitación práctica en el trabajo
O-94	on-track	bien engagé sur la bonne voie dont l'exécution se déroule comme prévu	bien encaminado encarrilado
O-95	OPEC, *see* Organization of the Petroleum Exporting Countries		
O-96	open capital account [IMF] *see also:* liberalization of the capital account	mouvements de capitaux exempts de restrictions absence de restrictions aux mouvements de capitaux mouvements de capitaux non réglementés	cuenta de capital abierta apertura de la cuenta de capital
O-97	open inflation	inflation ouverte inflation déclarée inflation caractérisée	inflación abierta inflación manifiesta
O-98	open lending policy	politique libérale de prêt	política liberal de crédito
O-99	Open Market Committee, *see* Federal Open Market Committee		
O-100	open market operation	opération d'open-market	operación de mercado abierto
O-101	open market price	prix de pleine concurrence	precio de mercado abierto precio de libre competencia
O-102	open position	position à découvert position ouverte	posición abierta posición en descubierto
O-103	open trade, *see* free trade		
O-104	open unemployment	chômage apparent chômage connu chômage visible chômage déclaré	desempleo abierto desempleo manifiesto desempleo declarado
O-105	open-end grant [public finance]	don de montant non déterminé subvention de montant non limité	subvención de monto indeterminado subvención ilimitada
O-106	open-end investment company, *see* mutual fund		
O-107	open-end investment fund, *see* mutual fund		

O-108	open-end investment trust, *see* mutual fund		
O-109	open-end mutual fund, *see* mutual fund		
O-110	opening, *see* vacancy		
O-111	opening assets	actif(s) d'ouverture	activo al inicio del ejercicio activo de apertura
O-112	opening liabilities	passif(s) d'ouverture	pasivo al inicio del ejercicio pasivo de apertura
O-113	opening remarks	allocution d'ouverture discours d'ouverture	palabras de apertura
O-114	openness	ouverture degré d'ouverture sur l'extérieur	apertura
O-115	operating account *see also:* income account	compte d'exploitation	cuenta de operaciones cuenta de explotación
O-116	operating balance operating profit or loss	résultat d'exploitation	resultado operativo resultado de operaciones saldo operativo saldo de operación resultado de explotación
O-117	operating budget	budget de fonctionnement budget d'exploitation	presupuesto operativo presupuesto operacional presupuesto de operaciones presupuesto de explotación presupuesto de operación
O-118	operating costs operational costs	coûts de fonctionnement coûts d'exploitation frais de fonctionnement charges d'exploitation	costos de operación costos de operaciones costos operativos costos de explotación
O-119	operating income operational income	recettes d'exploitation recettes de fonctionnement	ingresos de explotación ingresos de operación ingresos de operaciones ingreso por operaciones
O-120	operating profit or loss, *see* operating balance		
O-121	operation [IMF] *see also:* transaction [IMF]	opération	operación
O-122	operational balance, *see* operational fiscal balance		
O-123	operational budget [IMF]	budget des opérations et transactions	presupuesto de operaciones
O-124	operational costs, *see* operating costs		
O-125	operational fiscal balance operational balance	solde budgétaire opérationnel solde opérationnel des finances publiques	saldo operativo saldo operacional saldo fiscal operativo saldo fiscal operacional
O-126	operational income, *see* operating income		

O-127	operational leasing	location-exploitation	arrendamiento de explotación
O-128	operational risk	risque opérationnel	riesgo operativo
O-129	operational staff [IMF]	membres des services opérationnels du FMI	personal de operaciones
O-130	operations account [franc zone]	compte d'opérations compte d'opérations au Trésor français	cuenta de operaciones
O-131	Operations Division [IMF]	Division des opérations	División de Operaciones
O-133	operations research O.R. OR	recherche opérationnelle	investigación operativa investigación operacional
O-134	opportunity cost	coût d'opportunité coût d'option coût de substitution	costo de oportunidad
O-135	opt out [SDR]	exercer l'option de refus	ejercer la opción de rechazo optar por no recibir
O-136	optimal currency area [EMS] OCA optimum currency area	zone monétaire optimale	zona monetaria óptima ZMO
O-137	optimistic scenario, *see* better policies scenario		
O-138	optimistic scenario, *see* best-case scenario		

O-139	optimization of Fund reserve
	  management
		optimisation de la gestion des
		  réserves du FMI
			optimización de la gestión de las
			  reservas del FMI

O-140	optimum currency area, *see* optimal currency area		
O-141	optimum search strategy	stratégie de recherche optimale	estrategia de búsqueda óptima
O-142	option option contract	option contrat d'option	opción contrato de opciones
O-143	option contract, *see* option		
O-144	option exchange	marché d'options marché à options	mercado de opciones
O-145	O.R., *see* operations research		
O-146	OR, *see* operations research		
O-147	order instrument *see also:* bearer instrument; registered instrument order paper	instrument à ordre	instrumento a la orden título a la orden
O-148	order paper, *see* order instrument		

O-149	orderly liberalization of capital
	  movements
		libéralisation ordonnée des
		  mouvements de capitaux
			liberalización ordenada de los
			  movimientos de capital

O-150	orderly marketing agreement, *see* orderly marketing arrangement	

O-151	orderly marketing arrangement
	see also: voluntary export
	  restraints
	OMA
	orderly marketing agreement
	OMA
		accord de commercialisation avec
		  contingentement
		arrangement de commercialisation
		  ordonnée
		arrangement d'organisation
		  du marché
			acuerdo de comercialización
			  ordenada

O-152	ordinary least squares OLS	moindres carrés ordinaires MCO	mínimos cuadrados ordinarios MCO
O-153	ordinary resources [IMF] *see also:* borrowed resources	ressources ordinaires	recursos ordinarios

O-154	ordinary share, *see* common share	

O-155	Organisation for Economic
	  Co-operation and Development
	OECD
	Organization for Economic
	  Cooperation and Development
	Organization of Economic Co-
	  operation and Development
		Organisation de coopération
		  et de développement
		  économiques
		OCDE
			Organización para la Cooperación
			  y el Desarrollo Económicos
			OCDE

O-156	organization chart, *see* organizational chart	

O-157	Organization for Economic Cooperation and Development, *see* Organisation for Economic Co-operation and Development	

O-158	Organization of American States OAS	Organisation des États américains OEA	Organización de los Estados Americanos OEA

O-159	Organization of Economic Co-operation and Development, *see* Organisation for Economic Co-operation and Development	

O-160	Organization of the Petroleum
	  Exporting Countries
	OPEC
		Organisation des pays
		  exportateurs de pétrole
		OPEP
			Organización de Países
			  Exportadores de Petróleo
			OPEP

O-161	organizational chart organization chart	organigramme	organigrama

O-162	original cost, *see* historical cost	

O-163	original maturity initial maturity	échéance initiale durée de crédit initiale	vencimiento inicial vencimiento original plazo de vencimiento inicial plazo de vencimiento original
O-164	original member [IMF]	État membre originaire	país miembro fundador

O-165	OTC, *see* over-the-counter market	

O-166	OTC financial derivatives, *see* over-the-counter financial derivatives	

O-167	OTC option, *see* over-the-counter option	

O-168	other conventional fixed peg arrangements [IMF exchange rate classification system, 2006]	autres régimes conventionnels de parité fixe	otros regímenes convencionales de tipo de cambio fijo
O-169	other depository corporations see also: depository corporation	autres institutions de dépôt	otras sociedades de depósito
O-170	other holder of SDRs [IMF]	autre détenteur de DTS	otro tenedor de DEG
O-171	other things being equal, see ceteris paribus		
O-172	other things equal, see ceteris paribus		
O-173	OTM, see Office of Technical Assistance Management		
O-174	outflow of capital capital outflow	sortie de capitaux	salida de capital
O-175	outgoings outlay(s)	décaissements dépense(s) débours mise de fonds	desembolsos gastos egresos
O-176	outlay(s), see outgoings		
O-177	output see also: product	production produit (d'un facteur de production)	producto producción
O-178	output budget, see performance budget		
O-179	output gap production gap	écart de production écart conjoncturel de production écart entre la production effective et la production potentielle	brecha del producto brecha de producción brecha entre el producto efectivo y el potencial diferencia entre la producción efectiva y la producción potencial brecha entre el producto tendencial y el efectivamente observado
O-180	outright gift	don pur et simple	regalo propiamente dicho
O-181	outright purchase [IMF]	achat direct achat pur et simple	compra directa
O-182	outsourcing vendorization contracting out	externalisation sous-traitance	tercerización externalización contratación de servicios con terceros subcontratación
O-183	outstanding bonds outstanding securities	obligations en circulation titres en circulation	bonos en circulación valores en circulación
O-184	outstanding borrowing	encours des emprunts emprunts non remboursés	empréstitos pendientes de reembolso
O-185	outstanding claim	créance non éteinte droit (effectif)	crédito vigente
O-186	outstanding claim, see pending claim		

O-187	outstanding debt	encours de la dette dette non amortie	deuda pendiente deuda viva saldo de la deuda
O-188	outstanding debt by type of debt holder	encours de la dette par catégorie de créanciers	deuda pendiente por tipo de tenedor
O-189	outstanding debt by type of debt instrument	encours de la dette par catégorie d'instruments	deuda pendiente por tipo de instrumento
O-190	outstanding drawings (on the Fund)	encours des tirages (sur le FMI) tirages non remboursés	giros (contra el FMI) pendientes de reembolso
O-191	outstanding Fund credit outstanding use of Fund credit	encours des crédits du FMI encours de crédit du FMI utilisé crédit du FMI non remboursé	crédito del FMI pendiente de reembolso saldo del crédito del FMI
O-192	outstanding government debt, see outstanding public debt		
O-193	outstanding interest	intérêts échus intérêts à payer	intereses pendientes intereses por pagar
O-194	outstanding liabilities outstanding stock of liabilities	encours des engagements	saldo de los pasivos saldo total de pasivos obligaciones pendientes
O-195	outstanding loans	encours des prêts prêts non remboursés	préstamos pendientes de reembolso préstamos pendientes no amortizados saldo de los préstamos
O-196	outstanding obligation	obligation non acquittée	obligación pendiente
O-197	outstanding public debt outstanding government debt	encours de la dette publique	saldo de la deuda pública deuda pública pendiente deuda pública viva
O-198	outstanding purchases [IMF]	encours des achats achats non rachetés	compras pendientes de recompra
O-199	outstanding securities, see outstanding bonds		
O-200	outstanding stock of liabilities, see outstanding liabilities		
O-201	outstanding use of Fund credit, see outstanding Fund credit		
O-202	outward investment	investissements extérieurs investissements réalisés à l'étranger	inversiones en el exterior inversión de residentes en el extranjero
O-203	outward-looking economy, see outward-oriented economy		
O-204	outward-looking policy	politique économique orientée vers l'extérieur politique économique ouverte sur l'extérieur	política económica orientada hacia el exterior política económica de apertura al exterior política de fomento de las exportaciones
O-205	outward-oriented economy outward-looking economy	économie ouverte économie ouverte sur l'extérieur	economía orientada hacia el exterior economía abierta al exterior

| O-206 | outward-oriented growth strategy | stratégie de croissance orientée vers l'extérieur | estrategia de crecimiento orientada hacia el exterior |
| | | | estrategia de crecimiento basada en el fomento de las exportaciones |

O-207   overall balance, *see* overall fiscal balance

| O-208 | overall demand | demande globale | demanda global |

O-209	overall fiscal balance	solde budgétaire global	resultado fiscal global
	overall balance	solde global	saldo fiscal global
			saldo global

O-210   overall inflation, *see* headline inflation

O-211	overdraft	découvert	descubierto
		à découvert	giro en descubierto
			sobregiro

| O-212 | overdraft checking account | compte avec autorisation de découvert | cuenta corriente con autorización para girar en descubierto |

| O-213 | overdraft credit | crédit par découvert | crédito en descubierto |

| O-214 | overdue country [IMF] *see also:* arrears country | pays en situation d'impayés | país miembro con obligaciones financieras en mora |

| O-215 | overdue financial obligation to the Fund [IMF] overdue financial obligations | impayé au titre d'une obligation financière obligation financière impayée | obligación financiera en mora ante el FMI |

O-216   overdue financial obligations, *see* overdue financial obligation to the Fund

| O-217 | overdue payment to the Fund [IMF] | impayé envers le FMI | pago en mora ante el FMI |

| O-218 | overdue repurchase | impayé au titre d'un rachat rachat impayé rachat en arriéré | recompra en mora recompra vencida |

O-219   overemployment, *see* overstaffing

| O-220 | overexposed bank | banque ayant pris trop de risques banque surexposée aux risques | banco en situación de riesgo excesivo |

| O-221 | overexposure | engagement excessif | concentración excesiva de riesgos volumen excesivo de préstamos |

| O-222 | overhang, dollar | excédent de dollars | excedente de dólares |

| O-223 | overhead overhead expenses | frais généraux charges indirectes | gastos generales gastos fijos gastos indirectos |

O-224   overhead capital, *see* social overhead capital

O-225   overhead expenses, *see* overhead

O-226	overheating [economics]	surchauffe	recalentamiento recalentamiento de la economía sobrecalentamiento de la economía
O-227	overindebtedness	surendettement	sobreendeudamiento exceso de endeudamiento
O-228	overinvoicing	surfacturation	sobrefacturación datos sobrefacturados
O-229	overmanning, *see* overstaffing		
O-230	overnight call money rate, *see* cash rate		
O-231	overnight credit overnight loan overnight money overnight funds	crédit à un jour prêt à un jour argent au jour le jour fonds à un jour crédit à 24 heures	crédito día a día dinero de un día para otro préstamo de un día para otro fondos a un día
O-232	overnight funds, *see* overnight credit		
O-233	overnight loan, *see* overnight credit		
O-234	overnight money, *see* overnight credit		
O-235	overnight rate, *see* cash rate		
O-236	oversaving	surépargne épargne excessive	sobreahorro exceso de ahorro
O-237	oversee the international monetary system [IMF]	contrôler le système monétaire international	supervisar el sistema monetario internacional
O-238	overshooting	surajustement ajustement excessif surcompensation	reajuste excesivo reacción excesiva corrección excesiva
O-239	oversight	tutelle surveillance	supervisión fiscalización control
O-240	overstaffing overmanning overemployment	suremploi effectifs surnuméraires effectifs pléthoriques sureffectif	exceso de personal sobreempleo exceso de empleo
O-241	oversubscription	sursouscription souscription surpassée	exceso de suscripción
O-242	oversupply excess supply	offre excédentaire offre excessive excès d'offre	exceso de oferta sobreoferta
O-243	overt devaluation	dévaluation manifeste dévaluation patente dévaluation explicite	devaluación manifiesta
O-244	overt subsidy	subvention explicite	subvención explícita

O-245	over-the-counter financial derivatives OTC financial derivatives	dérivés financiers de gré à gré dérivés financiers hors cote	instrumentos financieros derivados extrabursátiles
O-246	over-the-counter market OTC	marché hors cote marché de gré à gré	mercado extrabursátil bolsín
O-247	over-the-counter option OTC option	option de gré à gré	opción extrabursátil
O-248	over-the-counter stock	action hors cote	acciones negociadas fuera de la Bolsa acciones negociadas en forma extrabursátil
O-249	overvaluation	surévaluation	sobrevaluación sobrevaloración
O-250	overvalued currency	monnaie surévaluée	moneda sobrevaluada moneda sobrevalorada
O-251	own funds, *see* capital		
O-252	own reserves, *see* nonborrowed reserves		
O-253	own saving	épargne propre	ahorro propio
O-254	own-account fixed capital formation	formation de capital fixe pour compte propre autoéquipement	formación de capital fijo por cuenta propia
O-255	owned reserves, *see* nonborrowed reserves		
O-256	owner equity, *see* net worth		
O-257	owners' equity, *see* net worth		
O-258	ownership country ownership borrower ownership program ownership	internalisation prise en charge maîtrise appropriation	identificación de los países con los programas identificarse con el programa sentido de propiedad de los prestatarios sentir el programa como propio autoría del programa

P

P-1	Paasche index, *see* current-weighted index		
P-2	Pacific Division [IMF]	Division Pacifique	División del Pacífico
P-3	Pacific Economic Cooperation Council *see also:* Asia-Pacific Economic Cooperation PECC	Conseil de coopération économique du Pacifique	Consejo de Cooperación Económica del Pacífico
P-4	Pacific Financial Community CFP	Communauté financière du Pacifique CFP	Comunidad Financiera del Pacífico CFP

P-5	package *see also:* financing package; policy package	série (de mesures) montage programme train (de mesures) batterie (de mesures)	conjunto de medidas paquete
P-6	paid-in capital, *see* paid-up capital		
P-7	paid-up capital paid-in capital	capital entièrement versé capital entièrement libéré	capital desembolsado capital pagado capital integrado
P-8	paired accounts	comptes couplés	cuentas emparejadas
P-9	palliative measure, *see* stopgap measure		
P-10	panel *see also:* fiscal panel expert panel	groupe d'experts panel	panel panel de expertos grupo de expertos grupo de consultores
P-11	panel expert [IMF]	expert expert consultant expert du fichier	experto experto consultor
P-12	paper [finance]	effets titres papier	efectos papeles comerciales títulos
P-13	paper currency paper money	papier-monnaie	papel moneda
P-14	paper money, *see* paper currency		
P-15	paperless security, *see* book-entry security		
P-16	par bond	obligation émise au pair	bono a la par

P-17	par bond exchange	échange d'obligations au pair
		échange de créances contre des
		    titres de même valeur nominale
			canje de bonos a la par
			operación de canje de bonos
			    a la par

P-18	par exchange	échange à parité	cambio a la par canje a la par
P-19	par value, *see* nominal value		
P-20	par value [currency]	pair parité	paridad
P-21	par value system	système des parités	sistema de paridades

P-22	parallel contingency financing	financement parallèle pour
		    imprévus
			financiamiento paralelo para
			    contingencias
			financiamiento paralelo para
			    imprevistos

P-23	parallel economy	économie parallèle	economía paralela
P-24	parallel financing side financing	financement parallèle	financiamiento paralelo

P-25	parallel market	marché parallèle	mercado paralelo
P-26	parapublic enterprise, *see* semipublic enterprise		
P-27	parent bank	banque d'origine banque mère	casa matriz
P-28	parent company parent corporation parent enterprise	maison mère société mère	casa matriz sociedad matriz empresa matriz
P-29	parent corporation, *see* parent company		
P-30	parent enterprise, *see* parent company		
P-31	pari passu clause [London Club]	clause *pari passu*	cláusula *pari passu* cláusula de igualdad de rango
P-32	Paris Club Secretariat	Secrétariat du Club de Paris	Secretaría del Club de París
P-33	Paris Office [IMF] EUO/PA	Bureau du FMI à Paris Bureau de Paris	Oficina del FMI en París
P-34	parity	parité	paridad relación de paridad
P-35	parity grid *see also:* divergence indicator; European Monetary System; European narrow margins arrangement; Exchange Rate Mechanism; intervention point grid of parities grid	grille de parités	parrilla de paridades red de relaciones de paridad
P-36	partial interest forgiveness	renoncement à une partie des intérêts dus remise d'une partie des intérêts dus	condonación parcial de los intereses adeudados
P-37	participant [IMF, SDR Department]	participant (au Département des DTS)	participante
P-38	participation rate labor participation rate labor force participation rate	taux d'activité économique taux de participation taux d'activité (de la population)	tasa de actividad tasa de participación tasa de participación en la fuerza laboral
P-39	participatory PRSP [PRGF] full participatory PRSP	établissement du DSRP selon un processus participatif établissement du DSRP selon un processus pleinement participatif	proceso plenamente participativo de elaboración del DELP
P-40	partner countries, *see* trading partners		
P-41	partnership	société de personnes société en nom collectif	sociedad sociedad colectiva asociación
P-42	pass on *see also:* onlending	rétrocéder	represtar

P-43	passbook account passbook savings account	compte sur livret compte d'épargne sur livret	cuenta en libreta de ahorro cuenta en cartilla de ahorros
P-44	passbook savings account, *see* passbook account		
P-45	passenger services	services fournis aux passagers	servicios de pasajeros
P-46	pass-through shifting of tax	répercussion translation	traslado traslación del impuesto repercusión del impuesto percusión del impuesto transmisión
P-47	pass-through basis, borrowing on a	rétrocession immédiate, emprunt avec	transferencia inmediata, préstamo con
P-48	pattern of trade trade patterns	structure du commerce structure des échanges configuration du commerce configuration des échanges courants d'échanges (commerciaux)	estructura del comercio estructura de los intercambios comerciales
P-49	pay parity *see also:* comparable worth	parité salariale parité des salaires	paridad salarial
P-50	pay scale, *see* salary scale		
P-51	pay schedule, *see* salary scale		
P-52	pay table, *see* salary scale		
P-53	pay-as-you-earn withholding PAYE	prélèvement à la source retenue à la source	retención del impuesto en la fuente retención en la fuente retención en el origen
P-54	pay-as-you-go system *see also:* funded system PAYG unfunded system unfunded pension plan	régime sans constitution de réserves régime de retraite par répartition régime de répartition régime sans capitalisation	régimen de reparto sistema de reparto régimen de financiación de los pagos con ingresos corrientes
P-55	PAYE, *see* pay-as-you-earn withholding		
P-56	PAYG, *see* pay-as-you-go system		
P-57	paying agency paying agent	agent payeur organisme payeur	organismo pagador organismo que efectúa el desembolso
P-58	paying agent, *see* paying agency		
P-59	payment arrears, *see* arrears		
P-60	payment in kind	paiement en nature prestation en nature	pago en especie
P-61	payment leads and lags	termaillage avances et retards dans les règlements décalage dans les paiements	adelantos y atrasos en los pagos

P-62	payments position, *see* balance of payments position		
P-63	payments restriction	restriction de(s) paiements restriction aux paiements restriction imposée sur les paiements	restricciones de pagos restricciones a los pagos
P-64	payments standstill, *see* debt moratorium		
P-65	payroll	état de paie	nómina planilla de liquidación de sueldos
P-66	payroll, *see* wage bill		
P-67	payroll cost(s), *see* wage cost(s)		

P-68	payroll tax
	see also: taxes on payroll or work
	  force
		impôt sur les salaires (à la charge
		  de l'employeur)
		cotisations sociales
		charges sociales
			impuestos sobre sueldos y salarios
			impuesto sobre la nómina
			cotizaciones salariales
			cargas sociales

P-69	PCE, *see* personal consumption expenditures		
P-70	PCRF, *see* Post-Conflict Reconstruction Fund		
P-71	PDP, *see* Policy Discussion Paper		
P-72	PDR, *see* Policy Development and Review Department		
P-73	PE ratio, *see* price-earnings ratio		
P-74	peak *see also:* trough	sommet point culminant crête maximum cyclique	nivel máximo nivel más alto cima del ciclo económico cresta
P-75	PECC, *see* Pacific Economic Cooperation Council		
P-76	peg [exchange rates]	monnaie de référence unité de référence	unidad de referencia moneda de referencia

P-77	peg a currency to
	see also: currency peg
		rattacher une monnaie à
		fixer le taux de change d'une
		  monnaie par rapport à
		déterminer le taux de change
		  d'une monnaie par référence à
		arrimer une monnaie à
			fijar la paridad
			vincular una moneda a
			establecer un tipo de cambio fijo
			  en relación con

P-78	pegged exchange rate	taux de change fixe parité fixe taux de change arrimé à	tipo de cambio fijo tipo de cambio fijo frente a otra moneda

P-79	pegged exchange rates within
	  horizontal bands
	[IMF exchange rate classification
	  system, 2006]
		rattachement à l'intérieur
		  de bandes horizontales
			tipos de cambio fijos dentro
			  de bandas horizontales

P-80	penalty charge [arrears]	commission de pénalisation pénalité	cargo punitivo comisión de penalización
P-81	penalty clause	clause pénale clause de pénalisation	cláusula penal cláusula de penalización

P-82	penalty interest *see also:* moratory interest penalty interest rate penalty rate	intérêt(s) de pénalisation	interés punitivo interés punitorio interés de penalización
P-83	penalty interest rate, *see* penalty interest		
P-84	penalty rate, *see* penalty interest		
P-85	pending claim outstanding claim	réclamation en instance	demanda pendiente
P-86	pension plan pension scheme	régime de retraite plan de retraite	plan de jubilaciones plan de pensiones fondo de pensiones caja de jubilaciones caja de pensiones
P-87	pension scheme, *see* pension plan		

P-88	pensionable salary
	pensionable wage
		salaire soumis à retenue pour
		  pension
			sueldo computable a efectos de la
			  jubilación
			salario computable a efectos
			  jubilatorios

P-89	pensionable wage, *see* pensionable salary		
P-90	pent-up demand	demande comprimée demande contenue demande refoulée	demanda reprimida
P-91	PER, *see* price-earnings ratio		
P-92	per capita per head	par habitant par personne	per cápita por habitante
P-93	per diem, *see* per night allowance		
P-94	per head, *see* per capita		
P-95	per night allowance [IMF] per diem	indemnité journalière per diem	viáticos dietas
P-96	percentage point	point (de pourcentage)	punto porcentual
P-97	perfect foresight model	modèle de prévision parfaite	modelo de previsión absoluta modelo de previsión perfecta
P-98	performance appraisal performance evaluation performance assessment	évaluation (du travail)	evaluación del desempeño
P-99	performance assessment, *see* performance appraisal		
P-100	performance benchmark, *see* benchmark		

P-101	performance bond	garantie de bonne fin
		caution de bonne exécution
		  (d'un contrat)
			fianza de cumplimiento
			  (de un contrato)
			garantía de cumplimiento
			garantía de ejecución

P-102	performance budget	budget de réalisation	presupuesto por resultados
	output budget	budget fonctionnel	sistema presupuestario en base
	performance budgeting	élaboration du budget sur la base	a resultados
	performance budgeting system	des résultats	
		système budgétaire basé sur les	
		résultats	

P-103   performance budgeting, *see* performance budget

P-104   performance budgeting system, *see* performance budget

P-105	performance contract	contrat d'objectifs	contrato por resultado
	management contract	contrat de performance	contrato de gestión
	development contract	contrat-plan	contrato de desarrollo
		contrat-programme	
		contrat de plan	
		contrat de prestations	
		contrat de développement	

P-106	performance criterion	critère de réalisation	criterio de ejecución
	[IMF]	critère d'exécution	
		critère de performance	

P-107   performance evaluation, *see* performance appraisal

| P-108 | performance of financial | exécution d'obligations financières | cumplimiento de obligaciones |
| | obligations | | financieras |

P-109   performing debt, *see* performing loan

P-110	performing loan	prêt productif	préstamo redituable
	performing debt		préstamo productivo
			préstamo en situación regular
			deuda al corriente

P-111	period of consent	délai de consentement	plazo de aceptación
	[IMF quota increase]	délai de notification du	plazo para notificar la aceptación
		consentement	plazo de notificación del
		délai d'acceptation	consentimiento
		délai de notification de	
		l'acceptation	

| P-112 | periodic charges | commissions périodiques | cargos periódicos |
| | [IMF] | | |

P-113	periodic consultation	consultations périodiques	consulta periódica
	[IMF]		
	see also: formal consultation		

P-114	periodicity	périodicité (des données)	periodicidad (de los datos)
	[IMF]		
	see also: frequency		

P-115	perpetual bond	obligation perpétuelle	bono perpetuo
	nonredeemable bond	rente perpétuelle	
	nonmaturing bond		
	annuity bond		
	consol		
	[GBR]		

P-116	perpetual inventory method perpetual inventory system	méthode de l'inventaire permanent	método de inventario permanente sistema de inventario perpetuo método de inventario perpetuo
P-117	perpetual inventory system, *see* perpetual inventory method		
P-118	personal allowance, *see* personal exemption		

P-119	Personal Assistant to the
	  Managing Director
	[IMF]
		Assistant personnel du Directeur
		  général
			Asistente Personal del Director
			  Gerente

P-120	personal consumption
	  expenditures
	PCE
	private consumption expenditure
		dépenses de consommation des
		  particuliers
		dépenses de consommation des
		  ménages
		consommation privée
			gastos de consumo personal
			gasto de consumo privado

P-121	personal effects personal property	effets personnels	efectos personales
P-122	personal exemption [taxation] personal allowance	abattement à la base	deducción por gastos personales o cargas de familia
P-123	personal income [macroeconomics]	revenu des ménages revenu des particuliers	renta personal ingreso personal renta de los particulares

P-124	personal income tax	impôt sur le revenu des personnes
		  physiques
		IRPP
			impuesto sobre la renta de las
			  personas físicas

P-125	personal loan, *see* signature loan		
P-126	personal property [taxation]	biens meubles biens mobiliers	bienes muebles
P-127	personal property, *see* personal effects		
P-128	personal savings	épargne des ménages épargne des particuliers	ahorro personal ahorro de los particulares
P-129	personal travel	voyages à titre personnel	viajes personales
P-130	Personnel Manager, Senior [IMF] SPM	responsable principal des ressources humaines	Gerente de Recursos Humanos
P-131	perverse effect	effet pervers effet pernicieux	efecto perverso efecto pernicioso
P-132	pessimistic scenario, *see* worse-policies scenario		
P-133	pessimistic scenario, *see* worst-case scenario		
P-134	PFI, *see* public financial institution		
P-135	PFP, *see* policy framework paper		
P-136	phase out	éliminer progressivement supprimer progressivement	eliminar por etapas abolir progresivamente

P-137	phasing [IMF] phasing of purchases	échelonnement échelonnement des achats	escalonamiento escalonamiento de las compras
P-138	phasing of purchases, *see* phasing		
P-139	Pigou effect, *see* real balances effect		
P-140	PIN, *see* Public Information Notice		
P-141	pioneer industry *see also:* frontier technology; high technology industry	industrie de pointe	industria de vanguardia industria pionera
P-142	PIP, *see* public investment program		
P-143	pipeline, in the	sous dossier (actif) dans la filière à l'étude en préparation en réserve	preparación, en tramitación, en
P-144	placement [securities]	placement	colocación

P-145	planning-programming-budgeting
	  system
	PPBS
	program-based budgeting system
		système de planification, de
		  programmation et de préparation
		  du budget
		rationalisation des choix
		  budgétaires
			sistema de planificación,
			  programación y presupuestación
			SPPP
			sistema de presupuesto
			  planificado de programas

P-146	plant and equipment	installations et outillage installations et équipements investissements productifs immobilisations	instalaciones y equipo
P-147	plant capacity, *see* installed capacity		
P-148	pledge, *see* pledged asset		
P-149	pledge [HIPC]	contribution annoncée engagement	contribución prometida aportación prometida
P-150	pledged account	compte assigné en gage compte gagé	cuenta comprometida
P-151	pledged asset pledge	nantissement caution garantie sûreté actif gagé	prenda activo dado en prenda activo prendado caución garantía
P-152	pledged gold	or mis en gage	oro en prenda
P-153	PMA, *see* Policy Monitoring Arrangement		
P-154	POD, *see* PRGF Operations Division		
P-155	point of valuation	lieu d'évaluation	punto de valoración
P-156	policies and practices of the IMF	politiques et pratiques du FMI politiques et usages du FMI	políticas y prácticas del FMI

P-157	policies and procedures of the Fund	principes et procédures du FMI	políticas y procedimientos del FMI
P-158	Policy Communication Division [IMF]	Division communication de la politique institutionnelle	División de Comunicaciones sobre Políticas
P-159	Policy Development and Review Department [IMF] PDR	Département de l'élaboration et de l'examen des politiques	Departamento de Elaboración y Examen de Políticas
P-160	Policy Discussion Paper [IMF] PDP	document de synthèse	documento de análisis de política económica
P-161	policy framework paper [IMF-IBRD] PFP	document-cadre de politique économique DCPE	documento sobre parámetros de política económica
P-162	policy instrument	instrument de politique (économique, monétaire, ...)	instrumento de política (económica, monetaria, ...)
P-163	policy interest rate, *see* policy rate		
P-164	policy issue [IMF]	question d'ordre général question de politique économique	cuestión de política cuestión de política económica
P-165	policy loans, *see* policy-based lending		
P-166	policy mix	dosage de mesures combinaison de mesures (de politique économique)	combinación de medidas (de política económica) articulación de las políticas
P-167	Policy Monitoring Arrangement PMA	arrangement de suivi des politiques ASP	Mecanismo de Seguimiento de las Políticas MSP
P-168	policy of emergency assistance to post-conflict countries, *see* emergency post-conflict assistance		
P-169	policy of restraint	politique de modération politique d'austérité	política de moderación política de austeridad
P-170	policy on enlarged access to the Fund's resources [IMF] EAP enlarged access policy	politique d'accès élargi aux ressources du FMI politique d'accès élargi	política de mayor acceso a los recursos del FMI política de mayor acceso
P-171	policy package *see also:* package	ensemble de mesures train de mesures	conjunto de medidas (de política) programa de medidas paquete de medidas
P-172	policy rate policy interest rate	taux directeur	tasa de interés de intervención tasa de intervención tasa de interés clave tasa de interés básica tasa de interés indicativa
P-173	Policy Review Division [IMF] PRD	Division examen des politiques	División de Examen de Políticas

P-174	policy statement	déclaration de politique générale	declaración de política
			declaración de principios
P-175	Policy Support Instrument	instrument de soutien à la politique	Instrumento de Apoyo a la Política
	[IMF]	économique	Económica
	PSI	ISPE	IAPE
		programme sans financement	
P-176	policy variable	variable de politique économique	variable de política
			variable de política económica
P-177	policy-based lending	prêts à l'appui de réformes	préstamos en apoyo de políticas
	[IBRD]	prêts à l'appui de mesures	
	policy loans	d'ajustement	
		prêts en faveur de réformes	
P-178	policymaker	responsable de la politique	autoridad responsable de la
		économique	política económica
		décideur	encargado de formular la política
		autorité	económica
		dirigeant	responsable de la política
			económica
P-179	policymaking	formulation de la politique	formulación de la política
		économique	económica
			formulación de políticas
P-180	political economy	économie politique	economía política
P-181	political risk, *see* sovereign risk		
P-182	poll tax, *see* head tax		
P-183	pool, *see* syndicate		
P-184	pooling arrangement	dispositif de mise en commun	acuerdo de mancomunación
		de ressources	de recursos
		accord de mise en commun	
		de ressources	
P-185	population pressure	pression démographique	presión demográfica
	demographic pressure	poussée démographique	
P-186	population pyramid	pyramide des âges	pirámide de población
	age pyramid		pirámide etaria
			árbol de población
P-187	port services	services portuaires	servicios portuarios
P-188	portfolio assets	actifs de portefeuille	activos en cartera
		actifs en portefeuille	
P-189	portfolio choice	choix d'un portefeuille	selección de la cartera
		choix de portefeuille	
P-190	portfolio choice theory	théorie des choix de portefeuille	teoría de la selección de carteras
P-191	portfolio debt flow	investissements de portefeuille	flujo de inversión de cartera
		en titres de créance	en títulos de deuda
			flujo de inversión de cartera
			en activos de renta fija

P-192	portfolio equity flow	investissements de portefeuille sous forme de participations	flujo de inversión de cartera en acciones flujo de inversión de cartera en activos de renta variable
P-193	portfolio flow	flux d'investissements de portefeuille	flujo de inversión de cartera
P-194	portfolio investment	investissement(s) de portefeuille	inversión de cartera inversiones de cartera
P-195	Portfolio Investment Survey, *see* Task Force on Coordinated Portfolio Investment Survey		
P-196	portfolio rebalancing, *see* rebalancing of portfolio		
P-197	portfolio reshuffling, *see* portfolio shift		
P-198	portfolio shift portfolio reshuffling portfolio switching	restructuration du portefeuille modification du portefeuille remodelage du portefeuille remaniement du portefeuille variation de la composition du portefeuille arbitrage de portefeuille	reestructuración de la cartera cambio de composición de la cartera
P-199	portfolio switching, *see* portfolio shift		
P-200	portfolio theory	théorie de portefeuille	teoría de la cartera
P-201	position	position solde situation	posición saldo situación
P-202	position data, *see* stock data		
P-203	position in the Fund net Fund position	position au FMI position nette au FMI	posición en el FMI saldo neto en el FMI posición neta en el FMI
P-204	positive bias, *see* upward bias		
P-205	positive externality external economy	économie externe avantage externe	externalidad positiva economía externa
P-206	Post SCA-2 Administered Account	Compte administré post-CSC-2	Cuenta Administrada Post CEC-2
P-207	post-conflict country *see also:* emergency post-conflict assistance	pays sortant d'un conflit	país en situación de posconflicto
P-208	Post-Conflict Reconstruction Fund [IBRD] PCRF	Fonds postconflit Fonds pour la reconstruction des pays sortant d'un conflit	Fondo para la Reconstrucción de Países en Etapa de Posconflicto Fondo Posconflicto
P-209	posted price	prix affiché prix coté	precio anunciado
P-210	posted value, *see* official value		
P-211	postpayment	paiement différé	pago diferido

P-212	post-program monitoring [IMF] PPM	suivi postprogramme	seguimiento posterior a un programa
P-213	potential growth	croissance potentielle	crecimiento potencial crecimiento posible
P-214	potential output [macroeconomics]	produit potentiel potentiel de production	producto potencial
P-215	potential output [microeconomics]	production potentielle	producción potencial
P-216	Poverty and Social Impact Analysis poverty and social impact assessment PSIA	analyse des impacts sur la pauvreté et le social AIPS	Análisis del Impacto Social y en la Pobreza

P-217 poverty and social impact assessment, *see* Poverty and Social Impact Analysis

P-218 poverty income threshold, *see* poverty line

P-219	poverty line poverty income threshold	seuil de pauvreté	línea de pobreza umbral de pobreza
P-220	Poverty Reduction and Growth Facility [IMF] PRGF	facilité pour la réduction de la pauvreté et pour la croissance FRPC	Servicio para el Crecimiento y la Lucha contra la Pobreza SCLP

P-221 PPBS, *see* planning-programming-budgeting system

P-222 PPF, *see* production frontier

P-223 PPI, *see* producer price index

P-224 PPM, *see* post-program monitoring

P-225 PPP, *see* purchasing power parity

P-226 PPP exchange rate, *see* purchasing power parity exchange rate

P-227 PR, *see* Press Release

P-228 practices of the Fund, *see* rules and practices of the Fund

P-229 PRD, *see* previously rescheduled debt

P-230 PRD, *see* Policy Review Division

P-231	precautionary balances [IMF]	encaisses de précaution encaisses-précaution	saldos precautorios saldos de precaución
P-232	precautionary demand for money	demande de monnaie pour des motifs de précaution	demanda de dinero por motivo de precaución demanda de dinero con fines de precaución demanda precautoria de dinero
P-233	precautionary motive	motif de précaution	motivo de precaución motivo precaución

P-234	predictive power	pouvoir prédictif capacité prédictive	poder de predicción capacidad de predicción
P-235	pre-emerging market country	pays préémergent	país de mercado preemergente
P-236	preference bond	obligation privilégiée	bono preferencial bono preferido obligación preferente obligación privilegiada
P-237	preference share, *see* preferred share		
P-238	preferential tariff arrangement *see also:* tariff preferences	accord tarifaire préférentiel	acuerdo arancelario preferencial
P-239	Preferential Trade Area for Eastern and Southern African States PTA	Zone d'échanges préférentiels des États de l'Afrique de l'Est et de l'Afrique australe ZEP	Zona de comercio preferencial para los Estados del África Oriental y del África Austral ZCP
P-240	preferred creditor	créancier privilégié	acreedor privilegiado
P-241	preferred share preferred stock preference share [GBR]	action privilégiée	acción privilegiada acción preferencial acción preferente acción que confiere preferencia
P-242	preferred stock, *see* preferred share		
P-243	pre-investment study	étude de préinvestissement étude de rentabilité étude de viabilité	estudio de preinversión
P-244	premium	report	prima
P-245	premium, at a	à prime avec prime	sobre la par por encima del valor nominal con prima
P-246	premium received	prime recouvrée	prima cobrada
P-247	premiums less claims	primes diminuées des indemnités	primas menos indemnizaciones
P-248	prepayment	paiement anticipé prépaiement	pago anticipado anticipo
P-249	prepayment clause	clause de remboursement anticipé	cláusula de reembolso anticipado
P-250	prepayment of debt debt prepayment	remboursement anticipé de la dette	pago anticipado de la deuda reembolso anticipado de deudas
P-251	prescribed holder of SDRs, *see* prescribed SDR holder		
P-252	prescribed operation [SDR]	opération agréée	operación autorizada
P-253	prescribed SDR holder [IMF] prescribed holder of SDRs	détenteur agréé de DTS	tenedor autorizado de DEG
P-254	prescription of currency, *see* prescription of currency requirements		

P-255	prescription of currency requirements [IMF] prescription of currency	monnaie de règlement	moneda que debe utilizarse en los pagos moneda de pago
P-256	present value, *see* current value		
P-257	Press Release [IMF] PR	communiqué de presse	comunicado de prensa
P-258	presumptive assessment [taxation]	imposition forfaitaire	liquidación sobre base presuntiva
P-259	pretax, *see* before taxes		
P-260	prevailing market rate *see also:* market rate going rate	taux du marché taux pratiqué sur le marché taux en vigueur sur le marché	tipo de cambio del mercado tipo de cambio vigente en el mercado
P-261	prevention [IMF] preventive action preventive measure	prévention mesure préventive action préventive	prevención acción preventiva medida preventiva
P-262	preventive action, *see* prevention		
P-263	preventive measure, *see* prevention		
P-264	previously rescheduled debt [Paris Club] PRD	dette précédemment rééchelonnée DPR	deuda previamente reprogramada DPR
P-265	PRGF, *see* Poverty Reduction and Growth Facility		
P-266	PRGF and HIPC Financing Division [IMF]	Division du financement de la FRPC et de l'initiative PPTE	División de Financiamiento del SCLP y la Iniciativa para los PPME
P-267	PRGF arrangement [IMF]	accord FRPC	acuerdo en el marco del SCLP
P-268	PRGF Operations Division [IMF] POD	Division opérations de la facilité pour la réduction de la pauvreté et pour la croissance Division opérations de la FRPC	División de Operaciones del Servicio para el Crecimiento y la Lucha contra la Pobreza División de Operaciones del SCLP
P-269	PRGF Trust *see also:* PRGF-ESF Trust [IMF]	compte de fiducie de la FRPC	Cuenta Fiduciaria del SCLP
P-270	PRGF Trust loan [IMF]	prêt financé sur ressources du compte de fiducie de la FRPC	préstamo de la Cuenta Fiduciaria del SCLP préstamo en el marco de la Cuenta Fiduciaria del SCLP
P-271	PRGF Trust Loan Account Loan Account	compte de prêts compte de prêts du compte de fiducie de la FRPC	Cuenta de Préstamos de la Cuenta Fiduciaria del SCLP Cuenta de Préstamos
P-272	PRGF Trust Reserve Account [IMF] Reserve Account	réserve du compte de fiducie de la FRPC réserve	Cuenta de Reservas de la Cuenta Fiduciaria del SCLP

P-273	PRGF Trust Subsidy Account
	Subsidy Account
		compte de bonification du compte
		  de fiducie de la FRPC
		compte de bonification
			Cuenta de Subvención de la
			  Cuenta Fiduciaria del SCLP
			Cuenta de Subvención

P-274	PRGF-ESF Trust	compte de fiducie FRPC–FCE	Cuenta Fiduciaria SCLP–SSE

P-275	PRGF-HIPC Trust
	[IMF]
		fonds fiduciaire FRPC–PPTE
		fonds fiduciaire pour les opérations
		  spéciales de la FRPC en faveur
		  des pays pauvres très endettés
		  et les opérations de la FRPC
		  intérimaire
			Fondo Fiduciario SCLP–PPME

P-276	price control *see also:* control	contrôle des prix réglementation des prix	control de precios regulación de los precios
P-277	price determination, *see* pricing		
P-278	price discrimination *see also:* pricing discriminatory pricing	différenciation des prix fixation de prix différentiels tarification discriminatoire	discriminación de precios fijación discriminatoria de precios
P-279	price elasticity	élasticité par rapport aux prix élasticité-prix	elasticidad con respecto al precio elasticidad-precio
P-280	price expectations	anticipations de prix	expectativas de precios expectativas con respecto a los precios
P-281	price fixing *see also:* pricing	entente sur le prix fixation du prix	fijación de precios por acuerdo pacto de imposición de precios
P-282	price follower *see also:* price leader	suiveur de prix	seguidor de precios
P-283	price freeze	blocage des prix gel des prix	congelación de precios
P-284	price incentive	incitation par les prix	incentivo de precios incentivo a través de los precios
P-285	price index	indice des prix	índice de precios
P-286	price inflation *see also:* cost inflation	hausse des prix inflation	inflación de precios

P-287	price leader
	see also: price follower
		agent économique qui influence le
		  prix
			líder de precios
			empresa líder en materia de
			  precios
			agente económico que impone el
			  precio

P-288	price maker
	see also: price taker
	price setter
		agent économique qui détermine le
		  prix
		fixeur de prix
		décideur de prix
			agente económico que determina
			  el precio
			formador de precios

P-289	price policy, *see* pricing policy		
P-290	price premium	surprix	sobreprecio
P-291	price range	fourchette des prix	escala de precios gama de precios

| P-292 | price sensitivity | sensibilité-prix | sensibilidad al precio |
| | | sensibilité aux prix | sensibilidad con respecto al precio |

P-293 price setter, *see* price maker

P-294 price setting, *see* pricing

P-295	price taker	agent économique n'ayant pas	agente económico sin influencia en
	see also: price maker	d'influence sur le prix	el precio
		preneur de prix	tomador de precios

P-296	price-earnings ratio	coefficient de capitalisation des	relación precio-beneficios
	PER	résultats	relación precio-ganancia
	PE ratio	CCR	
		ratio cours–bénéfices	

P-297	pricing	tarification	fijación de precios
	see also: price discrimination	établissement du prix	cálculo de precios
	price setting	calcul du prix	determinación de precios
	price determination	fixation du prix	
		détermination du prix	

| P-298 | pricing policy | politique des prix | política de fijación de precios |
| | price policy | politique de détermination des prix | política de precios |

P-299 pricing policy, *see* rate setting policy

P-300 primary balance, *see* primary fiscal balance

P-301 primary capital, *see* tier 1 capital

P-302 primary commodity, *see* primary product

| P-303 | primary exporting country | pays exportateur de produits | país exportador de productos |
| | | primaires | primarios |

| P-304 | primary fiscal balance | solde budgétaire primaire | saldo fiscal primario |
| | primary balance | solde primaire | resultado primario |

| P-305 | primary market | marché primaire | mercado primario |
| | *see also:* secondary market | marché des émissions | |

| P-306 | primary money | monnaie primaire | dinero primario |
| | *see also:* base money | | |

| P-307 | primary producing country | pays de production primaire | país de producción primaria |

P-308	primary product	produit primaire	producto primario
	see also: commodity	produit de base	
	primary commodity		
	commodity		

P-309 primary reserve assets, *see* primary reserves

P-310	primary reserves	actifs de réserve primaires	reservas primarias
	[USA]	instruments de réserve primaires	activos primarios de reserva
	primary reserve assets		

| P-311 | prime borrower | emprunteur de premier ordre | prestatario de primera clase |
| | | emprunteur bien coté | prestatario de primera línea |

P-312	prime rate base lending rate BLR	taux de base (des banques) TDB taux préférentiel	tasa de interés preferencial
P-313	principal office of the Fund, *see* headquarters		
P-314	principal reserve asset	principal instrument de réserve	principal activo de reserva
P-315	prior action(s) [IMF arrangements]	mesures préalables	acciones previas medidas previas
P-316	prior challenge (not subject to) [IMF] *see also:* unchallengeable use	ne pas opposer d'objection *a priori*	no objetar a priori

P-317	prioritization of debt
	ranking of claims
		traitement sélectif des créances
		classement des créances par
		  priorité
			establecimiento de un orden de
			  prelación de los créditos
			establecimiento de un orden de
			  precedencia de los créditos
			establecimiento de un orden de
			  prioridad de la deuda

P-318	prisoner's dilemma *see also:* game theory; Nash equilibrium; zero-sum game	dilemne des prisonniers	dilema del prisionero
P-319	private consumption expenditure, *see* personal consumption expenditures		
P-320	private equity	capital-investissement	capital de riesgo capital riesgo
P-321	private nonprofit institution	institution privée sans but lucratif	institución privada sin fines de lucro
P-322	private offering, *see* private placement		
P-323	private paper	effets privés	efectos privados títulos privados
P-324	private placement [securities] private offering	placement privé placement par voie privée emprunt réservé (aux investisseurs institutionnels)	colocación privada emisión privada suscripción restringida

P-325	private rate of return
	see also: social rate of return
	PRR
		taux de rentabilité du secteur privé
		taux de rentabilité pour le secteur
		  privé
			tasa de rentabilidad del sector
			  privado
			tasa de rentabilidad para el sector
			  privado
			tasa de retorno privada

P-326	privatization *see also:* divestiture (of enterprises)	privatisation désétatisation dénationalisation	privatización
P-327	privatization voucher	bon de privatisation	cupón de privatización
P-328	probability probability level	probabilité	probabilidad nivel de probabilidad
P-329	probability level, *see* probability		
P-330	problem bank	banque en difficulté	banco en situación problemática banco en dificultades

P-331	problem loan, *see* nonaccrual loan		
P-332	procedural guidelines [IMF Executive Board]	règles générales de procédure	normas de procedimiento
P-333	proceeds (from a sale)	produit (d'une vente)	producto (de una venta)
P-334	procurement	passation des marchés (publics)	adquisiciones
P-335	procurement price	prix officiel au producteur prix officiel au fournisseur	precio oficial al proveedor precio oficial al productor
P-336	procyclical	qui suit les mouvements de la conjoncture qui suit les mouvements cycliques procyclique	procíclico que sigue los movimientos de la coyuntura
P-337	producer good, *see* capital good		
P-338	producer price producer's price	prix au producteur prix à la production prix-producteurs prix départ-usine	precio al productor precio a la producción precio en fábrica
P-339	producer price index PPI	indice des prix à la production IPP	índice de precios al productor IPP índice de precios a la producción IPP índice de precios industriales IPI
P-340	producer surplus *see also:* consumer surplus; social surplus	surplus du producteur	superávit del productor
P-341	producer's price, *see* producer price		
P-342	producer's value	prix départ-usine prix à la production	valor a precio de productor
P-343	product *see also:* output	produit	producto
P-344	product wage	salaire en unités de produits	salario en unidades de producto
P-345	production account	compte de production	cuenta de producción
P-346	production factor *see also:* input factor of production factor input	facteur de production	factor de producción
P-347	production frontier production possibility frontier PPF production possibility boundary production possibility curve transformation curve	courbe des possibilités de production frontière des possibilités de production frontière de production	frontera de producción frontera de las posibilidades de producción curva de las posibilidades de producción
P-348	production function	fonction de production	función de producción

P-349	production gap, *see* output gap		
P-350	production incentive	incitation à la production encouragement à la production stimulants de la production	incentivo a la producción
P-351	production possibility boundary, *see* production frontier		
P-352	production possibility curve, *see* production frontier		
P-353	production possibility frontier, *see* production frontier		
P-354	production sharing contract PSC	contrat de partage de la production	contrato de repartición de la producción contrato de distribución de la producción
P-355	productive asset, *see* earning asset		
P-356	productive base	appareil de production base productive	base de producción base productiva
P-357	productivity gain	gain de productivité accroissement de la productivité	aumento de la productividad incremento de la productividad
P-358	productivity of labor, *see* labor productivity		
P-359	profit and loss statement, *see* income statement		
P-360	profit margin *see also:* markup	marge bénéficiaire marge de bénéfices	margen de ganancia margen de utilidad margen de beneficios
P-361	profit sharing	participation (aux bénéfices) intéressement (des salariés aux bénéfices de l'entreprise)	participación en las utilidades participación en las ganancias participación en los beneficios
P-362	profit squeeze	compression des bénéfices laminage des bénéfices	reducción de los márgenes de utilidad reducción de los márgenes de ganancia reducción de los márgenes de beneficio
P-363	profit taking	prise de bénéfice(s) vente bénéficiaire vente avec bénéfice	realización de utilidades toma de utilidades toma de ganancias realización de beneficios
P-364	profit tax	impôt sur les bénéfices	impuesto sobre las utilidades impuesto sobre las ganancias impuesto sobre los beneficios
P-365	profitability earning power	rentabilité	rentabilidad
P-366	profits	bénéfices profit(s)	utilidades ganancias beneficios lucro
P-367	profits of export or import monopolies	bénéfices des monopoles d'exportation ou d'importation	utilidades de los monopolios de exportación o de importación

P-368	profits of fiscal monopolies	bénéfices des monopoles fiscaux	utilidades de los monopolios fiscales
P-369	program budget	élaboration du budget en fonction des objectifs système budgétaire fondé sur des programmes budget-programme	presupuesto por programas presupuesto programa
P-370	program country [IMF]	pays appliquant un programme approuvé par le FMI pays sous programme avec le FMI	país que aplica un programa aprobado por el FMI
P-371	program loan	prêt-programme	préstamo para programas financiamiento para programas
P-372	program monitoring [IMF]	suivi du programme	supervisión de programas monitoreo de programas
P-373	program ownership, *see* ownership		
P-374	program trading [securities]	négociation informatisée négociation assistée par ordinateur gestion informatisée des portefeuilles	contratación programada de valores bursátiles
P-375	program-based budgeting system, *see* planning-programming-budgeting system		
P-376	progress report status report	rapport d'étape rapport d'avancement rapport d'activité rapport sur l'état des travaux rapport sur l'avancement des travaux rapport intérimaire	informe de avance informe de situación informe sobre la labor realizada informe sobre la marcha de los trabajos informe de progreso
P-377	progressive tax	impôt progressif	impuesto progresivo
P-378	progressivity [taxation]	progressivité	progresividad
P-379	project grant [public finance] project-specific grant	don-projet subvention pour un projet	subvención para proyectos
P-380	project-specific grant, *see* project grant		
P-381	prolonged user of IMF resources [IMF]	utilisateur persistant utilisateur de longue durée pays qui fait un usage prolongé des ressources du FMI	país que utiliza los recursos del FMI de manera prolongada
P-382	promissory note	billet à ordre	pagaré
P-383	prompt repurchase expectation, *see* early repurchase expectation		
P-384	propensity to consume	propension à consommer	propensión al consumo propensión a consumir
P-385	propensity to save	propension à épargner	propensión al ahorro propensión a ahorrar

P-386	property and assets of the Fund [IMF]	biens et avoirs du FMI	bienes y activos del FMI
P-387	property income	revenu de la propriété revenu du patrimoine	renta de la propiedad ingreso de la propiedad
P-388	property tax taxes on property	impôts sur le patrimoine impôt sur la propriété impôt foncier impôt sur la fortune	impuesto inmobiliario impuesto sobre la propiedad impuesto predial
P-389	proposed amendment [IMF] *see also:* draft amendment	proposition d'amendement amendement proposé proposition de modification modification proposée	propuesta de enmienda propuesta de modificación
P-390	proposed resolution [IMF] *see also:* draft resolution	résolution proposée	propuesta de resolución
P-391	protective tariff	tarif protectionniste tarif aux fins de protection	arancel proteccionista
P-392	protracted arrears (to the Fund) [IMF] *see also:* continuous arrears (to the Fund)	arriérés persistants (envers le FMI) arriérés prolongés (envers le FMI) arriérés de longue date (envers le FMI)	atrasos persistentes ante el FMI atrasos prolongados en los pagos al FMI
P-393	proven record, to establish a, *see* track record, to establish a positive		
P-394	provident fund	fonds de prévoyance	fondo de previsión
P-395	provision [GBR] *see also:* depreciation allowance; reserve accruals [USA]	provision	reserva provisión previsión
P-396	provisional administration [insolvency] *see also:* receivership conservatorship	administration judiciaire provisoire	administración provisional intervención administración judicial sindicatura
P-397	provisional administrator [insolvency] conservator	administrateur provisoire	administrador provisional interventor
P-398	provisioning establishment of provisions	provisionnement constitution de provisions	constitución de reservas aprovisionamiento constitución de provisiones
P-399	proxy, *see* proxy variable		
P-400	proxy variable proxy	variable de substitution variable représentative variable de remplacement	variable sustitutiva variable representativa
P-401	PRR, *see* private rate of return		

P-402	PRSP approach
	see also: Poverty Reduction
	  Strategy Paper
	PRSP process
	[PRGF]
		dispositif des DSRP
		processus d'élaboration des DSRP
		processus des DSRP
			proceso de los DELP
			proceso de elaboración de los
			  DELP
			mecanismo de los DELP

P-403	PRSP Preparation Status Report
	[IMF-IBRD]
	see also: PRSP Progress Report
		rapport d'avancement sur la
		  préparation du DSRP
			Informe de situación sobre la
			  preparación del DELP

P-404	PRSP process, *see* PRSP approach		

P-405	PRSP Progress Report
	see also: PRSP Preparation Status
	  Report
	Annual PRSP Progress Report
	[IMF, World Bank-IDA]
	APR
		rapport d'étape sur la mise en
		  œuvre du DSRP
		rapport d'étape annuel sur la mise
		  en œuvre du DSRP
			Informe anual de situación sobre la
			  preparación del DELP

P-406	prudential ratios [bank supervision]	ratios prudentiels ratios de liquidité et de solvabilité	coeficientes prudenciales
P-407	prudential regulation	réglementation prudentielle	regulación prudencial
P-408	prudential standards	normes prudentielles règles prudentielles règles de gestion prudente	normas prudenciales reglas prudenciales
P-409	PSBR, *see* public sector borrowing requirement(s)		
P-410	PSC, *see* production sharing contract		
P-411	PSI, *see* Policy Support Instrument		
P-412	PSIA, *see* Poverty and Social Impact Analysis		
P-413	PSIP, *see* public investment program		
P-414	PTA, *see* Preferential Trade Area for Eastern and Southern African States		
P-415	Public Affairs Division [IMF]	Division relations publiques	División de Relaciones Públicas
P-416	Public Affairs Officer [IMF]	agent de relations publiques	Oficial de Relaciones Públicas

P-417	Public Affairs Officer, Senior
	[IMF]
		agent principal de relations
		  publiques
			Oficial Principal de Relaciones
			  Públicas

P-418	public auction *see also:* public sale	adjudication publique enchères vente aux enchères	subasta pública remate público
P-419	public authorities	pouvoirs publics autorités puissance publique	autoridades públicas autoridades gubernamentales

P-420	public capital formation	formation de capital du secteur
		  public
			formación de capital del sector
			  público

P-421	public corporation, *see* public enterprise		

P-422	public debt	dette publique	deuda pública
P-423	public enterprise public corporation state enterprise state-owned enterprise SOE state-owned corporation government enterprise government corporation	entreprise publique entreprise d'État société publique	empresa estatal empresa del Estado empresa pública sociedad pública
P-424	public financial institution PFI	institution financière publique	institución financiera pública
P-425	Public Financial Management I, II Division [IMF] M1, M2	Division de la gestion des finances publiques I, II	División de Gestión de las Finanzas Públicas I, II
P-426	public good *see also:* global public goods; merit good	bien public	bien público
P-427	Public Information Notice [IMF] PIN	note d'information au public	nota de información al público
P-428	public investment program PIP public sector investment program PSIP	programme d'investissements publics PIP	programa de inversión pública PIP programa de inversiones del sector público
P-429	public nonmonetary enterprise	entreprise publique non monétaire	empresa pública no monetaria
P-430	public offering [securities] public placement	offre publique (de vente) placement de titres dans le public émission (publique) sur le marché	emisión pública
P-431	public or publicly guaranteed debt government or government- guaranteed debt	dette contractée ou garantie par l'État dette contractée ou avalisée par l'État	deuda contraída o garantizada por el Estado
P-432	public order and safety	ordre et sécurité publics	orden público y seguridad
P-433	public placement, *see* public offering		
P-434	public sale *see also:* public auction	offre publique de vente OPV	venta pública
P-435	public sector borrowing requirement(s) PSBR	besoin de financement du secteur public besoin d'emprunt du secteur public	necesidades de financiamiento del sector público NFSP
P-436	public sector investment program, *see* public investment program		
P-437	public service corporation, *see* utility		
P-438	public utility, *see* utility		
P-439	Publication Services Section [IMF]	Section des services de publications	Sección de Servicios de Publicaciones

P-440	publicly issued	émis en souscription publique en émission publique émis dans le public	emitido mediante suscripción pública emitido por suscripción pública
P-441	publicly traded share	action cotée en bourse	acción cotizada en bolsa
P-442	pump priming, *see* deficit financing		
P-443	punitive measure [IMF]	mesure punitive	medida punitiva
P-444	purchase [IMF]	achat	compra
P-445	purchaser's price	prix d'acquisition	precio de comprador precio de adquisición
P-446	purchasers' value	valeur d'acquisition	valor a precio de comprador
P-447	purchasing power parity PPP	parité de pouvoir d'achat PPA	paridad del poder adquisitivo paridad de poder de compra

P-448	purchasing power parity exchange
	  rate
	PPP exchange rate
		taux de change réel de parité de
		  pouvoir d'achat
		taux de change réel de PPA
			tipo de cambio basado en la
			  paridad del poder adquisitivo

P-449	pure economic rent	rente économique pure rente de situation	renta económica pura renta de situación
P-450	put, *see* put option clause		
P-451	put, *see* put option		
P-452	put option, *see* put option clause		
P-453	put option put	option de vente	opción de venta *put*
P-454	put option clause put option put	option d'encaissement anticipé droit d'encaissement par anticipation clause d'encaissement anticipé	cláusula de rescate anticipado opción de rescate anticipado

Q

Q-1	QMV, *see* qualified majority voting		
Q-2	*QNA Manual, see Quarterly National Accounts Manual--Concepts, Data Sources, and Compilation*		
Q-3	qualified *see also:* eligible	remplissant les conditions nécessaires	calificado cualificado idóneo
Q-4	qualified majority, *see* special majority		
Q-5	qualified majority voting QMV	vote à la majorité qualifiée	votación por mayoría especial votación por mayoría calificada votación por mayoría cualificada

Q-6	qualifying member	État membre remplissant les conditions requises	país miembro que reúne los requisitos país miembro habilitado
Q-7	quantification	chiffrage quantification évaluation chiffrée	cuantificación
Q-8	quantity sensitivity	sensibilité-volume	sensibilidad al volumen sensibilidad con respecto al volumen sensibilidad a la cantidad sensibilidad con respecto a la cantidad
Q-9	quantity theory of money	théorie quantitative de la monnaie	teoría cuantitativa del dinero
Q-10	quantum index	indice de quantités	número índice de cantidad
Q-11	Quarterly National Accounts Manual, *see* Quarterly National Accounts Manual--Concepts, Data Sources, and Compilation		
Q-12	Quarterly National Accounts Manual — Concepts, Data Sources, and Compilation [IMF] Quarterly National Accounts Manual QNA Manual	Manuel des comptes nationaux trimestriels — Concepts, sources des données et compilation Manuel des comptes nationaux trimestriels	Manual de cuentas nacionales trimestrales: Conceptos, fuentes de datos y compilación Manual de cuentas nacionales trimestrales
Q-13	quasi-corporate enterprise quasi-corporation quasicorporation	quasi-société	cuasisociedad cuasicorporación
Q-14	quasi-corporation, *see* quasi-corporate enterprise		
Q-15	quasicorporation, *see* quasi-corporate enterprise		
Q-16	quasi-fiscal	parafiscal quasi budgétaire	cuasifiscal
Q-17	quasi-money near-money	quasi-monnaie	cuasidinero cuasi-dinero
Q-18	quasi-money instrument near cash instrument	instrument quasi monétaire	instrumento cuasimonetario
Q-19	questionnaire, *see* survey form		
Q-20	quick asset ratio acid-test ratio quick ratio	ratio de liquidité relative ratio de trésorerie immédiate ratio de liquidité immédiate	coeficiente de liquidez coeficiente de solvencia inmediata
Q-21	quick asset(s) *see also:* current asset(s); liquid asset(s); quick asset(s)	actif(s) immédiatement réalisable(s) actif(s) sans préavis actif(s) liquide(s) disponibilités immédiates	activo(s) de liquidez inmediata activo(s) inmediatamente realizable(s)
Q-22	quick ratio, *see* quick asset ratio		
Q-23	quick-yielding project	projet à rendement rapide	proyecto de rápido rendimiento

Q-24	quinquennial review of quotas, *see* General Review of Quotas		
Q-25	quota, *see* membership quota		
Q-26	quota	plafond contingent	cuota
Q-27	quota [trade]	contingent	cuota contingente [OMC] cupo
Q-28	quota in the Fund, *see* membership quota		
Q-29	quota limit [IMF]	limite définie par référence à la quote-part limite exprimée en pourcentage de la quote-part	límite de acceso definido en función de la cuota
Q-30	quota review [IMF] *see also:* adjustment of quotas; General Review of Quotas review of quotas	révision des quotes-parts examen des quotes-parts	revisión de cuotas
Q-31	quota share [IMF] actual quota share share in actual quotas share in total quotas	part en pourcentage du total des quotes-parts quote-part relative quote-part effective quote-part actuelle	cuota relativa cuota efectiva relativa
Q-32	quota-based institution	institution dont les ressources proviennent principalement des quotes-parts	institución cuyos recursos provienen principalmente de las cuotas
Q-33	quoted price	prix coté	precio de cotización precio cotizado
Q-34	quoted security, *see* listed security		

R

R-1	RAD1, RAD2, *see* Revenue Administration Division I, II		
R-2	raider *see also:* takeover corporate raider	prédateur attaquant chevalier noir	depredador
R-3	RAM, *see* reverse mortgage		
R-4	rampant inflation *see also:* creeping inflation runaway inflation galloping inflation	inflation galopante inflation débridée	inflación galopante inflación desenfrenada
R-5	random variable	variable aléatoire	variable aleatoria
R-6	randomness	caractère aléatoire	aleatoriedad carácter aleatorio

R-7	range	fourchette gamme plage intervalle de variation	rango intervalo gama
R-8	ranking	classement	clasificación
R-9	ranking of claims, *see* prioritization of debt		
R-10	RAP, *see* rights accumulation program		
R-11	ratchet effect	effet (de) cliquet effet de crémaillère effet d'encliquetage	efecto trinquete efecto irreversible
R-12	rate of charge [IMF; SDR use]	taux de commission	tasa de cargos
R-13	rate of return	taux de rentabilité taux de rendement	tasa de rentabilidad tasa de rendimiento tasa de retorno
R-14	rate setting policy pricing policy	politique tarifaire	política de tarifas

R-15	rate tiering
	tiering
		différenciation par les taux
		écart entre les taux d'intérêt
		  appliqués aux prêts
			diferenciación por medio de las
			  tasas

R-16	rates [GBR] *see also:* head tax	impôts locaux	contribuciones impuestos municipales tarifas municipales
R-17	rating [securities] *see also:* AAA rating	cotation du risque	calificación calificación de valores clasificación de valores
R-18	rating agency, *see* credit rating agency		
R-19	rating services, *see* credit rating agency		
R-20	rational expectations	anticipations rationnelles	expectativas racionales
R-21	raw data crude data	données brutes données non traitées	datos brutos
R-22	R&D, *see* research and development		
R-23	real balances effect *see also:* wealth effect Pigou effect	effet d'encaisse(s) réelle(s)	efecto de saldos reales efecto de saldos reales en efectivo efecto Pigou
R-24	real economy *see also:* financial economy real sector	secteur réel de l'économie	economía real sector real sector real de la economía

R-25	real effective exchange rate index
	see also: effective exchange rate
	REER index
		indice du taux de change effectif
		  réel
			índice del tipo de cambio efectivo
			  real

R-26	real estate taxes	impôts fonciers impôts sur les biens immobiliers	impuestos sobre bienes raíces

R-27	real flow	flux réel	flujo real
R-28	real interest rate	taux d'intérêt réel	tasa de interés real
R-29	real sector, *see* real economy		
R-30	Real Sector Division [IMF]	Division secteur réel	División del Sector Real
R-31	real terms *see also:* nominal terms in real terms	en valeur réelle en termes réels à prix constants en volume	términos reales en términos reales en valores reales
R-32	real wage	salaire réel	salario real
R-33	realization of collateral, *see* enforcement of security		
R-34	realized price	prix réalisé prix obtenu	precio obtenido
R-35	rebalancing of portfolio [IMF] portfolio rebalancing	rééquilibrage du portefeuille	reequilibrio de la cartera
R-36	recapitalization	recapitalisation	recapitalización
R-37	recapture clause	clause de récupération	cláusula de recuperación
R-38	receiver [insolvency]	séquestre	síndico
R-39	receivership *see also:* provisional administration	mise sous séquestre	sindicatura
R-40	Recent Economic Developments [IMF] RED	évolution récente de l'économie	documento sobre la evolución económica reciente
R-41	reciprocal currency arrangement *see also:* swap arrangement cross-currency swap foreign currency swap swap arrangement currency swap arrangement swap	swap temporaire de devises accord de swap accord de crédit croisé	acuerdo de crédito recíproco acuerdo de swap crédito cruzado crédito de dobles crédito recíproco crédito swap operación de swap swap
R-42	reciprocal exchange guarantee	garantie de change réciproque	garantía cambiaria recíproca
R-43	reconcilement, *see* reconciliation		
R-44	reconciliation reconcilement conciliation	rapprochement concordance	conciliación armonización
R-45	reconciliation account	compte de rapprochement compte d'ajustement	cuenta de conciliación
R-46	reconciliation table *see also:* bridge table	tableau de concordance	cuadro de conciliación

R-47	reconstitution of SDR holdings	reconstitution des avoirs en DTS	reconstitución de las tenencias de DEG
R-48	recording system record-keeping system	système d'enregistrement système de comptabilisation	sistema de registro método de registro sistema de contabilización
R-49	record-keeping system, *see* recording system		
R-50	recovery, *see* economic recovery		
R-51	recovery [finance]	recouvrement	cobranza reembolso recuperación
R-52	Recruitment and Staffing Division [IMF] RSD	Division recrutement et affectations	División de Contratación y Asignación del Personal
R-53	recurrent budget	budget ordinaire budget des opérations courantes	presupuesto ordinario
R-54	recurrent expenditure recurrent expense recurrent outlay	dépenses courantes dépenses ordinaires dépenses de fonctionnement dépenses récurrentes	gasto ordinario
R-55	recurrent expense, *see* recurrent expenditure		
R-56	recurrent income, *see* recurrent revenue		
R-57	recurrent outlay, *see* recurrent expenditure		
R-58	recurrent receipts, *see* recurrent revenue		
R-59	recurrent revenue recurrent receipts recurrent income	recettes courantes recettes ordinaires recettes renouvelables	ingreso ordinario
R-60	recurrent taxes on immovable property	impôts périodiques sur la propriété immobilière	impuestos permanentes sobre bienes raíces impuestos recurrentes sobre la propiedad inmueble
R-61	recurrent taxes on net wealth	impôts périodiques sur la valeur du patrimoine net	impuestos permanentes sobre el patrimonio neto impuestos recurrentes sobre la riqueza neta
R-62	recycling [finance]	recyclage	reciclaje recirculación
R-63	RED, *see* Recent Economic Developments		
R-64	redemption retirement	remboursement amortissement	rescate amortización reembolso redención
R-65	redemption (of a pledge)	dégagement	liberación

R-66	redemption, right of	droit de remboursement	retroventa, derecho de
		réméré	
		droit de réméré	
R-67	redemption yield, *see* yield to maturity		
R-68	rediscount ceiling	plafond de réescompte	tope de redescuento
	[central banking]		límite de redescuento
	rediscount quota		cuota de redescuento
R-69	rediscount facility	guichet de réescompte	línea de redescuento
	[central banking]	facilité de réescompte	
R-70	rediscount quota, *see* rediscount ceiling		
R-71	rediscount rate	taux d'escompte (de la banque	tasa de redescuento
	see also: discount rate [central	centrale)	
	banking]		
R-72	redistributional transfer payments	transferts de redistribution	transferencias redistributivas
R-73	reduced-form equation	équation réduite	ecuación de forma reducida
		équation en forme réduite	
R-74	reduced interest par bond	échange de créances contre des	canje de créditos por bonos a la
	exchange	obligations de même valeur	par de interés reducido
		nominale à taux d'intérêt réduit	
R-75	REER index, *see* real effective exchange rate index		
R-76	reference currency	monnaie de référence	moneda de referencia
R-77	reference rate	taux de référence	tasa de referencia
	see also: commercial interest		
	reference rate		
R-78	reference scenario, *see* baseline scenario		
R-79	reference zone (of rates)	zone de référence	zona de referencia
R-80	refinancing	refinancement	refinanciamiento
			refinanciación
R-81	reflation	reflation	reflación
R-82	reflow	remboursement	reembolso de préstamos
R-83	reflows of flight capital	retour des capitaux enfuis	retorno del capital fugado
	return of flight capital	rapatriement des capitaux enfuis	regreso del capital fugado
	repatriation of flight capital	reflux des capitaux	repatriación del capital fugado
			repatriación de capitales
R-84	reflows, use of Trust Fund	utilisation des ressources	utilización de los recursos
	[IMF]	provenant des remboursements	procedentes de los reembolsos
		des prêts du fonds fiduciaire	del Fondo Fiduciario
			utilización de los reembolsos del
			Fondo Fiduciario
R-85	refund of charges	remboursement des commissions	reintegro de cargos
	[IMF]		
R-86	refunding	remboursement	reembolso

R-87	region of acceptance	région d'acceptation	región de aceptación
R-88	region of rejection	région critique	región de rechazo
R-89	regional balance of payments statement	état régional des balances des paiements	balanza de pagos regional presentación regional de la balanza de pagos
R-90	*Regional Economic Outlook* [IMF] *REO*	*Perspectives économiques régionales*	Perspectivas económicas regionales
R-91	Regional Office for Asia and the Pacific [IMF] OAP	Bureau régional Asie et Pacifique	Oficina Regional para Asia y el Pacífico
R-92	Regional Office for Central Europe and the Baltics [IMF]	Bureau régional Europe centrale et pays baltes	Oficina Regional para Europa Central y los Países Bálticos
R-93	register check, *see* registered check		
R-94	registered check *see also:* cashier's check; certified check register check	chèque de banque chèque de caisse	cheque de caja
R-95	registered instrument *see also:* bearer instrument; order instrument registered security	titre nominatif titre immatriculé titre enregistré	título nominativo
R-96	registered security, *see* registered instrument		
R-97	regression equation	équation de régression	ecuación de regresión
R-98	regression of Y on X	régression de Y dans X régression de Y en X régression de Y en fonction de X	regresión de Y sobre X regresión de Y en X
R-99	regressive tax	impôt régressif impôt dégressif	impuesto regresivo
R-100	regressivity [taxation]	caractère régressif	regresividad
R-101	regular consultation, *see* formal consultation		
R-102	regular election [IMF, Executive Directors]	élection ordinaire	elección ordinaria
R-103	regular meeting [IMF]	réunion ordinaire	reunión ordinaria
R-104	Regulation and Supervision Division [IMF]	Division réglementation et supervision	División de Regulación y Supervisión
R-105	regulatory agency	organisme de réglementation institution (internationale) disposant de pouvoirs réglementaires	organismo regulador organismo con potestad normativa

R-106	regulatory capture	captation réglementaire	captura regulatoria
R-107	regulatory forbearance	laxisme réglementaire	tolerancia en la aplicación de las normas tolerancia regulatoria dispensa de las normas aplicación poco estricta de las normas
R-108	regulatory power	pouvoir réglementaire pouvoir de réglementation	facultades reglamentarias facultades reguladoras facultades regulatorias potestad normativa
R-109	rehabilitation	réorganisation restructuration redressement réaménagement assainissement réhabilitation remise en état	rehabilitación reorganización saneamiento recuperación
R-110	rehabilitation program	programme d'assainissement programme de redressement programme de réorganisation programme de restructuration	programa de reorganización programa de saneamiento programa de reestructuración
R-111	reinvested earnings	bénéfices réinvestis	utilidades reinvertidas reinversión de utilidades reinversión de ganancias reinversión de beneficios
R-112	rejection error, *see* type I error		
R-113	relative share	parts relatives	participación relativa
R-114	relending *see also:* onlending	réutilisation des prêts réaffectation des prêts	représtamo reciclaje de los préstamos
R-115	remaining maturity, *see* residual maturity		
R-116	remedial action, *see* remedial measure		
R-117	remedial measure [IMF] corrective action corrective measure remedial action	mesure corrective action corrective mesure correctrice mesure de redressement	medida correctiva
R-118	remittance of funds	envoi de fonds remise de fonds	remesa de fondos
R-119	remittance recipient	pays bénéficiant d'envois de fonds	país receptor de remesas
R-120	remitted earnings	bénéfices rapatriés	utilidades remitidas
R-121	remunerated reserve tranche position [IMF]	position rémunérée dans la tranche de réserve	saldo remunerado en el tramo de reserva posición remunerada en el tramo de reserva

R-122	remuneration [IMF]	rémunération	remuneración
R-123	remuneration coefficient [IMF]	coefficient de rémunération	coeficiente de remuneración
R-124	remuneration, rate of [IMF]	taux de rémunération	tasa de remuneración
R-125	renewable replenishable reproducible	renouvelable reproductible	renovable reproducible
R-126	rent, *see* economic rent		
R-127	rental income	revenu locatif	renta por concepto de alquileres ingresos por alquiler renta locativa
R-128	rent-seeking *see also:* economic rent	recherche de rente	búsqueda de ventaja económica búsqueda de renta económica búsqueda de rentas oligopólicas afán de enriquecimiento
R-129	*REO, see Regional Economic Outlook*		
R-130	repatriation of flight capital, *see* reflows of flight capital		
R-131	repayment	remboursement amortissement	reembolso amortización
R-132	repayment capacity *see also:* borrowing capacity	capacité de remboursement	capacidad de pago capacidad de reembolso
R-133	repayment period [Paris Club]	période de remboursement	plazo de reembolso
R-134	repayment profile, *see* maturity profile		
R-135	repayment schedule	calendrier d'échéances échéancier	calendario de vencimientos calendario de reembolso
R-136	replacement cost, *see* current replacement cost		
R-137	replenish the Fund's holdings of currencies [IMF]	reconstituer les avoirs du FMI en monnaies	reponer las monedas en poder del FMI
R-138	replenishable, *see* renewable		
R-139	replenishment of Fund resources [IMF]	reconstitution des ressources du FMI	reposición de los recursos del FMI
R-140	replenishment of reserves	reconstitution des réserves	reconstitución de reservas
R-141	repo, *see* repurchase agreement		
R-142	report form, *see* bank call report form		
R-143	report of the Executive Board [IMF]	rapport du Conseil d'administration	informe del Directorio Ejecutivo

R-144	Report on the Observance of Standards and Codes [IMF] ROSC	rapport sur l'observation des normes et codes RONC	Informe sobre la Observancia de los Códigos y Normas IOCN ROSC
R-145	reporting [IMF] data reporting	communication de(s) données déclaration de(s) données transmission de données reporting	declaración de datos
R-146	reporting agency [IMF]	organisme déclarant organisme chargé de communiquer les données	organismo notificador
R-147	reporting country	pays déclarant pays communiquant les données pays recensé	país declarante
R-148	reporting economy	économie déclarante	economía declarante
R-149	reporting period	période de déclaration période sur laquelle porte la communication des données	período al cual se refiere la declaración de datos período de declaración de datos período que se declara
R-150	representation expenses, *see* business expenses		
R-151	representation of balance of payments financing need [IMF] representation of need declaration of BOP-related need declaration of need	déclaration de besoin de financement de la balance des paiements déclaration de besoin	declaración de necesidad de financiamiento de la balanza de pagos declaración de necesidad
R-152	representation of need, *see* representation of balance of payments financing need		
R-153	representative rate [IMF]	taux représentatif	tipo de cambio representativo
R-154	representative set of currencies [IMF]	ensemble représentatif de monnaies	conjunto representativo de monedas
R-155	Representative to the WTO [IMF]	Représentant auprès de l'OMC	Representante ante la OMC
R-156	repressed inflation, *see* suppressed inflation		
R-157	repricing period (for interest rates)	période de réajustement des taux d'intérêt	período de redeterminación de las tasas de interés
R-158	reproducible, *see* renewable		
R-159	repurchase [IMF]	rachat	recompra

R-160	repurchase agreement *see also:* reverse operation repo RP repurchase operation repurchase transaction	accord de pension opération de pension prise en pension (à l'initiative de la banque centrale) accord de rachat accord de rachat de titres pension livrée	acuerdo de recompra operación de reporto reporto operación de reporto activo operación de pase operación de pase activo operación con pacto de recompra repo
R-161	repurchase agreement [IMF]	accord de rachat	acuerdo de recompra
R-162	repurchase of accelerated set-aside amounts [IMF] *see also:* early repurchase of accelerated set-aside amounts accelerated set-aside amounts repurchase	rachat au titre d'achats accélérés de montants mis en réserve rachat au titre d'achats accélérés de montants préaffectés	recompra de montos consignados adquiridos de manera acelerada
R-163	repurchase operation, *see* repurchase agreement		
R-164	repurchase transaction, *see* repurchase agreement		
R-165	request for proposal [procurement] *see also:* invitation to bid RFP	demande de propositions	solicitud de propuestas llamado a licitación
R-166	required reserve ratio *see also:* reserve requirement minimum reserve ratio reserve requirement reserve ratio legal reserve ratio	ratio de réserves obligatoires coefficient de réserves obligatoires taux des réserves obligatoires taux de couverture	coeficiente de encaje legal encaje legal coeficiente de encaje encaje coeficiente de caja coeficiente de reservas obligatorias
R-167	required reserves, *see* reserve requirement		
R-168	requirement of need [IMF, SDR]	critère de besoin	principio relativo a la necesidad
R-169	requited current transfers	transferts courants contractuels	transferencias corrientes con contrapartida
R-170	requited payment	opération avec contrepartie	pago con contraprestación
R-171	RES, *see* Research Department		
R-172	Res. Rep., *see* Resident Representative		
R-173	rescheduler rescheduling country	pays dont la dette est en cours de rééchelonnement pays ayant obtenu des rééchelonnements pays négociant un rééchelonnement	país que reprograma su deuda
R-174	rescheduling, *see* debt rescheduling		
R-175	rescheduling country, *see* rescheduler		

R-176	research and development R&D	recherche-développement R-D	investigación y desarrollo I&D
R-177	Research Department [IMF] RES	Département des études	Departamento de Estudios
R-178	reservation price (of labor) reservation wage	prix d'intégration (de la main-d'œuvre) salaire d'intégration	precio de reserva de la mano de obra precio de reserva salario de reserva
R-179	reservation wage, *see* reservation price (of labor)		
R-180	reserve *see also:* depreciation allowance; provision	réserve provision	reserva provisión
R-181	Reserve Account, *see* PRGF Trust Reserve Account		
R-182	reserve asset	actif de réserve instrument de réserve avoir de réserve	activo de reserva
R-183	reserve creation	création de réserves	creación de reservas
R-184	reserve currency	monnaie de réserve	moneda de reserva
R-185	reserve cushion, *see* reserve ease		
R-186	reserve deficiency, *see* reserve inadequacy		
R-187	reserve ease reserve cushion	aisance des réserves aisance de la situation des réserves	amplitud de las reservas colchón de reservas
R-188	reserve inadequacy reserve deficiency	insuffisance des réserves	insuficiencia de reservas
R-189	reserve money, *see* base money		
R-190	reserve position	situation des réserves position des réserves	situación de las reservas nivel de las reservas saldo de las reservas
R-191	reserve ratio, *see* required reserve ratio		
R-192	reserve requirement *see also:* required reserve ratio; cash ratio requirement minimum reserve requirement required reserves	réserves obligatoires couverture obligatoire	encaje legal reservas obligatorias
R-193	reserve requirement, *see* required reserve ratio		
R-194	reserve stringency	étroitesse des réserves resserrement des réserves	escasez de reservas
R-195	reserve target [IMF]	objectif de réserves	monto de reservas fijado como objetivo

R-196	reserve tranche position [IMF]	position dans la tranche de réserve	saldo en el tramo de reserva posición en el tramo de reserva
R-197	reserve tranche purchase [IMF]	achat dans la tranche de réserve	compra en el tramo de reserva
R-198	reserve-related official borrowing	emprunts officiels liés aux réserves	préstamos oficiales relacionados con las reservas
R-199	reserve-related transaction	transaction relative aux réserves	transacción relacionada con las reservas
R-200	reserves adequacy, *see* adequacy of reserves		
R-201	residence of enterprises	résidence d'entreprises	residencia de las empresas
R-202	residence of individuals	résidence des particuliers résidence des personnes physiques	residencia de las personas físicas
R-203	resident official sector	secteur officiel résident	sector oficial residente
R-204	Resident Representative [IMF] Res. Rep.	représentant résident	Representante Residente
R-205	Resident Representative, Senior [IMF]	représentant résident principal	Representante Residente Principal
R-206	residential construction	construction de logements construction résidentielle	construcción de viviendas construcción residencial
R-207	residential demand	demande de logements	demanda de los hogares demanda de los particulares
R-208	resident-to-resident transaction	transaction entre résidents	transacción entre residentes
R-209	residual item	poste résiduel	partida residual
R-210	residual maturity remaining maturity	échéance résiduelle	vencimiento residual plazo residual vencimiento remanente
R-211	residual method	méthode des résidus	método de los residuos
R-212	resilience [economics]	résistance capacité d'adaptation capacité de récupération tenue	resiliencia resistencia capacidad de reacción flexibilidad capacidad de recuperación capacidad de adaptación
R-213	resilience [banking]	résilience	resiliencia capacidad de recuperación resistencia
R-214	resource allocation allocation of resources	affectation de(s) ressources allocation de(s) ressources répartition des ressources	asignación de (los) recursos
R-215	resource gap	déficit en ressources insuffisance des ressources	déficit de recursos insuficiencia de recursos

R-216	Resource Management Division [IMF]	Division gestion des ressources	División de Gestión de Recursos
R-217	resource rich countries	pays riches en ressources naturelles	países ricos en recursos naturales
R-218	respondent [IMF]	déclarant répondant	declarante
R-219	responsive	sensible qui réagit	sensible que reacciona
R-220	rest of the world account ROW Account rest of the world sector	compte du reste du monde	cuenta del resto del mundo
R-221	rest of the world sector, *see* rest of the world account		
R-222	restocking	reconstitution de(s) stocks réapprovisionnement	reposición de existencias
R-223	restricted deposit	dépôt restrictif	depósito restringido
R-224	restricted session [IMF] *see also:* executive session	séance restreinte	sesión restringida
R-225	restrictive business practices	pratiques commerciales restrictives	prácticas comerciales restrictivas
R-226	restructuring, *see* debt restructuring		
R-227	retail bank	banque de détail	banco minorista
R-228	retail price index RPI	indice des prix de détail	índice de precios al por menor índice de precios minoristas
R-229	retained earnings undistributed earnings undistributed profits retained gains	bénéfices non distribués	utilidades no distribuidas utilidades retenidas beneficios no distribuidos beneficios no repartidos
R-230	retained gains, *see* retained earnings		
R-231	retaliatory measure	mesure de rétorsion	medida de represalia medida de retorsión
R-232	retirement, *see* redemption		
R-233	retirement of outstanding debt	amortissement de la dette amortissement anticipé de la dette	amortización de la deuda amortización anticipada de la deuda rescate de la deuda rescate anticipado de la deuda
R-234	return of flight capital, *see* reflows of flight capital		
R-235	return of investment	reflux des capitaux investis retour des capitaux investis	rentabilidad de la inversión rendimiento del capital invertido retorno del capital invertido retorno de la inversión
R-236	return on capital employed, *see* return on investment		

R-237	return on capital invested, *see* return on investment		
R-238	return on investment ROI return on capital employed return on capital invested	rendement des capitaux engagés rendement des capitaux investis	rendimiento del capital invertido retorno de la inversión rendimiento de la inversión

R-239	returned exports and imports	exportations et importations
		  renvoyées à l'expéditeur
			exportaciones e importaciones
			  devueltas

R-240	returns to scale	rendements d'échelle	rendimientos de escala rendimientos a escala
R-241	revaluation	réévaluation revalorisation	revaluación revaloración revalorización
R-242	revaluation changes	variations dues à une réévaluation	variaciones por revaloración
R-243	revaluation counterpart, *see* counterpart to valuation changes		

R-244	Revenue Administration
	  Division I, II
	[IMF]
	RAD1, RAD2
		Division des recettes fiscales I, II	División de Administración de
			  Ingresos Fiscales I, II

R-245	revenue and expense account, *see* income account		
R-246	revenue collection	recouvrement des recettes mobilisation des recettes	recaudación de ingresos recaudación de rentas

R-247	revenue sharing
	tax revenue sharing
		partage des recettes fiscales
		péréquation des recettes (fiscales)
			participación en los ingresos
			  fiscales
			participación en los ingresos
			  tributarios
			coparticipación de ingresos

R-248	revenue sharing grant
	[public finance]
		transfert au titre du partage des
		  recettes fiscales
			transferencia a título de
			  participación en los ingresos
			  fiscales
			transferencia de coparticipación
			coparticipación

R-249	revenue shortfall	insuffisance de recettes manque à percevoir manque à gagner	déficit de ingresos insuficiencia de ingresos
R-250	revenue stamp tax stamp	timbre fiscal	timbre fiscal estampilla fiscal impuesto de sellos
R-251	revenue tariff, *see* fiscal tariff		
R-252	revenue-producing monopoly, *see* fiscal monopoly		
R-253	reversal of a loan [IMF]	dénouement d'un prêt	reintegro de un préstamo
R-254	reverse annuity mortgage, *see* reverse mortgage		

R-255	reverse mortgage *see also:* life annuity reverse annuity mortgage RAM	prêt hypothécaire inversé rente viagère	hipoteca inversa con renta vitalicia hipoteca inversa

R-256	reverse operation
	see also: repurchase agreement
	reverse repurchase operation
	reverse transaction
	matched sale-purchase agreement
	[USA]
	MSP
	reverse repo
		opération de cession temporaire
		opération de mise en pension
		  (à l'initiative de la banque
		  centrale)
			reporto pasivo
			operación de reporto pasivo
			pase pasivo
			operación de pase pasivo

R-257	reverse repo, *see* reverse operation		
R-258	reverse repurchase operation, *see* reverse operation		

R-259	reverse stand-by arrangement	accord de confirmation proposé
		  par le FMI
			acuerdo de derecho de giro
			  a iniciativa del FMI

R-260	reverse transaction, *see* reverse operation		
R-261	review [IMF]	revue (d'un accord avec le FMI) réexamen (d'une décision)	revisión (de un programa) examen (de un programa) reconsideración (de una decisión)
R-262	review mission (Fund)	mission (du FMI) pour la revue d'un programme	misión de revisión de un programa
R-263	review of quotas, *see* quota review		

R-264	reviews-based approach	suivi au moyen de revues
		  périodiques
			supervisión basada en revisiones
			  periódicas
			enfoque basado en revisiones

R-265	revised downward	corrigé à la baisse corrigé en baisse révisé à la baisse révisé en baisse	corregido a la baja revisado a la baja
R-266	revised upward	corrigé à la hausse corrigé en hausse révisé à la hausse révisé en hausse	corregido al alza revisado al alza
R-267	revolving character of resources [IMF]	nature rotative des ressources caractère temporaire (de l'utilisation) des ressources	carácter rotatorio de los recursos
R-268	revolving credit *see also:* rollover credit	crédit rotatif crédit automatiquement renouvelable crédit renouvelable crédit permanent	crédito rotativo crédito revolvente crédito rotatorio crédito renovable

R-269	revolving underwriting facility
	see also: note issuance facility
	RUF
		facilité à prise ferme renouvelable
		RUF
		facilité d'émission renouvelable
		facilité de souscription
		  renouvelable
		facilité de crédit spécial
			servicio de suscripción renovable
			suscripción renovable garantizada
			compromiso de suscripción
			  continuada
			RUF
			servicios de suscripción rotatorios

R-270	RFP, *see* request for proposal		
R-271	right to terminate participation [IMF]	droit de mettre fin à la participation	derecho a dar por terminada la participación
R-272	right to withdraw [IMF]	droit de retrait	derecho a retirarse derecho de retiro
R-273	rights accumulation program RAP	programme d'accumulation de droits PAD	programa de acumulación de derechos
R-274	"rights" approach [IMF] *see also:* encashment of rights; notional drawing right	méthode des droits	enfoque de los "derechos"
R-275	ring system [taxation]	système de suspension de taxe régime suspensif système suspensif	sistema de suspensión del impuesto
R-276	rising trend, *see* upward trend		
R-277	risk asset	actif à risque	activo de riesgo
R-278	risk avoider	agent économique pusillanime agent économique frileux	agente económico que rehuye el riesgo
R-279	risk capital, *see* venture capital		
R-280	risk diversification, *see* spreading of risks		
R-281	risk exposure exposure	(exposition à un) risque engagement montant de l'engagement niveau d'engagement volume de crédits volume de prêts exposition risque couru	riesgo vivo exposición cantidad prestada a un solo país o grupo riesgo bancario exposición al riesgo
R-282	risk of illiquidity, *see* illiquidity risk		
R-283	risk of insolvency, *see* insolvency risk		
R-284	risk premium, *see* risk premium on interest rates		
R-285	risk premium on interest rates risk premium	prime de risque	prima de riesgo sobre la tasa de interés prima de riesgo prima por riesgo
R-286	risk spreading, *see* spreading of risks		
R-287	risk taker	agent économique disposé à prendre des risques preneur de risques téméraire	agente económico dispuesto a asumir riesgos
R-288	risk-based capital, *see* risk-weighted capital		
R-289	risk-based capital ratio, *see* risk-weighted capital ratio		

R-290	risk-weighted capital risk-based capital	fonds propres pondérés en fonction des risques	capital ponderado en función del riesgo capital medido en función del riesgo
R-291	risk-weighted capital ratio risk-based capital ratio	ratio de fonds propres pondérés en fonction des risques	coeficiente de capital ponderado en función del riesgo
R-292	River Plate Division [IMF]	Division Rio de la Plata	División del Río de la Plata
R-293	ROI, *see* return on investment		
R-294	rollback commitment [WTO]	engagement de démantèlement	compromiso de desmantelamiento de restricciones
R-295	rollover	refinancement reconduction renouvellement	renovación refinanciación refinanciamiento
R-296	rollover credit *see also:* revolving credit	crédit reconductible (à taux variable) crédit renouvelable	crédito renovable
R-297	rollover risk	risque de refinancement	riesgo de refinanciamiento
R-298	ROSC, *see* Report on the Observance of Standards and Codes		
R-299	ROW Account, *see* rest of the world account		
R-300	RP, *see* repurchase agreement		
R-301	RPI, *see* retail price index		
R-302	RS, *see* baseline scenario		
R-303	RSD, *see* Recruitment and Staffing Division		
R-304	RTP, *see* IMF-AMF Regional Training Program		
R-305	RUF, *see* revolving underwriting facility		
R-306	rule of law	état de droit primauté du droit primauté de la loi	Estado de derecho imperio de la ley
R-307	rules and practices of the Fund [IMF] standard practices (of the Fund)	règles et pratiques du FMI	normas y prácticas del FMI
R-308	Rules and Regulations [IMF] *see also: By-Laws, Rules and Regulations*	Règles et Règlements	Reglamento
R-309	rules for designation [SDR]	règles de désignation	normas de designación
R-310	rules for reconstitution [SDR]	règles de reconstitution	normas de reconstitución

R-311	rules for repurchase [IMF]	règles de rachat	normas de recompra
R-312	run on a bank, *see* bank run		
R-313	run on a currency	mouvement spéculatif contre une monnaie effort pour se débarrasser d'une monnaie fuite devant une monnaie	movimiento especulativo contra una moneda corrida contra una moneda
R-314	runaway inflation, *see* rampant inflation		
R-315	rundown on inventories, *see* inventory rundown		

S

S-1	SAAR, *see* seasonally adjusted annual rate		
S-2	SAC, *see* structural adjustment credit		
S-3	SAF, *see* Structural Adjustment Facility (within the Special Disbursement Account)		
S-4	safeguard safeguard measure safeguard clause	mesures de sauvegarde clause de sauvegarde sauvegarde	salvaguardia medida de salvaguardia cláusula de salvaguardia
S-5	safeguard clause, *see* safeguard		
S-6	safeguard measure, *see* safeguard		
S-7	safeguards, *see* safeguards on the use of Fund resources		
S-8	safeguards assessment	évaluation des mesures de diligence évaluation des diligences évaluation du dispositif de sauvegarde évaluation des mesures de sauvegarde cadre d'évaluation des gardefous évaluation des sauvegardes	evaluación de las salvaguardias
S-9	Safeguards Assessments Division [IMF]	Division de l'évaluation des sauvegardes	División de Evaluación de Salvaguardias
S-10	safeguards on the use of Fund resources *see also:* adequate safeguards safeguards	sauvegardes diligences garanties	salvaguardias en relación con el uso de los recursos del FMI
S-11	safety net social safety net	dispositif de protection dispositif de protection sociale filet de protection sociale filet de sécurité	red de protección red de protección social medidas de protección social
S-12	SAL, *see* Structural Adjustment Lending		
S-13	salary *see also:* wage	traitement rémunération salaire solde	sueldo remuneración

S-14	salary scale	barème des traitements	escala de sueldos
	salary schedule	grille salariale	escala salarial
	wage scale	échelle des salaires	escala de salarios
	wage schedule	barème salarial	
	pay scale		
	pay schedule		
	pay table		
S-15	salary schedule, *see* salary scale		
S-16	sale value, *see* market value		
S-17	sales, *see* turnover		
S-18	sales tax	taxe sur les ventes	impuesto sobre las ventas
	turnover tax	taxe locale	impuesto a las ventas
S-19	SAMA, *see* Saudi Arabian Monetary Agency		
S-20	sample	échantillon	muestra
S-21	sample survey	enquête par sondage	encuesta por muestreo
			encuesta por sondeo
			encuesta muestral
S-22	sampling	sondage	muestreo
		échantillonnage	
		prélèvement d'échantillons	
S-23	satellite currency	monnaie satellite	moneda satélite
S-24	satisfactory, *see* unimpaired		
S-25	saturated market	marché saturé	mercado saturado
	filled market		
S-26	Saudi Arabian Monetary Agency	Agence monétaire de l'Arabie	Instituto Monetario de Arabia
	SAMA	Saoudite	Saudita
		SAMA	SAMA
S-27	saving	épargne	ahorro
	savings		
S-28	saving rate	taux d'épargne	tasa de ahorro
	saving(s) ratio		
S-29	savings, *see* saving		
S-30	savings account	compte d'épargne	cuenta de ahorro
			caja de ahorro
			banco de ahorro
			banco de ahorros
S-31	savings and loan association	association d'épargne et de prêt	asociación de ahorro y préstamo
	S&L	organisme d'épargne et de crédit	AAP
		institution d'épargne et de crédit	
S-32	savings bank	caisse d'épargne	caja de ahorros
		banque d'épargne	banco de ahorros
S-33	savings bond	bon d'épargne	bono de ahorro
		bon de caisse	

S-34	saving(s) ratio, *see* saving rate		
S-35	SBA, *see* Stand-By Arrangement		
S-36	SBC, *see* soft budget constraint		
S-37	SBO, *see* Stand-By Operations Division		
S-38	SCA-1, *see* Special Contingent Account 1		
S-39	SCA-2, *see* Special Contingent Account 2		
S-40	scale effect	effet d'échelle	efecto de escala
S-41	scale factor	facteur d'échelle	factor de escala
S-42	scale variable	variable d'échelle	variable de escala
S-43	scarce currency	monnaie rare	moneda escasa
S-44	scarcity rent	rente de rareté	renta de escasez renta derivada de la escasez
S-45	scarcity value	valeur de rareté	valor de escasez
S-46	scatter diagram	diagramme de dispersion graphique de dispersion nuage statistique nuage de points	diagrama de dispersión
S-47	scenario	scénario	escenario marco hipotético
S-48	schedular tax	impôt cédulaire	impuesto cedular
S-49	schedule of charges	barème des commissions	escala de cargos
S-50	schedule of repurchases	calendrier de(s) rachat(s) échéancier de rachat	calendario de recompras plan de recompras
S-51	scheduled item, *see* classified loan		
S-52	scheduled repurchase [IMF]	rachat prévu à l'échéancier	recompra programada plazo previsto en el plan de recompras
S-53	scrip issue, *see* stock dividend		
S-54	SCT, *see* serial correlation test		
S-55	SDA, *see* Special Disbursement Account		
S-56	SDDS, *see* Special Data Dissemination Standard		
S-57	SDR, *see* special drawing right		
S-58	SDR account, *see* SDR holdings account		

S-59	SDR allocation *see also:* general SDR allocation; special SDR allocation; special one-time allocation of SDRs allocation of SDRs	allocation de DTS	asignación de DEG
S-60	SDR as unit of account SDR qua unit of account	DTS (en tant qu')unité de compte	DEG como unidad de cuenta
S-61	SDR assessment assessment	prélèvement de DTS prélèvement pour la gestion du Département des DTS	contribución de DEG contribución para el funcionamiento del Departamento de DEG
S-62	SDR basket, *see* SDR interest rate basket		
S-63	SDR basket, *see* SDR valuation basket		
S-64	SDR charges	commissions sur DTS	cargos sobre las asignaciones de DEG
S-65	SDR Department	département des DTS	Departamento de DEG
S-66	SDR holdings account SDR account	compte DTS	cuenta de tenencias de DEG cuenta de DEG
S-67	SDR interest	taux du DTS taux d'intérêt du DTS	intereses sobre las tenencias de DEG
S-68	SDR interest rate	taux d'intérêt sur le DTS taux d'intérêt du DTS	tasa de interés del DEG
S-69	SDR interest rate basket SDR basket	panier du taux d'intérêt du DTS panier de détermination du taux d'intérêt du DTS	cesta de la tasa de interés del DEG cesta de cálculo de la tasa de interés del DEG
S-70	SDR qua unit of account, *see* SDR as unit of account		
S-71	SDR valuation	évaluation du DTS	valoración del DEG
S-72	SDR valuation basket SDR basket	panier servant au calcul de la valeur du DTS panier du DTS	cesta de valoración del DEG cesta del DEG
S-73	SDR weighted average interest rate	moyenne des taux d'intérêt pondérée selon la formule du DTS	tasa media ponderada del DEG tasa media de interés ponderada según la fórmula del DEG
S-74	SDR-denominated	libellé en DTS exprimé en DTS	denominado en DEG expresado en DEG
S-75	search unemployment, *see* frictional unemployment		
S-76	seasonal adjustment	correction des variations saisonnières	ajuste estacional desestacionalización
S-77	seasonal credit crop credit	crédit de campagne	crédito estacional crédito para una campaña agrícola

S-78	seasonal labor seasonal labor force seasonal workers migrant labor	travailleurs saisonniers	trabajadores de temporada trabajadores estacionales trabajadores migratorios
S-79	seasonal labor force, *see* seasonal labor		
S-80	seasonal unemployment	chômage saisonnier	desempleo estacional
S-81	seasonal workers, *see* seasonal labor		
S-82	seasonally adjusted	corrigé des variations saisonnières CVS désaisonnalisé	desestacionalizado
S-83	seasonally adjusted annual rate SAAR	taux annuel corrigé des variations saisonnières	tasa anual desestacionalizada
S-84	SEC, *see* Secretary's Department		
S-85	Second Special Contingent Account, *see* Special Contingent Account 2		
S-86	secondary capital, *see* tier 2 capital		
S-87	secondary market *see also:* primary market	marché secondaire second marché	mercado secundario
S-88	second-best optimum, *see* second-best solution		
S-89	second-best solution second-best optimum	optimum de second rang	segunda alternativa óptimo de segundo grado opción subóptima segunda opción óptima
S-90	second-best theory	théorie de l'optimum de second rang théorie de l'optimum second	teoría del segundo óptimo
S-91	secondment *see also:* assignment	détachement	envío en comisión de servicio adscripción
S-92	Secretary, Assistant [IMF]	Sous-Secrétaire	Secretario Adjunto
S-93	Secretary, Deputy [IMF]	Secrétaire adjoint	Subsecretario
S-94	Secretary for Conferences, Assistant [IMF]	Sous-Secrétaire chargé des conférences	Secretario Adjunto de Conferencias
S-95	Secretary (of the Fund) [IMF]	Secrétaire (du FMI)	Secretario (del FMI)
S-96	Secretary's Department [IMF] SEC	Département du Secrétariat	Departamento de Secretaría
S-97	sector	secteur filière	sector

S-98	sector GDP	PIB sectoriel PIB du secteur	PIB sectorial
S-99	sectorization	sectorisation ventilation par secteur	sectorización
S-100	sectorize	ventiler par secteur sectoriser	sectorizar
S-101	secular trend	tendance séculaire tendance à très long terme	tendencia secular tendencia a muy largo plazo
S-102	secured note [USA]	billet garanti billet gagé	pagaré garantizado
S-103	Securities Account [IMF]	compte titres	Cuenta de Valores
S-104	securities exchange stock exchange	bourse bourse des valeurs	bolsa bolsa de valores mercado de valores

S-105	securities index future
	stock index future
	share price index future
	index future
		contrat à terme d'indice boursier
		contrat sur indice boursier
		contrat à terme (négociable)
		  d'indice de valeurs mobilières
			futuro sobre índices de valores
			futuro sobre índices bursátiles
			futuro sobre índices de
			  cotizaciones de acciones
			contrato de futuro sobre índices de
			  valores
			contrato de futuro sobre índices
			  bursátiles
			contrato de futuro sobre índices de
			  cotizaciones de acciones

S-106	securitization	titrisation	titulización titularización bursatilización securitización
S-107	security [finance]	titre valeur valeur mobilière	título valor valor mobiliario
S-108	security [law]	garantie sûreté nantissement sécurité	garantía caución seguridad
S-109	Security Services Division [IMF]	Division services de sécurité	División de Servicios de Seguridad
S-110	seed capital start-up capital initial capital	capital de départ capital d'amorçage capital initial capital de lancement préinvestissement	capital inicial capital generador capital simiente
S-111	seigniorage	seigneuriage profits de la frappe des monnaies	señoreaje monedaje
S-112	seignorage, *see* inflation tax		
S-113	SELA, *see* Latin American Economic System		

S-114	*Selected Decisions of the International Monetary Fund and Selected Documents* [IMF]	*Recueil de décisions du Fonds monétaire international et Annexe*	*Recopilación seleccionada de decisiones del Fondo Monetario Internacional y otros documentos*
S-115	Selected Issues papers SI	documents de la série des «Questions générales» documents de la série des «Selected Issues»	documento de la serie "Selected Issues Papers"
S-116	selective excises on goods	taxes sur des produits déterminés	impuestos selectivos sobre la producción y el consumo de bienes
S-117	selective increase in quotas *see also:* incremental approach	augmentation sélective des quotes-parts	aumento selectivo de las cuotas
S-118	self-consumption	autoconsommation	consumo propio autoconsumo
S-119	self-employed independent labor force	travailleurs indépendants personnes travaillant pour leur propre compte	trabajadores independientes trabajadores por cuenta propia trabajadores autónomos
S-120	self-financing	autofinancement	autofinanciamiento
S-121	self-liquidating [projects]	autoamortissable financièrement autonome qui s'amortit automatiquement	autoamortizable
S-122	self-reliance, *see* self-sufficiency		
S-123	self-sufficiency [in general] self-reliance	autonomie capacité de subvenir à ses propres besoins indépendance (économique) prise en charge (par les intéressés) autodéveloppement	autosuficiencia independencia autonomía
S-124	self-sufficiency [economics]	autonomie autoapprovisionnement	autoabastecimiento autonomía
S-125	self-sustained, *see* self-sustaining		
S-126	self-sustained PRGF *see also:* interim PRGF	FRPC autofinancée FRPC autoalimentée	SCLP autofinanciado
S-127	self-sustaining self-sustained	autoalimenté autocentré autoentretenu autonome	autosostenido
S-128	sell short shorting	vendre court vendre à découvert vendre des titres avant de les acheter	vender en descubierto sobrevender especular a la baja
S-129	sellers' market	marché vendeur marché favorable au vendeur marché dominé par le(s) vendeur(s)	mercado de vendedores mercado favorable a los vendedores

S-130	seller's rate, *see* selling rate		
S-131	selling exchange rate, *see* selling rate		
S-132	selling rate selling exchange rate seller's rate offer rate	cours vendeur taux de vente	tipo de cambio vendedor tipo de cambio de venta
S-133	semidurable good	bien semi-durable	bien semiduradero
S-134	semifinished good semimanufacture unfinished good	produit semi-fini demi-produit bien semi-transformé	producto semimanufacturado producto semielaborado producto semiacabado
S-135	semimanufacture, *see* semifinished good		
S-136	semipublic enterprise parapublic enterprise mixed enterprise	entreprise d'économie mixte entreprise semi-publique	empresa mixta
S-137	semiskilled labor semiskilled manpower semiskilled worker	ouvrier spécialisé O.S.	mano de obra semicalificada trabajador semicalificado
S-138	semiskilled manpower, *see* semiskilled labor		
S-139	semiskilled worker, *see* semiskilled labor		
S-140	Senior ..., *see* ..., Senior [IMF]		
S-141	senior auditor	inspecteur principal des impôts	auditor principal
S-142	senior creditor	créancier privilégié créancier de premier rang	acreedor privilegiado acreedor de mayor rango
S-143	senior debt senior loan	créance privilégiée créance de premier rang créance de rang supérieur dette prioritaire	crédito privilegiado crédito de rango superior
S-144	senior loan, *see* senior debt		
S-145	senior officer, *see* senior official		
S-146	senior official high official senior officer [IMF]	haut fonctionnaire cadre de direction	alto funcionario alto cargo
S-147	senior staff [IMF]	cadres supérieurs cadres de direction	altos funcionarios altos cargos personal directivo
S-148	sense of the meeting, *see* collective judgment		
S-149	sensitivity analysis	analyse de sensibilité	análisis de sensibilidad
S-150	sequester appropriations, *see* impound appropriations		

S-151	sequestration	blocage des crédits	embargo presupuestario
		blocage automatique des crédits	embargo presupuestario automático
S-152	serial bond issue	émission d'obligations échéant par tranches	emisión de bonos en serie
		émission à échéances successives	emisión de obligaciones con vencimiento escalonado
		émission échéant en série	
S-153	serial correlation test	test de corrélation sériale	prueba de autocorrelación
	SCT		
S-154	serial multiyear rescheduling agreement, *see* serial multiyear rescheduling arrangement		
S-155	serial multiyear rescheduling arrangement	rééchelonnement pluriannuel en série	reprogramación multianual en serie
	serial MYRA	accord de rééchelonnement pluriannuel en série	acuerdo de reprogramación multianual en serie
	serial multiyear rescheduling agreement		
S-156	serial MYRA, *see* serial multiyear rescheduling arrangement		
S-157	service charge	commission de tirage	cargo por servicio
	service fee	rémunération des services	comisión por servicio
S-158	service economy	économie de services	economía de servicios
	tertiary economy	économie tertiaire	economía terciaria
S-159	service fee, *see* service charge		
S-160	service life, *see* economic life		
S-161	service payment, *see* debt service payment		
S-162	service provider	prestataire de services	proveedor de servicios
		fournisseur de services	
S-163	services on merchandise	services relatifs aux marchandises	servicios relacionados con mercancías
S-164	set off against each other	compenser des obligations financières	compensar obligaciones
		compenser des engagements	
S-165	set-aside account	compte de préaffectation	cuenta de recursos afectados
S-166	set-aside amount	montant(s) mis en réserve	recursos afectados
	set-aside(s)	montant(s) préaffecté(s)	
S-167	set-aside(s), *see* set-aside amount		
S-168	settlement currency	monnaie de règlement	moneda de pago
			moneda de liquidación
S-169	settlement of accounts	règlement des comptes	liquidación de cuentas
		apurement des comptes	
S-170	settlement of commitments	règlement d'engagements	liquidación de obligaciones
S-171	settlement of currency valuation adjustment	règlement de l'ajustement de valeur	liquidación del ajuste de valoración de la moneda
	see also: valuation adjustment		

S-172	settlement of disagreements [IMF] settlement of disputes	règlement de différends	arreglo de desacuerdos arreglo de diferencias
S-173	settlement of disputes, *see* settlement of disagreements		
S-174	settlement of financial obligations	règlement d'obligations financières	liquidación de las obligaciones financieras
S-175	settlement risk [securities settlement systems; public debt management]	risque de règlement risque de non-règlement	riesgo de liquidación riesgo de falta de pago
S-176	severance package, *see* severance pay		
S-177	severance pay severance package layoff pay severance payments	indemnité de licenciement indemnité de cessation d'emploi indemnité de départ	indemnización por despido
S-178	severance payments, *see* severance pay		
S-179	severance tax	taxe d'extraction	impuesto sobre la extracción (de productos minerales)
S-180	severely indebted country, *see* debt-distressed country		
S-181	severely indebted low-income countries SILICs	pays surendettés à faible revenu PSFR	países de bajo ingreso gravemente endeudados
S-182	severely indebted middle-income countries SIMICs	pays surendettés à revenu intermédiaire	países de ingreso mediano gravemente endeudados
S-183	SFA, *see* Special Facility for Sub-Saharan Africa		
S-184	SFF, *see* Supplementary Financing Facility		
S-185	SFF Subsidy Account, *see* Supplementary Financing Facility Subsidy Account		
S-186	SFSA, *see* Special Facility for Sub-Saharan Africa		
S-187	shadow economy gray economy underground economy	économie souterraine économie clandestine économie occulte	economía sumergida economía informal economía subterránea economía oculta economía irregular economía clandestina economía invisible economía negra economía no registrada economía gris
S-188	shadow exchange rate accounting exchange rate	taux de change de référence taux de change fictif taux de change comptable	tipo de cambio sombra tipo de cambio contable
S-189	shadow price *see also:* implicit cost	prix de référence prix virtuel prix fictif	precio sombra precio contable precio virtual

S-190	shadow program	programme d'essai	programa sombra
S-191	share	part participation titre action	acción participación
S-192	share capital capital stock	capital social capital-actions	capital social capital accionario
S-193	share in actual quotas, *see* quota share		
S-194	share in calculated quotas, *see* calculated quota share		
S-195	share in total quotas, *see* quota share		
S-196	share price index future, *see* securities index future		
S-197	share purchase warrant, *see* warrant		

S-198	sharing clause	clause de partage
		clause de partage des paiements
		   reçus des débiteurs
			cláusula de distribución equitativa
			cláusula de distribución
			cláusula de distribución de los
			   pagos recibidos de los deudores

S-199	shield package, *see* financial shield		
S-200	shift in demand, *see* shift in the demand curve		
S-201	shift in supply, *see* shift in the supply curve		

S-202	shift in the adequacy of global
	   reserves
		variation du montant adéquat de
		   réserves mondiales
		variation du volume nécessaire de
		   réserves mondiales
			variación de la suficiencia de las
			   reservas mundiales

S-203	shift in the demand curve shift in demand demand shift	déplacement de la demande	desplazamiento de la demanda desplazamiento de la curva de demanda
S-204	shift in the supply curve shift in supply supply shift	déplacement de l'offre	desplazamiento de la oferta desplazamiento de la curva de oferta
S-205	shifting of tax, *see* pass-through		
S-206	shifting of tax, *see* shifting of tax burden		
S-207	shifting of tax burden [tax policy] shifting of tax	déplacement de la charge fiscale	transferencia de la carga tributaria
S-208	shipment	expédition	embarques
S-209	shocks facility, *see* Exogenous Shocks Facility		
S-210	short position	position courte position à découvert position potentielle d'achat	posición sobrevendida posición corta posición en descubierto

S-211	shortfall *see also:* export shortfall	écart par rapport à l'objectif déficit insuffisance contre-performance moins-perçu	diferencia entre el resultado y lo previsto deficiencia disminución insuficiencia déficit pérdida
S-212	shorting, *see* sell short		
S-213	short-term asset(s) *see also:* current asset(s); liquid asset(s); quick asset(s)	actif à court terme actif mobilisable à court terme valeur réalisable	activo a corto plazo
S-214	short-term capital	capitaux à court terme	capital a corto plazo
S-215	short-term interest rate, *see* short-term rate		
S-216	short-term paper	effet à court terme titre à court terme	efectos comerciales a corto plazo títulos a corto plazo
S-217	short-term rate short-term interest rate	taux à court terme taux d'intérêt à court terme taux court	tasa a corto plazo tasa de interés a corto plazo
S-218	shuttle trade *see also:* border trade	commerce-navette navettage tourisme commercial	comercio de frontera turismo comercial comercio fronterizo
S-219	SI, *see* Selected Issues papers		
S-220	SIBOR, *see* Singapore interbank offered rate		
S-221	side financing, *see* parallel financing		
S-222	side letter	lettre complémentaire	carta complementaria
S-223	sight deposit, *see* demand deposit		
S-224	signaling	signalisation	emisión de señales señalización
S-225	signature loan unsecured loan personal loan character loan	crédit personnel prêt personnel prêt sur signature	préstamo personal préstamo sin garantía real préstamo a sola firma
S-226	significance level	seuil de signification significativité	nivel de significación nivel de significancia
S-227	SILICs, *see* severely indebted low-income countries		
S-228	SIMICs, *see* severely indebted middle-income countries		
S-229	simple interest rate *see also:* compound interest rate	taux d'intérêt simple	tasa de interés simple
S-230	simplifying assumption	hypothèse simplificatrice	supuesto simplificador
S-231	simulation model	modèle de simulation	modelo de simulación

S-232	Singapore interbank offered rate SIBOR	taux interbancaire offert à Singapour	tasa interbancaria de oferta de Singapur
S-233	single crop economy, *see* one-crop economy		
S-234	single currency link, *see* single peg		
S-235	single currency loan monocurrency loan	prêt en une seule monnaie prêt monodevise prêt en devise unique	préstamo en una sola moneda
S-236	single currency pegging, *see* single peg		

S-237	single peg
	single currency pegging
	single currency link
	unicurrency peg
	unicurrency pegging
		détermination du taux de change
		  par référence à une seule
		  monnaie
		rattachement à une seule monnaie
			tipo de cambio fijo en relación con
			  una sola moneda
			determinación del tipo de cambio
			  en relación con una sola moneda
			vinculación a una sola moneda

S-238	single tax identification number, *see* taxpayer identification number		

S-239	single-factor terms of trade	termes de l'échange factoriels
		  simples
			relación de intercambio de factor
			  único

S-240	single-purpose expenditure rule	principe de la spécialité budgétaire règle de la spécialité budgétaire	principio de especialidad presupuestaria
S-241	single-stage tax	taxe unique	impuesto monofásico impuesto de etapa única
S-242	single-tailed test, *see* one-tailed test		
S-243	sinking fund	caisse d'amortissement	fondo de amortización
S-244	SITC, *see* Standard International Trade Classification		
S-245	size of the Fund	volume des ressources du FMI	magnitud de los recursos del FMI monto de los recursos del FMI
S-246	"skeleton", *see* fiscal skeleton		
S-247	skilled labor skilled manpower skilled worker	main-d'œuvre qualifiée	mano de obra calificada trabajador especializado
S-248	skilled manpower, *see* skilled labor		
S-249	skilled worker, *see* skilled labor		
S-250	S&L, *see* savings and loan association		
S-251	slack [economics]	atonie stagnation ralentissement lourdeur de la conjoncture	atonía falta de dinamismo

S-252	slack capacity
	idle capacity
	underemployed capacity
		volant de ressources inutilisées
		capacité (de production) inutilisée
		capacité (de production)
		  inemployée
		capacité (de production) oisive
		capacité (de production) sous-
		  employée
		faible taux d'utilisation des
		  capacités (productives)
			capacidad no utilizada
			capacidad ociosa
			capacidad subutilizada

S-253	sliding parity, *see* gliding parity		
S-254	slippage	dérapage	desviación
S-255	SM, *see* Staff Memorandum		
S-256	small and medium-scale enterprises, *see* small and medium-sized enterprises		
S-257	small and medium-size enterprises, *see* small and medium-sized enterprises		

S-258	small and medium-sized
	  enterprises
	SMEs
	small and medium-size enterprises
	small and medium-scale
	  enterprises
	small and medium-sized industries
	SMIs
		petites et moyennes entreprises
		PME
		petites et moyennes industries
		PMI
			pequeña y mediana empresa
			PYME

S-259	small and medium-sized industries, *see* small and medium-sized enterprises		
S-260	small ingot *see also:* bar; ingot	lingotin [FRA] petit lingot [CHE, BEL]	pequeño lingote
S-261	small island economy	petite économie insulaire	pequeña economía insular
S-262	small low-income economies	petits pays à faible revenu	economías pequeñas de bajo ingreso
S-263	SMEs, *see* small and medium-sized enterprises		
S-264	SMIs, *see* small and medium-sized enterprises		

S-265	Smoot-Hawley Tariff Act of 1930
	see also: beggar-my-neighbor
	  policy
	Tariff Act of 1930
		loi Smoot-Hawley de 1930	Ley Smoot-Hawley de 1930 sobre
			  Aranceles

S-266	smoothing	lissage atténuation des variations aplanissement des variations	suavización atenuación de las variaciones
S-267	SMP, *see* staff-monitored program		
S-268	*SNA 1993, see System of National Accounts 1993*		
S-269	snake in the tunnel, *see* European narrow margins arrangement		
S-270	snake system, *see* European narrow margins arrangement		

S-271	social cost	coût social coût pour la collectivité coût collectif	costo social costo colectivo
S-272	social infrastructure	équipements collectifs équipements sociaux infrastructure sociale	infraestructura social
S-273	social overhead capital overhead capital	équipements collectifs fixes équipements publics fixes	capital social fijo capital nacional fijo
S-274	social rate of return *see also:* private rate of return SRR	taux de rentabilité sociale	tasa de rentabilidad social tasa de retorno social
S-275	social safety net, *see* safety net		
S-276	social security *see also:* welfare	sécurité sociale	seguridad social seguro social
S-277	social security contributions	cotisations de sécurité sociale	contribuciones a la seguridad social contribuciones al seguro social
S-278	social security funds	administrations de sécurité sociale caisses de sécurité sociale	fondos de seguridad social fondos de seguro social
S-279	social security scheme, *see* social security system		
S-280	social security system social security scheme	régime de sécurité sociale système de sécurité sociale	sistema de seguridad social régimen de seguridad social plan de seguridad social seguridad social
S-281	social surplus net social benefit of production	surplus collectif surplus social	superávit social
S-282	SOE, *see* public enterprise		
S-283	soft budget constraint *see also:* budget constraint; hard budget constraint SBC	faible contrainte budgétaire	limitación presupuestaria flexible limitación presupuestaria poco estricta
S-284	soft currency	monnaie faible	moneda débil
S-285	soft landing	atterrissage en douceur	aterrizaje suave
S-286	soft loan	prêt concessionnel prêt favorable	préstamo concesionario préstamo blando préstamo en condiciones concesionarias préstamo en condiciones favorables crédito en condiciones favorables crédito blando
S-287	soft patch	passage à vide	desaceleración temporal desaceleración transitoria
S-288	softening, *see* easing		

S-289	solve for x [equations]	redistribuer les termes de l'équation pour obtenir l'expression de x	despejar la x
S-290	sorting	tri classification	reparto clasificación
S-291	South/Central American I, II Division [IMF]	Division Amérique du Sud/Amérique centrale I, II	División de América del Sur/América Central I, II
S-292	Southeastern Division I, II, III [IMF]	Division Europe du Sud-Est I, II, III	División de Europa Sudoriental I, II, III
S-293	Southern Common Market MERCOSUR	Marché commun du Sud MERCOSUR	Mercado Común del Sur MERCOSUR
S-294	Southern I, II Division [IMF]	Division Europe du Sud I, II	División de Europa Meridional I, II
S-295	Sovereign Asset and Liability Management Division [IMF]	Division gestion des actifs et des passifs souverains	División de Gestión de Activos y Pasivos Soberanos
S-296	sovereign borrower	emprunteur souverain	prestatario soberano
S-297	sovereign credit	crédit souverain emprunt garanti par les pouvoirs publics	crédito soberano
S-298	sovereign debt	dette souveraine	deuda soberana
S-299	sovereign rating	notation d'un emprunteur souverain	calificación soberana calificación del prestatario soberano
S-300	sovereign risk political risk	risque de la dette souveraine risque souverain risque politique risque de souveraineté risque d'insolvabilité du pays emprunteur	riesgo soberano riesgo de la deuda soberana riesgo político
S-301	SPA, *see* Special Program of Assistance (for the Low-Income Debt-Distressed Countries in Sub-Saharan Africa)		
S-302	Spanish Division [IMF]	Division espagnole	División de Español
S-303	Special Advisor to the Managing Director [IMF]	Conseiller spécial du Directeur général	Asesor Especial del Director Gerente
S-304	special allocation of SDRs, *see* special SDR allocation		
S-305	Special Assistant to the Deputy Managing Director [IMF]	Assistant spécial du Directeur général adjoint	Asistente Especial del Subdirector Gerente
S-306	special charges [IMF] additional charges	commissions spéciales	cargos especiales cargos adicionales

S-307	Special Contingent Account 1 First Special Contingent Account SCA-1	compte spécial conditionnel 1 CSC-1	Primera Cuenta Especial para Contingencias CEC-1
S-308	Special Contingent Account 2 *see* Post SCA-2 Administered Account SCA-2 Second Special Contingent Account	compte spécial conditionnel 2 CSC-2	Segunda Cuenta Especial para Contingencias CEC-2
S-309	Special Data Dissemination Standard [IMF] *see also:* General Data Dissemination System SDDS special standard more demanding standard special data dissemination standard	norme spéciale de diffusion des données NSDD norme spéciale norme plus contraignante	Normas Especiales para la Divulgación de Datos NEDD normas especiales normas más rigurosas
S-310	special data dissemination standard, *see* Special Data Dissemination Standard		
S-311	Special Disbursement Account SDA	compte de versements spécial CVS	Cuenta Especial de Desembolsos CED
S-312	special drawing right SDR	droit de tirage spécial DTS	derecho especial de giro DEG
S-313	special election [IMF, Executive Directors]	élection extraordinaire	elección extraordinaria
S-314	special facility [IMF]	mécanisme spécial	servicio financiero especial
S-315	Special Facility for Africa, *see* Special Facility for Sub-Saharan Africa		
S-316	Special Facility for Sub-Saharan Africa [IBRD] SFSA Special Facility for Africa SFA Africa Facility	Fonds spécial d'aide à l'Afrique subsaharienne FSAAS Fonds d'aide à l'Afrique FAA	Servicio Especial de Asistencia para África al sur del Sahara SEAASS Servicio Especial para África SEA Servicio Africano
S-317	special majority qualified majority supermajority	majorité qualifiée supermajorité	mayoría especial mayoría calificada mayoría cualificada
S-318	special meeting [IMF]	réunion extraordinaire	reunión extraordinaria
S-319	special one-time allocation of SDRs *see also:* equity issue one-time special SDR allocation equity allocation of SDRs special SDR allocation	allocation spéciale de DTS à caractère exceptionnel	asignación especial de DEG de carácter excepcional

S-320	Special Program of Assistance (for the Low-Income Debt-Distressed Countries in Sub-Saharan Africa) [IBRD] SPA Special Program of Assistance (to Sub-Saharan Africa)	Programme spécial d'assistance (en faveur des pays surendettés à faible revenu d'Afrique subsaharienne)	Programa Especial de Asistencia (para los Países de Bajos Ingresos de África al Sur del Sahara Agobiados por la Deuda)
S-321	Special Program of Assistance (to Sub-Saharan Africa), see Special Program of Assistance (for the Low-Income Debt-Distressed Countries in Sub-Saharan Africa)		
S-322	special purpose grant, see categorical grant		
S-323	Special Representative to the EU [IMF]	Représentant spécial auprès de l'UE	Representante Especial ante la UE
S-324	special SDR allocation see also: SDR allocation special allocation of SDRs	allocation spéciale de DTS	asignación especial de DEG
S-325	special SDR allocation, see special one-time allocation of SDRs		
S-326	special standard, see Special Data Dissemination Standard		
S-327	Special Trade Representative/Director [IMF]	Représentant spécial pour les questions commerciales/Directeur	Representante Especial para Asuntos Comerciales/Director
S-328	specialized agency [UN]	institution spécialisée	organismo especializado
S-329	specific assessment framework, see dataset-specific quality assessment framework		
S-330	speculation motive	motif de spéculation	motivo especulación
S-331	spending agency spending department spending unit budgetary unit	organisme dépensier ministère dépensier entité dépensière unité budgétaire	organismo ejecutor del gasto organismo que efectúa los gastos ministerio que efectúa los gastos unidad ejecutora de gasto unidad presupuestaria
S-332	spending department, see spending agency		
S-333	spending unit, see spending agency		
S-334	split, see stock split		
S-335	split exchange rates, see multiple exchange rates		
S-336	split pricing differential pricing	prix multiples régime de prix multiples	diferenciación de precios desdoblamiento de precios
S-337	split system, see income-split tax system		
S-338	split-up, see stock split		
S-339	SPM, see Personnel Manager, Senior		
S-340	spot exchange transaction, see spot transaction		
S-341	spot market cash market	marché du disponible marché au comptant	mercado de entrega inmediata mercado spot mercado al contado

S-342	spot price spot quotation spot rate cash price	cours au comptant prix au comptant prix du disponible prix du marché libre	precio de entrega inmediata cotización al contado tipo de cambio al contado tipo al contado
S-343	spot quotation, *see* spot price		
S-344	spot rate, *see* spot price		
S-345	spot transaction spot exchange transaction	opération de change au comptant	operación de cambio al contado
S-346	spread	écart différence marge écart de cours	*spread* diferencial diferencia margen
S-347	spread effect	effet de propagation effet d'entraînement	efecto de propagación
S-348	spread over Libor	marge au-dessus du Libor	margen por encima de la Libor
S-349	spreading of risks risk spreading risk diversification	répartition des risques diversification des risques	diversificación de los riesgos distribución de los riesgos
S-350	spreadsheet	tableur tableau de calcul	hoja de cálculo planilla electrónica
S-351	spurious correlation	corrélation factice corrélation illusoire	correlación espuria
S-352	SRF, *see* Supplemental Reserve Facility		
S-353	SRP, *see* Staff Retirement Plan		
S-354	SRR, *see* social rate of return		
S-355	SSA, *see* sub-Saharan Africa		
S-355a	STA, *see* Statistics Department		
S-356	STABEX, *see* Stabilization System for Export Earnings		
S-357	stabilization fund [IMF]	fonds de stabilisation caisse de stabilisation	fondo de estabilización
S-358	stabilization measure	mesure de stabilisation mesure stabilisatrice	medida de estabilización
S-359	Stabilization System for Export Earnings [Lomé Convention] STABEX	Système de stabilisation des recettes d'exportation STABEX	Sistema de estabilización de los ingresos de exportación STABEX
S-360	stable but adjustable par values	parités stables mais ajustables	paridades estables pero ajustables
S-361	staff [IMF] Fund staff	fonctionnaires du FMI services du FMI personnel du FMI membres des services du FMI	personal técnico del FMI cuerpo técnico del FMI funcionarios del FMI personal del FMI

S-362	staff development	valorisation du personnel valorisation des ressources humaines perfectionnement du personnel gestion des carrières	perfeccionamiento del personal
S-363	Staff Development Division [IMF]	Division perfectionnement du personnel	División de Perfeccionamiento del Personal

S-364	staff estimates
	[IMF]
		estimations des services du FMI	estimaciones de los funcionarios
			  del FMI
			estimaciones del personal técnico
			  del FMI

S-365	staff member [IMF]	membre des services du FMI membre du personnel fonctionnaire	funcionario
S-366	Staff Memorandum [IMF] SM staff report	mémorandum des services du FMI SM	memorando del personal técnico del FMI
S-367	staff mission [IMF]	mission des services du FMI	misión del personal técnico del FMI misión del FMI

S-368	staff projections
	[IMF]
		projections des services du FMI	proyecciones de los funcionarios
			  del FMI
			proyecciones del personal técnico
			  del FMI

S-369	staff report, *see* Staff Memorandum		
S-370	Staff Retirement Plan [IMF] SRP	régime de retraite du personnel	Plan de Jubilación del Personal
S-371	staff-monitored program SMP Fund-monitored program	programme de référence	programa supervisado por el FMI
S-372	stage one [IMF, safeguards assessment]	phase un première étape	primera etapa
S-373	stage two [IMF, safeguards assessment]	phase deux deuxième étape	segunda etapa
S-374	stagflation	stagflation	estanflación
S-375	stagnation	marasme stagnation torpeur	estancamiento
S-376	stamp tax	droit de timbre	impuesto de timbre impuesto de sellos
S-377	standard component	composante type	componente normalizado
S-378	standard deviation	écart-type	desviación estándar desviación normal desviación típica

S-379	*Standard International Trade Classification* [UN] *SITC*	Classification type pour le commerce international CTCI	Clasificación Uniforme para el Comercio Internacional CUCI
S-380	standard of value	étalon de valeur	patrón de valor
S-381	standard practices (of the Fund), *see* rules and practices of the Fund		
S-382	standard value, *see* official value		
S-383	standardization	normalisation standardisation	normalización estandarización estandardización
S-384	Stand-By Arrangement [IMF] SBA	accord de confirmation	acuerdo de derecho de giro acuerdo *stand-by*
S-385	stand-by charge [IMF] *see also:* commitment fee [IMF]	commission d'engagement	cargo por acuerdo de derecho de giro
S-386	stand-by credit stand-by loan	crédit accordé dans le cadre d'un accord de confirmation	crédito en el marco de un acuerdo de derecho de giro
S-387	stand-by loan, *see* stand-by credit		
S-388	Stand-By Operations Division [IMF] SBO	Division opérations relatives aux accords de confirmation	División de Operaciones relativas a Acuerdos de Derecho de Giro
S-389	standing committee	commission permanente comité permanent	comisión permanente comité permanente
S-390	standstill agreement [WTO]	accord de maintien du *statu quo*	acuerdo de mantenimiento del statu quo
S-391	standstill agreement, *see* standstill on payments		
S-392	standstill on payments *see also:* stay of payments standstill agreement	suspension de paiements (par accord mutuel) sursis de paiements (par accord mutuel)	moratoria de pagos (por acuerdo mutuo) moratoria autorizada
S-393	staple crop	culture vivrière de base	cultivo básico
S-394	staples, *see* basic foodstuffs		
S-395	start-up capital, *see* seed capital		
S-396	start-up cost	frais d'établissement frais initiaux coûts de démarrage	costos iniciales costos de puesta en marcha
S-397	state enterprise, *see* public enterprise		
S-398	stated interest rate, *see* nominal interest rate		
S-399	statement of account [banking] account statement	relevé de compte extrait de compte	estado de cuenta extracto de cuenta

S-400	statement of assets and liabilities, *see* balance sheet		
S-401	statement of condition, *see* balance sheet		
S-402	statement of financial condition, *see* balance sheet		
S-403	statement of financial position, *see* balance sheet		
S-404	statement of income, *see* income statement		
S-405	statement of income and expenses, *see* income statement		
S-406	state-owned corporation, *see* public enterprise		
S-407	state-owned enterprise, *see* public enterprise		
S-408	statistical correspondent [IMF] correspondent on statistical matters	correspondant statistique correspondant des services statistiques	corresponsal de estadísticas corresponsal encargado de estadísticas
S-409	statistical data source	source de données statistiques	fuente de los datos estadísticos
S-410	statistical discrepancy	écart statistique discordance disparité différence non-concordance	discrepancia estadística
S-411	statistical inference	induction statistique	inferencia estadística
S-412	Statistics Department [IMF] STA	Département des statistiques	Departamento de Estadística
S-413	status, immunities, and privileges [IMF]	statut, immunités et privilèges	condición jurídica, inmunidades y privilegios
S-414	status of the Fund *see also:* Articles of Agreement	statut juridique du FMI	condición jurídica del Fondo
S-415	status report, *see* progress report		
S-416	statutory ceiling	plafond légal plafond réglementaire limite légale	límite legal
S-417	statutory power	pouvoir conféré par la loi pouvoir légal pouvoir statutaire	poder legal facultad legal
S-418	statutory reserve statutory reserves legal reserve legal reserves	réserve légale réserves légales	reserva legal reservas legales encaje legal
S-419	statutory reserves, *see* statutory reserve		

S-420	stay of payments
	see also: standstill agreement
		suspension de paiements
		  (accordée par les créanciers)
		moratoire
		sursis de paiements (accordé par
		  les créanciers)
			suspensión de pagos con acuerdo
			  de los acreedores
			suspensión de pagos

S-421	steady state	état stable état d'équilibre à long terme	estado estable
S-422	steady-state growth	croissance en état stable croissance à taux constant	crecimiento en estado estable crecimiento a una tasa constante
S-423	steering committee, *see* bank advisory committee		
S-424	step depreciation discrete depreciation one-off depreciation discrete step depreciation	dépréciation ponctuelle	depreciación discreta
S-425	step devaluation, *see* discrete devaluation		
S-426	sterilization [central banking]	stérilisation monétaire neutralisation	esterilización esterilización monetaria neutralización
S-427	sterilize	stériliser geler bloquer	esterilizar
S-428	sterilized intervention [central banking]	intervention stérilisée	intervención esterilizada
S-429	STF, *see* Systemic Transformation Facility		
S-430	STI, *see* IMF-Singapore Regional Training Institute		
S-431	stickiness downward rigidity	viscosité inflexibilité à la baisse rigidité rigidité à la baisse inélasticité à la baisse	inflexibilidad a la baja rigidez adhesividad rigidez a la baja
S-432	stock *see also:* flow	stock encours	stock masa saldo tenencias
S-433	stock, *see* inventory		
S-434	stock cycle inventory cycle	cycle des stocks	ciclo de existencias ciclo de inventario
S-435	stock data *see also:* flow data position data	données de stocks données d'encours	datos de saldos datos sobre saldos
S-436	stock dividend [USA] *see also:* bonus share; stock split scrip issue [GBR]	dividende (payé) en actions dividende sous forme d'actions (gratuites)	dividendo en acciones

S-437	stock exchange, *see* securities exchange		
S-438	stock index future, *see* securities index future		
S-439	stock index option contract	contrat d'options sur indice boursier	contrato de opción basado en índices bursátiles
S-440	stock of money, *see* money supply		
S-441	stock option plan	programme d'options d'achat d'actions programme d'options de souscription d'actions régime d'actionnariat plan d'options sur titre plan d'option de souscription (d'actions)	plan de opción de compra de acciones
S-442	stock purchase warrant, *see* warrant		
S-443	stock split *see also:* stock dividend split split-up	fractionnement d'actions	fraccionamiento de acciones
S-444	stock variable	variable de stock	variable de stock variable de saldo
S-445	stock warrant, *see* warrant		
S-446	stockbuilding	constitution de stocks stockage formation de stocks restockage	acumulación de existencias
S-447	stockholder equity, *see* net worth		
S-448	stock-of-debt operation [Paris Club] debt stock agreement	opération sur le stock de la dette opération sur l'encours de la dette	operación sobre el saldo de la deuda operación de reducción del saldo de la deuda
S-449	stockpiling	accumulation de stocks constitution de stocks de réserve	acumulación de existencias de reserva acumulación de existencias estratégicas
S-450	stocks and flows	stocks et flux encours et flux	saldos y flujos tenencias y flujos stocks y flujos
S-451	stop and go, *see* stop-go (policy)		
S-452	stop-filer [taxation]	non-déclarant	contribuyente omiso
S-453	stopgap measure palliative measure	solution provisoire solution d'attente palliatif	medida de emergencia paliativo medida provisional

S-454	stop-go (policy) stop and go	politique faisant alterner freinage et relance de l'expansion alternance de phases d'accélération et de freinage alternance du recours au frein et à l'accélérateur	política de avance intermitente alternancia rápida de medidas de expansión y contracción
S-455	stop-out price, *see* minimum acceptable bid		
S-456	store of value	réserve de valeur	reserva de valor
S-457	straight bond	obligation ordinaire obligation classique obligation à taux fixe	bono ordinario
S-458	straight debt	instruments classiques de la dette dette constituée par des instruments classiques	deuda ordinaria
S-459	Strategic Issues Division [IMF]	Division questions stratégiques	División de Asuntos Estratégicos
S-460	strengthened cooperative strategy, *see* intensified cooperative approach		
S-461	strengthened cooperative strategy on arrears, *see* intensified cooperative approach		
S-462	strengthened cooperative strategy on overdue financial obligations, *see* intensified cooperative approach		
S-463	strengthened debt strategy [IMF]	stratégie renforcée en matière de dette	estrategia reforzada ante la deuda
S-464	strike	grève	huelga paro
S-465	strike price, *see* exercise price		
S-466	striking price, *see* exercise price		
S-467	stripped bond *see also:* zero coupon bond	obligation coupon détaché obligation démembrée obligation démantelée	bono desprovisto de cupón bono sin cupón título desmantelado
S-468	structural adjustment credit [IBRD] SAC	crédit à l'ajustement structurel	crédito para ajuste estructural
S-469	Structural Adjustment Facility (within the Special Disbursement Account) *see also:* Enhanced Structural Adjustment Facility; Poverty Reduction and Growth Facility SAF	facilité d'ajustement structurel (établie dans le cadre du compte de versements spécial) FAS	Servicio de Ajuste Estructural (en el marco de la Cuenta Especial de Desembolsos) SAE
S-470	Structural Adjustment Lending [IBRD] SAL	prêts à l'ajustement structurel PAS	préstamo para (fines de) ajuste estructural
S-471	structural conditionality	conditionnalité structurelle	condicionalidad estructural
S-472	structural deficit, *see* underlying deficit		

S-473	structural equation [econometrics]	équation structurelle	ecuación estructural
S-474	structural inflation, *see* trend inflation		
S-475	structural inflexibility, *see* structural rigidity		
S-476	structural rigidity structural inflexibility	rigidité structurelle	rigidez estructural inflexibilidad estructural
S-477	structural unemployment	chômage structurel	desempleo estructural
S-478	Student's *t*-statistic, *see* *t*-statistic		
S-479	stunted growth	croissance freinée croissance retardée croissance ralentie	crecimiento frenado crecimiento retardado
S-480	stylized fact	exemple stylisé fait stylisé	hecho estilizado generalización
S-481	subcontract	contrat de sous-traitance	subcontrato
S-482	submission of bids	soumission d'offres	presentación de ofertas
S-483	subnational government	administration infranationale collectivité territoriale collectivité locale	gobierno subnacional niveles inferiores de gobierno
S-484	subordinated debt junior debt	créance de rang inférieur créance subordonnée créance non privilégiée	deuda subordinada crédito de rango inferior
S-485	subordinated loan	prêt non privilégié prêt subordonné prêt participatif	préstamo subordinado
S-486	subpar asset, *see* substandard asset		
S-487	sub-Saharan Africa SSA	Afrique subsaharienne	África subsahariana África al sur del Sahara
S-488	subscript	indice inférieur	subíndice
S-489	subscription warrant, *see* warrant		
S-490	subscriptions of members [IMF]	souscriptions des États membres	suscripciones de los países miembros
S-491	subsidiary subsidiary enterprise incorporated branch	filiale	filial
S-492	subsidiary enterprise, *see* subsidiary		
S-493	subsidized interest rate	intérêt bonifié taux d'intérêt bonifié	tasa de interés subvencionada tasa de interés subsidiada
S-494	subsidy	subvention	subvención subsidio
S-495	Subsidy Account, *see* PRGF Trust Subsidy Account		

S-496	subsidy resources *see also:* loan resources	ressources de bonification	recursos para subvenciones
S-497	subsistence income	revenu de subsistance minimum vital	ingreso de subsistencia ingreso mínimo vital
S-498	substandard asset subpar asset	actif de qualité inférieure	activo de calidad inferior activo inferior
S-499	substitute substitute good competitive good	substitut produit de substitution	bien sustitutivo sucedáneo sustituto
S-500	substitute good, *see* substitute		
S-501	substitution effect *see also:* income effect	effet de substitution	efecto de sustitución
S-502	successful bidder successful tenderer	adjudicataire	adjudicatario
S-503	successful tenderer, *see* successful bidder		
S-504	summary accounting	comptabilité de synthèse	contabilidad sintética
S-505	summary proceedings summary record	compte rendu analytique	acta resumida
S-506	summary record, *see* summary proceedings		
S-507	summary statement [IMF]	état récapitulatif	estado resumido
S-508	summary table	récapitulation tableau récapitulatif	cuadro sintético
S-509	sunset act, *see* sunset legislation		
S-510	sunset legislation [USA] sunset act	loi à durée déterminée loi de temporarisation	ley de caducidad automática ley con disposición de extinción automática
S-511	supermajority, *see* special majority		
S-512	superscript	indice supérieur	índice superior
S-513	supervisory data source	source de données pour le contrôle bancaire	fuente de los datos de supervisión
S-514	supplement reserves, need to [IMF]	nécessité d'ajouter aux réserves	necesidad de complementar las reservas
S-515	Supplemental Reserve Facility [IMF] SRF	facilité de réserve supplémentaire FRS	Servicio de Complementación de Reservas SCR
S-516	supplementary budget	loi de finances rectificative collectif budgétaire budget supplémentaire rallonge budgétaire	presupuesto complementario
S-517	supplementary capital, *see* tier 2 capital		

S-518	Supplementary Financing Facility [IMF] SFF	mécanisme de financement supplémentaire MFS	Servicio de Financiamiento Suplementario SFS
S-519	Supplementary Financing Facility Subsidy Account [IMF] SFF Subsidy Account	compte de bonification du mécanisme de financement supplémentaire	Cuenta de Subvención del Servicio de Financiamiento Suplementario
S-520	supplier industry upstream industry	industrie d'amont industrie fournisseuse	industria abastecedora
S-521	supplier's credit	crédit-fournisseur	crédito de proveedores
S-522	supplies and equipment	fournitures et matériel	suministros y equipo
S-523	supply	offre approvisionnement	oferta abastecimiento aprovisionamiento
S-524	supply and use	ressources et emplois	oferta y utilización
S-525	supply bottleneck	goulet d'étranglement au niveau de l'offre goulet d'étranglement de l'offre	estrangulamiento de la oferta estrangulamiento en el suministro
S-526	supply curve	courbe d'offre	curva de oferta
S-527	supply elasticity, *see* elasticity of supply		
S-528	supply of money, *see* money supply		
S-529	supply schedule	tableau de l'offre	tabla de oferta
S-530	supply shift, *see* shift in the supply curve		
S-531	supply-side economics	économie de l'offre doctrine économique axée sur l'offre	economía de oferta doctrina macroeconómica basada en la oferta ofertismo
S-532	supply-side policy	politique de stimulation de l'offre politique d'expansion de l'offre politique d'incitation de l'offre politique d'action sur l'offre	política de incentivos a la oferta política de oferta política de estímulo a la oferta
S-533	support intervention [central banking]	intervention de soutien	intervención de apoyo
S-534	support price	prix de soutien prix garanti	precio de apoyo precio de subvención precio garantizado precio sostén
S-535	support ratio *see also:* dependency ratio	ratio actifs/inactifs nombre d'actifs par retraité	razón población activa/población inactiva
S-536	support services [IMF]	services de soutien services d'appui	servicios de apoyo

S-537	support staff [IMF]	personnel d'appui personnel auxiliaire services généraux	personal auxiliar personal de apoyo
S-538	supporting document	pièce justificative	documentación probatoria documentación justificativa comprobante
S-539	suppressed inflation repressed inflation	inflation refoulée inflation contenue inflation latente inflation réprimée	inflación reprimida inflación contenida inflación latente
S-540	supranational authorities	autorités supranationales	autoridades supranacionales
S-541	surcharge to the basic rate of charge [IMF]	commission additionnelle	sobretasa adicional a la tasa de cargos básica
S-542	surplus country	pays excédentaire	país con superávit país superavitario
S-543	surrender of foreign exchange	rétrocession de devises cession de devises	cesión de divisas entrega de divisas liquidación de divisas
S-544	surveillance	surveillance	supervisión
S-545	Surveillance Operations Division [IMF]	Division opérations de surveillance	División de Operaciones de Supervisión
S-546	surveillance over exchange arrangements [IMF]	surveillance de la politique de change	supervisión de los regímenes de cambios
S-547	Surveillance Review Division [IMF]	Division examen de la surveillance	División de Examen de la Supervisión
S-548	survey form questionnaire	questionnaire formulaire	cuestionario
S-549	survey on capital markets [IMF]	examen de la situation des marchés de capitaux	panorama de los mercados de capital
S-550	suspense account *see also:* memorandum account transit account clearing account	compte d'attente compte provisoire compte de passage compte d'imputation provisoire compte d'affectation temporaire	cuenta suspensiva cuenta de suspensión cuenta transitoria cuenta provisoria
S-551	sustainability	viabilité soutenabilité	sostenibilidad viabilidad sustentabilidad
S-552	sustainable debt	dette viable dette soutenable	deuda sostenible deuda viable deuda sustentable
S-553	sustainable development	développement durable développement viable	desarrollo sostenible desarrollo viable desarrollo sustentable

S-554	sustainable growth	croissance durable croissance soutenable croissance viable	crecimiento sostenible crecimiento viable crecimiento sustentable
S-555	sustained growth	croissance régulière croissance soutenue	crecimiento duradero crecimiento continuo
S-556	swap, *see* reciprocal currency arrangement		
S-557	swap, *see* swap arrangement		
S-558	swap arrangement, *see* reciprocal currency arrangement		
S-559	swap arrangement swap	accord de swap échange financier swap	acuerdo de swap swap canje permuta permuta financiera operación de pase pase operación de canje
S-560	swing credit	découvert réciproque	crédito recíproco al descubierto línea de crédito a muy corto plazo
S-561	swing line, *see* bridge financing		
S-562	swing loan, *see* bridge financing		
S-563	switching policy, *see* expenditure switching policy		
S-564	syndicate *see also:* underwriters consortium pool	consortium consortium bancaire syndicat syndicat financier syndicat bancaire	consorcio bancario consorcio de bancos
S-565	syndicate leader, *see* lead manager		
S-566	syndicated credit, *see* syndicated loan		
S-567	syndicated loan syndicated credit	crédit consortial crédit syndiqué	préstamo de un consorcio bancario préstamo suscrito por un consorcio bancario préstamo sindicado
S-568	system of information notices, *see* information notice system		
S-569	*System of National Accounts 1993* [UN] *SNA 1993*	*Système de comptabilité nationale 1993* *SCN 1993*	*Sistema de Cuentas Nacionales 1993* *SCN 1993*
S-570	systematic risk market risk undiversifiable risk	risque systématique risque de marché	riesgo sistemático riesgo de mercado riesgo no diversificable
S-571	Systemic Issues and Crisis Resolution Division [IMF]	Division questions systémiques et résolution des crises	División de Cuestiones Sistémicas y Resolución de Crisis

| S-572 | Systemic Transformation Facility [IMF] STF | facilité de transformation systémique facilité pour la transformation systémique FTS | Servicio para la Transformación Sistémica STS |

T

| T-1 | TA Advisor, *see* Technical Assistance Advisor | | |

| T-2 | takeoff [economics] | décollage démarrage | despegue arranque reactivación impulso |

| T-3 | takeover *see also:* hostile takeover (of a company); raider | prise de contrôle opération de prise de contrôle rachat reprise absorption | toma de control adquisición absorción |

| T-4 | takeover bid, *see* tender offer | | |

| T-5 | tangible assets | actifs corporels actifs visibles avoirs corporels avoirs visibles | activos materiales activos tangibles activos físicos |

| T-6 | tap issue | émission continuelle émission permanente émission à guichets ouverts émission continue | emisión continua |

| T-7 | target group | groupe-cible groupe ciblé | grupo beneficiario grupo escogido como meta grupo meta |

| T-8 | target income, *see* income target | | |

| T-9 | target range | fourchette-objectif fourchette fixée fourchette retenue intervalle de variation-objectif | banda meta banda fijada como meta |

| T-10 | target variable | variable-objectif variable-cible variable choisie comme objectif variable prise pour cible | variable objetivo variable meta |

| T-11 | target zone [exchange rates] | zone-objectif zone de référence monétaire zone d'objectifs de change | zona meta banda cambiaria zona de referencia |

| T-12 | tariff, *see* customs tariff | | |

| T-13 | Tariff Act of 1930, *see* Smoot-Hawley Tariff Act of 1930 | | |

| T-14 | tariff barrier | barrière tarifaire barrière douanière obstacle tarifaire | barrera arancelaria obstáculo arancelario |

T-15	tariff binding	consolidation des droits de douane consolidation tarifaire concession tarifaire plafonnement tarifaire	consolidación arancelaria
T-16	tariff escalation	progressivité des droits escalade tarifaire	progresividad arancelaria escalada de los aranceles progresión arancelaria
T-17	tariff item	position tarifaire	partida arancelaria
T-18	tariff preferences *see also:* preferential tariff arrangement	préférences tarifaires	preferencias arancelarias
T-19	tariff schedule	barème barème des droits liste tarifaire	arancel de aduanas
T-20	tariff union, *see* customs union		
T-21	TAS, *see* Technical Assistance Secretariat		
T-22	Task Force on Coordinated Portfolio Investment Survey [IMF]	Groupe d'étude pour l'enquête coordonnée sur les investissements de portefeuille	Grupo de Trabajo del FMI para la Realización de una Encuesta Coordinada sobre la Inversión de Cartera
T-23	Task Force on Implementation of Standards [FSF]	Groupe de travail du FSF sur l'application des normes	Grupo de Trabajo sobre la Aplicación de las Normas
T-24	*tâtonnement*, *see* trial and error		
T-25	tax abatement	abattement d'impôt	rebaja de impuestos
T-26	tax administration [agency] tax bureau	administration fiscale	administración de impuestos administración tributaria administración impositiva
T-27	tax administration	administration de l'impôt administration fiscale	administración tributaria administración impositiva administración de impuestos
T-28	tax assessment assessment	détermination de la base d'imposition évaluation de la base d'imposition établissement de l'assiette établissement du rôle assiette	determinación de la base imponible cálculo del impuesto tasación base imponible
T-29	tax audit	contrôle fiscal vérification fiscale	inspección tributaria inspección de hacienda auditoría impositiva auditoría fiscal
T-30	tax avoidance *see also:* tax evasion	évasion fiscale (non frauduleuse) incivisme fiscal	elusión fiscal evasión no ilegal de impuestos
T-31	tax base *see also:* basis of assessment; tax incidence	matière imposable assiette de l'impôt	base imponible base impositiva base tributaria

T-32	tax benefit, *see* tax concession		
T-33	tax bracket	tranche d'imposition tranche de revenu imposable tranche du barème de l'impôt	tramo (de la escala impositiva) categoría tributaria
T-34	tax break, *see* tax relief		

T-35	tax buoyancy
	see also: built-in elasticity of a tax
	  system; elasticity of a tax system;
	  tax elasticity
	buoyancy of a tax system
	buoyancy of tax revenue
		élasticité globale d'un système
		  fiscal
		réponse de la fiscalité à une
		  augmentation de la base
			elasticidad tributaria global
			elasticidad global de un sistema
			  tributario
			flexibilidad tributaria

T-36	tax burden *see also:* tax ratio	pression fiscale charge fiscale poids de l'impôt charge des prélèvements obligatoires	presión fiscal carga fiscal carga impositiva carga tributaria
T-37	tax bureau, *see* tax administration		
T-38	tax clearance tax clearing certificate	quitus fiscal licence	certificado de pago de impuestos
T-39	tax clearing certificate, *see* tax clearance		
T-40	tax collection *see also:* tax enforcement	perception de l'impôt	recaudación de impuestos
T-41	tax compliance, *see* taxpayer compliance		
T-42	tax concession tax benefit	allégements dégrèvements fiscaux avantage fiscal	ventaja tributaria
T-43	tax credit credit against (a) tax	crédit d'impôt imputation sur un impôt imputation sur l'impôt avoir fiscal	crédito tributario descuento impositivo
T-44	tax deductible	déductible de la matière imposable déductible du revenu imposable	deducible a efectos tributarios deducible de impuestos
T-45	tax deduction	dégrèvement abattement	deducción impositiva
T-46	tax deferral	ajournement d'impôt moratoire fiscal report d'impôt	aplazamiento del pago de los impuestos
T-47	tax effort, *see* fiscal effort		
T-48	tax elasticity *see also:* tax buoyancy	élasticité de l'impôt élasticité fiscale	elasticidad tributaria
T-49	tax enforcement *see also:* tax collection enforced collection	application des lois fiscales exécution des dispositions fiscales mise en recouvrement recouvrement de l'impôt	ejecución de las leyes tributarias aplicación de las leyes tributarias prevención de la evasión tributaria recaudación coercitiva de impuestos

T-50	tax equity tax fairness	équité fiscale équité de l'impôt justice fiscale	equidad tributaria
T-51	tax evasion *see also:* tax avoidance	fraude fiscale évasion fiscale (frauduleuse)	evasión fiscal evasión ilegal de impuestos
T-52	tax expenditure *see also:* forgone revenue	dépenses fiscales moins-value fiscale	gasto tributario gasto fiscal ingreso fiscal sacrificado ingreso fiscal no percibido
T-53	tax fairness, *see* tax equity		
T-54	tax haven	paradis fiscal refuge fiscal	paraíso tributario paraíso fiscal
T-55	tax holiday	exonération temporaire d'impôt trêve fiscale	exoneración temporal de impuestos tregua tributaria
T-56	tax identification number, *see* taxpayer identification number		
T-57	tax incentive	incitation fiscale encouragement fiscal stimulant fiscal	incentivo tributario incentivo fiscal estímulo tributario
T-58	tax incidence *see also:* basis of assessment; tax base incidence of taxation	incidence de l'impôt	incidencia del impuesto incidencia impositiva incidencia tributaria
T-59	tax liability	cotisation fiscale montant de l'impôt exigible assujettissement à l'impôt	deuda tributaria
T-60	tax loophole	niche fiscale échappatoire fiscale	laguna tributaria escapatoria fiscal

T-61	tax loss carryback
	carryback
	loss carryback
		report en arrière
		imputation à un exercice antérieur
		report de pertes sur les exercices
		  antérieurs
		report de perte rétrospectif
		report de pertes en amont
			imputación a un ejercicio anterior
			traslado a un ejercicio anterior
			traslado de pérdidas al ejercicio
			  anterior
			retrotraer pérdidas
			pérdida traspasada al ejercicio
			  anterior

T-62	tax loss carryforward, *see* carryforward		
T-63	tax loss carryover, *see* carryforward		
T-64	tax on wealth, *see* wealth tax		
T-65	Tax Policy Division [IMF]	Division politique fiscale	División de Política Tributaria
T-66	tax rate	taux d'imposition	tasa impositiva tasa del impuesto alícuota del impuesto tipo fiscal

T-67	tax ratio *see also:* tax burden	coefficient fiscal coefficient de pression fiscale niveau de la fiscalité pression fiscale ratio des impôts au PIB	presión fiscal presión tributaria presión impositiva
T-68	tax receipts, *see* tax revenue		
T-69	tax refund	remboursement d'impôts	reintegro de impuestos devolución de impuestos
T-70	tax relief tax break	abattement dégrèvement fiscal allégement fiscal	exoneración fiscal desgravación reducción impositiva
T-71	tax return	déclaration d'impôts déclaration de revenus déclaration au fisc	declaración de impuestos declaración de renta
T-72	tax revenue tax receipts	recettes fiscales rentrées fiscales	ingresos tributarios ingresos impositivos recaudación tributaria recaudación impositiva
T-73	tax revenue sharing, *see* revenue sharing		
T-74	tax shelter	refuge fiscal abri fiscal	refugio tributario
T-75	tax sparing, *see* tax sparing credit		
T-76	tax sparing credit tax sparing	crédit d'impôt fictif imputation fictive déduction d'impôt fictif	descuento por impuesto exonerado ahorro de impuesto por exenciones
T-77	tax stamp, *see* revenue stamp		
T-78	tax wedge	prélèvement fiscal écart (de prix) introduit par la fiscalité coin fiscal	cuña fiscal cuña tributaria discrepancia impositiva
T-79	tax withholding *see also:* withholding tax withholding at source	retenue à la source prélèvement à la source	retención en la fuente retención en el origen
T-80	tax year base year fiscal year	année d'imposition année de référence	año gravable
T-81	taxable capacity ability to pay	capacité contributive faculté contributive	capacidad contributiva capacidad tributaria
T-82	taxable event	fait générateur	hecho imponible
T-83	taxable income	revenu imposable	renta imponible renta gravable ingreso imponible

T-84	taxation	fiscalité imposition impôt(s) contributions	tributación impuestos sistema tributario fiscalidad
T-85	tax-based income policies, *see* tax-based income policy		
T-86	tax-based income policy tax-based incomes policy TIP tax-based income policies	politique des revenus à base fiscale politique basée sur la fiscalité	política de ingresos basada en los impuestos política de ingresos basada en la tributación
T-87	tax-based incomes policy, *see* tax-based income policy		
T-88	taxes on corporate net wealth	impôts sur l'actif net des sociétés	impuestos sobre el patrimonio neto de las sociedades de capital
T-89	taxes on goods and services	taxes sur les biens et services	impuestos sobre los bienes y servicios impuestos sobre bienes y servicios
T-90	taxes on income, profits, and capital gain	impôts sur le revenu, les bénéfices et les gains en capital	impuestos sobre el ingreso, las utilidades y las ganancias de capital impuestos sobre la renta, las utilidades y las ganancias de capital
T-91	taxes on payroll or work force *see also:* payroll tax	impôts sur les salaires et la main-d'œuvre	impuestos sobre la nómina o la fuerza de trabajo
T-92	taxes on personal net wealth	impôts sur le patrimoine net des personnes physiques	impuestos sobre el patrimonio neto de las personas físicas
T-93	taxes on property, *see* property tax		
T-94	taxpayer	contribuable assujetti	contribuyente
T-95	taxpayer compliance tax compliance	civisme fiscal respect des obligations fiscales discipline fiscale	cumplimiento tributario
T-96	taxpayer identification number TIN tax identification number single tax identification number	numéro d'identification fiscale unique identifiant fiscal unique numéro d'identification du contribuable NIC	número de identificación tributaria NIT código de identificación fiscal número de identificación fiscal NIF
T-97	T-bill, *see* treasury bill		
T-98	T-bond, *see* treasury bond		
T-99	Technical Assistance Advisor [IMF] TA Advisor	Conseiller en matière d'assistance technique	Asesor en Asuntos de Asistencia Técnica
T-100	Technical Assistance Secretariat [IMF] TAS	Secrétariat de l'assistance technique	Secretaría de Asistencia Técnica
T-101	technical memorandum, *see* Technical Memorandum of Understanding		

T-102	Technical Memorandum of Understanding [IMF] TMU technical memorandum	protocole d'accord technique PAT aide-mémoire technique	Memorando Técnico de Entendimiento memorando técnico
T-103	technical reserves	réserve technique réserves techniques provisions techniques	reservas técnicas
T-104	Technology and General Services Department [IMF] TGS	Département de la technologie et des services généraux	Departamento de Tecnología y Servicios Generales
T-105	technology transfer transfer of technology	transfert de technologie	transferencia de tecnología
T-106	Temporary Acting Managing Director, *see* Managing Director, Temporary Acting [IMF]		
T-107	Temporary Alternate Governor, *see* Governor, Temporary Alternate		
T-108	temporary employment temporary occupation	emploi temporaire	empleo temporal trabajo temporario
T-109	temporary occupation, *see* temporary employment		
T-110	tender offer takeover bid	offre publique d'achat OPA	oferta pública de adquisición opa
T-111	tender rate [GBR treasury bills]	taux d'adjudication taux de soumission	tasa de adjudicación
T-112	tenderer, *see* bidder		
T-113	term of maturity maturity life	durée délai de remboursement échéance	vencimiento plazo de vencimiento
T-114	term sheet	descriptif des termes et conditions	hoja de condiciones hoja de plazos y condiciones
T-115	term structure, *see* yield curve		
T-116	term structure of interest rates, *see* yield curve		
T-117	termination	résiliation	extinción rescisión resolución
T-118	terms and conditions	modalités modalités et conditions conditions termes et conditions clauses cahier des charges	condiciones términos y condiciones pliego de condiciones

T-119	terms of reference TOR	mandat instructions attributions	términos de referencia mandato objeto de la misión instrucciones atribuciones
T-120	terms of trade	termes de l'échange	términos del intercambio términos de intercambio relación de intercambio relación de precios de intercambio
T-121	territorial change	modification territoriale	cambio territorial
T-122	tertiary economy, *see* service economy		
T-123	tested cable	télégramme portant numéro de contrôle	cable cifrado
T-124	TFP, *see* total factor productivity		
T-125	TGS, *see* Technology and General Services Department		
T-126	thin market, *see* narrow market		
T-127	three-year arrangement [PRGF]	accord triennal	acuerdo trienal
T-128	thrift, *see* thrift institution		
T-129	thrift institution thrift	institution d'épargne établissement d'épargne	institución de ahorro
T-130	tied aid	aide liée	ayuda condicionada ayuda vinculada
T-131	tier 1 capital *see also:* tier 2 capital capital tier one core capital primary capital [EU]	fonds propres de base fonds propres de première catégorie noyau dur du capital capital de base	capital de nivel 1 capital básico capital primario capital de base
T-132	tier 2 capital *see also:* tier 1 capital capital tier two supplementary capital secondary capital [EU]	fonds propres complémentaires	capital de nivel 2 capital suplementario
T-133	tiering, *see* rate tiering		
T-134	tight labor market	pénurie de main-d'œuvre pénurie d'offre de main-d'œuvre	escasez de oferta de mano de obra tensión en el mercado laboral
T-135	tight market, *see* narrow market		
T-136	tight monetary policy, *see* monetary tightening		
T-137	tight money, *see* monetary tightening		
T-138	tight money policy, *see* monetary tightening		

T-139	tightening, *see* monetary tightening		
T-140	tightening of credit, *see* credit crunch		

T-141	tightening of policy
	hardening of policy
		resserrement d'une politique
		durcissement d'une politique
			intensificación de la política
			  restrictiva
			imposición de una política más
			  restrictiva
			endurecimiento de una política

T-142	TIM, *see* Trade Integration Mechanism		
T-143	time deposit fixed-term deposit certificate of deposit CD	dépôt à terme dépôt à durée déterminée certificat de dépôt CD	depósito a plazo depósito a plazo fijo depósito a término fijo DTF certificado de depósito CD
T-144	time lag, *see* lag		
T-145	time of recording	date d'enregistrement date de comptabilisation chronologie	momento de registro
T-146	time path	profil temporel sentier temporel	trayectoria en el tiempo
T-147	time preference	préférence temporelle préférence intertemporelle préférence pour le présent	preferencia cronológica preferencia temporal
T-148	time regression	régression temporelle	regresión temporal
T-149	time series analysis	analyse temporelle analyse de séries temporelles analyse de séries chronologiques analyse longitudinale	análisis de series cronológicas análisis de series temporales

T-150	time-based repurchase
	  expectations
	[IMF]
		principe du rachat par anticipation
		  à échéance prédéterminée
		principe des rachats modulés dans
		  le temps
			expectativa de recompra en un
			  plazo establecido

T-151	timeliness (of data) [IMF]	ponctualité (des données) degré d'actualité (des données)	puntualidad (en la divulgación de los datos)
T-152	timing adjustment	ajustement chronologique	ajuste del momento de registro
T-153	TIN, *see* taxpayer identification number		
T-154	TIP, *see* tax-based income policy		
T-155	TMU, *see* Technical Memorandum of Understanding		
T-156	T-note, *see* treasury note		

T-157	tombstone	encart publicitaire d'émission consortiale	anuncio de emisión efectuada
		avis financier	esquela
		avis d'émission d'obligations	
		avis de prêts syndiqués	
		épitaphe d'émission	
T-158	topping up [Paris Club]	topping-up	complemento de concesionalidad
		complément de concessionnalité	aporte de fondos complementarios
		supplément d'aide	
T-159	TOR, *see* terms of reference		
T-160	total factor productivity TFP	productivité globale des facteurs	productividad total de los factores
		productivité totale des facteurs	PTF
T-161	total voting power [IMF]	nombre total des voix attribuées	total de votos
			número total de votos
T-162	track record, to establish a positive [IMF; HIPC Initiative]	établir des antécédents positifs	establecer un historial positivo
		faire ses preuves	establecer una trayectoria positiva
	proven record, to establish a	démontrer résultats à l'appui	demostrar un buen historial
T-163	tradable goods	biens échangeables	bienes transables
	tradables	biens exportables	bienes comerciables
		biens pouvant faire l'objet d'échanges (internationaux)	bienes comercializables
		biens négociables	
T-164	tradables, *see* tradable goods		
T-165	trade	commerce international	comercio
	foreign trade	commerce extérieur	comercio exterior
	international trade	échanges commerciaux	comercio internacional
	cross-border trade	échanges internationaux	intercambios comerciales
		échanges transfrontaliers	comercio transfronterizo
T-166	trade arrears *see also:* commercial arrears	arriérés commerciaux	atrasos comerciales
T-167	trade balance, *see* balance of trade		
T-168	trade barrier	obstacle au commerce	barrera comercial
	trade impediment	obstacle aux échanges	obstáculo al comercio
T-169	trade creation	création d'échanges	creación de comercio
			creación de corrientes comerciales
T-170	trade credit *see also:* commercial lending trade financing commercial credit trade loan	crédit commercial	crédito comercial financiamiento del comercio exterior
T-171	trade currency	monnaie utilisée dans les échanges (internationaux)	moneda utilizada en el intercambio
T-172	trade cycle, *see* business cycle		
T-173	trade deepening	intensification des échanges commerciaux	profundización del comercio exterior
			intensificación del comercio

T-174	trade deficit trade gap	déficit commercial déficit de la balance commerciale	déficit comercial déficit de la balanza comercial

T-175	trade diversion	réorientation des courants
		  d'échanges
		détournement des échanges
			desviación del comercio
			desviación de corrientes
			  comerciales

T-176	trade financing, *see* trade credit		
T-177	trade gap, *see* trade deficit		
T-178	trade impediment, *see* trade barrier		

T-179	Trade Integration Mechanism
	TIM
		mécanisme d'intégration
		  commerciale
		MIC
			Mecanismo de Integración
			  Comercial
			MIC

T-180	trade loan, *see* trade credit		
T-181	trade patterns, *see* pattern of trade		
T-182	Trade Policy Division [IMF]	Division politique commerciale	División de Política Comercial
T-183	trade restriction trade restrictive practice	restriction au commerce restriction aux échanges pratique commerciale restrictive	restricción comercial práctica comercial restrictiva
T-184	trade restrictive practice, *see* trade restriction		
T-185	trade sanction	sanction commerciale	sanción comercial
T-186	trade statistics	statistiques du commerce extérieur	estadísticas del comercio exterior estadísticas de comercio exterior
T-187	traded good	bien échangé bien faisant l'objet d'échanges (internationaux)	bien comerciado bien que es objeto de intercambio bien transado bien comerciable

T-188	trade-off	arbitrage
		dosage
		compromis
		mise en balance
		option
		alternative
		compensation réciproque
		balance des avantages et
		  inconvénients
		substituabilité
			solución de compromiso (entre ...)
			relación de correspondencia
			relación de sustitución
			elección entre opciones
			relación inversa
			relación de compensación
			compensación (de ventajas y
			  desventajas)
			disyuntiva

T-189	trade-weighted	pondéré par le commerce extérieur
		pondéré en fonction du commerce
		  extérieur
			ponderado según el comercio
			  exterior

T-190	trading floor, *see* trading room		
T-191	trading floor, *see* trading pit		
T-192	trading officer, *see* foreign exchange dealer		

T-193	trading partners partner countries	partenaires commerciaux	socios comerciales países que mantienen relaciones comerciales países que comercian entre sí
T-194	trading pit trading floor	corbeille parquet	recinto de operaciones parqué
T-195	trading profits, *see* business profits		
T-196	trading room [banking] trading floor	salle des opérations salle de(s) marché(s) salle de(s) cotations	recinto de operaciones sala de operaciones

T-197	traditional debt relief mechanisms	mécanismes traditionnels
		  d'allégement (de la dette)
			mecanismos tradicionales de alivio
			  de la deuda

T-198	tranche policy [IMF]	politique des tranches	política de tramos
T-199	tranche position [IMF]	position de tranche position dans les tranches	posición en los tramos
T-200	transaction [IMF] *see also:* operation [IMF]	transaction	transacción
T-201	transaction arranged by the IMF, *see* arranged transaction		
T-202	transaction balances	encaisses de transaction encaisses-transaction encaisses-trésorerie	saldos para transacciones
T-203	transaction by agreement [IMF] *see also:* arranged transaction	transaction par accord	transacción mediante acuerdo transacción por acuerdo
T-204	transaction cost	coût de transaction	costo de transacción
T-205	transaction currency	monnaie de transaction	moneda de transacción

T-206	transaction demand for money	demande de monnaie aux fins de
		  transactions
		demande transactionnelle de
		  monnaie
			demanda de dinero por motivo
			  transacción
			demanda de dinero para
			  transacciones

T-207	transaction money, *see* narrow money		
T-208	transaction value	valeur de transaction prix de transaction	valor de transacción precio de transacción
T-209	transaction with designation [IMF] designated transaction	transaction avec désignation	transacción por designación
T-210	transactions account [USA]	compte de transactions	cuenta de transacciones
T-211	transactions basis	sur la base des transactions	sobre la base de transacciones

T-212	transactions in goods, services,
	  and income
		transactions sur biens, services
		  et revenus
			transacciones de bienes, servicios
			  y renta

T-213	transactions plan, *see* financial transactions plan		
T-214	transactor *see also:* economic agent	agent économique partie (à une transaction) intervenant opérateur	parte (de la transacción) agente partícipe
T-215	transborder claim, *see* cross-border claim		
T-216	transborder interbank claim, *see* cross-border claim		
T-217	transfer cost	coût de transfert coût de mutation	costo de transferencia
T-218	transfer in kind	transfert en nature	transferencia en especie
T-219	transfer income	revenus de transferts revenus provenant de transferts	ingreso por transferencias
T-220	transfer of real resources	transfert de ressources réelles	transferencia de recursos reales
T-221	transfer of technology, *see* technology transfer		
T-222	transfer payment	paiement de transfert	pago de transferencia
T-223	transfer price transfer pricing	prix de transfert établissement de prix de transfert prix de cession interne établissement de prix de cession interne	precio de transferencia fijación de precios de transferencia
T-224	transfer pricing, *see* transfer price		
T-225	transfer pricing	manipulation de prix entre sociétés affiliées	precio de transferencia
T-226	transfer risk	risque de transfert	riesgo de transferencia
T-227	transfer tax	impôt sur le transfert de biens droits de mutation	impuestos sobre la transferencia de bienes
T-228	transferable deposit	dépôt transférable	depósito transferible
T-229	transferable security	valeur mobilière cessible valeur mobilière négociable	valor mobiliario transferible valor negociable título transferible
T-230	transformation curve, *see* production frontier		
T-231	transit account, *see* suspense account		
T-232	transit trade	commerce de transit	comercio de tránsito
T-233	transition country [IMF country classification] country in transition transition economy	pays en transition économie en transition	país en transición economía en transición
T-234	transition economy, *see* transition country		
T-235	transitional arrangements [IMF]	dispositions transitoires	régimen transitorio

T-236	transitional procedures [IMF]	procédure transitoire	procedimiento de transición procedimiento durante la transición procedimiento transitorio
T-237	transitional provisions [IMF]	dispositions transitoires	disposiciones transitorias
T-238	transitional unemployment, *see* frictional unemployment		
T-239	transnational enterprise, *see* multinational enterprise		
T-240	*t*-ratio, *see* *t*-statistic		
T-241	treasurer's check, *see* cashier's check		
T-242	treasury bill T-bill	bon du Trésor	letra del Tesoro letra de Tesorería
T-243	treasury bond *see also:* agency bond T-bond	obligation du Trésor	bono del Tesoro bono de Tesorería
T-244	treasury note T-note	obligation du Trésor certificat du Trésor	pagaré del Tesoro pagaré de Tesorería
T-245	Treaty on European Union Maastricht Treaty	Traité sur l'Union européenne Traité de Maastricht	Tratado de la Unión Europea Tratado de Maastricht
T-246	trend analysis	analyse de la tendance	análisis de tendencia análisis de la tendencia
T-247	trend GDP	PIB tendanciel	PIB tendencial PIB de tendencia
T-248	trend inflation structural inflation	inflation tendancielle inflation structurelle	inflación tendencial inflación estructural
T-249	trend line	ligne de tendance	línea de tendencia
T-250	trend scenario, *see* baseline scenario		
T-251	trend value	valeur tendancielle valeur de tendance	valor tendencial valor de tendencia
T-252	trial and error *tâtonnement*	par tâtonnement(s) méthode expérimentale	método de ensayo y error por tanteo
T-253	triangular trade *see also:* merchanting	commerce triangulaire	comercio triangular
T-254	trickle down theory	théorie des effets de percolation théorie des effets de retombée	teoría del efecto de filtración
T-255	trigger *see also:* activate	déclencher (automatiquement)	disparar activar (automáticamente)
T-256	trigger price	prix d'intervention prix de déclenchement	precio de intervención
T-257	trillion [IMF-IBRD; USA]	billion mille milliards	billón

T-258	trough *see also:* peak	creux (cyclique) minimum cyclique étiage	mínimo (cíclico) punto mínimo punto más bajo sima
T-259	troy ounce of fine gold, *see* fine ounce		
T-260	trust account fiduciary account	compte de fiducie	cuenta en fideicomiso cuenta fiduciaria
T-261	Trust for Special ESAF Operations for the Heavily Indebted Poor Countries and Interim ESAF Subsidy Operations, *see* ESAF-HIPC Trust		
T-262	Trust Fund [IMF]	fonds fiduciaire	Fondo Fiduciario
T-263	Trust Fund Instrument [IMF]	Instrument portant création du fonds fiduciaire	Instrumento de creación del Fondo Fiduciario
T-264	trustee	fiduciaire mandataire fidéicommis	fideicomisario administrador fiduciario fiduciario depositario
T-265	trustee savings bank	caisse d'épargne privée	caja de ahorro en fideicomiso
T-266	*t*-statistic Student's *t*-statistic *t*-ratio	coefficient *t* coefficient de Student	estadístico *t* coeficiente de Student coeficiente *t*
T-267	turnaround, *see* turning point		
T-268	turning point turnaround change point	point de retournement infléchissement changement d'orientation changement de direction	punto de inflexión cambio de rumbo cambio de tendencia momento decisivo
T-269	turnover sales	chiffre d'affaires CA ventes	volumen de ventas volumen de negocios ventas cifra de negocios
T-270	turnover [personnel]	rotation renouvellement	rotación de personal movimiento de personal
T-271	turnover [securities]	volume du marché boursier	volumen de operaciones
T-272	turnover ratio	taux de rotation	velocidad de circulación coeficiente de rotación
T-273	turnover tax, *see* sales tax		
T-274	turnover tax	taxe sur le chiffre d'affaires TCA impôt sur le chiffre d'affaires ICA ICHA	impuesto sobre los ingresos brutos impuesto sobre el volumen de venta impuesto sobre la cifra de negocios
T-275	TWG, *see* IMF Terminology Working Group		
T-276	two-sided test, *see* two-tailed test		

T-277	two-stage least squares	doubles moindres carrés	mínimos cuadrados dobles
			mínimos cuadrados en dos etapas
T-278	two-tailed test	test bilatéral	prueba bilateral
	two-sided test	test à deux queues	prueba a dos extremos
			verificación bilateral
			verificación a dos extremos
T-279	two-tier banking system	système bancaire à deux niveaux	sistema bancario de dos niveles
T-280	two-tier market	double marché	mercado doble
			mercado segmentado
T-281	two-way breakdown	décomposition bipartite	desglose doble
T-282	two-way transaction	accord à deux volets	transacción de compraventa
	[SDR]	accord permettant d'acheter et de	
		vendre des DTS	
T-283	type I error	erreur de première espèce	error de primer tipo
	error of the first kind	erreur du premier type	error de primera especie
	rejection error	risque de première espèce	riesgo de primera clase
	type one error		error de rechazo
T-284	type II error	erreur de deuxième espèce	error de segundo tipo
	error of the second kind	erreur du second type	error de segunda especie
	acceptance error	risque de seconde espèce	riesgo de segunda clase
	type two error		error de aceptación
	false negative		
T-285	type one error, *see* type I error		
T-286	type two error, *see* type II error		

U

U-1	UDC, *see* underdeveloped country		
U-2	UFR, *see* use of IMF resources		
U-3	ULC-based real effective exchange rate, *see* unit labor cost-based real effective exchange rate		
U-4	UMICS, *see* higher-middle-income country		
U-5	UN, *see* Fund Office in the United Nations		
U-6	UN, *see* United Nations		
U-7	unbiased estimator	estimateur sans biais	estimador insesgado
		estimateur sans distorsion	
U-8	unchallengeable use	utilisation non contestable	uso inobjetable
	[SDR]		
	see also: prior challenge		
	(not subject to)		
U-9	UNCITRAL, *see* United Nations Commission on International Trade Law		
U-10	uncommitted resources	ressources non engagées	recursos no comprometidos
U-11	unconditional grant, *see* nonconditional grant		

U-12	unconditional liquidity	liquidité inconditionnelle	liquidez incondicional
U-13	UNCTAD, *see* United Nations Conference on Trade and Development		
U-14	undeclared employment *see also:* moonlighting unreported employment	travail au noir	empleo no declarado
U-15	underdeveloped country UDC	pays sous-développé PSD	país subdesarrollado PSD
U-16	underemployed capacity, *see* slack capacity		
U-17	underemployment	sous-emploi	subempleo
U-18	underground economy, *see* shadow economy		
U-19	underinvestment	sous-investissement	subinversión inversión insuficiente
U-20	underinvoicing	sous-facturation	subfacturación
U-21	underlying	tendanciel sous-jacent fondamental de base	subyacente tendencial fundamental básico
U-22	underlying deficit structural deficit	déficit structurel	déficit estructural déficit subyacente
U-23	underlying inflation, *see* core inflation		
U-24	underlying instrument, *see* underlying security		
U-25	underlying security [derivatives] underlying instrument	instrument sous-jacent sous-jacent support	instrumento subyacente
U-26	undershooting	résultat en deçà de l'objectif sous-ajustement	subreacción reajuste insuficiente
U-27	underutilization, *see* capacity underutilization		
U-28	underwriters *see also:* syndicate underwriting consortium underwriting group underwriting pool issue syndicate underwriting bank	syndicat de prise ferme syndicat de placement membres d'un syndicat de prise ferme membres d'un syndicat d'émission membres d'un syndicat de garantie syndicataire groupe de souscripteurs	consorcio asegurador de emisiones sindicato de emisión agente de colocación y sucripción de valores
U-29	underwriter	preneur ferme placeur souscripteur	garante de emisión suscriptor asegurador
U-30	underwriting [securities]	garantie de souscription garantie de placement souscription (d'une émission) prise ferme	colocación en firme garantía de emisión
U-31	underwriting bank, *see* underwriters		

U-32	underwriting commission, *see* underwriting fee		
U-33	underwriting consortium, *see* underwriters		
U-34	underwriting fee underwriting commission	commission de garantie commission de placement	comisión de suscripción
U-35	underwriting group, *see* underwriters		
U-36	underwriting pool, *see* underwriters		
U-37	undisbursed debt	crédits non versés crédits non décaissés montant non décaissé montant de crédit non décaissé	préstamos no desembolsados
U-38	undistributed earnings, *see* retained earnings		
U-39	undistributed profits, *see* retained earnings		
U-40	undiversifiable risk, *see* systematic risk		
U-41	UNDP, *see* United Nations Development Programme		
U-42	undrawn balance	solde non tiré solde non utilisé	saldo no desembolsado saldo no utilizado
U-43	unearned income	revenu ne provenant pas du travail	renta no derivada del trabajo ingreso no derivado del trabajo renta no salarial ingreso no salarial renta no ganada
U-44	uneconomic	antiéconomique contraire au bon sens économique contraire à la logique économique	antieconómico
U-45	uneconomical	non rentable	antieconómico no rentable
U-46	unemployed	chômeurs effectifs en chômage	desempleado parado desocupado
U-47	unemployment	chômage sous-emploi	desempleo paro desocupación
U-48	unemployment benefit unemployment compensation	indemnisation du chômage prestation d'assurance chômage	indemnización por desempleo indemnización de paro
U-49	unemployment compensation, *see* unemployment benefit		
U-50	unemployment insurance	assurance chômage indemnisation du chômage	seguro de desempleo seguro de paro
U-51	unenforceable	non exécutoire	inexigible
U-52	unfair competition	concurrence déloyale	competencia desleal
U-53	unfair competitive advantage	avantage compétitif indu avantage compétitif déloyal	ventaja competitiva desleal

U-54	unfinished good, *see* semifinished good		
U-55	unfunded benefits unfunded social benefits unfunded employee social benefits	prestations non capitalisées prestations sociales directes prestations sociales non capitalisées	prestaciones sociales no basadas en fondos especiales prestaciones sociales directas prestaciones sociales para los asalariados no basadas en fondos especiales
U-56	unfunded employee social benefits, *see* unfunded benefits		
U-57	unfunded liabilities	engagements non capitalisés engagements basés sur la répartition	pasivos sin financiamiento previsto pasivos no capitalizados
U-58	unfunded mandate [USA]	obligation de dépense sans financement fédéral	obligación de gasto sin financiamiento previsto
U-59	unfunded pension plan, *see* pay-as-you-go system		
U-60	unfunded social benefits, *see* unfunded benefits		
U-61	unfunded system, *see* pay-as-you-go system		
U-62	unicurrency peg, *see* single peg		
U-63	unicurrency pegging, *see* single peg		
U-64	uniform norm, *see* uniform norm for remuneration		
U-65	uniform norm for remuneration [IMF] uniform norm	norme uniforme de rémunération norme uniforme	norma uniforme de remuneración norma uniforme
U-66	unimpaired [bank supervision] satisfactory	sans risque non classé «à risque»	sin problemas en situación regular satisfactorio
U-67	unincorporated business, *see* unincorporated enterprise		
U-68	unincorporated enterprise unincorporated business	entreprise non constituée en société entreprise individuelle	empresa no constituida en sociedad
U-69	unincorporated government enterprise, *see* unincorporated public enterprise		
U-70	unincorporated public enterprise unincorporated government enterprise	entreprise publique non constituée en société	empresa pública no constituida en sociedad
U-71	union contract, *see* collective bargaining agreement		
U-72	unit elasticity unitary elasticity	élasticité égale à l'unité élasticité unitaire élasticité-unité	elasticidad unitaria elasticidad igual a la unidad
U-73	unit labor cost	coût unitaire de (la) main-d'œuvre coût unitaire du travail coût salarial par unité produite	costo unitario de la mano de obra costo unitario del trabajo

U-74	unit labor cost-based real effective exchange rate ULC-based real effective exchange rate	taux de change effectif réel basé sur les coûts unitaires de main-d'œuvre	tipo de cambio efectivo real basado en el costo unitario de la mano de obra
U-75	unit of account, *see* accounting unit		
U-76	unit of output unit produced	unité produite	unidad de producto unidad producida
U-77	unit of value	unité de valeur	unidad de valor
U-78	unit produced, *see* unit of output		
U-79	unit trust, *see* mutual fund		
U-80	unit value	valeur unitaire	valor unitario
U-81	unit value index	indice de valeur unitaire	índice de valor unitario
U-82	unitary elasticity, *see* unit elasticity		
U-83	United Nations UN	Organisation des Nations Unies ONU Nations Unies	Organización de las Naciones Unidas
U-84	United Nations Commission on International Trade Law UNCITRAL	Commission des Nations Unies pour le droit commercial international CNUDCI	Comisión de las Naciones Unidas para el Derecho Mercantil Internacional CNUDMI
U-85	United Nations Conference on Trade and Development UNCTAD	Conférence des Nations Unies sur le commerce et le développement CNUCED	Conferencia de las Naciones Unidas sobre Comercio y Desarrollo UNCTAD
U-86	United Nations Development Programme UNDP	Programme des Nations Unies pour le développement PNUD	Programa de las Naciones Unidas para el Desarrollo PNUD
U-87	United Nations Monetary and Financial Conference [IMF-IBRD] Bretton Woods Conference	Conférence monétaire et financière des Nations Unies Conférence de Bretton Woods	Conferencia Monetaria y Financiera de las Naciones Unidas Conferencia de Bretton Woods
U-88	universal, *see* global		
U-89	universal bank, *see* multipurpose bank		
U-90	universality of Fund membership [IMF]	dimension universelle du FMI caractère universel du FMI	dimensión universal del FMI carácter universal del FMI
U-91	unlisted security unquoted security	titre non inscrit à la cote officielle titre non admis à la cote officielle titre non coté	valor no cotizado en bolsa valor no admitido a cotización
U-92	unpaid charge [IMF]	commission non payée commission non réglée	cargo impagado cargo impago
U-93	unpeg the rate	ne plus ancrer le taux de change décrocher le taux de change	dejar que fluctúe el tipo de cambio liberar el tipo de cambio
U-94	unquoted security, *see* unlisted security		

U-95	unremitted earnings	bénéfices non rapatriés	utilidades no remitidas
U-96	unremunerated reserve tranche position [IMF]	position non rémunérée dans la tranche de réserve	posición no remunerada en el tramo de reserva saldo no remunerado en el tramo de reserva
U-97	unreported employment, *see* undeclared employment		
U-98	unrequited payment	versement sans contrepartie	pago sin contrapartida pago sin contraprestación
U-99	unrequited transaction	transaction unilatérale opération sans contrepartie	transacción unilateral
U-100	unrequited transfer	transfert sans contrepartie transfert non contractuel	transferencia unilateral transferencia sin contrapartida
U-101	unsecured loan, *see* signature loan		
U-102	unsecured loan	prêt non garanti prêt non gagé	préstamo no garantizado
U-103	unskilled labor unskilled manpower unskilled worker	main-d'œuvre non qualifiée	mano de obra no calificada trabajador no especializado
U-104	unskilled manpower, *see* unskilled labor		
U-105	unskilled worker, *see* unskilled labor		
U-106	unsoundness *see also:* insolvency	fragilité précarité	fragilidad
U-107	untapped resource	ressource inexploitée	recurso inexplotado
U-108	untied aid	aide non liée	ayuda no condicionada ayuda no vinculada
U-109	untying of aid	déliement de l'aide	desvinculación de la ayuda
U-110	unwinding of global imbalances	résorption des déséquilibres mondiaux correction des déséquilibres mondiaux réduction des déséquilibres mondiaux	corrección de los desequilibrios mundiales
U-111	upgrading	reclassement	mejorar la calificación reclasificación en una categoría superior reclasificación en una categoría más alta
U-112	upper credit tranches [IMF]	tranches supérieures de crédit	tramos superiores de crédito
U-113	upper-middle-income countries, *see* higher-middle-income country		

U-114	upside risk	possibilité que les résultats dépassent les prévisions chances que les résultats dépassent les prévisions chances de révision à la hausse des prévisions	riesgo de que los resultados sean superiores a lo previsto probabilidad de que las cifras reales sean mayores de las que indican las proyecciones probabilidad de que los resultados superen las proyecciones riesgo al alza
U-115	upstream industry, *see* supplier industry		
U-116	upstream integration	intégration en amont	integración vertical hacia arriba
U-117	upsurge, *see* upturn		
U-118	upswing, *see* upturn		
U-119	uptrend, *see* upward trend		
U-120	upturn upswing upsurge	phase ascendante (du cycle économique) phase d'expansion amélioration de la conjoncture essor conjoncturel reprise redressement	recuperación reactivación iniciación de la fase ascendente fase ascendente fase de expansión movimiento ascendente
U-121	upward adjustment	ajustement en hausse	ajuste al alza
U-122	upward bias positive bias	erreur systématique par excès biais par excès distorsion par excès	sesgo por exceso sesgo alcista sesgo al alza
U-123	upward pressure	pression à la hausse poussée à la hausse tendance à la hausse	presión al alza presión alcista
U-124	upward trend rising trend uptrend	tendance ascendante tendance à la hausse évolution à la hausse	tendencia ascendente tendencia al alza
U-125	upward-sloping curve	courbe ascendante courbe croissante	curva ascendente curva de pendiente ascendente
U-126	Uruguay Round (of Multilateral Trade Negotiations) [GATT]	Cycle de négociations commerciales multilatérales d'Uruguay Cycle d'Uruguay Uruguay Round	Ronda Uruguay (de negociaciones comerciales multilaterales)
U-127	usable national currency	monnaie nationale utilisable	moneda nacional utilizable
U-128	USAID, *see* Agency for International Development		
U-129	use of Fund credit use of IMF credit	utilisation des crédits du FMI recours aux crédits du FMI	uso del crédito del FMI uso de crédito del Fondo
U-130	use of Fund resources, *see* use of IMF resources		
U-131	use of IMF credit, *see* use of Fund credit		

U-132	use of IMF resources [IMF] use of Fund resources UFR	utilisation des ressources du FMI utilisation du crédit du FMI recours aux ressources du FMI	uso de los recursos del FMI
U-133	useful life, *see* economic life		
U-134	user cost	coût d'usage	costo para el usuario costo de utilización
U-135	user fee	redevance d'utilisation	tasa que paga el usuario de un servicio tasa de un servicio tasa de uso de un servicio
U-136	utility public service corporation public utility	services publics entreprise de services publics service d'intérêt public service d'utilité publique équipements collectifs	empresa de servicios públicos

V

V-1	vacancy job vacancy opening job opening	emploi vacant emploi non pourvu vacance d'emploi	vacante
V-2	validation, *see* expenditure validation		
V-3	valuable	objet de valeur	objeto de valor
V-4	valuation *see also:* point of valuation	évaluation valorisation	valoración valuación

V-5	valuation adjustment
	[IMF]
	see also: settlement of currency
	    valuation adjustment
	currency valuation adjustment
	CVA
		réévaluation
		ajustement de valeur
		ajustement de valeur des avoirs en
		    monnaie
		réévaluation des avoirs du FMI en
		    monnaie d'un pays membre
		réévaluation des avoirs du FMI en
		    une monnaie donnée
			ajuste de valoración
			ajuste de valoración de la moneda

V-6	valuation basis	base d'évaluation base de valorisation	base de valoración criterio de valoración
V-7	valuation effects	incidence des variations de (taux de) change effets de valorisation	efectos de valoración
V-8	value-added deflator	déflateur de la valeur ajoutée	deflactor del valor agregado deflactor del valor añadido [ESP]

V-9	value added in manufacturing	valeur ajoutée manufacturière
		VAM
		valeur ajoutée dans l'industrie
		    manufacturière
			valor agregado en la industria
			    manufacturera
			valor añadido en la industria
			    manufacturera
			[ESP]

V-10	value added tax, *see* value-added tax		

V-11	value-added tax VAT value added tax	taxe sur la valeur ajoutée TVA taxe à la valeur ajoutée	impuesto sobre el valor agregado IVA impuesto al valor agregado IVA impuesto sobre el valor añadido [ESP] IVA
V-12	value date [IMF]	date de valeur	fecha de valor
V-13	value index	indice de valeur	índice de valor
V-14	variable rate, *see* floating interest rate		
V-15	variable uniform norm, *see* variable uniform norm for remuneration		

V-16	variable uniform norm
	  for remuneration
	[IMF]
	variable uniform norm
		norme uniforme modifiable
		  de rémunération
		norme uniforme modifiable
			norma uniforme variable
			  de remuneración
			norma uniforme variable

V-17	variance	variance	varianza
V-18	VAT, *see* value-added tax		
V-19	vault cash cash in vault	billets et pièces en caisse encaisses des banques numéraire en caisse	reservas en efectivo reservas en metálico
V-20	velocity of circulation velocity of money	vitesse de circulation de la monnaie	velocidad de circulación del dinero velocidad del dinero
V-21	velocity of money, *see* velocity of circulation		
V-22	vendorization, *see* outsourcing		
V-23	venture capital risk capital	capital-risque capital à risque	capital de riesgo capital-riesgo
V-24	VER, *see* voluntary export restraints		
V-25	verification, *see* expenditure verification		
V-26	visiting fellow, *see* visiting scholar		
V-27	visiting professor, *see* visiting scholar		
V-28	visiting scholar [IMF] visiting professor visiting fellow	professeur invité expert invité	profesor visitante profesor invitado
V-29	volatile capital	capitaux instables capitaux fébriles capitaux mouvants	capital volátil capital inestable
V-30	volume index	indice de volume indice de quantité	índice de volumen índice de cantidad índice de quántum

V-31	voluntary contribution account [IMF arrears]	compte de contributions volontaires	cuenta de aportaciones voluntarias
V-32	voluntary departure program voluntary departure scheme	programme de départs volontaires	programa de retiro voluntario
V-33	voluntary departure scheme, *see* voluntary departure program		
V-34	voluntary export restraints *see also:* orderly marketing arrangement VER	limitation volontaire des exportations autolimitation des exportations	limitación voluntaria de las exportaciones restricciones voluntarias a la exportación
V-35	voluntary repayment [IMF]	remboursement volontaire	reembolso voluntario
V-36	voluntary repurchase [IMF]	rachat volontaire	recompra voluntaria
V-37	vote by proxy [IMF]	vote par procuration	votación por poder
V-38	voting power [IMF] *see also:* allotted number of votes	nombre de voix attribuées pouvoir de vote	número de votos poder de voto
V-39	voting without meeting	vote sans réunion vote par correspondance	votación sin reunión
V-40	vulnerabilities	facteur de vulnérabilité source de vulnérabilité	aspectos vulnerables vulnerabilidades factores de vulnerabilidad
V-41	vulnerability assessment	évaluation de la vulnérabilité	evaluación de la vulnerabilidad
V-42	vulnerability indicator	indicateur de vulnérabilité	indicador de vulnerabilidad
V-43	vulture fund *see also:* hedge fund	fonds vautour	fondo buitre

W

W-1	WADB, *see* West African Development Bank		
W-2	WAEC, *see* West African Economic Community		
W-3	WAEMU, *see* West African Economic and Monetary Union		
W-4	wage *see also:* salary wage rate	salaire traitement solde rémunération	salario
W-5	wage bill payroll	masse salariale total des salaires versés dépenses de personnel	masa salarial gasto en remuneraciones
W-6	wage cost(s) payroll cost(s)	coûts salariaux charges salariales	costo de los salarios costos salariales
W-7	wage creep, *see* wage drift		

W-8	wage differential	écart des salaires disparité salariale éventail des salaires	disparidad salarial diferencia salarial desigualdad de remuneración
W-9	wage drift *see also:* grade drift wage creep	dérive salariale dérive des salaires	diferencia entre el pago básico y la remuneración total diferencial de salarios
W-10	wage earner	salarié travailleur salarié	asalariado
W-11	wage equalization	péréquation des salaires	equiparación de salarios
W-12	wage moderation, *see* wage restraint		
W-13	wage policy wages policy	politique salariale	política salarial
W-14	wage rate, *see* wage		
W-15	wage restraint wage moderation	modération des salaires modération salariale	moderación salarial moderación de los aumentos salariales contención salarial restricción salarial austeridad salarial
W-16	wage scale, *see* salary scale		
W-17	wage schedule, *see* salary scale		
W-18	wage wedge	ratio salaires bruts/salaires nets	razón sueldo bruto/sueldo neto
W-19	wage-price spiral	spirale prix–salaires course des salaires et des prix	espiral salarios-precios espiral de precios y salarios
W-20	wage-push inflation	inflation par les salaires	inflación salarial inflación producida por los salarios
W-21	wages and salaries	traitements et salaires	sueldos y salarios
W-22	wages policy, *see* wage policy		
W-23	waive	déroger (à une clause) autoriser une dérogation renoncer (à un droit)	dispensar del cumplimiento de una obligación eximir de una obligación renunciar a un derecho
W-24	waiver	dispense dérogation exemption renonciation (à un droit) abattement	dispensa exención renuncia a un derecho
W-25	WAMA, *see* West African Monetary Agency		
W-26	warning sign, *see* warning signal		
W-27	warning signal warning sign	signal d'alarme clignotant	señal de alerta señal de advertencia señal de prevención

W-28	warrant stock warrant equity warrant subscription warrant stock purchase warrant share purchase warrant	certificat d'option bon de souscription warrant	*warrant* *warrant* financiero certificado para la compra de valores
W-29	warranted unemployment rate, *see* natural rate of unemployment		
W-30	WB, *see* World Bank		
W-31	WCO, *see* World Customs Organization		
W-32	wealth	patrimoine richesse	riqueza patrimonio
W-33	wealth effect *see also:* real balances effect	effet de patrimoine effet de richesse	efecto riqueza efecto de riqueza
W-34	wealth tax tax on wealth	impôt sur la fortune impôt sur la richesse	impuesto al patrimonio impuesto a la riqueza impuesto sobre el patrimonio
W-35	weight	pondération coefficient de pondération poids	ponderación coeficiente de ponderación peso
W-36	weighted voting system	système de vote pondéré	sistema de votación ponderada
W-37	weighting pattern	structure de pondération	estructura de ponderación
W-38	welfare, *see* economic welfare		
W-39	welfare *see also:* social security	aide sociale protection sociale	asistencia social bienestar social
W-40	welfare well-being	bien-être mieux-être	bienestar
W-41	welfare economics	économie du bien-être collectif théorie économique du bien-être théorie de l'optimum économique	economía del bienestar
W-42	welfare payment	prestation sociale prestation d'assistance sociale	prestación de asistencia social subsidio de asistencia social
W-43	welfare state	État-providence	Estado de bienestar Estado benefactor Estado asistencial Estado providente
W-44	well-being, *see* welfare		
W-45	WEMD, *see* World Economic and Market Developments		
W-46	*WEO, see World Economic Outlook*		
W-47	*WEO* exercise	études sur les perspectives de l'économie mondiale	estudio de las perspectivas de la economía mundial

W-48	West African Development Bank WADB	Banque ouest-africaine de développement BOAD	Banco de Desarrollo de África Occidental BOAD
W-49	West African Division I, II [IMF]	Division Afrique de l'Ouest I, II	División de África Occidental I, II
W-50	West African Economic and Monetary Union WAEMU	Union économique et monétaire ouest-africaine UEMOA	Unión Económica y Monetaria del África Occidental UEMAO
W-51	West African Economic Community WAEC CEAO	Communauté économique de l'Afrique de l'Ouest CEAO	Comunidad Económica del África Occidental CEAO
W-52	West African Monetary Agency WAMA	Agence monétaire de l'Afrique de l'Ouest AMAO	Organismo Monetario del África Occidental WAMA
W-53	Western Division [IMF]	Division Europe de l'Ouest	División de Europa Occidental
W-54	Western Hemisphere Department [IMF] WHD	Département Hémisphère occidental	Departamento del Hemisferio Occidental
W-55	Western Hemisphere Division [IMF]	Division Hémisphère occidental	División del Hemisferio Occidental
W-56	Western Hemisphere Regional Division [IMF]	Division Amériques	División de la Región del Hemisferio Occidental
W-57	WFP, *see* World Food Programme		
W-58	WHD, *see* Western Hemisphere Department		
W-59	WHO, *see* World Health Organization		
W-60	wholesale bank	banque de gros	banco mayorista
W-61	wholesale price index WPI	indice des prix de gros	índice de precios al por mayor índice de precios mayoristas
W-62	wholly owned subsidiary fully owned subsidiary	filiale à 100 % filiale en propriété exclusive	filial de propiedad absoluta filial de propiedad exclusiva
W-63	widening of capital, *see* capital widening		
W-64	windfall profit *see also:* excess profit	bénéfice exceptionnel gain fortuit gain inattendu superbénéfice	ganancias inesperadas ganancias extraordinarias beneficios imprevistos utilidades imprevistas
W-65	winding down, *see* liquidation		
W-66	winding up, *see* liquidation		
W-67	window dressing	habillage de bilan présentation du bilan sous un jour favorable	maquillaje de las cifras retoque del balance presentación cosmética manipulación de la contabilidad

W-68	WIPO, *see* World Intellectual Property Organization		
W-69	wire transfer	transfert télégraphique virement télégraphique	giro telegráfico transferencia telegráfica
W-70	withdrawal from membership [IMF]	retrait (d'un État membre)	retiro de un país miembro

W-71	withhold tax
	see also: collect tax; deposit
	  withheld tax with government
	collect withholding tax for the
	  government
		prélever à la source
		recouvrer à la source
			retener impuestos en la fuente
			recaudar impuestos en la fuente

W-72	withholding at source, *see* tax withholding		
W-73	withholding tax *see also:* tax withholding	impôt retenu à la source impôt déduit à la source précompte précompte fiscal	impuesto retenido en la fuente
W-74	workers' remittances	envois de fonds des travailleurs	remesas de trabajadores
W-75	workforce, *see* labor force		
W-76	workforce [enterprises]	effectifs personnel	personal dotación de personal plantilla
W-77	working-age population	population d'âge actif population en âge de travailler	población en edad laboral población en edad de trabajar
W-78	working balances	fonds de roulement	saldos para operaciones saldos de operación fondos para operaciones
W-79	working capital	fonds de roulement capital circulant	capital de trabajo capital circulante capital de explotación
W-80	working group working party	groupe de travail	grupo de trabajo

W-81	Working Group on Capital Flows
	[FSF]
		Groupe de travail du FSF sur les
		  flux de capitaux
			Grupo de Trabajo sobre los Flujos
			  de Capital

W-82	Working Group on Offshore
	  Financial Centers
	[FSF]
		Groupe de travail du FSF sur les
		  centres financiers offshore
			Grupo de Trabajo sobre los
			  Centros Financieros
			  Extraterritoriales

W-83	working hypothesis	hypothèse de travail	hipótesis de trabajo
W-84	working life	vie active	vida activa
W-85	Working Paper [IMF] WP IMF Working Paper	document de travail du FMI	documento de la serie "IMF Working Papers" documento de trabajo del FMI
W-86	working paper	document de travail	documento de trabajo
W-87	working party, *see* working group		

W-88	Working Party on the Measurement of International Capital Flows	Groupe de travail sur l'évaluation des flux de capitaux internationaux	Grupo de Trabajo sobre la Medición de las Corrientes Internacionales de Capital
W-89	Working Party on the Statistical Discrepancy in World Current Account Balances [IMF, BIS, EUROSTAT, OECD]	Groupe de travail sur l'écart statistique dans les comptes courants globaux des balances des paiements	Grupo de Trabajo sobre la Discrepancia Estadística en los Saldos Mundiales en Cuenta Corriente
W-90	working population	population active	población activa
W-91	workout, *see* debt workout		
W-92	workout, *see* corporate sector workout		
W-93	workshop [IMF]	travaux pratiques [FMI] atelier travaux dirigés TD séminaire groupe de travail	trabajo práctico [FMI] curso práctico prácticas seminario taller
W-94	world, *see* global		
W-95	World Bank [World Bank Group] *see also:* International Bank for Reconstruction and Development WB	Banque mondiale	Banco Mundial
W-96	World Bank Group	Groupe de la Banque mondiale	Grupo del Banco Mundial
W-97	world current account discrepancy world current account statistical discrepancy	écart statistique dans les comptes des transactions courantes de la balance mondiale des paiements	discrepancia estadística en los saldos mundiales en cuenta corriente
W-98	world current account statistical discrepancy, *see* world current account discrepancy		
W-99	World Customs Organization WCO	Organisation mondiale des douanes OMD	Organización Mundial de Aduanas OMA
W-100	World Economic and Market Developments [IMF] WEMD	Évolution de l'économie mondiale et des marchés	Evolución de la economía y los mercados mundiales
W-101	*World Economic Outlook* [IMF] *WEO*	*Perspectives de l'économie mondiale*	*Perspectivas de la economía mundial*
W-102	World Economic Studies Division [IMF]	Division études économiques internationales	División de Estudios Económicos Internacionales
W-103	World Food Programme [UN-FAO] WFP	Programme alimentaire mondial PAM	Programa Mundial de Alimentos
W-104	World Health Organization WHO	Organisation mondiale de la santé OMS	Organización Mundial de la Salud OMS

W-105	World Intellectual Property Organization WIPO	Organisation mondiale de la propriété intellectuelle OMPI	Organización Mundial de la Propiedad Intelectual OMPI
W-106	world market price world price	cours mondial	precio del mercado mundial precio mundial
W-107	world price, *see* world market price		
W-108	World Trade Organization WTO	Organisation mondiale du commerce OMC	Organización Mundial del Comercio OMC
W-109	worse-policies scenario [*WEO*] worst-policies scenario pessimistic scenario	scénario fondé sur des politiques plus défavorables scénario pessimiste	escenario de medidas de política desfavorables
W-110	worst-case scenario pessimistic scenario	scénario pessimiste scénario catastrophe scénario fondé sur les hypothèses les plus défavorables	escenario pesimista escenario más desfavorable marco hipotético pesimista marco hipotético más desfavorable
W-111	worst-policies scenario, *see* worse-policies scenario		
W-112	WP, *see* Working Paper		
W-113	WPI, *see* wholesale price index		
W-114	write down (an asset) *see also:* write off (an asset) write-down	réduire la valeur amortir partiellement	castigar reducir el valor en libros castigar contablemente bajar el precio de
W-115	write off (an asset) *see also:* write down (an asset) charge off	passer par pertes et profits passer en charges annuler	pasar a pérdidas y ganancias cancelar en libros amortizar una deuda incobrable cancelación contable traslado a pérdidas y ganancias
W-116	write-down, *see* write down (an asset)		
W-117	write-down	réduction de la valeur comptable	castigo castigo contable
W-118	write-off, *see* write-off value		
W-119	write-off amount, *see* write-off value		
W-120	write-off value write-off amount write-off	valeur non encaissable passée par pertes et profits	valor pasado a pérdidas y ganancias valor incobrable amortizado valor cancelado en libros cancelación contable
W-121	written-down value, *see* carrying value		
W-122	WTO, *see* World Trade Organization		

Y

| Y-1 | yearly rate | taux annuel | tasa anual |
| | | taux rapporté à l'année | elevado a tasa anual |

Y-2 year-on-year basis, on a, *see* year-to-year basis, on a

Y-3	year-on-year change	variation d'une année sur l'autre	variación interanual
			variación de un año al otro
			variación en relación con igual período del año anterior

Y-4	year-to-year basis, on a	en glissement annuel	interanual
	see also: annual basis, on an	d'une année sur l'autre	de un año a otro
	year-on-year basis, on a		
	y/y		

Y-5	yield	produit	rendimiento
		rendement	rentabilidad
		rapport	

Y-6	yield curve	structure par échéance(s)	curva de rendimientos
	see also: inverse yield curve	structure par échéances des taux d'intérêt	estructura de las tasas de interés
	term structure of interest rates	courbe de(s) taux	
	interest rate structure	courbe de(s) rendement(s)	
	term structure	hiérarchie des taux d'intérêt	

Y-7	yield to maturity	taux de rendement actuariel	rendimiento al vencimiento
	YTM	rendement à l'échéance	
	redemption yield		

Y-8 YTM, *see* yield to maturity

Y-9 y/y, *see* year-to-year basis, on a

Z

Z-1 ZBB, *see* zero base budget

Z-2	zero base budget	budget base zéro	presupuesto base cero
	[IMF]	BBZ	presupuesto en base cero
	ZBB		
	zero-based review		

| Z-3 | zero-coupon bond | obligation à coupon zéro | bono de cupón cero |
| | *see also:* stripped bond | obligation sans coupon | bono cupón cero |

| Z-4 | zero growth | croissance zéro | crecimiento cero |
| | | croissance nulle | crecimiento nulo |

| Z-5 | zero saving | épargne nulle | ahorro nulo |
| | | | ahorro igual a cero |

Z-6 zero-based review, *see* zero base budget

| Z-7 | zero-sum game | jeu à somme nulle | juego de suma cero |
| | *see also:* game theory; Nash equilibrium; prisoner's dilemna | jeu de somme nulle | |

2-1 2015 targets, *see* International Development Goals

APPENDIX I

Currency Units
Unités monétaires
Unidades monetarias

The following table, prepared by the Reference, Terminology and Documentation Section (RTD) of the IMF TGS-Language Services, reflects standard IMF usage. It is sorted alphabetically by country name, followed by currency name, subsidiary unit, adjective, abbreviation and ISO-3 Code. Accordingly, a dash in the place of these fields indicates that it is not used with the currency. The notation (inv.) indicates that the currency name is invariable, otherwise the plural is shown within parentheses. Some currencies carry (m.) or (f.) in French identifying the gender, when not clear. The adjective listed is the form to be used with the currency, if appropriate; it is not necessarily the adjective of nationality. Endnotes follow this section in numerical order.

Afghanistan	Afghanistan	Afganistán
Afghani(s) [1]	afghani(s)	afgani(s)
pul(s)	pul(s)	pul(es)
-	-	-
Af	Af	Af
AFA		
Albania	**Albanie**	**Albania**
lek(s)	lek(s)	lek(s)
qindar(ka)	qindar(ka)	qindar(s)
Albanian	albanais	albanés
lek	lek	lek
ALL		
Algeria	**Algérie**	**Argelia**
dinar(s)	dinar(s)	dinar(es)
centime(s)	centime(s)	céntimo(s)
Algerian	algérien	argelino
DA	DA	DA
DZD		
Andorra	**Andorre**	**Andorra**
euro(s) [2]	euro(s)	euro(s)
cent(s)	cent(s)	céntimo(s)
-	-	-
EUR or €	EUR ou €	EUR o €
EUR		
Angola	**Angola**	**Angola**
kwanza(s)	kwanza(s)	kwanza(s)
cêntimo(s)	cêtimo(s)	céntimo(s)
Angolan	angolais	angoleño
Kz	Kz	Kz
AOA		
Anguilla	**Anguilla**	**Anguila**
dollar(s) [3]	dollar(s)	dólar(es)
cent(s)	cent(s)	centavo(s)
Eastern Caribbean	des Caraïbes orientales	del Caribe Oriental
EC$	EC$	EC$
XCD		
Antigua and Barbuda	**Antigua-et-Barbuda**	**Antigua y Barbuda**
dollar(s) [3]	dollar(s)	dólar(es)
cent(s)	cent(s)	centavo(s)
Eastern Caribbean	des Caraïbes orientales	del Caribe Oriental
EC$	EC$	EC$
XCD		
Argentina	**Argentine**	**Argentina**
peso(s)	peso(s)	peso(s)
centavo(s)	centavo(s)	centavo(s)
Argentine	argentin	argentino
Arg$	$Arg	$ o Arg$
ARS		
Armenia	**Arménie**	**Armenia**
dram(s)	dram(s)	dram(s)
luma(s)	luma(s)	luma(s)
Armenian	arménien	armenio
dram	dram	dram
AMD		
Aruba	**Aruba**	**Aruba**
florin(s)	florin(s)	florín (florines)
cent(s)	cent(s)	centavo(s)
Aruban	de Aruba	de Aruba
Af.	Af.	Af.
AWG		

Australia	**Australie**	**Australia**
dollar(s)	dollar(s)	dólar(es)
cent(s)	cent(s)	centavo(s)
Australian	australien	australiano
$A	$A	A$
AUD		
Austria	**Autriche**	**Austria**
euro(s) [2]	euro(s)	euro(s)
cent(s)	cent(s)	céntimo(s)
-	-	-
EUR or €	EUR ou €	EUR o €
EUR		
Azerbaijan	**Azerbaïdjan**	**Azerbaiyán**
manat	manat(s)	manat(s)
kepik(s)	kepik(s)	gopik(s)
Azerbaijan	d'Azerbaïdjan	de Azerbaiyán
manat	manat	manat
AZN		
Azores	**Açores**	**Azores**
euro(s) [2]	euro(s)	euro(s)
cent(s)	cent(s)	céntimo(s)
-	-	-
EUR or €	Açores	EUR o €
EUR	EUR ou €	
Bahamas, The	**les Bahamas**	**Las Bahamas**
dollar(s)	dollar(s)	dólar(es)
cent(s)	cent(s)	centavo(s)
Bahamian	des Bahamas	de las Bahamas
B$	B$	B$
BSD		
Bahrain	**Bahreïn**	**Bahrein**
dinar(s)	dinar(s)	dinar(es)
fils (inv.)	fils	fils (inv.)
Bahrain	de Bahreïn	de Bahrein
BD	BD	DB
BHD		
Bangladesh	**Bangladesh**	**Bangladesh**
taka	taka	taka(s)
poisha	poisha	poisha(s)
Bangladesh	du Bangladesh	de Bangladesh
Tk	Tk	Tk
BDT		
Barbados	**Barbade (la)**	**Barbados**
dollar(s)	dollar(s)	dólar(es)
cent(s)	cent(s)	centavo(s)
Barbados	de la Barbade	de Barbados
BDS$	BDS$	BDS$
BBD		
Belarus	**Bélarus**	**Belarús**
rubel(s) [4]	rouble(s)	rublo(s)
-	-	kipek(s)
Belarussian	bélarussien	belaruso
Rbl	Rbl	Rbl
BYR		
Belgium	**Belgique**	**Bélgica**
euro(s) [2]	euro(s)	euro(s)
cent(s)	cent(s)	céntimo(s)
-	-	-
EUR or €	EUR ou €	EUR o €
EUR		

Belize	**Belize**	**Belice**
dollar(s)	dollar(s)	dólar(es)
cent(s)	cent(s)	centavo(s)
Belize	du Belize	de Belice
BZ$	BZ$	BZ$
BZD		
Benin	**Bénin**	**Benin**
CFA franc(s) [5]	franc(s) CFA	franco(s) CFA
centime(s)	centime(s)	céntimo(s)
-	-	-
CFAF	FCFA	FCFA
XOF		
Bermuda	**Bermudes**	**Bermudas**
dollar(s)	dollar(s)	dólar(es)
cent(s)	cent(s)	centavo(s)
Bermuda	des Bermudes	de las Bermudas
Ber$	Ber$	Ber$
BMD		
Bhutan	**Bhoutan**	**Bhután**
ngultrum	ngultrum	ngultrum(s)
chhetrum	chetrum	chetrum(s)
Bhutanese	du Bhoutan	de Bhután
Nu	Nu	Nu
BTN		
Bolivia	**Bolivie**	**Bolivia**
boliviano(s)	boliviano(s)	boliviano(s)
centavo(s)	centavo(s)	centavo(s)
-	-	-
Bs	Bs	Bs
BOB		
Bosnia and Herzegovina	**Bosnie-Herzégovine**	**Bosnia y Herzegovina**
convertible marka	mark convertible	marco(s) convertible(s)
pfening(a)	pfening(a)	penique(s)
-	-	-
KM	KM	KM
BAM		
Botswana	**Botswana**	**Botswana**
pula	pula	pula(s)
thebe	thebe	thebe(s)
Botswana	du Botswana	de Botswana
P	P	P
BWP		
Brazil	**Brésil**	**Brasil**
real (reais) [6]	real (reais)	real(es)
centavo(s)	centavo(s)	centavo(s)
Brazilian	brésilien	brasileño
R$	R$	R$
BRL		
British Virgin Islands	**Îles Vierges britanniques**	**Islas Vírgenes Británicas**
dollar(s)	dollar(s)	dólar(es)
cent(s)	cent(s)	centavo(s)
U.S.	E.U.	de EE.UU.
British Virgin Islands	Îles Vierges britanniques	S$
$ or US$ [7]	$ ou $E.U.	
USD		
Brunei Darussalam	**Brunéi Darussalam**	**Brunei Darussalam**
dollar(s)	dollar(s)	dólar(es)
cent(s)	cent(s)	centavo(s)
Brunei	du Brunéi	de Brunei
B$	B$	B$
BND		

Bulgaria
lev(a)
stotinka (stotinki)
Bulgarian
lev
BGN

Burkina Faso
CFA franc(s) [5]
centime(s)
-
CFAF
XOF

Burundi
franc(s)
centime(s)
Burundi
FBu
BIF

Cambodia
riel
sen (inv)
Cambodian
CR
KHR

Cameroon
CFA franc(s) [8]
centime(s)
-
CFAF
XAF

Canada
dollar(s)
cent(s)
Canadian
Can$
CAD

Canary Islands
euro(s) [2]
cent(s)
-
EUR or €
EUR

Cape Verde
escudo(s)
centavo(s)
Cape Verde
CVEsc
CVE

Cayman Islands
dollar(s)
cent(s)
Cayman Islands
C$
KYD

Central African Republic
CFA franc(s)
centime(s)
-
CFAF
XAF

Bulgarie
lev(a)
stotinka (stotinki)
bulgare
lev

Burkina Faso
franc(s) CFA
centime(s)
-
FCFA

Burundi
franc(s)
centime(s)
burundais
FBu

Cambodge
riel
sen (inv.)
du Cambodge
CR

Cameroun
franc(s) CFA
centime(s)
-
FCFA

Canada
dollar(s)
cent(s)
canadien
$Can

Îles Canaries
euro(s)
cent(s)
-
Îles ou €

Cap-Vert
escudo(s)
centavo(s)
du Cap-Vert
Cap- C.V.

Îles Caïmans
dollar(s)
cent(s)
des îles Caïmans
C$

République Centrafricaine
franc(s) CFA
centime(s)
-
FCFA

Bulgaria
lev(s)
stotinka(s)
búlgaro
lev

Burkina Faso
franco(s) CFA
céntimo(s)
-
FCFA

Burundi
franco(s)
céntimo(s)
de Burundi
FBu

Camboya
riel(es)
sen(s)
de Camboya
CR

Camerún
franco(s) CFA
céntimo(s)
-
FCFA

Canadá
dólar(es)
centavo(s)
canadiense
Can$

Islas Canarias
euro(s)
céntimo(s)
-
Islas o €

Cabo Verde
escudo(s)
centavo(s)
de Cabo Verde
Cabo.V.

Islas Caimán
dólar(es)
centavo(s)
de las Islas Caimán
C$

República Centroafricana
franco(s) CFA
céntimo(s)
-
FCFA

Chad
CFA franc(s)
centime(s)
-
CFAF
XAF

Tchad
franc(s) CFA
centime(s)
-
FCFA

Chad
franco(s) CFA
céntimo(s)
-
FCFA

Chile
peso(s)
centavo(s)
Chilean
Ch$
CLP

Chili
peso(s)
centavo(s)
chilien
$Ch

Chile
peso(s)
centavo(s)
chileno
$ o Ch$

China
yuan [9]
fen (inv.) [10]
Chinese
¥
CNY

Chine
yuan
fen (inv.)
chinois
¥

China
yuan(es)
fen(es)
chino
¥

Colombia
peso(s)
centavo(s)
Colombian
Col$
COP

Colombie
peso(s)
centavo(s)
colombien
$Col

Colombia
peso(s)
centavo(s)
colombiano
$ o Col$

Comoros
franc(s)
centime(s)
Comorian
CF
KMF

Comores
franc(s)
centime(s)
comorien
FC

Comoras
franco(s)
céntimo(s)
comorano
FC

Congo, Democratic Republic of the
franc(s)
centime(s)
Congo
CGF
CDF

République démocratique du Congo
franc(s)
centime(s)
congolais
FCG

República Democrática del Congo
franco(s)
céntimo(s)
congoleño
FCG

Congo, Republic of
CFA franc(s)
centime(s)
-
CFAF
XAF

République du Congo
franc(s) CFA
centime(s)
-
FCFA

República del Congo
franco(s) CFA
céntimo(s)
-
FCFA

Costa Rica
colón (colones)
céntimo(s)
Costa Rican
C
CRC

Costa Rica
colon (colones)
centimo(s)
costa-ricien
C

Costa Rica
colón (colones)
céntimo(s)
costarricense
¢

Côte d'Ivoire
CFA franc(s) [5]
centime(s)
-
CFAF
XOF

Côte d'Ivoire
franc(s) CFA
centime(s)
-
FCFA

Côte d'Ivoire
franco(s) CFA
céntimo(s)
-
FCFA

Croatia
kuna(s)
lipa (inv.)
Croatian/Croat
HRK
HRK

Croatie
kuna(s)
lipa (inv.)
croate
HRK

Croacia
kuna(s)
lipa(s)
croata
HRK

Cuba
peso(s)
centavo(s)
Cuban
$
CUP

Cyprus
pound(s)
cent(s)
Cyprus
£C
CYP

Czech Republic
koruna (koruny)
halér(e)
Czech
CZK
CZK

Denmark
krone(r)
øre
Danish
DKr
DKK

Djibouti
franc(s)
centime(s)
Djibouti
DF
DJF

Dominica
dollar(s) [3]
cent(s)
Eastern Caribbean
EC$
XCD

Dominican Republic
peso(s)
centavo(s)
Dominican
RD$
DOP

Ecuador
dollar(s)
cenftavo(s)
U.S.
$ or US$ [7]
USD

Egypt
pound(s)
piastre(s) [11]
Egyptian
LE
EGP

El Salvador
colón (colones) [12]
centavo(s)
Salvadoran
¢
SVC

Cuba
peso(s)
centavo(s)
cubain
$

Chypre
livre(s)
cent(s)
chypriote
£C

République tchèque
couronne(s)
halér(e)
tchèque
CZK

Danemark
couronne(s)
øre
danoise
DKr

Djibouti
franc(s)
centime(s)
djiboutien
FD

Dominique
dollar(s)
cent(s)
des Caraïbes orientales
EC$

République Dominicaine
peso(s)
centavo(s)
dominicain
$RD

Équateur
dollar(s)
centavo(s)
E.U.
$ ou $E.U.

Égypte
livre(s)
piastre(s)
égyptienne
LE

El Salvador
colon (colones)
centavo(s)
salvadorien
¢

Cuba
peso(s)
centavo(s)
cubano
$

Chipre
libra(s)
centavo(s)
chipriota
£C

República Checa
corona(s)
haler(s)
checa
CZK

Dinamarca
corona(s)
ore(s)
danesa
DKr

Djibouti
franco(s)
céntimo(s)
de Djibouti
FD

Dominica
dólar(es)
centavo(s)
del Caribe Oriental
EC$

República Dominicana
peso(s)
centavo(s)
dominicano
$ o RD$

Ecuador
dólar(es)
centavo(s)
de EE.UU.
$ o US$

Egipto
libra(s)
piastra(s)
egipcia
LE

El Salvador
colón (colones)
centavo(s)
salvadoreño
¢

El Salvador
dollar(s)
cent(s)
U.S.
$ or US$ [7]
USD

Equatorial Guinea
CFA franc(s)
centime(s)

-
CFAF
XAF

Eritrea
nakfa
cent(s)
Eritrean
ERN
ERN

Estonia
kroon(i)
sent(i)
Estonian
EEK
EEK

Ethiopia
birr
cent(s)
Ethiopian
Br
ETB

Faeroe Islands
krone(r)
øre
Danish
DKr
DKK

Falkland Islands
pound(s)
penny (pence)
Falkland Islands
£
FKP

Fiji
dollar(s)
cent(s)
Fiji
F$
FJD

Finland
euro(s) [2]
cent(s)

-
EUR or €
EUR

France
euro(s) [2]
cent(s)

-
EUR or €
EUR

El Salvador
dollar(s)
cent(s)
E.U.
$ ou $E.U.

Guinée Équatoriale
franc(s) CFA
centime(s)

-
FCFA

Érythrée
nakfa
cent(s)
d'Érythrée
ERN

Estonie
couronne(s)
sent(i)
estonienne
EEK

Éthiopie
birr
cent(s)
éthiopien
Br

Îles Féroé (Faeroe)
couronne(s)
øre
danoise
DKr

Îles Falkland (Malouines)
livre(s)
penny (pence)
des îles Falkland
£

Fidji
dollar(s)
cent(s)
de Fidji
F$

Finlande
euro(s)
cent(s)

-
EUR ou €

France
euro(s)
cent(s)

-
EUR ou €

El Salvador
dólar(es)
centavo(s)
de EE.UU.
$ o US$

Guinea Ecuatorial
franco(s) CFA
céntimo(s)

-
FCFA

Eritrea
nakfa(s)
centavo(s)
de Eritrea
ERN

Estonia
corona(s)
sent(s)
estonia
EEK

Etiopía
birr(s)
centavo(s)
etíope
Br

Islas Feroe
corona(s)
ore(s)
danesa
DKr

Islas Malvinas
libra(s)
penique(s)
de las Islas Malvinas
£

Fiji
dólar(es)
centavo(s)
de Fiji
F$

Finlandia
euro(s)
céntimo(s)

-
EUR o €

Francia
euro(s)
céntimo(s)

-
EUR o €

French Guiana	**Guyane française**	**Guayana Francesa**
euro(s) [2]	euro(s)	euro(s)
cent(s)	cent(s)	céntimo(s)
-	-	-
EUR or €	Guyane €	EUR o €
EUR		
French Polynesia	**Polynésie française**	**Polinesia Francesa**
CFP franc(s)	franc(s) CFP	franco(s) CFP
centime(s)	centime(s)	céntimo(s)
-	-	-
CFPF	FCFP	FCFP
XPF		
Gabon	**Gabon**	**Gabón**
CFA franc(s)	franc(s) CFA	franco(s) CFA
centime(s)	centime(s)	céntimo(s)
-	-	-
CFAF	FCFA	FCFA
XAF		
Gambia, The	**Gambie**	**Gambia**
dalasi(s)	dalasi(s)	dalasi(s)
butut(s)	butut(s)	butut(s)
Gambian	gambien	gambiano
D	D	D
GMD		
Georgia	**Géorgie**	**Georgia**
lari	lari	lari(s)
tetri (inv.)	tetri (inv.)	tetri(s)
Georgian	géorgien	georgiano
lari	lari	lari
GEL		
Germany	**Allemagne**	**Alemania**
euro(s) [2]	euro(s)	euro(s)
cent(s)	cent(s)	céntimo(s)
-	-	-
EUR or €	EUR ou €	EUR o €
EUR		
Ghana	**Ghana**	**Ghana**
cedi(s)	cedi(s)	cedi(s)
pesewa(s)	pesewa(s)	pesewa(s)
Ghanaian	ghanéen	ghanés
¢	¢	¢
GHC		
Gibraltar	**Gibraltar**	**Gibraltar**
pound(s)	livre(s)	libra(s)
penny (pence)	penny (pence)	penique(s)
Gibraltar	de Gibraltar	de Gibraltar
£	£	£
GIP		
Greece	**Grèce**	**Grecia**
euro(s) [2]	euro(s)	euro(s)
cent(s)	cent(s)	céntimo(s)
-	-	-
EUR or €	EUR ou €	EUR o €
EUR		
Greenland	**Groenland**	**Groenlandia**
krone(r)	couronne(s)	corona(s)
øre	øre	ore(s)
Danish	danoise	danesa
DKr	DKr	DKr
DKK		

Grenada
dollar(s) [3]
cent(s)
Eastern Caribbean
EC$
XCD

Guadeloupe
euro(s) [2]
cent(s)
-
EUR or €
EUR

Guatemala
quetzal(es)
centavo(s)
Guatemalan
Q
GTQ

Guinea
franc(s) [4]
-
Guinean
GF
GNF

Guinea-Bissau
CFA franc(s) [5]
centime(s)
-
CFAF
XOF

Guyana
dollar(s)
cent(s)
Guyana
G$
GYD

Haiti
gourde(s)
centime(s)
Haitian
G
HTG

Honduras
lempira(s)
centavo(s)
Honduran
L
HNL

Hong Kong SAR
dollar(s)
cent(s)
Hong Kong
HK$
HKD

Hungary
forint
fillér
Hungarian
Ft
HUF

Grenade
dollar(s)
cent(s)
des Caraïbes orientales
EC$

Guadeloupe
euro(s)
cent(s)
-
EUR ou €

Guatemala
quetzal(es)
centavo(s)
guatémaltèque
Q

Guinée
franc(s)
-
guinéen
FG

Guinée-Bissau
franc(s) CFA
centime(s)
-
FCFA

Guyana
dollar(s)
cent(s)
guyanais
G$

Haïti
gourde(s)
centime(s)
haïtienne
G

Honduras
lempira(s)
centavo(s)
hondurien
L

Région administrative spéciale de Hong Kong
dollar(s)
cent(s)
de Hong Kong
HK$

Hongrie
forint
fillér
hongrois
Ft

Granada
dólar(es)
centavo(s)
del Caribe Oriental
EC$

Guadalupe
euro(s)
céntimo(s)
-
EUR o €

Guatemala
quetzal(es)
centavo(s)
guatemalteco
Q

Guinea
franco(s)
céntimo(s)
guineo
FG

Guinea-Bissau
franco(s) CFA
céntimo(s)
-
FCFA

Guyana
dólar(es)
centavo(s)
de Guyana
G$

Haití
gourde(s)
céntimo(s)
haitiano
G

Honduras
lempira(s)
centavo(s)
hondureño
L

RAE de Hong Kong
dólar(es)
centavo(s)
de Hong Kong
HK$

Hungría
forint(s)
filler(s)
húngaro
Ft

Iceland	**Islande**	**Islandia**
króna (krónur)	couronne(s)	corona(s)
eyrir (aurar)	eyrir (aurar)	eyrir (aurar)
Icelandic	islandaise	islandesa
ISK	ISK	ISK
ISK		
India	**Inde**	**India**
rupee(s)	roupie(s)	rupia(s)
paisa (paise)	paisa (paise)	paisa(s)
Indian	indienne	india
Rs [13]	Rs	Rs
INR		
Indonesia	**Indonésie**	**Indonesia**
rupiah	rupiah	rupia(s)
sen	sen	sen(s)
Indonesian	indonésienne	indonesia
Rp	Rp	Rp
IDR		
Iran, Islamic Republic of	**République islamique d'Iran**	**República Islámica del Irán**
rial(s) [4]	rial(s)	rial(es)
-	-	-
Iranian	iranien	iraní
Rls [14]	Rls	Rls
IRR		
Iraq	**Iraq**	**Iraq**
dinar(s) [15]	dinar(s)	dinar(es)
fils (inv.)	fils (inv.)	fils (inv.)
Iraqi	iraquien	iraquí
ID	KD	DI
IQD		
Ireland	**Irlande**	**Irlanda**
euro(s) [2]	euro(s)	euro(s)
cent(s)	cent(s)	céntimo(s)
-	-	-
EUR or €	EUR ou €	EUR o €
EUR		
Israel	**Israël**	**Israel**
new sheqel (new sheqalim)	nouveau sheqel (nouveaux sheqalim)	nuevo(s) sheqel(s)
agora (agorot)	agora (agorot)	agorá(s)
Israeli	israélien	israelí
NIS	NSI	NSI
ILS		
Italy	**Italie**	**Italia**
euro(s) [2]	euro(s)	euro(s)
cent(s)	cent(s)	céntimo(s)
-	-	-
EUR or €	EUR ou €	EUR o €
EUR		
Jamaica	**Jamaïque**	**Jamaica**
dollar(s)	dollar(s)	dólar(es)
cent(s)	cent(s)	centavo(s)
Jamaica	jamaïquain	de Jamaica
J$	J$	J$
JMD		
Japan	**Japon**	**Japón**
yen	yen	yen(es)
sen (inv.)	sen	sen(s)
Japanese	japonais	japonés
¥	¥	¥
JPY		

Jordan
dinar(s)
fils (inv.)
Jordanian
JD
JOD

Kazakhstan
tenge
tiyn(s)
Kazakhstani
T
KZT

Kenya
shilling(s)
cent(s)
Kenya
K Sh
KES

Kiribati
dollar(s)
cent(s)
Australian
$A
AUD

Korea, Democratic People's Republic of
won
chun (inv.)
Korean Democratic People's Republic
-
KRW

Korea, Republic of
won
chun
Korean
W
KRW

Kuwait
dinar(s)
fils (inv.)
Kuwaiti
KD
KWD

Kyrgyzstan
som(s)
tyiyn(s)
Kyrgyz
som
KGS

Lao People's Democratic Republic
kip [4]
-
Lao (inv.)
KN
LAK

Jordanie
dinar(s)
fils (inv.)
jordanien
JD

Kazakhstan
tenge
tiyn(s)
kazakh
T

Kenya
shilling(s)
cent(s)
du Kenya
K Sh

Kiribati
dollar(s)
cent(s)
australien
$A

République populaire démocratique de Corée
won
chun (inv.)
de la République populaire démocratique de Corée
-

République de Corée
won
chun
coréen
W

Koweït
dinar(s)
fils
koweïtien
KD

Kirghizistan (le)
som(s)
tyiyn(s)
kirghize
som

République démocratique populaire lao
kip
-
lao
NK

Jordania
dinar(es)
fils (inv.)
jordano
DJ

Kazajstán
tenge(s)
tiyn(s)
kasako
T

Kenya
chelín (chelines)
centavo(s)
keniano
Sh K

Kiribati
dólar(es)
centavo(s)
australiano
A$

República Popular Democrática de Corea
won(s)
chun(s)
de la República Popular Democrática de Corea
-

República de Corea
won(s)
chun(s)
coreano
W

Kuwait
dinar(es)
fils (inv.)
kuwaiti
DK

República Kirguisa
som(s)
tyiyn(s)
kirguís
som

República Democrática Popular Lao
kip(s)
att(s)
lao
KN

Latvia	Lettonie	Letonia
lats	lats	lats (inv.)
santims (inv.)	santims	santims (inv.)
Latvian	letton	letón
LVL	LVL	LVL
LVL		

Lebanon	**Liban**	**Líbano**
pound(s) [4]	livre(s)	libra(s)
-	-	-
Lebanese	libanaise	libanesa
LL	LL	LL
LBP		

Lesotho	**Lesotho**	**Lesotho**
loti (maloti) [16]	loti (maloti)	loti(s)
sente (lisente)	sente (lisente)	sente(s)
Lesotho	du Lesotho	de Lesotho
M	M	M
LSL		

Liberia	**Libéria**	**Liberia**
dollar(s)	dollar(s)	dólar(es)
cent(s)	cent(s)	centavo(s)
Liberian	libérien	liberiano
$	$	L$
LRD		

Libyan Arab Jamahiriya	**Jamahiria arabe libyenne**	**Jamahiriya Árabe Libia**
dinar(s)	dinar(s)	dinar(es)
dirham(s)	dirham(s)	dirham(s)
Libyan	libyen	libio
LD	LD	DL
LYD		

Liechtenstein	**Liechtenstein**	**Liechtenstein**
franc(s)	franc(s)	franco(s)
centime(s)	centime(s)	céntimo(s)
Swiss	suisse	suizo
Sw F	FS	FS
CHF		

Lithuania	**Lituanie**	**Lituania**
litas (litai)	litas (litai)	litas (inv.)
centas (centai)	centas (centai)	centas (inv.)
Lithuanian	lituanien	lituana
LTL	LTL	LTL
LTL		

Luxembourg	**Luxembourg**	**Luxemburgo**
euro(s) [2]	euro(s)	euro(s)
cent(s)	cent(s)	céntimo(s)
-	-	-
EUR or €	EUR ou €	EUR o €
EUR		

Macao SAR	**Macao, RASRPC**	**Macao, RAE**
pataca(s)	pataca(s)	pataca(s)
avo(s)	avo(s)	avo(s)
Macao	de Macao	de Macao
P	P	P
MOP		

Madagascar	**Madagascar**	**Madagascar**
ariary	ariary	ariary (ariaries)
iraimbilanja (inv.)	iraimbilanja (inv.)	iraimbilanja(s)
Malagasy	malgache	malgache
Ar	Ar	Ar
MGA		

Madeira	**Madère**	**Madeira**
euro(s) [2]	euro(s)	euro(s)
cent(s)	cent(s)	céntimo(s)
-	-	-
EUR or €	EUR ou €	EUR o €
EUR		
Malawi	**Malawi**	**Malawi**
kwacha	kwacha	kwacha(s)
tambala (inv.)	tambala (inv.)	tambala(s)
Malawi	malawien	malawiano
MK	MK	MK
MWK		
Malaysia	**Malaisie**	**Malasia**
ringgit	ringgit	ringgit(s)
sen	sen	sen(s)
Malaysian	malaisien	malasio
RM	RM	RM
MYR		
Maldives	**Maldives**	**Maldivas**
rufiyaa	rufiyaa	rufiyaa(s)
laari	laari	laari(s)
Maldivian	des Maldives	maldiva
Rf	Rf	Rf
MVR		
Mali	**Mali**	**Malí**
CFA franc(s) [5]	franc(s) CFA	franco(s) CFA
centime(s)	centime(s)	céntimo(s)
-	-	-
CFAF	FCFA	FCFA
XOF		
Malta	**Malte**	**Malta**
lira (liri)	lire(s)	lira(s)
cent(s) [17]	cent(s)	céntimo(s)
Maltese	maltaise	maltesa
Lm	Lm	Lm
MTL		
Marshall Islands	**Îles Marshall**	**Islas Marshall**
dollar(s)	dollar(s)	dólar(es)
cent(s)	cent(s)	centavo(s)
U.S.	E.U.	de EE.UU.
$ or US$ [7]	$ ou $E.U.	$ o US$
USD		
Martinique	**Martinique**	**Martinica**
euro(s) [2]	euro(s)	euro(s)
cent(s)	cent(s)	céntimo(s)
-	-	-
EUR or €	EUR ou €	EUR o €
EUR		
Mauritania	**Mauritanie**	**Mauritania**
ouguiya(s) [18]	ouguiya	ouguiya(s)
khoum(s)	khoum(s)	khoum(s)
Mauritanian	mauritanienne	mauritano
UM	UM	UM
MRO		
Mauritius	**Maurice**	**Mauricio**
rupee(s)	roupie(s)	rupia(s)
cent(s)	cent(s)	centavo(s)
Mauritian	mauricienne	mauriciana
MUR	MUR	MUR
MUR		

Mexico	Mexique	México
peso(s)	peso(s)	peso(s)
centavo(s)	centavo(s)	centavo(s)
Mexican	mexicain	mexicano
Mex$	$Mex	$ o Mex$
MXN		

Micronesia, Federated States of	États fédérés de Micronésie	Estados Federados de Micronesia
dollar(s)	dollar(s)	dólar(es)
cent(s)	cent(s)	centavo(s)
U.S.	E.U.	de EE.UU.
$ or US$ [7]	$ ou $E.U.	$ o US$
USD		

Moldova, Republic of	République de Moldova	República de Moldova
leu (lei) [19]	leu (lei)	leu (lei)
ban(i)	ban(i)	ban(i)
Moldovan	moldove	moldavo
MDL	MDL	MDL
MDL		

Monaco	Monaco	Mónaco
euro(s) [2]	euro(s)	euro(s)
cent(s)	cent(s)	céntimo(s)
-	-	-
EUR or €	EUR ou €	EUR o €
EUR		

Mongolia	Mongolie	Mongolia
togrog(s)	togrog(s)	togrog(s)
möngö	möngö	mongo(s)
Mongolian	mongol	mongol
Tog	Tog	Tog
MNT		

Montenegro	Monténégro	Montenegro
euro(s) [2, 20]	euro(s)	euro(s)
cent(s)	cent(s)	cent(s)
-	-	-
EUR or €	EUR ou €	EUR o €
EUR		

Montserrat	Montserrat	Montserrat
dollar(s) [3]	dollar(s)	dólar(es)
cent(s)	cent(s)	centavo(s)
Eastern Caribbean	des Caraïbes orientales	del Caribe Oriental
EC$	EC$	EC$
XCD		

Morocco	Maroc	Marruecos
dirham(s)	dirham(s)	dirham(s)
centime(s)	centime(s)	céntimo(s)
Moroccan	marocain	marroquí
DH	DH	DH
MAD		

Mozambique	Mozambique	Mozambique
metical (meticais)	metical (meticais)	metical(es)
centavo(s)	centavo(s)	centavo(s)
Mozambican	du Mozambique	de Mozambique
Mt	Mt	Mt
MZM		

Myanmar	Myanmar	Myanmar
kyat(s)	kyat(s)	kyat(s)
pya(s)	pya(s)	pya(s)
Myanmar	du Myanmar	de Myanmar
K	K	K
MMK		

Namibia
dollar(s) [21]
cent(s)
Namibia
N$
NAD

Namibia
rand
cent(s)
South African
R
ZAR

Nauru
dollar(s)
cent(s)
Australian
$A
AUD

Nepal
rupee(s)
paisa (inv.)
Nepalese
Nr [22]
NPR

Netherlands Antilles
guilder(s)
cent(s)
Netherlands Antillean
NA f.
ANG

Netherlands
euro(s) [2]
cent(s)
-
EUR or €
EUR

New Caledonia
CFP franc(s)
centime(s)
-
CFPF
XPF

New Zealand
dollar(s)
cent(s)
New Zealand
$NZ
NZD

Nicaragua
córdoba(s)
centavo(s)
Nicaraguan
C$
NIO

Niger
CFA franc(s) [5]
centime(s)
-
CFAF
XOF

Namibia
dollar(s)
cent(s)
Namibia
N$

Namibie
rand
cent(s)
sud-africain
R

Nauru
dollar(s)
cent(s)
australien
$A

Népal
roupie(s)
paisa (paise)
népalaise
Nr

Antilles néerlandaises
florin(s)
cent(s)
des Antilles néerlandaises
NA f.

Pays-Bas
euro(s)
cent(s)
-
EUR ou €

Nouvelle-Calédonie
franc(s) CFP
centime(s)
-
FCFP

Nouvelle-Zélande
dollar(s)
cent(s)
néo-zélandais
$NZ

Nicaragua
cordoba(s)
centavo(s)
nicaraguayen
C$

Niger
franc(s) CFA
centime(s)
-
FCFA

Namibia
dólar(es)
centavo(s)
de Namibia
N$

Namibia
rand(s)
centavo(s)
sudafricano
R

Nauru
dólar(es)
centavo(s)
australiano
A$

Nepal
rupia(s)
paisa(s)
nepalesa
Nr

Antillas Neerlandesas
florín (florines)
centavo(s)
de las Antillas Neerlandesas
NA f.

Países Bajos
euro(s)
céntimo(s)
-
EUR o €

Nueva Caledonia
franco(s) CFP
céntimo(s)
-
FCFP

Nueva Zelandia
dólar(es)
centavo(s)
neozelandés
NZ$

Nicaragua
córdoba(s)
centavo(s)
nicaragüense
C$

Níger
franco(s) CFA
céntimo(s)
-
FCFA

Nigeria
naira
kobo (inv.)
Nigerian
N
NGN

Norway
krone(r)
øre
Norwegian
NKr
NOK

Macedonia, former Yugoslav Republic of
denar(s)
deni (inv.)
Macedonian
MDen
MKD

Oman
rial(s) Omani
baisa(s)
-
RO
OMR

Pakistan
rupee(s)
paisa(s)
Pakistan
PRs
PKR

Palau
dollar(s)
cent(s)
U.S.
$ or US$ [7]
USD

Panama
balboa(s)
centésimo(s)
Panamanian
B
PAB

Papua New Guinea
kina
toea (inv.)
Papua New Guinea
K
PGK

Paraguay
guaraní(es)
céntimo(s)
Paraguayan
G
PYG

Peru
nuevo(s) sol(es)
céntimo(s)
Peruvian
S/.

Nigéria
naira
kobo (inv.)
nigérien
N

Norvège
couronne(s)
øre
norvégienne
NKr

ex-république yougoslave de Macédoine
denar
deni (inv.)
de Macédoine
MDen

Oman
rial(s) omani
baisa(s)
-
RO

Pakistan
roupie(s)
paisa(s)
pakistanaise
PRs

Palau
dollar(s)
cent(s)
E.U.
$ ou $E.U.

Panama
balboa(s)
centesimo(s)
panaméen
B

Papouasie-Nouvelle-Guinée
kina
toea (inv.)
papouan-néo-guinéen
K

Paraguay
guaraní (guaranies)
centimo(s)
paraguayen
G

Pérou
nouveau(x) sol(es)
centimo(s)
péruvien
S/.

Nigeria
naira(s)
kobo(s)
nigeriano
N

Noruega
corona(s)
ore(s)
noruega
NKr

ex República Yugoslava de Macedonia
denar(es)
deni(s)
macedonio
MDen

Omán
rial(es) omaní(es)
baisa(s)
-
RO

Pakistán
rupia(s)
paisa(s)
pakistaní
PRs

Palau
dólar(es)
centavo(s)
de EE.UU.
$ o US$

Panamá
balboa(s)
centésimo(s)
panameño
B/

Papua Nueva Guinea
kina(s)
toea(s)
de Papua Nueva Guinea
K

Paraguay
guaraní(es)
céntimo(s)
paraguayo
G

Perú
nuevo(s) sol(es)
céntimo(s)
peruano
S/.

Philippines	**Philippines**	**Filipinas**
peso(s)	peso(s)	peso(s)
centavo(s)	centavo(s)	centavo(s)
Philippine	philippin	filipino
-	-	-
PHP		
Poland	**Pologne**	**Polonia**
zloty(s)	zloty(s)	zloty(s)
grosz(y)	grosz(y)	grosz(y)
Polish	polonais	polaco
Zl	Zl	Zl
PLN		
Portugal	**Portugal**	**Portugal**
euro(s) [2]	euro(s)	euro(s)
cent(s)	cent(s)	céntimo(s)
-	-	-
EUR or €	EUR ou €	EUR o €
EUR		
Qatar	**Qatar**	**Qatar**
riyal(s)	riyal(s)	riyal(es)
dirham(s)	dirham(s)	dirham(s)
Qatar	qatarien	de Qatar
QR	QR	QR
QAR		
Réunion	**Réunion (la)**	**Reunión**
euro(s) [2]	euro(s)	euro(s)
cent(s)	cent(s)	céntimo(s)
-	-	-
EUR or €	EUR ou €	EUR o €
EUR		
Romania	**Roumanie**	**Rumania**
leu (lei) [4]	leu (lei)	leu (lei)
-	-	ban(i)
Romanian	roumain	rumano
leu	leu	leu
ROL		
Russia	**Russie**	**Rusia**
ruble(s)	rouble(s)	rublo(s)
kopek(s)	kopek(s)	kopek(s)
Russian	russe	ruso
Rub	Rub	Rub
RUB		
Rwanda	**Rwanda**	**Rwanda**
franc(s)	franc(s)	franco(s)
centime(s)	centime(s)	céntimo(s)
Rwanda	rwandais	rwandés
RF	FR	FR
RWF		
Saint Helena	**Sainte-Hélène**	**Santa Elena**
pound(s) [23]	livre(s)	libra(s)
new penny (new pence)	penny (pence)	penique(s)
sterling	sterling	esterlina
£ or £ stg.	£ ou £ stg.	£ o £ stg.
SHP		
Saint Kitts and Nevis	**Saint-Kitts-et-Nevis**	**Saint Kitts y Nevis**
dollar(s) [3]	dollar(s)	dólar(es)
cent(s)	cent(s)	centavo(s)
Eastern Caribbean	des Caraïbes orientales	del Caribe Oriental
EC$	EC$	EC$
XCD		

Saint Lucia	**Sainte-Lucie**	**Santa Lucía**
dollar(s) [3]	dollar(s)	dólar(es)
cent(s)	cent(s)	centavo(s)
Eastern Caribbean	des Caraïbes orientales	del Caribe Oriental
EC$	EC$	EC$
XCD		
Saint Pierre and Miquelon	**Saint-Pierre-et-Miquelon**	**San Pedro y Miquelón**
euro(s) [2]	euro(s)	euro(s)
cent(s)	cent(s)	céntimo(s)
-	-	-
EUR or €	EUR ou €	EUR o €
EUR		
Saint Vincent and the Grenadines	**Saint-Vincent-et-les-Grenadines**	**San Vicente y las Granadinas**
dollar(s) [3]	dollar(s)	dólar(es)
cent(s)	cent(s)	centavo(s)
Eastern Caribbean	des Caraïbes orientales	del Caribe Oriental
EC$	EC$	EC$
XCD		
Samoa	**Samoa**	**Samoa**
tala	tala	tala(s)
sene	sene	sene(s)
Samoa	du Samoa	de Samoa
SAT	SAT	SAT
WST		
San Marino	**Saint-Marin**	**San Marino**
euro(s) [2]	euro(s)	euro(s)
cent(s)	cent(s)	céntimo(s)
-	-	-
EUR or €	EUR ou €	EUR o €
EUR		
São Tomé and Príncipe	**São Tomé-et-Principe**	**Santo Tomé y Príncipe**
dobra(s)	dobra(s)	dobra(s)
céntimo(s)	céntimo(s)	céntimo(s)
São Tomé and Príncipe	de São Tomé-et-Principe	de Santo Tomé y Príncipe
Db	Db	Db
STD		
Saudi Arabia	**Arabie Saoudite**	**Arabia Saudita**
riyal(s)	riyal(s)	riyal(es)
halala(s)	halala(s)	halala(s)
Saudi Arabian	saoudien	árabe saudita
SRls [24]	SRls	SRls
SAR		
Senegal	**Sénégal**	**Senegal**
CFA franc(s) [5]	franc(s) CFA	franco(s) CFA
centime(s)	centime(s)	céntimo(s)
-	-	-
CFAF	FCFA	FCFA
XOF		
Serbia	**Serbie**	**Serbia**
dinar(s)	dinar(s)	dinar(es)
para	para	para(s)
Serbian	serbe	serbio
SRD	SRD	DSR
RSD		
Seychelles	**Seychelles**	**Seychelles**
rupee(s)	roupie(s)	rupia(s)
cent(s)	cent(s)	centavo(s)
Seychelles	seychelloises	de Seychelles
SR	SR	SR
SCR		

Sierra Leone
leone(s)
cent(s)
Sierra Leonean
Le
SLL

Singapore
dollar(s)
cent(s)
Singapore
S$
SGD

Slovak Republic
koruna (koruny)
halĕr(e)
Slovak
Sk
SKK

Slovenia
euro(s) [2, 25]
cent(s)
-
EUR or €
EUR

Solomon Islands
dollar(s)
cent(s)
Solomon Islands
SI$
SBD

Somalia
shilling(s)
cent(s)
Somali
So. Sh.
SOS

South Africa
rand
cent(s)
South African
R
ZAR

Spain
euro(s) [2]
cent(s)
-
EUR or €
EUR

Sri Lanka
rupee(s)
cent(s)
Sri Lanka
SL Rs
LKR

Sudan
dinar(s)
piastre(s)
Sudanese
SD
SDD

Sierra Leone
leone(s)
cent(s)
de Sierra Leone
Le

Singapour
dollar(s)
cent(s)
singapourien
S$

République slovaque
couronne(s)
halĕr(e)
slovaque
Sk

Slovénie
euro(s)
cent(s)
-
EUR ou €

Îles Salomon
dollar(s)
cent(s)
des îles Salomon
SI$

Somalie
shilling(s)
cent(s)
somali
So. Sh.

Afrique du Sud
rand
cent(s)
sud-africain
R

Espagne
euro(s)
cent(s)
-
EUR ou €

Sri Lanka
roupie(s)
cent(s)
sri-lankaise
Sri Rs

Soudan
dinar(s)
piastre(s)
soudanaise
SD

Sierra Leona
leone(s)
centavo(s)
de Sierra Leona
Le

Singapur
dólar(es)
centavo(s)
de Singapur
S$

República Eslovaca
corona(s)
haler(s)
eslovaca
Sk

Eslovenia
euro(s)
céntimo(s)
-
EUR o €

Islas Salomón
dólar(es)
centavo(s)
de las Islas Salomón
SI$

Somalia
chelín (chelines)
centavo(s)
somalí
Sh. So.

Sudáfrica
rand(s)
centavo(s)
sudafricano
R

España
euro(s)
céntimo(s)
-
EUR o €

Sri Lanka
rupia(s)
centavo(s)
de Sri Lanka
Sri Rs

Sudán
dinar(es)
piastra(s)
sudanés
DS

Sudan	**Soudan**	**Sudán**
pound(s)	pound(s)	pound(s)
piastre(s)	piastre(s)	piastra(s)
SD	soudanaise	sudanés
SDG	-	-
Suriname	**Suriname**	**Suriname**
dollar(s) [26]	dollar(s)	dólar(es)
cent(s)	cent(s)	centavo(s)
Suriname	surinamais	surinamés
SRD	SRD	SRD
SRD		
Swaziland	**Swaziland**	**Swazilandia**
lilangeni (emalangeni)	lilangeni (emalangeni)	lilangeni (emalangeni)
cent(s)	cent(s)	centavo(s)
Swaziland	du Swaziland	de Swazilandia
E	E	E
SZL		
Sweden	**Suède**	**Suecia**
krona (kronor)	couronne(s)	corona(s)
öre	öre	ore(s)
Swedish	suédoise	sueca
SKr	SKr	SKr
SEK		
Switzerland	**Suisse**	**Suiza**
franc(s)	franc(s)	franco(s)
centime(s)	centime(s)	céntimo(s)
Swiss	suisse	suizo
Sw F	FS	FS
CHF		
Syrian Arab Republic	**République arabe syrienne**	**República Árabe Siria**
pound(s)	livre(s)	libra(s)
piastre(s)	piastre(s)	piastra(s)
Syrian	syrienne	siria
LS	LS	LS
SYP		
Taiwan Province of China	**Taiwan, province chinoise de**	**Taiwan, Provincia china de**
new Taiwan dollar(s)	nouveau(x) dollar(s) de Taiwan	nuevo(s) dólar(es) de Taiwan
fen	fen	fen(s)
-	-	-
NT$	NT$	NT$
TWD		
Tajikistan	**Tadjikistan**	**Tayikistán**
somoni	somoni	somoni(s)
diram(s)	diram(s)	diram(s)
Tajik	du Tadjikistan	de Tayikistán
SM	SM	SM
TJS		
Tanzania	**Tanzanie**	**Tanzanía**
shilling(s)	shilling(s)	chelín (chelines)
cent(s)	cent(s)	centavo(s)
Tanzania	tanzanien	tanzaniano
T Sh	T Sh	Sh T
TZS		
Thailand	**Thaïlande**	**Tailandia**
baht	baht	baht(s)
satang (inv.)	satang	satang(s)
Thai	thaïlandais	tailandés
B	B	B
THB		

Timor-Leste dollar(s) cent(s) U.S. $ or US$ [7] USD	**Timor-Leste** dollar(s) cent(s) E.U. $ ou $E.U.	**Timor-Leste** dólar(es) centavo(s) de EE.UU. $ o US$
Togo CFA franc(s) [5] centime(s) - CFAF XOF	**Togo** franc(s) CFA centime(s) - FCFA	**Togo** franco(s) CFA céntimo(s) - FCFA
Tonga pa'anga seniti (inv.) Tongan T$ TOP	**Tonga, les** pa'anga seniti des Tonga T$	**Tonga** pa'anga(s) seniti(s) de Tonga T$
Trinidad and Tobago dollar(s) cent(s) Trinidad and Tobago TT$ TTD	**Trinité-et-Tobago** dollar(s) cent(s) de la Trinité-et-Tobago TT$	**Trinidad y Tabago** dólar(es) centavo(s) de Trinidad y Tabago TT$
Tunisia dinar(s) millime(s) Tunisian D TND	**Tunisie** dinar(s) millime(s) tunisien D	**Túnez** dinar(es) milésimo(s) tunecino D
Turkey lira(s) kurus Turkish TL TRL	**Turquie** livre(s) kurus turque TL	**Turquía** nueva(s) lira(s) nuevo(s) kurus turca YTL
Turkmenistan manat tenge Turkmen manat TMM	**Turkménistan (le)** manat tenge (inv.) turkmene manat	**Turkmenistán** manta(s) tenge (inv.) turcomano manat
Turks and Caicos Islands dollar(s) cent(s) U.S. $ or US$ [7] USD	**Îles Turques et Caïques** dollar(s) cent(s) E.U. $ ou $E.U.	**Islas Turcas y Caicos** dólar(es) centavo(s) de EE.UU. Islas S$
Tuvalu dollar(s) cent(s) Australian $A AUD	**Tuvalu** dollar(s) cent(s) australien $A	**Tuvalu** dólar(es) centavo(s) australiano A$
Uganda shilling(s) cent(s) Uganda U Sh UGX	**Ouganda (l')** shilling(s) cent(s) ougandais U Sh	**Uganda** chelín (chelines) centavo(s) ugandés Sh U

Ukraine	**Ukraine**	**Ucrania**
hryvnia(s)	hryvnia	grivna(s)
kopiyka (kopiyky)	kopiyka (kopiyky)	kopika(s)
Ukrainian	ukrainienne	ucraniana
Hrv	Hrv	Hrv
UAH		
United Arab Emirates	**Émirats arabes unis**	**Emiratos Árabes Unidos**
dirham(s)	dirham(s)	dirham(s)
fils (inv.)	fils	fils (inv.)
U.A.E.	des É.A.U.	de los E.A.U.
Dh	Dh	Dh
AED		
United Kingdom	**Royaume-Uni**	**Reino Unido**
pound(s) [23]	livre(s)	libra(s)
penny (pence)	penny (pence)	penique(s)
sterling	sterling (invar.)	esterlina
£ or £ stg.	£ ou £ stg.	£ o £ stg.
GBP		
United States	**États-Unis**	**Estados Unidos**
dollar(s)	dollar(s)	dólar(es)
cent(s)	cent(s)	centavo(s)
U.S.	E.U.	de EE.UU.
$ or US$ [7]	$ ou $E.U.	$ o US$
USD		
Uruguay	**Uruguay**	**Uruguay**
peso(s)	peso(s)	peso(s)
centésimo(s)	centesimo(s)	centésimo(s)
Uruguayan	uruguayen	uruguayo
Ur$	$Ur	$ o Ur$
UYIU		
Uzbekistan	**Ouzbékistan**	**Uzbekistán**
sum	sum	sum(s)
tiyin	tiyin	tiyin(s)
Uzbek	ouzbek	uzbeko
SUM	SUM	Uzbekistán
UZS		SUM
Vanuatu	**Vanuatu**	**Vanuatu**
vatu [4]	vatu	vatu(s)
-	-	-
Vanuatu	de Vanuatu	de Vanuatu
VT	VT	VT
VUV		
Venezuela, República Bolivariana de Venezuela	**République bolivarienne du Venezuela**	**República Bolivariana de Venezuela**
bolívar(es)	bolívar(es)	bolívar(es)
céntimo(s)	centavo(s)	céntimo(s)
Venezuelan	vénézuélien	venezolano
Bs	Bs	Bs
VEB		
Vietnam	**Vietnam**	**Vietnam**
dong [4]	dong	dong(s)
-	-	xu(s)
Vietnamese	vietnamien	vietnamita
D	D	D
VND		
Wallis and Futuna Islands	**Îles Wallis-et-Futuna**	**Islas Wallis y Futuna**
CFP franc(s)	franc(s) CFP	franco(s) CFP
centime(s)	centime(s)	céntimo(s)
-	-	-
CFPF	FCFP	FCFP
XPF		

Yemen, Republic of
  rial
  fils
  Yemeni
  YRls [27]
  YER

Zambia
  kwacha
  ngwee
  Zambian
  K
  ZMK

Zimbabwe
  dollar(s)
  cent(s)
  Zimbabwe
  Z$
  ZWD

République du Yémen
  rial
  fils
  yéménite
  YRls

Zambie
  kwacha
  ngwee
  zambien
  K

Zimbabwe
  dollar(s)
  cent(s)
  zimbabwéen
  Z$

República del Yemen
  rial(es)
  fils (inv.)
  yemení
  YRls

Zambia
  kwacha(s)
  ngwee(s)
  zambiano
  K

Zimbabwe
  dólar(es)
  centavo(s)
  de Zimbabwe
  Z$

ENDNOTES

1. Currency units are not capitalized, except for Afghanis.

2. Use the term "euro area," not "euro zone." It is incorrect to refer to the euro by nationality, for example, as an Austrian euro or a Belgian euro. However, one may refer to a country's holdings of euros, for example, euro (France) or euro (Germany). Use the euro symbol (€) for publications.

3. The EC$ (East Caribbean dollar) is the legal tender in the following member countries of the East Caribbean Central Bank (ECCB): Anguilla, Antigua & Barbuda, Dominica, Grenada, Montserrat, St. Kitts and Nevis, St. Lucia, St. Vincent and the Grenadines.

4. Has no subsidiary unit.

5. The CFA (Communauté financière d'Afrique) franc is the currency issued by the Central Bank of West African States (BCEAO). It is legal tender in Benin, Burkina Faso, Côte d'Ivoire, Guinea-Bissau, Mali, Niger, Senegal and Togo. If it is necessary to make an explicit distinction with the CFA (Coopération financière en Afrique Centrale), the abbreviation CFAF (BEAC) or CFAF (BCEAO) can be used.

6. The word "real" should be italicized to avoid confusion in such phrases as "the real's real exchange rate".

7. Use US$ instead of $ when it is not clear that the reference is to the U.S. dollar.

8. The CFA (Coopération financière en Afrique Centrale) franc is the currency issued by the Bank of Central African States (BEAC). It is legal tender in Cameroon, Central African Republic, Chad, Congo Republic of, Equatorial Guinea and Gabon. If it is necessary to make an explicit distinction with the CFA (Communauté financière d'Afrique), the abbreviation CFAF (BEAC) or CFAF (BCEAO) can be used.

9. The currency is the renminbi, while the currency unit is the yuan.

10. Second subsidiary currency unit: jiao; 10 fen = 1 jiao; 10 jiao = 1 yuan.

11. Second subsidiary currency: millième; 10 millièmes = 1 piastre

12. The dollar is the legal tender and circulates freely at a fixed rate of ¢8.75 per $1 per $1. Payments may be made in either dollars or colones.

13. Singular: Re. Plural: Rs.

14. Singular: Rl. Plural: Rls.

15. The currency of Iraq is the Iraqi dinar. Effective October 15, 2003, new banknotes were introduced, replacing the "Saddam dinars" at a rate of 1:1 and the Swiss dinars at a rate of 150 Swiss dinars per 1 new Iraqi dinar.

16. The loti is interchangeable with the South African rand, which is also legal tender in Lesotho.

17. Second subsidiary currency: mil; 10 mils = 1 cent.

18. In French, the singular and plural are the same; in Arabic and English the plural form is used.

19. Use the plural form "lei" before a figure (lei 100).

20. Montenegro is not a formal member of the euro zone.

21. Both the South African rand and the Namibia dollar are legal tender in Namibia.

22. Singular: Nr. Plural: Nrs.

23. "Sterling" is at times used in place of "pounds." When used as an adjective to describe the currency, "sterling" follows "pounds" (i.e., "pounds sterling").

24. Singular: SRl. Plural: SRls.

25.   The "euro" became the currency of Slovenia—replacing the "tolar"—as of January 1, 2007 (International Standard Organization (ISO) MA Secretariat, 8/4/06.)

26.   Effective January 1, 2004, the currency of Suriname is the Suriname dollar—replacing the guilder. The conversion between two currencies is effected at a rate of SRD 1 per Sf1,000.

27.   Singular: YRI. Plural: YRIs.

APPENDIX II

Organizational Chart
Organigramme
Organigrama

IMF Organization Chart
As of December 2006

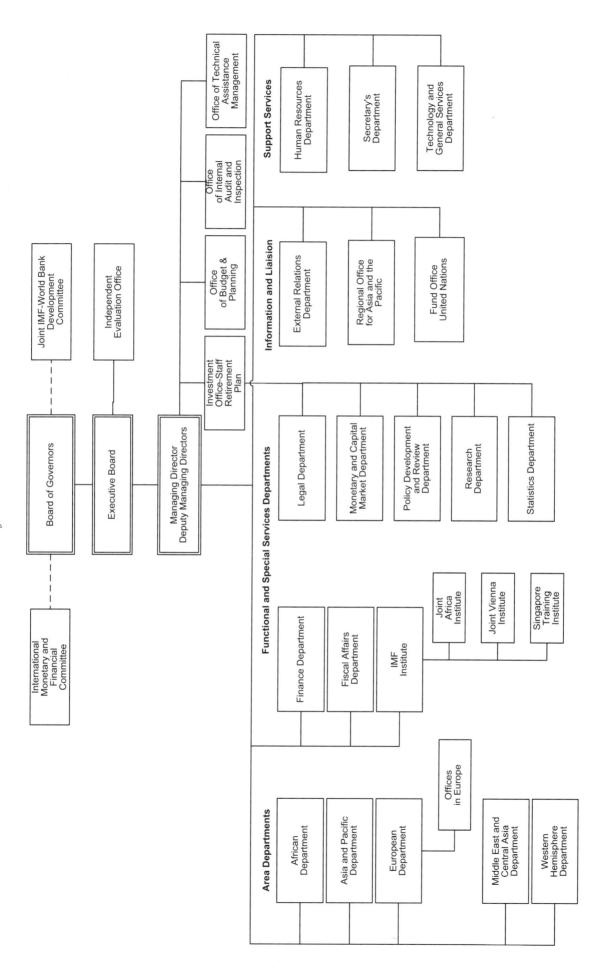

FMI : organigramme
décembre 2006

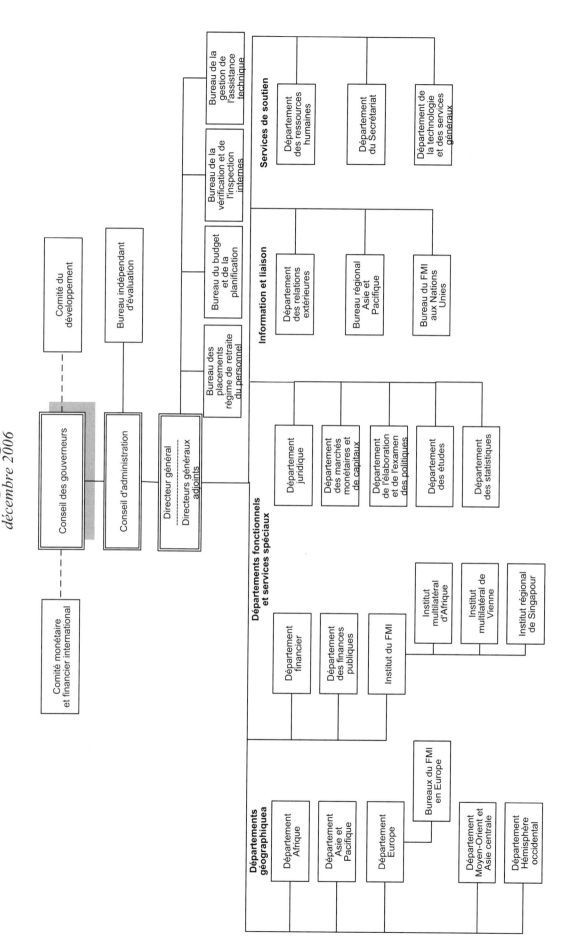

Comité monétaire et financier international

Comité du développement

Conseil des gouverneurs

Bureau indépendant d'évaluation

Conseil d'administration

Directeur général
Directeurs généraux adjoints

Bureau des placements régime de retraite du personnel

Bureau du budget et de la planification

Bureau de la vérification et de l'inspection internes

Bureau de la gestion de l'assistance technique

Départements géographiquea

Département Afrique

Département Asie et Pacifique

Département Europe

Bureaux du FMI en Europe

Département Moyen-Orient et Asie centrale

Département Hémisphère occidental

Départements fonctionnels et services spéciaux

Département financier

Département des finances publiques

Institut du FMI

Institut multilatéral d'Afrique

Institut multilatéral de Vienne

Institut régional de Singapour

Département juridique

Département des marchés monétaires et de capitaux

Département de l'élaboration et de l'examen des politiques

Département des études

Département des statistiques

Information et liaison

Département des relations extérieures

Bureau régional Asie et Pacifique

Bureau du FMI aux Nations Unies

Services de soutien

Département des ressources humaines

Département du Secrétariat

Département de la technologie et des services généraux

Organigrama del FMI
diciembre 2006

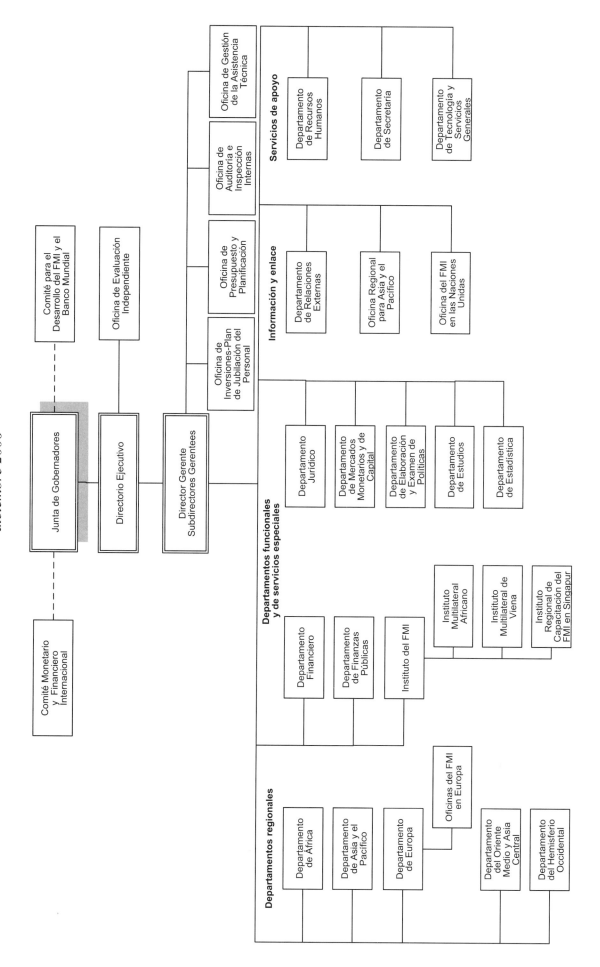

365

APPENDIX III

French Index
Index Français

A

actifs classés à risque C-627
actifs corporels T-5
actif(s) de clôture C-256
actifs de portefeuille P-188
actifs de réserve primaires P-310
actif(s) d'ouverture O-111
actifs en capital C-43
actifs en portefeuille P-188
actifs financiers C-43
actifs fixes F-170
actif(s) immédiatement réalisable(s) Q-21
actifs incorporels I-200
actifs liquides L-114
actif(s) liquide(s) Q-21
actif(s) sans préavis Q-21
actifs sous forme de dépôts D-158
actifs visibles T-5
action S-191
action anticyclique C-545
action contracyclique C-545
action corrective R-117
action cotée en bourse P-441
action des consommateurs C-450
action du FMI (dans un pays) E-159
action gratuite B-173
action hors cote O-248
action ordinaire C-350
action préventive P-261
action privilégiée P-241
actions ordinaires C-350
activer A-67
activité bancaire B-63
activité des banques B-63
activité hors marché N-154
activité industrielle et commerciale B-290
activité non marchande N-154
activités des banques centrales C-174
activités du FMI (dans un pays) E-159
activités réductrices d'importations I-69
à découvert O-211
adéquation des réserves A-87
adéquation du capital aux besoins C-40
adjudicataire S-502
adjudication à la baisse D-359
adjudication à la hollandaise D-359
adjudication au prix marginal décroissant D-359
adjudication de(s) devises F-228
adjudication publique P-418
administrateur E-362
administrateur électif E-100
administrateur élu E-99
administrateur nommé A-238
administrateur provisoire P-397
administrateur suppléant E-361
administration A-162
administration centrale C-176
administration de l'impôt T-27
administration fiscale T-26, T-27
administration infranationale S-483
administration judiciaire provisoire P-396
administration locale L-158
administration publique centrale C-176

administration publique centrale — comptes budgétaires B-255
administration publique centrale consolidée C-426
administration publique locale L-158
administration territoriale L-158
administrations de sécurité sociale S-278
administrations publiques G-36, G-109
administrations publiques consolidées C-427
admis à bénéficier de E-104
admis au réescompte D-241
admissibilité E-103
admissible E-104
admission de titres à la cote officielle L-134
adosser à des garanties C-279
ad valorem A-81
AE E-414
AELE E-288
AER E-177
affacturage F-11
affacturage à forfait F-250
affectation A-302
affectation de(s) ressources R-214
affectation (d'une somme à ...) B-230
affecter A-184, E-12
affermissement H-6
à fort effet de levier L-87
à forte composante d'importations I-75
à forte consommation d'énergie E-152
à forte intensité capitalistique C-84
à forte intensité de capital C-84
à forte intensité de main-d'œuvre L-15
à forte intensité de travail L-15
à forte intensité d'importations I-75
Afrique subsaharienne S-487
AFRITAC A-156
AGE G-27
agence de cotation C-604
agence de notation C-604
agence d'évaluation des sociétés C-604
Agence internationale de l'énergie I-263
Agence monétaire de l'Afrique de l'Ouest W-52
Agence monétaire de l'Arabie Saoudite S-26
Agence multilatérale de garantie des investissements M-246
Agence pour le développement international A-165
agent C-412
agent d'assiette A-296
agent de change F-229
agent de perception A-296
agent de relations publiques P-416
agent économique E-37, T-214
agent économique disposé à prendre des risques R-287
agent économique frileux R-278
agent économique n'ayant pas d'influence sur le prix P-295
agent économique pusillanime R-278
agent économique qui détermine le prix P-288
agent économique qui influence le prix P-287
agent financier F-128
agent payeur P-57
agent principal de la Division de l'information I-162
agent principal de relations publiques P-417

agrégat monétaire M-178
agrégat monétaire large B-213
agriculture, sylviculture, pêche et chasse A-178
AID A-165, I-261
aide à des conditions concessionnelles C-392
aide au développement D-195
aide concessionnelle C-392
aide d'urgence E-114
aide d'urgence à la suite de catastrophes
  naturelles E-115
aide d'urgence aux pays sortant d'un conflit E-118
aide d'urgence postconflit E-118
aide de trésorerie C-128
aide financière G-140
aide liée T-130
aide non liée U-108
aide publique au développement O-36
aide sociale W-39
aide-mémoire A-182
aide-mémoire technique T-102
AIE I-263
AIPS P-216
aisance de la situation des réserves R-187
aisance des réserves R-187
ajournement d'impôt T-46
ajustement F-167
ajustement à la baisse D-321
ajustement à la base caisse A-99
ajustement à la base encaissements-
  décaissements A-99
ajustement (au titre du) coût de la vie C-535
ajustement axé sur la croissance G-183
ajustement chronologique T-152
ajustement dans la croissance A-102
ajustement de valeur V-5
ajustement de valeur des avoirs en monnaie V-5
ajustement des commissions A-94
ajustement des quotes-parts A-95
ajustement en baisse D-321
ajustement en fonction du coût de la vie C-535
ajustement en hausse U-121
ajustement excessif O-238
ajustement fiscal à la frontière B-182
ajustement pour tenir compte des variations
  (de taux) de change E-356
ajuster une tendance F-168
à l'étude P-143
à la valeur A-81
aléa de moralité M-222
aléa moral M-222
aléas C-462
ALENA N-208
aliénation D-263
alignement des monnaies C-661
alignement monétaire E-342
allégement de dette D-61
allégement de la dette D-61
*Allégement de la dette des pays à faible revenu —
L'Initiative renforcée en faveur des pays pauvres
très endettés* D-62
allégement fiscal T-70
allégements T-42
allocation cumulative nette N-45

allocation de crédits budgétaires A-185
allocation de devises E-322
allocation de DTS S-59
allocation de(s) ressources R-214
allocation générale de DTS G-44
allocation pour enfant à charge C-214
allocation spéciale de DTS S-324
allocation spéciale de DTS à caractère
  exceptionnel S-319
allocations familiales D-153
allocution d'ouverture O-113
allouer A-184
alternance de phases d'accélération
  et de freinage S-454
alternance d'expansion et de récession B-293
alternance du recours au frein
  et à l'accélérateur S-454
alternative T-188
AMAO W-52
amélioration de la conjoncture U-120
amélioration de la cote du crédit E-163
amélioration de la qualité des créances E-163
amélioration de la qualité du DTS E-173
amélioration de la qualité d'une obligation E-167
amélioration de la signature E-163
amélioration de la situation de liquidité C-128
amélioration des conditions du crédit E-163
amélioration du crédit E-163
aménagement agricole L-23
aménagement du territoire L-23
aménagement foncier L-23
amendement A-197
amendement (des Statuts) A-198
amendement proposé P-389
AMGI M-246
amortir partiellement W-114
amortissement A-203, D-169, R-64, R-131
amortissement accéléré A-14
amortissement anticipé de la dette R-233
amortissement cumulé A-55
amortissement de la dette R-233
amortissement (des immobilisations
  corporelles) D-169
amortissement financier A-204
amortissement(s) A-55
analyse bilancielle B-25
analyse comparative entre pays C-641
analyse coûts–avantages C-539
analyse de la tendance T-246
analyse de sensibilité S-149
analyse de séries chronologiques T-149
analyse de séries temporelles T-149
analyse de soutenabilité de la dette D-79
analyse de viabilité de la dette D-79
analyse des impacts sur la pauvreté
  et le social P-216
analyse en coupe instantanée C-647
analyse explicative de la croissance G-181
analyse longitudinale T-149
analyse multinationale C-641
analyse par coupe transversale C-647
analyse portant sur plusieurs pays C-641
analyse rétrospective et prospective E-304

Assistant du Secrétaire A-305
Assistant personnel du Directeur général P-119
Assistant spécial du Directeur général adjoint S-305
association collective C-354
association de crédit mutuel C-615
association d'épargne et de prêt S-31
Association des nations de l'Asie du Sud-Est A-311
Association européenne de libre-échange E-288
Association internationale de développement I-261
association sans but lucratif N-172
assujetti T-94
assujettissement à l'impôt T-59
assurance chômage U-50
assurance contre les risques de change E-351
assurance de financement F-109
assurance des dépôts D-159
assurance responsabilité civile L-93
assurances en matière de financement F-109
assurances financières F-109
asymétrie des échéances M-96
asymétrie des taux d'intérêt I-218
atelier W-93
ATF F-273
atonie S-251
attaquant R-2
atténuation des variations S-266
atterrissage en douceur S-285
attribuer A-184
attributions T-119
au coût des facteurs F-5
«au-dessous de la ligne» B-120
au-dessous du pair D-235
«au-dessus de la ligne» A-8
au-dessus de la parité A-7
au-dessus de la valeur nominale A-6
au-dessus du pair A-6
audit A-318
audit dans l'entreprise F-43
audit sur place F-43
auditeur bancaire I-250
auditeur externe E-426
auditeur interne I-250
audits préalables D-352
augmentation au mérite M-140
augmentation de l'importance des circuits
    financiers F-69
augmentation des quotes-parts I-112
augmentation des ressources A-327
augmentation des ressources disponibles E-172
augmentation du stock de capital C-79
augmentation équiproportionnelle des quotes-
    parts G-38
augmentation générale des quotes-parts G-38
augmentation sélective des quotes-parts S-117
AUPC E-118
austérité budgétaire F-135
autoalimenté S-127
autoamortissable S-121
autoapprovisionnement S-124
autocentré S-127
autoconsommation S-118
autodéveloppement S-123

autoentretenu S-127
autoéquipement O-254
autofinancement S-120
autolimitation des exportations V-34
autonome S-127
autonomie S-123, S-124
autonomisation E-133
autorisation de crédits budgétaires A-242
autorisation de dépenses E-385
autoriser une dérogation W-23
autorité P-178
autorités P-419
autorités bancaires B-65
autorités de contrôle bancaire B-57
autorités monétaires M-184
autorités supranationales S-540
autre détenteur de DTS O-170
autres institutions de dépôt O-169
autres régimes conventionnels de parité fixe O-168
aval G-187
avance A-119, L-138
avances à vue C-14
avances et retards dans les règlements P-61
avant impôt(s) B-113
avantage B-126
avantage absolu A-11
avantage comparatif C-356
avantage compétitif C-366
avantage compétitif déloyal U-53
avantage compétitif indu U-53
avantage concurrentiel C-366
avantage externe P-205
avantage fiscal T-42
avantages indirects F-308
avantages sociaux F-308
avec garantie or G-99
avec prime P-245
avis d'appel d'offres I-308
avis de mise en adjudication I-308
avis de prêts syndiqués T-157
avis d'émission d'obligations T-157
avis des commissaires aux comptes A-321
avis financier T-157
avoir A-297
avoir conditionnel C-471
avoir de réserve R-182
avoir en banque C-129
avoir extérieur E-423
avoir fiscal T-43
avoir monétaire M-183
avoir non productif N-134
avoir productif E-16
avoir sur l'extérieur E-423
avoirs A-301
avoirs corporels T-5
avoirs du FMI en devises C-671
avoirs du FMI en monnaies C-671
avoirs en compte au FMI F-360
avoirs en devises F-227
avoirs exclus E-359
avoirs extérieurs nets N-54
avoirs incorporels I-200

bénéfices des monopoles fiscaux P-368
bénéfices distribués D-269
bénéfices industriels et commerciaux B-297
bénéfices non distribués R-229
bénéfices non rapatriés U-95
bénéfices ou pertes brutes d'exploitation G-163
bénéfices rapatriés R-120
bénéfices réinvestis R-111
BERD E-279
besoin de balance des paiements B-16
besoin de financement B-193, F-113, N-39
besoin de financement de la balance des paiements B-16
besoin de financement du secteur public P-435
besoin de financement non couvert F-111
besoin de financement résiduel F-111
besoin de soutien à la balance des paiements B-16
besoin d'emprunt B-193
besoin d'emprunt du secteur public P-435
besoin global d'ajouter aux instruments de réserve G-78
besoin net de financement N-39
biais B-134, B-135
biais dû à l'agrégation A-170
biais par défaut D-322
biais par excès U-122
biais résultant de l'agrégation A-170
biaisé B-136
Bibliothécaire en chef L-100
Bibliothèque commune (de la Banque et du FMI) J-19
BIC B-296, B-297
BID I-209, I-319
BIE I-120
bien commercialisable M-72
bien consomptible N-133
bien de capital C-58
bien de consommation durable C-443
bien de production C-58
bien d'équipement C-58
bien d'équipement des ménages C-443
bien d'intérêt social M-139
bien durable D-356
bien échangé T-187
bien engagé O-94
bien faisant l'objet d'échanges (internationaux) T-187
bien gratuit F-287
bien libre F-288
bien marchand M-72
bien ne faisant pas l'objet d'échanges internationaux N-197
bien non commercialisé N-197
bien non durable N-133
bien non échangé N-197
bien non exporté N-197
bien non marchand F-287
bien non taxé F-288
bien public P-426
bien semi-durable S-133
bien semi-transformé S-134
bien sous tutelle M-139
bien tutélaire M-139
bien-être W-40

bien-être économique E-63
biens autres que les biens d'équipement N-118
biens communautaires C-352
biens de capital fixe F-170
biens d'origine intérieur H-58
biens échangeables T-163
biens en consignation G-105
biens et avoirs du FMI P-386
biens et services marchands C-333
biens exportables T-163
biens manufacturés M-36
biens meubles P-126
biens mobiliers P-126
biens ne pouvant faire l'objet d'échanges internationaux N-195
biens négociables T-163
biens non échangeables N-195
biens non exportables N-195
biens pouvant faire l'objet d'échanges (internationaux) T-163
biens publics mondiaux G-79
biens, services et revenus G-106
bilan B-24
billet N-217
billet à ordre P-382
billet gagé S-102
billet garanti S-102
billet(s) à ordre C-309
billet(s) de trésorerie C-309
billets et pièces B-71, C-659
billets et pièces en caisse V-19
billets et pièces en circulation C-672
billion T-257
BIRD I-252
BIsD I-319
BIT I-269
«blindage financier» F-97
blocage automatique des crédits S-151
blocage des crédits S-151
blocage des prix P-283
bloquer S-427
bloquer des crédits I-76
BOAD W-48
bon B-165, D-18, N-217
bon à prime d'émission D-236
bon d'épargne S-33
bon d'option multidevises C-645
bon de caisse C-121, C-149, S-33
bon de privatisation P-327
bon de sortie E-370
bon de souscription W-28
bon du Trésor T-242
bon mobilisable en devises C-689
bonification d'intérêts I-236
bonification du taux d'intérêt I-236
bonne gestion de la chose publique G-103
bonne gestion des affaires publiques G-103
bonne gestion publique G-103
bonne gouvernance G-103
bourse S-104
bourse de commerce C-337

dispositif de protection S-11

dispositif de protection sociale S-11

dispositif des DSRP P-402

dispositions A-262

dispositions de change E-323

dispositions de Lyon L-183

dispositions de Naples N-7

dispositions d'exception E-119

dispositions financières contraignantes F-91

dispositions générales des régimes de change G-35

dispositions transitoires T-235, T-237

dissuasion D-189

distorsion D-268

distorsion entre les prix des facteurs F-12

distorsion par défaut D-322

distorsion par excès U-122

distribution de fréquences F-305

distribution uniforme (des tirages, mesures, etc.)
  pendant la durée du programme F-187

distribution uniforme (des tirages, mesures, etc.)
  sur la période F-187

distribution/répartition du/des revenu(s) D-272

diversification des circuits financiers F-69

diversification des risques S-349

diversification des services financiers F-63

diversification du marché M-53

dividende (payé) en actions S-436

dividende sous forme d'actions (gratuites) S-436

dividendes E-218

Division 1, 2, 3, ... D-281

Division administrative A-111

Division Afrique A-144, A-151

Division Afrique de l'Ouest I, II W-49

Division Amérique centrale C-170

Division Amérique du Nord N-207

Division Amérique du Sud/Amérique
  centrale I, II S-291

Division Amériques W-56

Division anglaise, chinoise et portugaise C-216

Division arabe et russe A-251

Division Asie A-283

Division Asie et Pacifique A-281

Division Atlantique A-312

Division banques centrales C-175

Division Caraïbes I, II C-100

Division communication de la politique
  institutionnelle P-158

division comptable A-42

Division coordination et normes C-501

Division de la balance des paiements et de la dette
  extérieure I, II B-12

Division de la gestion des finances
  publiques I, II P-425

Division de la politique et de la surveillance
  des finances publiques F-148

Division de l'évaluation des sauvegardes S-9

Division des dépenses et du contrôle
  administratifs A-112

Division des études macroéconomiques M-9

Division des opérations O-131

Division des recettes fiscales I, II R-244

Division développement D-200

Division développement des marchés de capitaux
  et infrastructure financière C-66

Division du financement de la FRPC et de l'initiative
  PPTE P-266

Division espagnole S-302

Division études économiques internationales W-102

Division études financières F-102

Division Europe E-278, E-285

Division Europe centrale I, II, III C-177

Division Europe de l'Ouest W-53

Division Europe du Nord N-210

Division Europe du Nord-Est N-209

Division Europe du Sud I, II S-294

Division Europe du Sud-Est I, II, III S-292

Division examen de la surveillance S-547

Division examen des données par pays C-558

Division examen des politiques P-173

Division finances publiques G-117

Division française F-302

Division gestion des actifs et des passifs
  souverains S-295

Division gestion des installations F-2

Division gestion des ressources R-216

Division Hémisphère occidental W-55

Division infrastructure I-166

Division institutions financières I, II F-77

Division Mexique et pays latins des Caraïbes M-143

Division modèles économiques E-56

Division Moyen-Orient M-149

Division Moyen-Orient et Asie centrale M-148

Division normes de diffusion des données D-2

Division opérations de financement officiel O-40

Division opérations de finances
  publiques I, II, III F-145

Division opérations de la facilité pour la réduction
  de la pauvreté et pour la croissance P-268

Division opérations de la FRPC P-268

Division opérations de surveillance S-545

Division opérations et déclarations financières F-84

Division opérations relatives aux accords
  de confirmation S-388

Division Pacifique P-2

Division perfectionnement du personnel S-363

Division politique commerciale T-182

Division politique de rémunérations et de
  prestations C-358

Division politique des dépenses publiques E-389

Division politique des ressources générales
  et des DTS G-41

Division politique du secteur financier F-94

Division politique fiscale T-65

Division politiques de l'Union européenne E-261

Division publications périodiques C-701

Division questions stratégiques S-459

Division questions systémiques et résolution
  des crises S-571

Division recrutement et affectations R-52

Division rédaction et publication E-76

Division réforme budgétaire B-246

Division régimes monétaires et régimes
  de change M-181

Division réglementation et supervision R-104

Division relations avec les médias M-115

Division relations publiques P-415

Division résolution des crises C-626

Division Rio de la Plata R-292

393

monde des affaires B-291

mondial G-67

mondialisation G-81

monétisation M-201

monétisation de la dette publique M-202

monétisation (de l'économie) M-204

monnaie C-659, M-206

monnaie à cours forcé F-40

monnaie à grande puissance B-80

monnaie à haute puissance B-80

monnaie acceptable par le FMI C-660

monnaie au sens étroit N-9

monnaie au sens large B-213

monnaie au sens strict N-9

monnaie centrale B-80

monnaie de couverture H-22

monnaie (de la) banque centrale B-80

monnaie de référence P-76, R-76

monnaie de règlement P-255, S-168

monnaie de réserve R-184

monnaie de transaction T-205

monnaie d'intervention I-284

monnaie en circulation (dans le public) C-672

monnaie entrant dans la composition
   (du panier du DTS) C-378

monnaie étrangère F-222

monnaie faible S-284

monnaie fiduciaire C-659, F-40

monnaie flottante F-195

monnaie forte H-2

monnaie librement utilisable F-301

monnaie métallique C-268

monnaie nationale D-291

monnaie nationale utilisable U-127

monnaie officiellement convertible F-260

monnaie oisive I-20

monnaie primaire P-306

monnaie rare S-43

monnaie satellite S-23

monnaie scripturale B-49

monnaie surévaluée O-250

monnaie utilisée dans les échanges
   (internationaux) T-171

monnaie-marchandise C-336

monnaies autres que les monnaies de réserve N-188

monnaies détenues par le FMI C-671

monnaies qui composent C-669

monnayage C-267

monopole discriminant D-247

monopole fiscal F-144

montage P-5

montage de protection financière F-97

montage financier F-112

montant cumulé des amortissements A-55

montant de crédit non décaissé U-37

montant de la dette I-119

montant de l'accès (aux ressources du FMI) A-206

montant de l'engagement R-281

montant de l'impôt exigible T-59

montant effectivement reçu (par l'emprunteur) D-230

montant immédiatement exigible A-208

montant nominal N-104

montant non décaissé U-37

montants à payer A-45

montants à recevoir A-46

montant(s) mis en réserve S-166

montant(s) préaffecté(s) S-166

moratoire S-420

moratoire de la dette D-53

moratoire fiscal T-46

motif de précaution P-233

motif de spéculation S-330

mouvement de capitaux équilibrant E-204

mouvement de capitaux stabilisateur E-204

mouvement spéculatif contre une monnaie R-313

mouvements de capitaux C-53

mouvements de capitaux exempts
   de restrictions O-96

mouvements de capitaux non réglementés O-96

mouvements de fonds C-126, F-203

moyen de paiement M-113

moyen de production I-174

moyen d'échange M-117

moyenne A-258

moyenne arithmétique A-258

moyenne des soldes quotidiens A-333

moyenne des taux d'intérêt pondérée
   selon la formule du DTS S-73

moyenne mobile M-233

moyens d'action L-85

moyens de paiement en cours d'encaissement F-193

MSMF M-182

MULTIMOD M-258

multinationale M-251

multiplicateur de plein emploi F-329

multiplicateur du commerce extérieur F-245

multiplicateur du revenu I-96

multiplicateur dynamique D-362

multiplicateur monétaire M-212

mutuelle de crédit C-615

N

NAE N-77

nantissement C-275, P-151, S-108

nantissement de l'or G-95

Nations Unies U-83

nature rotative des ressources R-267

navettage S-218

n.c.a. N-213

NCCD N-98

NCM M-248

n.d. N-212

n.d.a. N-214

NDB N-98

ne pas opposer d'objection *a priori* P-316

ne plus ancrer le taux de change U-93

ne plus avoir besoin de faire appel aux ressources
   de l'IDA G-136

ne portant pas intérêts N-151

néant N-211

nécessité d'ajouter aux réserves S-514

négociation assistée par ordinateur P-374

négociation informatisée P-374

négociation(s) collective(s) C-286

négociations commerciales multilatérales M-248

APPENDIX IV

Spanish Index
Índice Español

A

flujo de caja C-126
flujo de capital C-53
flujo de capital concesionario C-395
flujo de capital de carácter no concesionario N-126
flujo de capital no concesionario N-126
flujo de capital no generador de deuda N-132
flujo de capital no relacionado con la deuda N-132
flujo de capital oficial O-41
flujo de capital que contribuye al equilibrio E-204
flujo de efectivo C-126
flujo de fondos C-126, F-203
flujo de inversión de cartera P-193
flujo de inversión de cartera en acciones P-192
flujo de inversión de cartera en activos de renta fija P-191
flujo de inversión de cartera en activos de renta variable P-192
flujo de inversión de cartera en títulos de deuda P-191
flujo financiero no destinado a inversión en acciones N-135
flujo financiero no destinado a inversión en participaciones de capital N-135
flujo monetario M-192
flujo real R-27
flujos de asistencia financiera A-181
flujos de ayuda A-181
flujos oficiales de capital O-41
FMA A-250
FMAM G-73
FMI I-273
f.o.b. F-290a
fomento de la exportación E-406
fondeo F-356
Fondo Africano de Desarrollo A-150
Fondo Árabe de Desarrollo Económico y Social A-249
fondo buitre V-43
fondo común F-87
fondo común de inversión M-266, M-266
fondo común de recursos financieros F-87
fondo de amortización S-243
fondo de cobertura H-23
fondo de comercio G-107
fondo de contrapartida C-547
fondo de equiparación E-201
fondo de estabilización S-357
fondo de estabilización anticíclica A-228
fondo de estabilización cambiaria F-230
fondo de estabilización monetaria F-230
fondo de inversión I-299
fondo de inversión colectiva M-266
fondo de inversión de alto riesgo H-23
fondo de inversión especulativo H-23
fondo de inversiones abierto M-266
fondo de inversiones cerrado I-304
fondo de pensiones P-86
fondo de previsión P-394
fondo de reserva C-466
fondo de retorno absoluto H-23
fondo especulativo de cobertura H-23
Fondo Europeo de Desarrollo E-284
fondo extrapresupuestario E-437

Fondo Fiduciario T-262
Fondo Fiduciario para el Medio Ambiente Mundial G-74
Fondo Fiduciario para las operaciones especiales en el marco del SRAE a favor de los países pobres muy endeudados y las operaciones de subvención en el marco del SRAE transitorio E-239
Fondo Fiduciario para los PPME H-41
Fondo Fiduciario SCLP-PPME P-275
Fondo Fiduciario SRAE-PPME E-239
Fondo Monetario Árabe A-250
Fondo Monetario Internacional I-273
fondo multilateral para la reducción de la deuda D-58
fondo para contingencias C-466
Fondo para el Medio Ambiente Mundial G-73
Fondo para la Reconstrucción de Países en Etapa de Posconflicto P-208
fondo para la reducción de la deuda D-58
Fondo para la reducción de la deuda de países que solo pueden recibir financiamiento de la AIF D-57
Fondo Posconflicto P-208
Fondo Social Europeo E-292
fondos a un día O-231
fondos de seguridad social S-278
fondos de seguro social S-278
fondos disponibles en bancos C-129
fondos para operaciones W-78
fondos prestables L-70
fondos presupuestados B-264
fondos propios C-36, C-513
forfaiting F-250
forfetización F-250
formación bruta de capital fijo G-157, G-157
formación de capital C-54
formación de capital del sector público P-420
formación de capital fijo F-174
formación de capital fijo por cuenta propia O-254
formación del ahorro G-49
formación excesiva de capital E-310
formación neta de capital N-40
formador de mercado M-61
formador de precios P-288
formulación de la política económica P-179
formulación de políticas P-179
formulación del presupuesto B-265
formular una queja (contra un país miembro) I-323
formulario de declaración de datos B-42
formulario de declaración de datos de los bancos B-42
Foro de Cooperación Económica Asia-Pacífico A-284
Foro sobre Estabilidad Financiera F-100
fortalecimiento H-6
fortalecimiento de las capacidades C-29
fraccionamiento de acciones S-443
fragilidad U-106
franco a bordo F-290a
franquicia F-282
franquicia comercial F-282
frecuencia F-304
freno fiscal F-137
front office F-310
frontera aduanera C-717
frontera de las posibilidades de producción P-347

manufacturas M-36, M-37

maquila O-61

maquiladora I-86, O-62

maquillaje de las cifras W-67

marco basado en la adopción de objetivos de
inflación I-153

Marco de Evaluación de la Calidad de los Datos D-4

marco de política monetaria M-196

marco específico de evaluación de la calidad de los
datos D-8

marco general para el análisis de la calidad de los
datos G-52

marco hipotético S-47

marco hipotético más desfavorable W-110

marco hipotético optimista B-129

marco hipotético pesimista W-110

marco legal y reglamentario L-59

marco legal y regulatorio L-59

margen M-39, S-346

margen de beneficio M-83

margen de beneficios P-360

margen de caja C-136

margen de comercialización M-83

margen de crédito recíproco B-207

margen de fluctuación F-206

margen de ganancia P-360

margen de tesorería C-136

margen de utilidad M-83, P-360

margen entre el tipo de cambio comprador
y vendedor B-144

margen inicial I-170

margen por encima de la Libor S-348

masa S-432

masa de capital C-72

masa monetaria M-216

masa monetaria en sentido amplio B-213

masa salarial W-5

MATIF F-303

matriz de insumo-producto I-177

mayor acceso a los recursos del FMI E-177

mayoría calificada S-317

mayoría cualificada S-317

mayoría especial S-317

MCCA C-169

MCO O-152

MECAD D-4

mecanismo A-262

mecanismo de auditoría externa; estructura
e independencia jurídicas (del banco central);
presentación de información financiera;
mecanismo de auditoría interna y sistema
de controles internos E-425

mecanismo de contingencia para el ajuste
de las metas C-468

mecanismo de cooperación monetaria C-495

mecanismo de distribución de la carga B-289

mecanismo de financiamiento F-110

mecanismo de financiamiento de emergencia E-117

Mecanismo de Integración Comercial T-179

mecanismo de los DELP P-402

Mecanismo de Seguimiento de las Políticas P-167

mecanismo de tipos de cambio E-339

mecanismo de tipos de cambio 2 E-340

mecanismo ELRIC de evaluación de las
salvaguardias E-425

mecanismo financiero F-110

mecanismos tradicionales de alivio de la
deuda T-197

media A-258

media aritmética A-258

media móvil M-233

mediana M-116

medida administrativa A-109

medida anticíclica C-545

medida contingente C-467

medida correctiva R-117

medida de compresión de la demanda D-126

medida de disuasión D-189

medida de emergencia S-453

medida de estabilización S-358

medida de represalia R-231

medida de retorsión R-231

medida de salvaguardia S-4

medida de zona gris G-143

medida disuasoria D-189

medida no arancelaria N-191

medida para contingencias C-467

medida para hacer frente a imprevistos C-467

medida preventiva P-261

medida provisional S-453

medida punitiva P-443

medidas de protección social S-11

medidas previas P-315

medio circulante N-9

medio de cambio M-117

medio de pago M-113

medio de transmisión C-412

medios de comercialización M-79

medios empresariales B-291

MEFP G-119

mejora de tierras y terrenos L-23

mejoramiento de la situación de liquidez C-128

mejoramiento de tierras y terrenos L-23

mejorar la calificación U-111

MEMF M-182

memorando de entendimiento M-132

Memorando de Política Económica
y Financiera M-133

memorando del personal técnico del FMI S-366

memorando técnico T-102

Memorando Técnico de Entendimiento T-102

menú de opciones M-134

mercado a la baja B-108

mercado a plazo F-270

mercado a término F-270

mercado accionario E-223

mercado al alza B-280

mercado al contado S-341

mercado alcista B-280

mercado bajista B-108

mercado cambiario F-231

Mercado Común Centroamericano C-169

Mercado Común del Caribe C-98

Mercado Común del Sur S-293

mercado de acciones E-223

oferta fuera de concurso N-121
oferta mínima aceptable M-160
oferta monetaria M-216
oferta monetaria en sentido amplio B-213
oferta monetaria en sentido estricto N-9
oferta no competitiva N-121
oferta pública de adquisición T-110
oferta pública inicial I-172
oferta sin cotización de precio N-121
oferta y utilización S-524
ofertismo S-531
Oficial de Relaciones Públicas P-416
Oficial Principal de Información I-162
Oficial Principal de Relaciones Públicas P-417
oficina centralizadora O-81
Oficina de Auditoría A-320
Oficina de Auditoría e Inspección Internas O-25
Oficina de Conferencias del Banco y del Fondo B-62
Oficina de Ética E-259
Oficina de Evaluación Independiente I-120a
Oficina de Gestión de la Asistencia Técnica O-26
Oficina de Inversiones I-302
Oficina de Presupuesto y Planificación O-22
oficina de servicios auxiliares B-1
Oficina del Director I-51
Oficina del Director Gerente O-28
Oficina del FMI en Bruselas B-223
Oficina del FMI en Ginebra G-54
Oficina del FMI en las Naciones Unidas F-347
Oficina del FMI en París P-33
Oficina del Secretario Ejecutivo del Comité Ministerial
  Conjunto para el Desarrollo O-24
Oficina del Subdirector Gerente O-27
Oficina Internacional del Trabajo I-269
Oficina Regional para Asia y el Pacífico R-91
Oficina Regional para Europa Central y los Países
  Bálticos R-92
Oficinas de los Directores Ejecutivos O-23
Oficinas del FMI en Europa O-29
OIT I-269, I-270
OMA W-99
Ombudsman O-75
OMC W-108
OMGI M-246
OMPI W-105
OMS W-104
ONG N-147
onza de oro fino F-115
onza troy de oro fino F-115
opa T-110
opa hostil H-62
opción O-142
opción de compra C-16
opción de compra de bonos B-169
opción de renovación C-18
opción de rescate anticipado P-454
opción de venta P-453
opción del menú M-135
opción extrabursátil O-247
opción sobre futuros F-365
opción subóptima S-89
OPEP O-160

operación O-121
operación a plazo F-271, F-364
operación a término F-271, F-364
operación activa A-298
operación autorizada P-252
operación cambiaria a plazo F-267
operación con pacto de recompra R-160
operación conjunta J-25
operación de cambio a término F-267
operación de cambio al contado S-345
operación de canje S-559
operación de canje de bonos a la par P-17
operación de intercambio de deuda por bonos D-85
operación de mercado abierto O-100
operación de pase R-160, S-559
operación de pase activo R-160
operación de pase pasivo R-256
operación de reducción del saldo de la deuda S-448
operación de reporto R-160
operación de reporto activo R-160
operación de reporto pasivo R-256
operación de swap R-41
operación extrapresupuestaria O-19
operación pasiva L-94
operación sobre el saldo de la deuda S-448
operaciones bancarias B-63
operaciones basadas en información
  privilegiada I-182
operaciones consolidadas del gobierno central C-426
operaciones consolidadas del gobierno
  general C-427
operaciones de los bancos centrales C-174
operaciones de reducción de la deuda D-59
operaciones de reducción de la deuda basadas
  en el mercado M-75
operaciones internacionales de préstamo I-271
operador bursátil D-16
operador de valores D-16
opinión colectiva C-288
opinión de la mayoría C-288
opinión general C-288
optar por no recibir O-135
optimismo B-285
optimización de la gestión de las reservas
  del FMI O-139
óptimo de segundo grado S-89
Orden Administrativa General G-23
orden público y seguridad P-432
ordenamiento jurídico L-59
organigrama O-161
organismo A-162
organismo con potestad normativa R-105
organismo de verificación de antecedentes de
  crédito C-603
organismo descentralizado D-96
organismo ejecutor del gasto S-331
organismo especializado S-328
organismo estatal G-110
organismo fiscal F-128
organismo gubernamental G-110
organismo ministerial D-151
Organismo Monetario del África Occidental W-52

plan de transacciones financieras F-104
plan empresarial B-295
planilla de liquidación de sueldos P-65
planilla electrónica S-350
plantilla W-76
plaza financiera F-64
plazo I-188
plazo contractual C-482
plazo de aceptación P-111
plazo de adaptación L-18
plazo de notificación del consentimiento P-111
plazo de reembolso R-133
plazo de vencimiento D-351, T-113
plazo de vencimiento inicial O-163
plazo de vencimiento original O-163
plazo para notificar la aceptación P-111
plazo previsto en el plan de recompras S-52
plazo residual R-210
plena convertibilidad de las monedas F-325
plena participación en la sociedad E-133
pleno ejercicio de los derechos E-133
pleno empleo F-326
pliego de condiciones T-118
pluriempleo M-221
plusvalía C-55
plusvalía adquirida G-107
plusvalía mercantil G-107
PMA L-55
PMD L-74
PNB G-162
PNB agregado real A-169
PNN N-60
PNUD U-86
población activa L-4, W-90
población económicamente activa L-4
población en edad de trabajar W-77
población en edad laboral W-77
poder L-85
poder de importación de las exportaciones I-61
poder de mercado M-62
poder de negociación B-74
poder de predicción P-234
poder de sanción por incumplimiento E-157
poder de voto V-38
poder legal S-417
poder multiplicador G-21
polígono industrial I-134
política acomodaticia A-29
política cambiaria E-341
política contraccionista C-481
política contractiva C-481
política crediticia C-601
política de acceso A-24
política de acceso a los recursos del FMI A-24
política de austeridad C-481, P-169
política de avance intermitente S-454
política de concesión de préstamos a países con
   atrasos L-71
política de crédito C-601
política de dinero abundante C-206
política de dinero barato C-206
política de egoísmo nacional B-114

política de empobrecimiento del vecino B-114
política de estímulo a la oferta S-532
política de expansión E-379
política de expansión monetaria C-206
política de fijación de precios P-298
política de fomento de las exportaciones O-204
política de incentivos a la oferta S-532
política de ingresos I-97
política de ingresos basada en la tributación T-86
política de ingresos basada en los impuestos T-86
política de mayor acceso P-170
política de mayor acceso a los recursos del
   FMI P-170
política de moderación P-169
política de modificación de la composición del
   gasto E-390
política de oferta S-532
política de precios P-298
política de reorientación del gasto E-390
política de salida (del mercado) E-373
política de tarifas R-14
política de tipos de cambio E-341
política de tramos T-198
política de tramos de crédito C-613
política discrecional A-69
política económica de apertura al exterior O-204
política económica orientada hacia el exterior O-204
política expansionista E-379
política expansiva E-379
política favorable a la economía de mercado M-76
política fiscal F-147
política liberal de crédito O-98
política macroprudencial M-11
política monetaria acomodaticia A-29
política monetaria restrictiva M-200
política orientada al mercado M-76
política relativa a los tramos de crédito C-613
política restrictiva C-481
política salarial W-13
políticas y prácticas del FMI P-156
políticas y procedimientos del FMI P-157
ponderación W-35
ponderación del comercio bilateral B-151
ponderado según el comercio exterior T-189
poner en marcha A-67
por debajo de la línea B-120
por debajo del valor nominal D-235
por encima de la línea A-8
por encima de la paridad A-7
por encima del par A-6
por encima del valor nominal A-6, P-245
por habitante P-92
por tanteo T-252
porcentaje que corresponde a un país en el total
   de cuotas calculadas C-7
posición P-201
posición abierta O-102
posición acreedora C-619
posición bruta (de un país miembro) en el FMI G-158
posición cambiaria F-233
posición corta S-210
posición de inversión internacional I-268

reflación R-81
reforma A-197
reforma agraria L-27
refuerzo de los recursos financieros E-172
refuerzo del crédito E-163
refuerzo del DEG E-173
refuerzo monetario de los activos E-171
refugio tributario T-74
regalo propiamente dicho O-180
régimen A-262
régimen cambiario E-323
régimen cambiario dual D-348
régimen de caja de conversión C-666
régimen de cambio E-323
régimen de cambios doble D-348
régimen de capitalización F-354
régimen de convertibilidad C-666
régimen de financiación de los pagos con ingresos
    corrientes P-54
régimen de flotación independiente I-122
régimen de metas de inflación I-153
régimen de plena capitalización F-354
régimen de política monetaria M-196
régimen de precios dobles D-347
régimen de reparto P-54
régimen de seguridad social S-280
régimen de suspensión condicional del
    impuesto C-409
régimen de tipos de cambio E-323
régimen legal y reglamentario L-59
régimen monetario cooperativo C-495
régimen transitorio T-235
regímenes cooperativos (para mantener el valor
    de las monedas) C-496
regímenes de cambio sin una moneda nacional
    de curso legal E-324
regímenes generales de cambios G-35
región de aceptación R-87
región de rechazo R-88
registro E-185
registro base caja C-118
registro bruto G-166
registro de cambios F-234
registro de operaciones cambiarias F-234
registro en base devengado A-47
registro en cifras brutas G-166
registro en cifras netas N-69
registro neto N-69, N-76
registro tributario A-294
regla de oro de acumulación de capital G-100
Reglamento R-308
reglamento interno B-311
reglas prudenciales P-408
regresión de Y en X R-98
regresión de Y sobre X R-98
regresión múltiple M-256
regresión temporal T-148
regresividad R-100
regreso del capital fugado R-83
regulación C-484
regulación cambiaria E-327
regulación de la demanda D-138
regulación de la liquidez L-121

regulación de los precios P-276
regulación del tipo de cambio E-338
regulación monetaria M-194
regulación prudencial P-407
rehabilitación R-109
reintegro de cargos R-85
reintegro de impuestos T-69
reintegro de los derechos de aduana D-332
reintegro de un préstamo R-253
reinversión de beneficios R-111
reinversión de ganancias R-111
reinversión de utilidades R-111
relación capital propio/préstamos C-89
relación capital/deuda C-81
relación capital/producto C-90
relación capital/trabajo C-88
relación de compensación T-188
relación de correspondencia T-188
relación de intercambio T-120
relación de intercambio de factor único S-239
relación de paridad P-34
relación de precios de intercambio T-120
relación de sustitución T-188
relación del FMI con el país E-159
relación depósitos/préstamos D-165
relación deuda/capital propio D-89
relación entre el FMI y el país E-159
relación entre el servicio de la deuda y la
    exportación D-73
relación entre el valor presente neto de la deuda
    y la exportación N-66
relación entre el VPN de la deuda
    y la exportación N-66
relación entre la deuda y la exportación D-91
relación importaciones/consumo I-71
relación inversa T-188
relación marginal capital-producto I-115
relación marginal trabajo-producto I-117
relación precio-beneficios P-296
relación precio-ganancia P-296
relación préstamos desembolsados y pendientes-
    capital y reservas G-21
relación trabajo/producto L-16
remate público P-418
remesa de fondos R-118
remesas de emigrantes M-156
remesas de migrantes M-156
remesas de trabajadores W-74
remisión de la deuda D-47
rémora fiscal F-137
remuneración E-19, R-122, S-13
remuneración a los empleados C-359
remuneración de asalariados C-359
remuneración de empleados C-359
remuneración de los asalariados C-359
remuneración de los factores de producción F-9
remunerado I-237
rendición de cuentas A-31
rendimiento Y-5
rendimiento al vencimiento Y-7
rendimiento constante C-434
rendimiento de la inversión R-238
rendimiento de mercado M-71

RUF R-269

S

SAE S-469
SAF E-418
sala de operaciones T-196
salario W-4
salario computable a efectos jubilatorios P-88
salario de reserva R-178
salario en unidades de producto P-344
salario mínimo vital M-163
salario nominal M-219
salario real R-32
saldo A-207, P-201, S-432
saldo acreedor C-588, C-619
saldo acreedor neto N-44
saldo comercial B-22
saldo de caja C-119
saldo de la balanza de pagos B-17
saldo de la balanza de pagos en cuenta
    corriente C-692
saldo de la balanza en cuenta corriente C-692
saldo de la deuda D-37, O-187
saldo de la deuda pública O-197
saldo de las reservas R-190
saldo de los pasivos O-194
saldo de los préstamos O-195
saldo de operación O-116
saldo del crédito del FMI O-191
saldo del presupuesto F-130
saldo deudor D-23, D-93
saldo deudor neto N-47
saldo en cuenta corriente C-692
saldo en efectivo C-119, C-142
saldo en el tramo de reserva R-196
saldo fiscal F-130
saldo fiscal global O-209
saldo fiscal operacional O-125
saldo fiscal operativo O-125
saldo fiscal primario P-304
saldo global O-209
saldo medio diario A-333
saldo neto en el FMI P-203
saldo no desembolsado U-42
saldo no remunerado en el tramo de reserva U-96
saldo no utilizado U-42
saldo operacional O-125
saldo operativo O-116, O-125
saldo por cuenta corriente C-692
saldo presupuestario F-130
saldo primario P-304
saldo remunerado en el tramo de reserva R-121
saldo según liquidaciones oficiales O-45
saldo total de pasivos O-194
saldos de operación W-78
saldos de precaución P-231
saldos deudores en el exterior F-247
saldos en dólares D-288
saldos en el exterior F-247
saldos en manos de no residentes F-247
saldos inactivos I-18
saldos para operaciones W-78

saldos para transacciones T-202
saldos precautorios P-231
saldos y flujos S-450
salida de capital O-174
salud H-16
salvaguardia S-4, S-4
salvaguardias adecuadas A-88
salvaguardias en relación con el uso de los recursos
    del FMI S-10
SAMA S-26
sanción comercial T-185
saneamiento R-109
saneamiento de las finanzas públicas F-132
sanidad H-16
satisfactorio U-66
saturación del mercado M-60
SCLP P-220
SCLP autofinanciado S-126
SCN 1993 S-569
SCR S-515
SEA S-316
SEAASS S-316
Sección de Servicios de Publicaciones P-439
Secretaría Conjunta J-23
Secretaría de Asistencia Técnica T-100
Secretaría del Club de París P-32
Secretario Adjunto S-92
Secretario Adjunto de Conferencias S-94
Secretario (del FMI) S-95
Secretario Ejecutivo E-363
secreto bancario B-55
sector I-139, S-97
sector bancario B-66
sector de cooperativas C-499
sector de empresas no financieras constituidas en
    sociedades y cuasisociedades de capital N-141
sector de exportación E-410
sector de hogares H-68
sector de instituciones financieras F-78
sector de unidades familiares H-68
sector financiero F-72
sector financiero de la economía F-72
sector financiero informal N-149
sector financiero no estructurado N-149
sector financiero paralelo N-149
sector formal F-258
sector gobierno G-109
sector gobierno general G-36
sector informal I-158
sector líder L-49
sector no bancario N-116
sector no gubernamental N-148
sector no público N-176
sector oficial O-44
sector oficial extranjero F-242
sector oficial residente R-203
sector público no financiero N-143
sector que fija las pautas L-49
sector real R-24
sector real de la economía R-24
sectorización S-99
sectorizar S-100

votación formal F-259
votación por mayoría calificada Q-5
votación por mayoría cualificada Q-5
votación por mayoría especial Q-5
votación por poder V-37
votación sin reunión V-39
voto básico B-93
voto computable E-109
voto que cuenta para la elección E-109
VPN N-65
vulnerabilidades V-40

W

WAMA W-52
warrant W-28
warrant financiero W-28

Z

ZCP P-239
ZMO O-136
Zona de comercio preferencial para los Estados
  del África Oriental y del África Austral P-239
zona de depresión económica D-172
zona de libre comercio F-296
zona de moneda común C-690
zona de procesamiento para la exportación E-405
zona de referencia R-79, T-11
zona del franco C-187
zona del franco CFA C-187
zona deprimida D-172
zona desfavorecida D-172
Zona Económica Europea E-286
zona franca F-296, F-297
zona franca industrial E-405
zona franca para la industria de exportación E-405
zona maquiladora E-405
zona meta T-11
zona monetaria C-690
zona monetaria óptima O-1